BEYOND LEICHHARDT

...CHHARDT

...CLAREN

After the white settlement of Australia, British scientific societies clamoured for more knowledge of this new and strange continent. Questions about landforms, flora, fauna and the land's original inhabitants bombarded the early colonists as they struggled to come to terms with their place of exile.

Beyond Leichhardt is an account of Australia's first century of exploration, concentrating not so much on where the explorers went as how they went, how they learned, or failed to learn from experience, and how they overcame their fear of the unknown and came to be at home in one of the planet's most hostile environments.

At the centre of this story of enterprise, endurance, courage, and occasional foolhardiness and stupidity, stands the figure of Ludwig Leichhardt, a man driven to explore the unknown, blazing clear trails for his successors. Was he a genius or a fool? An experienced bushman or a hapless blunderer? A true polymath or an ineffectual dabbler?

Cover photograph: Richard Woldendorp, *Mongers Lake*, courtesy Photo Index.

Glen McLaren was born in York, Western Australia, in 1948. He received a Diploma of Agriculture in 1965 and spent the next ten years developing a farm property, as well as working as a shearer, bulldozing contractor and farm manager. He commenced full-time studies at the University of Western Australia in 1977, graduating with a Bachelor of Science in 1979. While studying he began riding racehorses to keep fit, and this interest rapidly grew into a full-time horse-breaking business, which he still operates. Continuing his studies part-time over the ensuing years, he was finally awarded a Doctorate of Philosophy by Curtin University of Technology in 1995, for the thesis upon which this book is based.

BEYOND LEICHHARDT

BUSHCRAFT AND THE EXPLORATION OF AUSTRALIA

GLEN MCLAREN

FREMANTLE ARTS CENTRE PRESS

First published 1996 by
FREMANTLE ARTS CENTRE PRESS
193 South Terrace (PO Box 320), South Fremantle
Western Australia 6162.

Reprinted 1997.

Consultant Editor Bryce Moore.
Designed by John Douglass.
Production Coordinator Linda Martin.
Index by Bill Phippard, Professional Editing Services, Adelaide.

Typeset in Times Roman
by Fremantle Arts Centre Press
and printed by Lamb Print, Perth, Western Australia.

National Library of Australia
Cataloguing-in-publication data

McLaren, Glen.

Beyond Leichhardt: Bushcraft and the Exploration of Australia

ISBN 1 86368 131 0.

1. Leichhardt, Ludwig, 1813–1848 — Journeys — Australia.
2. Survival skills — Australia — History. 3. Discovery and Exploration. I. Title.

919.4042

This work is dedicated to the memory of Ludwig Leichhardt — bushman, explorer and field scientist — a courageous and innovative man.

Acknowledgements

I would like to acknowledge my debt to the following: firstly to my Supervisor, Associate Professor Bill Cooper, whose patient, incisive comments, broad range of knowledge of Australian history and geography and genuinely strong interest in the project complemented my work so well and helped maintain my enthusiasm. Secondly, to the Royal Geographical Society of Queensland and to Mrs Hilary Russell of Jimbour House Station on the Darling Downs, for their kindness, physical and financial support, and strong belief in the value of my project. Thirdly, to Curtin University of Technology, which awarded me a Post-Graduate Scholarship, and the School of Social Sciences, which assisted with funding for my field research expenses. Fourthly, to Liza Bradbury, who graciously accepted my almost silent preoccupations and periodic disappearances to the Northern Territory for over four years, to Adam and Dot Clark of Taroom, Queensland, Brian and Mardi Sands of Wandowan, Queensland, and Frank and Daphne Clark of Seven Emus Station in the Northern Territory, all of whom encouraged and assisted me with paddocking for my horses and invaluable local information. Fifthly, to Terry Rose, who helped me carry out much of the fieldwork in the more remote areas of Queensland and the Northern Territory. And finally, to my friend and long-suffering typist, Janice Yarrow, whose skill and professionalism enabled her to quickly make fair copy of my, at times, appalling manuscripts.

The State of Western Australia has made an investment in this project through the Department for the Arts.

Department for theArts
Western Australia

Australia Council for the Arts

Publication of this title was assisted by the Commonwealth Government through the Australia Council, its arts funding and advisory body.

Contents

1. The Scientific Societies of Britain.......................... 11
2. Slow and Painful Progress — Settlement and Early Exploration to 1815.. 18
3. Feeling the Way — Developments to the Early 1830s.. 53
4. The 1830s and the Failure to Benefit from Experience.. 92
5. Harder Country, Harder Men — The Quantum Leap in Bushmanship 130
6. Leichhardt Revisited... 179
7. Exploring the Central Desert Region 224
8. The Final Task — The Deserts of Western Australia 260

Endnotes 273

Index 305

1

THE SCIENTIFIC SOCIETIES OF BRITAIN

The origins of the British scientific societies can be traced back to the Italian academies of the sixteenth and seventeenth centuries.[1] While scientific research was not unknown, nor gifted researchers a rarity at that time, institutions such as the Accademia del Cimento in Florence, and the Accademia del Lincei in Rome brought researchers together into organisations of common interest for the first time. By November 1660 the astronomer and architect Christopher Wren and his colleagues were discussing the desirability of forming a similar society in Britain, for 'the promoting of experimentall philosophy.'[2]

Such a Society was formed, and a charter was drawn up incorporating it as The Royal Society. In 1663 a second charter nominated it as The Royal Society of London for Improving Natural Knowledge.[3] As the all-embracing nature of the title indicates, science in the seventeenth century was not the world of intense specialisation that it so often is today. By that time, although British scientists were aware of the necessity for experimental analysis of specific paradigms, experimental methodology had not yet been formally developed. Only towards the latter part of the eighteenth century did narrow specialisation became a feature of scientific life in Britain.

In contrast to the major continental scientific societies, the Royal Society was not subsidised by the Government, which would demonstrate little interest in pure science for at least two centuries. It was necessary, therefore, not only to establish a sound financial base by other means, but also to secure social acceptance and facilitation at the highest levels. A good proportion of the Royal Society's members were, therefore, in the tradition of gentleman scientists, interested in '... natural science ... as patrons or dilettanti rather than practitioners.'[4]

By the time of Sir Joseph Banks' accession to the Presidency of the Royal Society in 1778, the dissemination of scientific research findings had been formalised into the practice of papers being read at meetings on a wide range of scientific subjects, though discussion was not necessarily a feature of such meetings. The reading of papers played an important role in the gradual development of scientific professionalism. Papers were reviewed, and those deemed inadequate were rejected. Those accepted were printed and distributed within the society and to its major overseas counterparts. The Royal Society saw international dissemination of research findings as a major responsibility, despite the costs involved. Indexing of research papers, which gradually grew in sophistication, was also considered essential in order to allow researchers to keep abreast of developments in their fields.

Despite the Royal Society's considerable achievements in formalising and advancing the role of scientists and scientific research in Britain, the breadth of its scope began to cause dissatisfaction among scientists in the late eighteenth and early nineteenth centuries. As a consequence, scientifically specialised groups constantly formed and re-formed. The corollary to the decline of the Society for Promoting Natural History, for example, was formation of the Linnean Society of London in 1788.

Outside London, in places like Oxford, Cambridge and Manchester, there was a comparable growing awareness and appreciation of science and its practice, and an increasing level of participation in scientific and learned debates. As with their London counterparts, these regional societies did not attempt to exclude interested and educated non-practitioners from their meetings.

From this point, however, two major shifts of emphasis in scientific research can be discerned. Firstly, science gradually become less wide-ranging and all-encompassing. As data accumulated from worldwide scientific investigations, its volume alone began to preclude competence over a range of fields. Theoretical development, which made scientific competence more demanding, was both cause and effect of this accumulation of data. Hutton's theory of geological time, The Theory of the Earth, published in 1788, is a clear example of this trend, for it would require extensive geological field sampling from Australia to help vindicate its claims.

The gradual specialisation of many of the areas of natural science led to the establishment of specialist branches of scientific societies. Although the Royal Society of Edinburgh originally subdivided natural history into meteorology, hydrography, geology, mineralogy, botany and zoology, with the growth of knowledge, further specialisation became inevitable. Indeed, each of these six subjects became a separate discipline, to which others were progressively added.

The second change in emphasis of certain scientific societies and scientific researchers was a greater interest in applied research. Whereas experimental science had flowered during the seventeenth century to the extent that early Royal Society Fellows were often satirised for their impracticality,[5] by 1800 the prevailing ethos had changed towards the direct application of science for commercial and humanitarian purposes. A measure of the extent to which the Royal Institution wished to harness scientific research to practical ends can be seen in its appointment of Humphrey Davy as an assistant lecturer and researcher. Davy was a Fellow of the Royal Society, who had been awarded its Copley Medal in 1805 for his electrical research, yet at the Royal Institution he worked for the first six years on practical chemical investigations, including the principles underlying the tanning of leather and the dyeing and printing of different types of cloth. Such research was vital, for at the beginning of the nineteenth century leather-making was possibly the fourth most important secondary industry in Britain. Tannin was in short supply, so a cheaper substitute had to be found.[6]

Although best known for his patronage of non-commercial scientific research, Joseph Banks was also a pragmatic and successful farmer and entrepreneur, who played a major role in acquiring and establishing the British merino flock. As the British woollen industry at this time accounted for £3.5 million in exports, or more than iron and cotton combined, and gave employment to a million people, the value to Britain of an indigenous fine wool industry is apparent.[7]

Banks was also associated with many commercially oriented research ventures. For example, the Kew Botanical Gardens were conceived on the basis of becoming '... the depository of every known plant that could be useful or ornamental in a climate like our own ...'[8] He also experimented with New Zealand flax and spinach plants. Consequently it is not difficult to agree with Patrick O'Brian's assessment that if Banks' 'many collectors ... happened to chance upon some plant of great economic value, so much the better.'[9]

As President of the Royal Society and one of three Honorary Fellows of the Linnean Society, Banks also had a strong influence on scientific research and the development of scientific institutions in the late eighteenth and early nineteenth centuries. He was particularly active and influential in regard to scientific field research and exploration in Australia, and can perhaps be seen as the embodiment of the linkage between British science and Australian exploration.

His childhood interest in botany was quickened through undergraduate lectures at Oxford and, three years after graduating, at the age of twenty-three, he made trips to Newfoundland and Portugal where he engaged in collecting and classifying a diversity of botanical and zoological specimens. In the following year he made two field trips to Wales. These excursions were particularly valuable inasmuch as they prepared Banks for his best-known and scientifically most rewarding field research, during the expedition to the South Seas with Captain James Cook in the *Endeavour*. The official purpose of this journey was to observe the transit of Venus, on behalf of the Royal Society. Cook was also instructed confidentially to search for the southern land mass believed to exist from earlier Portuguese and Dutch sightings and landings.

The *Endeavour* sailed via the Cape to Tahiti and stayed for three months, until the necessary observations had been made. The exploration then proceeded to New Zealand and Australia. Continuing on via Java, Timor and the Cape, the party returned to England after an absence of nearly three years.

During the *Endeavour*'s time in Australia, Cook surveyed most of the eastern coastline, and several large incursions were made, the most well-known being at Botany Bay. Banks and his botanist Solander, who was a pupil of Linnaeus, the assistant naturalist Sporing, and the two landscape artists and scientific illustrators, Roberts and Briscoe, worked assiduously the whole time. They recorded general impressions of Australia's east coast, as well as collecting, pressing, preserving, sketching and painting samples of plants, molluscs, reptiles, insects, birds, fish and so on. As well, extensive ethnographic data was collected on the local Aborigines and samples taken of their weapons and implements.

Banks made several other smaller journeys by sea and land, but none compared with his *Endeavour* experience, and he retired from field research at the age of thirty.

The second, somewhat more sedentary phase of Banks' life was an intensely productive period, in which he employed his wealth, social position and scientific status to attain an eminent position in several scientific societies and government advisory committees. Besides his prominence in the Royal Society and the Linnean Society, he was Director of the Kew Botanical Gardens and Vice-President of the Royal Institution. He developed his private residence as a resource centre with extensive facilities, including a scientific library, museum and herbarium, and it became a meeting place for scientists and students. By the late 1770s Banks' wealth, disposition and achievements had raised him to an extremely powerful and influential position in British society:

> ... Banks occupied the premier position in the scientific world, was persona grata at Court, possessed ample means, and a knowledge gained by actual experience of the resources, as yet

> largely untapped, of the globe. To these were added an attractive and powerful personality, good health, and an intense enthusiasm for doing things and getting things done.[10]

Thus, when the loss of the American colonies forced the British Government to seek alternative destinations for its convicts, Banks, with his knowledge of the eastern coast of Australia, was asked to comment on its suitability as a penal settlement. When examined by a Parliamentary Committee he 'reported most favourably as to the soil and climate, recommending Botany Bay as a place where a colony would readily become self-supporting.'[11] He also drew attention to the relative absence of wild beasts and the sufficiency of fish, water and grass. Nevertheless, his recommendations were not couched in terms of expected economic gains.

Although the argument over the motives underlying the choice of New South Wales as a convict colony will not be pursued in detail here, it cannot be ignored. Indeed, in attempting to outline the factors influencing the course of scientific research and exploration in early colonial Australia, the effects of such motives upon scientific research field goals are highly relevant.

In 1783 the former American loyalist James Maria Matra, who had been a midshipman on Cook's *Endeavour*, was a lifelong friend of Banks and would soon be appointed British Consul General at Tangier, forwarded a proposal for establishing a settlement in New South Wales.[12] Initially his plan was to provide asylum for expatriate Americans like himself but, as an inducement to have his plan more favourably received, Matra also outlined the economic gains which Britain could expect from participation in such a venture. Furthermore, he detailed strategic and wider trade opportunities which might be anticipated. He saw the settlement as being '... designed to increase the wealth of the parent country ...'[13] This concentration on economic rewards is particularly interesting, because at this stage there was no mention of New South Wales being settled as a convict colony.

Matra's proposal was not accepted, but a similar plan put forward in 1786 by Lord Sydney nominated the major purpose of the establishment of a settlement in New South Wales as '... effectually disposing of (the) convicts and rendering their transportation reciprocally beneficial both to themselves and to the State.'[14] Sydney further attempted to render the proposal more acceptable by asserting that there would also be economic returns from the establishment of such a colony. He stated explicitly that he expected commercial benefits in the form of flax and timber for the British fleet in India.[15]

Clearly, the originally accepted explanation that Australian settlement was almost exclusively related to convict transportation appears dubious.

Ged Martin's *The Founding of Australia*, which takes up the challenge of this ambiguity, includes articles by proponents and antagonists of the argument that convict transportation was the sole reason for the settlement of Australia. Dallas, Rowe and Blainey argue that a colony in Australia would have provided mercantilist opportunities, as well as flax for naval sails and ropes and Norfolk Island pines for masts.

In contrast, Martin attacks the economic argument, stating that the British Government's intentions in regard to economic ventures in the new settlement of New South Wales were to be 'simple self sufficiency'[16] and, only possibly, the production of flax and timber for the requirements of the Royal Navy.[17] Bolton is similarly disposed, arguing that:

> Convicts were ... the main reason why the Home Office promoted Botany Bay. Yet I would not wish to discount the commercial factor entirely.[18]

In a more recent article, although Martin continues to attack the economic arguments for the settlement of New South Wales, he shifts his ground somewhat, to include the possibility that Botany Bay was envisaged as a British entrepot trading station.[19]

Given the difficulty of discerning motives underlying complicated political decisions from a distance of over two centuries, with incomplete records to draw from, the complex of reasons influencing settlement in Australia may never be satisfactorily resolved. It appears reasonable to note, however, that while there were no explicitly commercial motivations, the wishes or beliefs expressed by a number of promoters of settlement indicate some underlying hope of economic gain. This sentiment would become more explicit once the settlement was established. It is therefore possible to argue that economic factors did affect the ethos of scientific research in colonial Australia.

Overall, it is clear that in eighteenth-century Britain much of the research in the natural sciences was descriptive in nature; Joseph Banks had a pragmatic and commercial aspect to his scientific interests and he played a definite part in the selection of New South Wales as a site for convict settlement; and there were underlying expectations of and desires for economic gain from the settlement of New South Wales. As a consequence, exploration and field research carried out in Australia during the first hundred years of white settlement were not primarily motivated by theoretical interest but, particularly after the early successes of the pastoral industry, by the search for grazing land.

Accordingly, the following chapters will examine the influence which official and individual desires for economic gain had upon the nature and location of exploration and field research. They will also show that, while science in Britain was very slowly becoming the province of professionals and specialists, early field research in Australia remained primarily in the hands of amateurs and was non-theoretical and descriptive in nature. For almost a century, it seems that scientists in the metropolitan country were happy to be the theorists, using their colonial counterparts merely as collectors. The subordinate relationship of field science to bushcraft, whereby the expertise of field scientists in most instances trailled that of bushmen, upon who they were vitally dependent, will also be outlined.

2

Slow and Painful Progress — Settlement and Early Exploration to 1815

Scientific field research, and the development of bushmanship in Australia, began officially with Governor Arthur Phillip's first minor explorations in April 1788. Even in these earliest ventures Phillip attempted to work towards the Blue Mountains, but his expeditions did not get within two days' march of the ranges. In the following year Phillip and Captain John Hunter sailed up the Hawkesbury River as far as the falls, some ten kilometres below the future settlement of Penrith, and Captain Watkin Tench worked his way westward from Parramatta, discovering the same stream further south and naming it the Nepean.

Following Phillip's exploration of the country surrounding the settlement, Lieutenant Dawes led a party in early 1790 which crossed the Nepean and attempted to reach the Blue Mountains. They were driven back after covering only twenty-four kilometres in five days. This was slow progress and Phillip commented that:

> ... after the first day's journey they met with such a constant succession of deep ravines, the sides of which were frequently inaccessible, that they returned.[1]

Dawes' attempts on the Blue Mountains were followed by those of Bass, Barrallier and Caley, but it was not until 1813 that Blaxland, Wentworth and Lawson were successful. Later in that year Deputy Surveyor-General George Evans retraced and extended their route and discovered the headwaters of the Macquarie River.

From 1788 until Evans' discovery of the Lachlan River in 1815 exploration was in an arc outwards from Sydney. Much of the country traversed in the immediate vicinity of the new settlement, and towards the foothills of the Blue Mountains, was broken and difficult and the earliest explorers were physically, materially and psychologically ill-equipped to cope with it. That these earliest attempts at exploration and field research were amateurish was inevitable.

There were other factors influencing the nature of exploration during this first quarter century of white settlement. In the first place, by the turn of the century Sir Joseph Banks had acquired a wide-ranging and influential role in planning and running the New South Wales colony. He corresponded regularly with the government, discussing proposed explorations and their rationale, as well as analysing and incorporating the findings. Furthermore, Banks received and distributed to the appropriate bodies a considerable volume of samples from field researchers in Australia. In the process, he had altered his values from those expressed when he gave evidence some years previously to the Parliamentary Committee. In a letter to Under-Secretary King, for example, Banks wrote:

> We have now possessed the country of New South Wales more than ten years and so much has the discovery of the interior been neglected that no one article has hitherto been discover'd by the importation of which the mother country can receive any degree of return for the cost of founding and hitherto maintaining the colony.[2]

By this stage the British government had expended a considerable amount of money on the colony and some return was deemed extremely desirable. An earlier covert wish for economic gain from the New South Wales settlement was now an overt desire. By 1798, Banks' expression of this desire was quite explicit:

> ... there are many objects, both in the vegetable and mineral kingdoms, hitherto undiscover'd that will, when brought forward, become objects of national importance and lay the foundation of a trade profitable to the mother country with that hitherto unproductive colony.[3]

This quest for economic recompense was not merely a wish of Banks but was also expressed by a number of senior officials. The Duke of Portland, in his letter to Acting-Governor King in 1800, outlined the means by which an area of the coastline was to be explored by the boat *Lady Nelson*. His instructions included ascertaining rivers, bays, harbours, magnetic variations, tides, currents and so on, but the main thrust of the instructions was:

> ... to land as often as he sees reason ... and to examine the country as far inland ... whenever there appears to him a probability of discovering anything useful to the commerce of

manufactories of Great Britain.[4]

This was not to say, however, that the emphasis was exclusively commercial, for Portland also outlined how natural history samples and data were to be gathered on such '... specimens of vegetables, animals and minerals as he shall think likely to prove interesting to naturalists at home.'[5]

Locally-inspired and economically-oriented field research during this period included searching for coal, small supplies of which had already been discovered in the Wollongong area in May 1797 by three survivors of the wrecked *Sydney Cove* who were attempting to walk northwards back to Sydney.[6] A successful find was made shortly afterwards in the Hunter River region and in 1798 Governor Hunter reported to Portland:

> There was a considerable quantity of coal discovered to the southward of this harbour and, I directed it to be examined; specimens were accordingly brought, which I sent to Sir Joseph Banks by the last China ship.[7]

The search for coal was accelerated for, as Portland noted to Hunter late in 1798, the cost of shipping coal from Britain to the colony at the Cape was '... attended with a very heavy expence to the public. I cannot but think that a great saving may be made by sending them (ie. ships) to the Cape from New South Wales.'[8]

By 1801 King was able to report to Portland that he had employed an experienced miner and eleven men in boring in the most likely places, and one month later that he had bartered a load of coal for produce from the master of the *Cornwallis*, 'this being the first natural produce of the colony that has tended to any advantage. I have enclosed the Commissary's statement of that exchange.'[9]

It was also hoped that the coalmines would form the basis of a viable iron-smelting industry, using ore from deposits already discovered in the colony. However, within a few years more sober assessments were being made of the commercial realities of Australia's known natural resources. Coal was not considered economically reliable, as the Cape of Good Hope, which was the only market, was only accessible in times of peace with the French. Markets for iron were not available. King commented on the colony's extremely narrow resource base at that time, though he expected that wool and linen exports would increase and that cotton and indigo would be useful crops later on when areas with the correct climatic conditions were settled and cleared.[10] He had earlier contended that '... if I except the ship timber, with which this part of the territory abounds, we possess no known staple whatever.'[11] The increasingly pressing need for economically advantageous discoveries was reflected in the nature of exploration and field research in early colonial Australia.

The second factor affecting pre-1815 scientific investigation was the dependence upon non-professional researchers. Governor Phillip's report of the first official exploration in April 1788, in the immediate hinterland of the new settlement, best describes the local unavailability of professional scientific expertise:

> ... here, my Lord, I must beg leave to observe, with regret, that being myself without the smallest knowledge of botany, I am without one botanist, or even an intelligent gardener, in the colony; it is not therefore in my power to give more than a very superficial account of the produce of this country, which has such variety of plants that I cannot, with all my ignorance, help being convinced that it merits the attention of the naturalist and the botanist.[12]

Phillip's findings were, inevitably, superficial, wide-ranging and purely descriptive. He was not a scientist, nor did he have scientists with him on his field expeditions. His reports are those of a layman attempting to cope with a volume and complexity of material beyond his technical capacity. He noted ethnographic data on the diet, eating and cooking habits of the local Aborigines, their cleanliness, courage, clothing, hunting and fishing utensils and so on. He commented in an elementary fashion on the vegetation, soil, mineralogy and presence of game.[13] In short, he acknowledged his inadequacies. Nevertheless, these first tentative expeditions, though materially ill-equipped and scientifically inadequate, allowed Phillip to gain an overview of the nature of the country.

Two years later Captain Tench found himself similarly ill-prepared to deal with field research in his limited excursions inland from the settlement. Tench appears to have been given no instructions for specific scientific research and — as with Phillip's reports — his findings were wide-ranging. He too commented on the absence of a botanist, but was also concerned with the lack of a mineralogist, for rock samples could not be evaluated. He claimed that:

> ... from specimens of ore seen in many of the stones picked up here ... I cannot quit this subject without regretting, that someone capable of throwing a better light on it, is not in the colony. Nor can I help being equally concerned that an experienced botanist was not sent out, for the purpose of collecting and describing the rare and beautiful plants with which the country abounds.[14]

Tench was also aware of the immense amount of information on Australian natural history which was unrecorded and basically unknown in Britain: '... to the Naturalist this country holds out many invitations.'[15]

Despite Tench's lack of scientific training, his narrative outlined the bird life, with particular reference to the internal and external anatomical differences between emus and other birds, and provided an analysis of information on kangaroos. Ethnographic data on the local Aborigines, meteorological observations and analyses of the soil types and their suitability for agriculture were also given, but almost without exception the data was purely descriptive. Apart from collecting soil samples in bags on one expedition near Broken Bay 'in order that by analysis its qualities might be ascertained,'[16] the nature of his scientific reportage and his general approach to scientific research were hesitant. Tench was aware of his own and his associates' shortcomings, in contrast to at least one member of one of his expeditions:

> I am going, on Monday next, in company with Capt Tench and Lieut Dawes, of the marines, on a week's excursion, to explore westward ... They are gentlemen whose minds are highly cultivated and of great scientific knowledge.[17]

Perhaps the best indication of Tench's awareness of his lack of scientific expertise can be seen in his tentative description of the kangaroo:

> Of the natural history of the kangaroo we are still very ignorant. We may, however venture ... a strong presumptive proof ... we know not.[18]

In short, Tench epitomises the enthusiastic amateur.

On some of his earlier explorations in the immediate surrounds of the settlement, Phillip was accompanied by Captain John Hunter, who later became Governor of New South Wales. Hunter was a keen amateur natural scientist, who encouraged explorers to collect samples and data, for which he often arranged transport to Sir Joseph Banks for his perusal and appropriate dispersal. Hunter too was aware of his own scientific inadequacies, particularly when there was so much work to be done in identification, description and classification.

> The vast variety of beautiful plants and flowers, which are to be found in this country, may hereafter afford much entertainment to the curious in the science of botany; but I am wholly unqualified to describe the different sorts with which we find the woods to abound ...[19]

His reporting of his first four years in the colony is very similar to that of Phillip and Tench: wide ranging, descriptive and elementary:

> Of insects there are as great a variety here as of birds; the scorpion, centipede, spider, ant and many others; the ants are of various sizes, from the smallest known in Europe, to the size of near an inch long; some are black, some white and others, of the largest sort, reddish; those of this kind are really a formidable little animal.[20]

Nevertheless, in Hunter's writings is the first recorded example since Banks of a theoretical, if ingenuous, approach to the interpretation of Australian field research data:

> It would appear, from the great similarity in some part or other of the different quadrupeds which we find here, that there is a promiscuous intercourse between the different sexes of all those different animals.[21]

Some ten years later there was still no resident botanist in Australia, despite successive governors noting the necessity for one. The position had been initially filled, in a fashion, by David Burton, a government gardener who collected specimens for the Kew Botanical Gardens.[22] Unfortunately, he died from a shooting accident within seven months of his arrival in the colony and botanical collecting was left to amateurs such as Governor King, who forwarded a steady flow of specimens to Banks. Banks' self-taught botanist, George Caley, was the first researcher in Australia with a background in that discipline, but because he did not have scientific qualifications, he could do little more than collect, briefly describe and forward specimens to Britain. As Banks noted, he had some smattering of knowledge in other sciences and had:

> ... studied practical botany and horticulture under my direction and ... has, without the advantages of what is called a liberal education, made a considerable progress in both these branches of usefull knowledge.[23]

Caley was well aware of his limitations, particularly in the classification of samples:

> I have tried of late to use the language of Linnaeus in making descriptions, but I have to lament that this is above my reach and I am afraid it will not be so easily understood.[24]

Caley's scientific shortcomings were often noted by scientists in Britain, who commented that, although his collections and notes on birds were extensive, his groupings were '... without any predilection for system, and in consonance merely with what appeared to him to be their natural affinities.'[25] The real scientific work on Caley's samples was carried out in Britain, where they were assessed by experts and incorporated into the systematic framework of the various scientific disciplines.

At the same time as Caley's pioneering efforts, Lieutenant Francis Barrallier of the New South Wales Corps made a number of explorations inland from Sydney, culminating in his attempt to cross the Blue Mountains. Though Barrallier's journal outlined his findings in a purely descriptive fashion, they were recorded in a more sophisticated manner than in the earlier journals. Barrallier appears to have been the first explorer to record direction and distance for each leg of the daily route, and minimum and maximum temperatures. His concise, precise and fluent recording of the equipment carried by Aboriginal women exemplifies the general quality of his work, and his journal is the best example of that genre prior to the arrival of professional scientists:

> During their marches the women are obliged to carry the children and have in addition a net in the form of a sack hanging on their back in which they have to carry opossums and all tools necessary to their husbands, such as kangaroo bones, which they use as chisels; bivalve shells which they employ for sharpening the point of their spears; and other utensils, as well as lines of various descriptions, gum etc.[26]

By the early 1800s the standard of scientific expertise and reporting in New South Wales had improved little. The major reason for this limited progress can be seen in Governor King's instructions to Lieutenant Grant, who was sent to examine the Hunter River region in 1801. Through a lack of professional personnel, King was forced to assign a miner to appraise the coal deposits, and two sawyers, presumably to evaluate the stands of timber. Consequently Grant's report of the expedition was of limited value, as the following extract suggests:

> The soil is black, but mixed with a sort of sand or marley substance ... The ash, gum-trees of all sorts ... fish also are plenty, and I suppose, from their leaping, are of the trout kind.[27]

In this light King, in his report to Hobart in 1803, commented on the impossibility of identifying and evaluating commercial mineral deposits, and pointed out that the only attempt to ascertain the commercial properties of the colony's iron ore had been made by French mineralogists.

He further noted that during Barrallier's expedition to the Blue Mountains he had found what may have been a 'perfect Ore', but that:

> ... not having any Person in the Colony capable of ascertaining these points I have sent the Specimens in a Box with these Despatches. I have not a doubt that if a good Mineralogist was sent out to reside here that some very useful discoveries would be made of Minerals.[28]

As a result of this and similar comments, the Colonial Office became more actively involved in the appointment of professional scientists and ordered that field researchers be granted facilities, physical assistance, transport, equipment and food.

During Caley's expedition on the brig *Bee* which, with the *Lady Frances*, was part of Lieutenant Grant's 1801 coastal survey, he was assigned a soldier who was '... always to attend him on shore' and he was to be taken ashore in any places likely to be productive.[29] Similarly, William H Humphrey, who was appointed in early 1803 as Government Mineralogist of New South Wales, was to be afforded:

> ... whatever protection and assistance of labour he may require ... in the incursions he may make into the country ... (for) the result of his labours will be productive of considerable benefit to the settlements.[30]

Despite such official support as Caley's expeditions received, they were ill-equipped affairs which usually lacked specific goals. Moreover, they were of an all-embracing exploratory style dictated as much by ignorance of terrain, weather and game and by a shortage of pack animals, as by Caley's scientific inadequacies. Until supplies, equipment, horse numbers, local knowledge and bush skills improved, field researchers and explorers were rarely in control of their work.

Examples of the equipment problems which frustrated Caley's field research included a critical shortage of drying paper, which meant that he was periodically prevented from gathering botanical specimens when they were in flower. As he often only traversed an area once, this simple deficiency meant that his collections were frequently incomplete. Caley's research also suffered from the want of small articles which, though neither sophisticated nor complex, were often unavailable in Australia. These included:

> ... pocket knives, ... a small pocket blow-pipe, a small quantity of various sized fish-hooks, a few pins for insects, a few nests of boxes, a small pocket barometer for ascertaining the heights of

> mountains, ... some small bottles with wide necks ... some fine glazed gun powder and various sized shot (to avoid destroying small birds).[31]

Caley occupies a special place in Australian scientific field research and exploration history, though. He had sufficient innate desire and drive to endure hardship, to develop techniques for coping with the Australian bush, to collect and dry samples in a professional manner and to pack and forward them with valuable accompanying notes. But he set himself an unrealistic task by attempting to cover both the systematic and spatial characteristics of the environment, despite inadequate training and equipment and the painstaking necessity of learning essential bush skills. Caley realised the drawbacks of over-extension:

> ... the misfortune is, they who study geography are very indifferent botanists, and vice-versa. For my part I should never have employed myself in a geographical pursuit.[32]

His poignant assessment of his shortcomings in taxidermy not only exemplifies his own lack of training, practical skills and equipment, but also indicates the standard of scientific research in the colony before 1815.

> ... in another box is a few skins of birds, but many of the specimens are not so good as I could wish, by not having any materials for to cure them with, and from which I have had many good skins spoiled, as the flies here are so destructive. ... I feel by practice that ... much [may be] overcome, and have reason to believe that a good and experienced stuffer might take up the extended parts without being perceived. I have aimed at saving the eyes and tongue and noticing the sex, but unfortunately the birds have oftentimes been much damaged by the shot.[33]

Contemporaneous with Caley's efforts was the voyage of the *Investigator*, the first scientifically planned, properly equipped and adequately staffed exploration and research project to be based in Australia. Although it was primarily a marine operation, with little relevance to land exploration history and the evolution of bushmanship, it warrants analysis, for it provides some insights into the problems researchers faced as field work became more sophisticated. It is also a yardstick with which to judge the scientific standard of previous and subsequent land explorations.

Banks played a considerable part in the planning, staffing and equipping of the voyage, the stated purpose of which was to examine the 'natural productions of New Holland'.[34] Economic pragmatism, so pervasive at that time, could not be denied. Indeed, Banks was even more explicit in a letter written in January 1801, in which he stated that the voyage was expected to produce economic results. He pointed out that he expected that the scientists and field researchers involved would be rewarded for their discoveries.

> It is a safe and a very interesting voyage and one very likely to make the fortune of the person who engages in the mineral line. There seems to me every prospect of minerals of the greatest value, and Government will, no doubt, if valuable mines are discovered in situations where they can be worked, employ the discoverer in some lucrative part of the working of them.[35]

Matthew Flinders was chosen as commander of the *Investigator*, which was fitted out extensively in Britain for the purpose of exploring, gathering, storing and transporting specimens of natural history. By 1801 Banks had enlisted an astronomer, a naturalist, a gardener and two painters of botanical specimens, and commented '... I may say I have my choice of twenty at least very able young men.'[36] The botanist's position was given to Robert Brown, a medical practitioner who had become attracted to, and qualified in, botany. Brown was to supervise the scientific research on the trip and plan the gathering of botanical, zoological and mineralogical specimens.

As carrying capacity was less of a problem on a substantial sailing vessel than with packhorses, Brown could afford to include equipment which would allow for better results to be obtained. Banks provided the Admiralty with a list of the scientific equipment he felt necessary for the standard of research which he expected from Brown. In contrast to Caley and his earlier problems, Brown was in the enviable position of being able to specify the type and quantity of paper he required for drying plant specimens and to carry as much as he felt he needed:

> The kind of paper I wish to have is Imperial brown paper. It is fully the size of cartridge and in many respects is much superior, both for drying and preserving specimens, especially of the rigid shrubs of this country and, what is no small advantage in our situation, mice do not eat it.[37]

He also was able to purchase at the government's expense and carry with him an extensive range of the latest reference texts available, an advantage not shared by Caley, who had pointed out in June 1799 that lack of access to the literature was a serious liability which detracted from his professional field research capacity. 'All that I have at the present to trust to is memory, as I cannot get to any of my books.'[38] Brown's ability to function as a professional scientist was infinitely superior to that of his untrained, ill-equipped and frequently physically stressed predecessors in Australian land-based scientific field research.

There was considerable space on board for dried and living botanical samples, as well as for mineral and zoological specimens. Flinders had had alterations made to the *Investigator* in England which reduced his own living space in order to obtain an extra cabin for the storage of specimens.[39] Special boxes constructed to convey living plants were not particularly successful, however, for by May 1802, sixty of the seventy samples had died. Ocean transport of such specimens was always difficult, for salt spray tended to kill them.

Because the *Investigator* was periodically in contact with other vessels, samples could be forwarded to Sydney for storage. Brown requested that the boxes containing them be periodically moved about to discourage mice, and that small fires be occasionally lit to prevent dampness, which encouraged the growth of mould.[40] This technique contrasts with the Prussian explorer Ludwig Leichhardt's later practice of encasing sample trunks in raw green-hide from the bullocks as they were slaughtered and allowing the untreated leather to set hard as a means of protecting the samples during up to fourteen months' travelling through thick scrub and the accompanying heat, dust, rain and high humidity.

Despite its undoubted success, the voyage of the *Investigator* had its shortcomings. The strategy of periodic incursions on shore from a marine operation was not without problems. Both at Albany and at a later site, Brown was hampered by sore legs which 'prevented me from attempting any very extensive incursions.'[41] Due to their lack of knowledge of the seasons of the various districts, the *Investigator*'s party arrived in many instances after the plants had finished flowering for the year. Furthermore, Brown was well aware of his own zoological and mineralogical shortcomings:

> In zoology I have done but little, the time necessarily employed in collecting, preserving and describing plants, preventing me from paying half the attention to the animal kingdom which its great importance deserves.
>
> In mineralogy I have hitherto merely collected what presented itself on the surface, never having been in a situation where it was necessary to sink a shaft.[42]

Although the findings of the *Investigator* voyage were extensive, there were clearly flaws in its planning, mainly because not enough was known in advance of the region, the seasons and habitats. Brown's work was in many respects merely a more sophisticated and seaborne version of the earliest traverses of country and the random gathering of samples.

Little scientific field research was carried out between Caley's field expeditions and the explorations of Deputy Surveyor-General George Evans in 1813 and 1815. Evans was probably the last of the public amateurs. His intellectual and technical limitations are apparent in his report, which was inferior to those of Barrallier, Caley and Robert Brown. He had no inkling of geology and lacked the descriptive capacity necessary to impart a picture of the country to Governor Lachlan Macquarie and the authorities in Britain. He was aware of his shortcomings, as his description of the Blue Mountains demonstrates: 'The hills around are fine indeed; it requires a clever person to describe this Country properly.'[43]

In 1815 Evans was sent by Macquarie on a second expedition over the Blue Mountains:

> ... I have sanguine Hope that he will meet with some great River which may probably fall into the Sea on that part of the Coast, bearing in a South-Easterly Direction from Spencers Gulph.[44]

This statement is significant, for it demonstrates that sufficient was now known about the pattern of landforms in south-eastern Australia for Macquarie to be able to piece together the information and construct a hypothesis about its drainage system. Until proven correct, his theory was to shape the direction of subsequent field exploration in that region. Indeed, the overall emphasis of exploration was slowly moving away from the gathering of an overview of previously unknown country, towards the testing of geographical theories. It was to be the 1840s, however, before sufficient data was collected to allow for overviews of terrain, climate, botany and zoology to be established, and for expeditions with specific scientific field research goals to be planned. It would be even longer before field exploration in Australia could overcome problems of mobility, carrying capacity and staffing, so that results comparable to those achieved by the *Investigator* could become a reality.

Perhaps the most important factor which inhibited early exploration and field research in Australia was the lack of mobility caused by the shortage of riding and packhorses, and pack and draught bullocks. In a letter to England in July 1790, Captain Hill criticised the first explorers for their failure to use even the limited number of horses which could have been made available to them:

> I look upon it as unpardonable, not having a greater knowledge of the country, the same pains that have been taken to explore would, if rightly planned, have been successful. A party is sent out with a few days' provisions on their backs, perhaps as much as they can well carry; this, with other impediments, prevents them from getting over much ground and they consequently are obliged to return with the knowledge only of a few miles of country; yet there are two or three colts and their dams in the colony that would be the better for gentle work and to burthen them but slightly with provisions would be a means of penetrating 20 times as far as we already have [and thus Governor Phillip] ... might by this period have transmitted to England an ample knowledge of a great part of this territory.[45]

When the First Fleet called at the Cape of Good Hope for supplies, en route to Botany Bay, it also took on board four mares, one stallion, one colt and two fillies, as well as sheep, cattle, goats, poultry and fodder. The fleet sailed from the Cape on 11 November 1787 and disembarked the male convicts, marines and livestock on 28 January 1788. Only six horses were unloaded, the fillies having died on the voyage.[46]

Similar losses occurred in later voyages, with the *Britannia*, for example, losing ten out of forty-one horses in 1795.[47] Not surprisingly, the horse population of New South Wales grew at an extremely slow rate. By 1796 there were only fifty-seven horses, all of which were owned by the authorities or by civil or military officers. Ten years after settlement there were still only 117 horses in the colony.

Of the several factors contributing to the slow growth of the horse population, relative utility is perhaps the most important. Because the development of a herd sufficient to sustain the colony's meat requirements was of critical importance, the importation of breeding cattle was given precedence over that of horses. Governor Hunter's 1796 letter to the Duke of Portland, after he was taken to task for importing bullocks instead of breeding stock, corroborates this point.

> ... it is certainly true, my Lord, that the importation of oxen into a colony which was wholly without breeding cattle is a measure which cannot well be defended ...[48]

Another inhibiting factor was the high cost of importation. In 1797, for example, a quotation was given for the shipment of cattle from the Cape to the colony — fodder, insurance and handling included — at a cost of £35 per head. This figure was actually quoted on a loss basis, the contract being conditional on the carrier getting a guarantee of government freight on the return voyage.[49] Since horses are larger, more prone to injury and infection and more difficult to transport than cattle, it is safe to assume that the cost of shipping them would be substantially higher than the quoted figure. As the typical wage for a labourer in 1797 was fifteen shillings per week, the minimum cartage cost for a horse, without taking the purchase price into account, was equivalent to at least a year's work for a farm labourer or, in 1990s values, more than $20,000.

By 1806 there were 552 horses in the colony, all of which had either originated in or been bred from stock imported from the Cape or India, apart from one stallion and one mare which were brought from Britain in 1802. The comment was frequently made that the descendants of these horses, which were bred and reared in New South Wales, were '... far superior to the original stock, both in strength and in beauty.'[50] The descendants of the Cape horses were found to be smaller though hardier than the Indian stock which, being more 'hotly' bred with Arab blood, required better feed. At this point the purchase price of horses was still considerable, ranging from £100 to £150 for an ordinary mare from 13.2 to 15 hands high.[51]

Horses were at their highest price at about 1806, although, as the data available on prices is meagre, this result may be atypical. Perhaps the most useful indicator of the relative costs of horses is the purchase price expressed in the number of weeks of a labourer's wage. In 1800, at £50 per horse and 15/- per week, a horse's value would have been equal to sixty-seven weeks of a labourer's wage, in 1806 approximately 126 weeks, in 1825 approximately fifty weeks and by 1837 approximately twenty-seven weeks. By 1844 there were 56,685 horses in New South Wales and prices had dropped to the point where importation, blood stock excepted, was no longer economic.

As a result, in the earlier years of the colony the high cost of horses slowed exploration immeasurably, both in regard to the amount of supplies and equipment which could be carried and to the distance which could be covered. Commissary Palmer's bills-of-account, drawn on the British Treasury in 1804, for instance, show that a horse hired for government usage from a private owner for forty-eight days, presumably for exploration purposes 'in the mountains',[52] cost £60, which was the equivalent of approximately eighty weeks' wages for a labourer. It is not surprising, therefore, that exploration parties were not, as a general rule, fully mounted until after the expeditions of Captain Charles Sturt, Surveyor-General Sir Thomas Mitchell and Leichhardt in the mid-1840s.

Nevertheless, packhorses were soon being used to carry supplies and equipment on expeditions, whose members also were, in some cases at least, mounted. In December 1803 Governor King and a party visited the area above the Nepean River known as the Cowpastures, a district to which straying cattle had migrated, settled, bred prolifically and prospered. For the first time on an official reconnaissance, all members of the party were on horseback.

When Barrallier attempted to cross the Blue Mountains in the early 1800s, his method of conveyance was novel in the Australian context, for he used a wagon drawn by two oxen. The practicality of this mode of conveyance over broken, trackless terrain is questionable for, in many cases, creek and river banks in their natural state were too precipitous to negotiate easily. It would be only after several years of occupation by herds of grazing cattle that such steep banks would be broken down and made more easily negotiable. On reaching the Nepean River on 6 November, Barrallier's men had to unyoke the bullocks and manhandle the provisions and the wagon down the almost vertical bluffs, across the shallow running stream with its heavy sand bed and up the steep bank on the other side. They covered only six more kilometres that day, then rested, 'feeling rather indisposed.'[53] The same problem occurred again on 8 November and presumably on the trip home as well.

Caley also appears to have suffered from a shortage of pack animals in his explorations of the hinterland of Sydney and the foothills of the Blue Mountains. Although he was normally supplied with a packhorse and a convict assistant, the carrying capacity of a single animal and the lack of mobility caused by the lack of a riding horse limited his expeditions in both duration and extent.

In scientific field research, the problem of carrying capacity is magnified, for the collection of specimens dictates that a means of transport be available to return them. Since Caley's single packhorse was primarily laden with food, bedding and cooking equipment, little space was available for note and specimen paper, for ink and pens, for glass jars and phials for insects and so on, let alone for carrying the specimens home. In 1845, when Leichhardt lost four horses in two days through poisoning and drowning near the end of his 5,000-kilometre expedition, he decided to burn his botanical samples, which numbered more than 3,000, since he now had no spare pack animals to carry them. This event was perhaps the greatest single loss in Australian scientific field research history.

Even though horses became more readily available after 1805, the 1813 crossing of the Blue Mountains was still impeded by a shortage of mounts, which meant that the seven expedition members and a local guide had to proceed on foot. On the other hand, since they had four packhorses to transport their provisions, it appears that the men were not required to carry knapsacks, making their passage through the rugged Blue Mountains considerably less arduous.

Besides the difficulties caused by a shortage of pack and riding horses, early explorers were also hampered by their lack of bush skills. Their field journals are valuable, if inadvertent, sources of information about the painful and often protracted learning process they were forced to undergo.

Before beginning an analysis of the development of bushmanship from the first settlement to 1815, two points need to be made. Firstly, bushmanship is an all-embracing term which includes the application of all the skills, knowledge and equipment necessary for survival and to provide a degree of facility in daily dealings with life in the bush. Should it include, as in Sturt's, the Gregory brothers' and Mitchell's cases, a determination never to give Myall Aborigines an opportunity for duplicity, such an approach is a manifestation of bushmanship. Secondly, the development of bushmanship is a slow process of accretion of learning, based upon previous experiences of success and failure. Bushmanship is the composite of the wide range of slowly and often painfully acquired skills which evolved from the amateurish efforts of the earliest explorers.

It is not surprising that little bushmanship was apparent in Phillip's earliest explorations, for he and his men were quite ill-equipped to cope with the country. They were military personnel who, in all probability, had never been off the beaten track. In addition, they had no knowledge of the local climate and consequently suffered during their first venture into the bush, being unprepared for the rains of autumn, which is the wettest season in coastal New South Wales.

Phillip's extremely limited rate of progress indicates his party's lack of proficiency. In his second expedition, after a full day's struggling on foot, his men were unable to penetrate the scrub and were forced to return to their starting point.[54] After five days they had to return home when their provisions ran out, yet they had penetrated only about thirty miles inland, at an effective rate of six miles per day. As Phillip remarked, because they could not count on finding water, they carried each day's supplies and this, combined with '... the provisions, arms and a couple of tents, obliged every officer and man to carry a very heavy load.'[55] Under such circumstances, little could be expected of Phillip's explorations.

Tench's accounts of several field expeditions between 1788 and 1792 indicate that, although some improvements were apparent on Phillip's earlier efforts, the outcomes were still extremely limited. Most of Tench's exploratory work was to the west and north-west of Sydney, where he attempted to ascertain the course of the rivers and generally gain an overview of the country.[56]

Tench and his peers could scarcely be described as bushmen. As soldiers they could not be expected to move freely through the Australian bush and their awkwardness, in contrast to the agility of their Aboriginal guides, soon became a sore point:

> Our natives continued to hold out stoutly. The hindrances to walking by the riverside, which plagued and entangled us so much, seemed not to be heeded by them, and they wound through them with ease; but to us they were intolerably tiresome. Our perplexities afforded them an inexhaustible fund of merriment and derision; — did the sufferer, stung at once with nettles and ridicule and shaken nigh to death by his fall, use an angry expression to them, they retorted in a moment, by calling him by every opprobrious name which their language affords.[57]

In fairness, it should be noted that, as the Aborigines were not weighted down with equipment and did not have to push themselves and their packs, bed rolls and rifles through the bush, they could be expected to be more proficient at traversing it. But Tench's party were to demonstrate their inexperience in other ways as well. In his description of their camping techniques, for example, the explorer outlines how they used their hatchets to build 'wigwams' for cover and to cut their nightly firewood. Persisting with this second task indicates how little they had learnt for, where dry timber abounds, experienced bushmen do not cut it, but burn it in half, then in quarters and so on, until it is reduced to manageable lengths.

In addition, from a brief survey of Tench's narrative, it appears that the majority of his expeditions were undertaken between April and July, a period when bleak, wet weather is to be expected in New South Wales. Knowledge of the seasons was then incomplete and — as with Phillip's earlier expeditions — the explorers suffered accordingly. Tench's amazement at the temperature falling to twenty-three degrees Fahrenheit in mid-July in inland New South Wales is a clear indication of his lack of knowledge of the climatic conditions which could be expected away from the coast. Under the circumstances it was an excusable shortcoming: 'Nothing but demonstration could have convinced me, that so severe a degree of cold ever existed in this low latitude.'[58]

Despite some difficulties, however, Tench penetrated considerably further inland than Phillip. He and his fellow explorers usually travelled by dead reckoning, drawing up a map of their traverse at the end of each day:

> Our method, on these expeditions, was to steer by compass, noting the different courses as we proceeded; and counting the number of paces, of which 2,200, on good ground, were allowed to be a mile. At night when we halted, all these courses were separately cast up and worked by a traverse table, in the manner a ship's reckoning is kept; so that by observing this precaution, we always knew exactly where we were and how far from home: an unspeakable advantage in a new country, where one hill and one tree, is so like another, that fatal wanderings would ensue without it.[59]

Obviously they were not sufficiently confident of either their feeling for the landscape or their sense of distance and direction to work in any other way, despite having the Blue Mountains as a barrier to the west. If lost, all they had to do was travel east until they reached the coast, which was rarely more than fifty miles away. Tench's inability to gauge direction was highlighted on a later expedition when he outlined how, when they finally gained a view of the ranges they were searching for, they saw their objective '... in a contrary direction from what we had been proceeding upon.'[60]

Twenty years later, Blaxland, Wentworth and Lawson would experience similar problems crossing the Great Divide. Given the broken nature of the terrain and its thick covering of forest through which a view of landmarks could rarely be found, it is not surprising that they had difficulty in maintaining their sense of direction. Since Blaxland had only had a few years' bush experience prior to embarking on this expedition, Wentworth a negligible amount and Lawson had been engaged in explorations to the north of Bathurst, their skills in coping with unknown country were poorly developed. On the inland side of the ranges, Blaxland and one of the convicts nearly became lost following a kangaroo too far. On the return journey, the whole expedition had considerable difficulty finding its way back through the forest from the foothills to the Nepean River. The danger of laxity in not carefully noting one's course in timbered plains or mountain country cannot be overemphasised. Leichhardt commented on this same problem in his Journal thirty-one years later, when John Roper went five hundred metres from a campsite to cut tent poles and was later found by the Aboriginal guide, Charley Fisher, some five hours and eight kilometres later, heading 180° in the wrong direction. Although he was only about eight kilometres east of the foothills of Expedition Range, Roper was unable to see these landmarks through the ten to twelve metre brigalow forest which grows in this area:

> Accidents of this kind happen very easily in a wooded country, where there is no leading range or watercourse to guide the

> rambler, or when sufficient care is not taken to mark and keep the direction of the camp.[61]

In April 1789, Tench participated in an expedition to the north of Sydney with twenty other persons, including the Governor and two Aborigines. The latter were taken because it was expected that they would be a useful source of information on the country to be traversed, '... as no-one doubted that they were acquainted with every part of it between the sea coast and the River Hawkesbury.'[62] The Aborigines failed to live up to expectations. After only a short distance had been covered, they advised the expedition leaders that they were unfamiliar with the country, '... so that the farther they went, the more dependent on us they became, being absolute strangers inland.'[63] According to Tench, at one point the Aborigines became so disoriented through being outside their home territory that, when the party came to the banks of a stream, they were completely bemused.

> Our natives had evidently never seen this river before: they stared at it with surprise and talked to each other. Their total ignorance of the country and of the direction in which they had walked, appeared, when they were asked which way Rose Hill lay; for they pointed almost oppositely to it.[64]

In addition to using the Aborigines as guides, the whites had hoped to learn from them '... their manner of living in the woods and the resources they rely upon in their journies. Nothing, however, of this sort had yet occurred ...'[65] It therefore appears that, although the objective of employing and observing the Aborigines as a means of learning bushmanship was logical, in practice it was not effective.

Perhaps the most useful information on the development of bushmanship before 1800 comes from the journals of two expeditions which Governor John Hunter encouraged and assisted. The work of an unnamed youth, they describe journeys on foot for up to a 160 kilometres to the west and south-west of the settlement, often through rocky and rugged range country. Most significantly, on the second expedition the youth and his fellow explorers remained in the field for twenty-five days, through supplementing their supplies with game. The original scope of the expedition was much more limited, for its leader, Wilson, had merely asked if each expedition member '... was willing to go to the S.W. part of the country for nine or ten days.'[66] Furthermore, they did not know whether game was available, nor the topography of the country to be covered. As it happened, their confidence in their ability led eventually to an uncomfortable shortage of substantial food. They were reduced to a limited supply of biscuits, which they rationed at two each per day, and finally:

> ... we concluded to return back, for fear that we should not have biscuits enough to bring us back ... having had no signs of a kangaroo for three days ... we really believe that there never was a native in this part of the country.[67]

The point remains, however, that these men were able to survive for an extended period of time compared to the earlier efforts which were of between three and ten days' duration. Here perhaps were the first signs by explorers of confidence in their ability to strike out across unknown country, to know where they were at any given moment, to be clear about where they wished to go and to be able to determine the general route to be taken. Without such skills, which can be developed over time, one is loath to make extended excursions, particularly in forest country where landmarks are usually very difficult to see. Thus, after only a decade of white settlement there were signs of emerging confidence and skill, at least amongst some bushmen.

Three years later, when Barrallier requested permission to attempt to cross the Blue Mountains, Governor King readily agreed, for he had 'been at some pains, seemingly, to know something more of the country.'[68] There are several features about this expedition which warrant attention, for they indicate the first methodical attempt to overcome the constraints which had hampered previous attempts. For one thing, Barrallier spent a few days in a reconnaissance of the plains country towards the foothills, for he intended establishing a series of depots to use as food supply bases, in order to extend his range. This done, in early November 1802 he, four soldiers, five convicts and a small group of Aborigines set off from Parramatta.

Although his Aboriginal guides came and went, Barrallier was one of the first explorers to use them advantageously. On occasions they showed him shortcuts of up to six miles through arduous mountain country. He does not appear to have been intimidated by gatherings of Aborigines, with whom he attempted to remain on good terms, for he realised the danger of upsetting these people in their own country:

> It is not of any advantage but, on the contrary, it is very dangerous to offer any insult to the natives. They avenge themselves of it sooner or later and the first white man they meet without means of defence becomes their victim. They make use of the most cruel tortures on the one they can catch, whoever he might be, without troubling in the least about enquiring whether he belonged or not to the party who ill-treated them.[69]

Through using a planned approach involving depots of food and being able to procure a certain amount of game, Barrallier's party was able to travel further and stay in the field longer than any previous expedition. However, the military style of his progress — slow moving, unmounted and relying on frequent returns to supply dumps — was not suited to the country and helped account for his lack of success. At the time of Barrallier's departure, Caley asserted in a letter to Sir Joseph Banks that the essential elements of travelling in New South Wales were lightness, speed and packhorse transport:

> The same gentleman is upon the eve of setting off again with a larger party and instead of horses he takes out two bullocks. He means this time of fixing stations, from which a regular supply is to be forwarded. By what I already know of travelling in this country gives me room to suspect that this journey will not accomplish the design. ... in my opinion it will fail, for they cannot go above 2 days' journey before they must part with the bullocks and then every man must carry his own provisions and he must be a very strong man that can carry 20lb extra of his gun, ammunition and etc. ... I am so vain as to think that with another man besides myself and a horse, that I can go further than what this party will, provided the weather is favourable.[70]

Caley, the son of a British horse-dealer, naturally appreciated the mobility offered by saddle horses. Furthermore, he had the skills necessary to ride through rugged country and to care for his horses in that environment. It appears, however, that his ideas were slow to gain acceptance, partly because of the shortage of horses.

It is useful to trace the development of Caley's bushmanship, for he probably achieved more than any previous explorer in New South Wales, no matter how well equipped. Like Barrallier, Caley used initial field trips of limited extent as a means of training for longer expeditions. He notes that in his earlier excursions he was usually beaten back by 'little provisions and meeting with wet weather'[71] and in part blamed this on Governor King, who — he raged to Banks — often made him wait for hours outside his office before seeing him, abused him and supplied him poorly with equipment. Notwithstanding such treatment, Caley's results were so satisfactory that, towards the end of his Australian service, Banks commended him for his efforts, commenting that he deserved 'some reward from me for your diligence and activity.'[72]

Initially Caley compiled maps based on pace and compass measurements, not only to provide a record of his journeying, but also to allow him to find his way home. He found that the compass with which he had been supplied was inadequate and indicated that, on his return to Britain, he intended to design and have manufactured a model more suited to Australian bush conditions. His maps were all the more inaccurate and rudimentary because, never having learnt to use a sextant, he was unable to measure latitude. With time his confidence and sense of direction improved, to the extent that, by 1802, he had few qualms about negotiating unknown country and staying out for extended periods. On one occasion, for example, when south-west of Sydney he wrote:

> ... I mean to proceed to the sea-shore, which must also be near at hand. If I find out its source in the time I reckon I shall proceed to the SSW if the land is favourable. If not, I shall try a west course.[73]

Like Barrallier, Caley appreciated the useful qualities of the Aborigines, although he did not personally require their services as guides:

> Respecting the natives themselves, it would be the means of bringing them over to our customs much sooner, and respecting natural history, we should be made acquainted with many animals at present unknown to us. ... There would be no danger of the collectors getting lost or bewildered, which is too oftentimes the case, for the native would trace back their footsteps. He would likewise foresee whether any danger was to be expected from the natives of that part. He would point out the tracks of different animals, which would be unnoticed by a European. Many new birds would be readily obtained, as the natives in general are excellent marksmen and quicker-sighted than our people. The specimens of the different trees might be procured which would otherwise have been missed or left for want of a climber.[74]

Consequently, as Caley noted to Banks, 'I mean to keep a bush native constant soon.'

Although Caley's role in the development of Australian bushmanship was important, he failed to develop the capacity to stay in the field for extended periods of time. By 1805, however, several other men had already acquired such skills. In that year Governor King equipped a party and promised to reward its members if they could take Caley over the ranges to the west of the Hawkesbury, where, they said, a large plain existed. By King's description these were:

> ... men who had been in the practice of frequenting that part of

> the mountains ... (and were) four of the strongest men of the colony, who had been accustomed to live in the woods.[75]

King called these men bushrangers, a term which, at that time, had no criminal connotations. By 1807 the term had acquired much of its modern meaning. In that year, Colonel Paterson, who had been responsible for establishing the British settlement at Launceston, outlined to Under-Secretary Sullivan how ten Van Diemen's Land convicts had absconded to the mountains, taking their masters' kangaroo dogs with them. These men rapidly became self-sufficient. By 1809 there were approximately sixty bushrangers in the area, some of them armed. They used their firearms and dogs to hunt kangaroo which they surreptitiously bartered with townspeople for grain, sugar and other commodities.[76] Unlike later bushrangers, these men were fugitives, rather than active criminals.

As early as 1805 there were white men capable of living for extended periods of time in the Australian bush, without the facilities normally offered by settled societies, and in such men, and in their hard-learnt skills, can be seen the origins of the Australian bushmen and of Australian bushmanship. Henceforth, bushmanship was to develop apace, for there was now a base of knowledge upon which to build and a group of practitioners from whom to learn.

Caley's most valuable contribution to the progress of Australian exploration came from his open mind and flexibility in regard to assessing and helping develop a technique for exploration that, once the Blue Mountains were crossed and the relatively open forest and plains country of inland Australia were exposed, would come into its own. It was only then that the advantages of high mobility through small, completely and adequately mounted expeditions with sufficient pack animal capacity, became fully apparent. As Caley himself commented:

> ... as a traveller in this country [being an experienced horseman] has given me an advantage over all others. When Mr. Barrallier returned I perceived his loss for the want of the like. ... Upon a horse I can take 100lb of food extra of all other articles for my pursuit. I am not afraid to travel by having only another person besides myself. By this I have not the incumbrance that will always be found in a large party.[77]

Explorers were slow to learn the lesson. In 1813, although Evans had sufficient packhorses to carry the supplies and equipment on his first retracing of Blaxland, Wentworth and Lawson's route, he had no spares.

Their absence constituted a severe problem, for horses cannot be relied upon to be constantly fit for work. Unlike a vehicle, which can be repaired, a horse, once lame, will often not heal, or heal at a slower rate, if forced to keep moving. Leichhardt encountered this same difficulty on his first expedition, when a horse went lame in the Suttor Creek area, after about one fifth of the journey had been completed and could scarcely hobble behind, unladen, for the remainder of the journey. On his second expedition Leichhardt's grey riding horse became sore and, despite the ministrations of the expedition's veterinarian, eventually went so lame that it had to be left behind. Its corpse was found on the return journey, having scarcely moved from the point at which it was left. Consequently, later expeditions, when horses were considerably cheaper, were all equipped with spare riding and packhorses.

Evans did not handle his horses well. Because the pack saddles were not lined with serge, the animals became badly galled on their withers and he was forced to give them days off, slowing his rate of progress. As well, by working them while they were unfit and under arduous circumstances, he accelerated their loss of condition. To counter the problem of galling, Evans and his men used their woollen blankets under the saddles.[78] Presumably some notice was taken of this problem, for no later references have been found of pack saddles not being correctly lined with woollen serge.

Furthermore, Evans does not appear to have developed a satisfactory technique for securing his horses overnight. During his first expedition, on 28 November 1813, he notes that they 'left the horses in the valley', which indicates the animals were unsecured. It is almost certain that he would have mentioned the mode of securing them if one had been employed, as it would have differed from the normal British practice of not fettering one's horses. It is likely that the horses were not tempted to stray overnight only because they were exhausted from carrying heavy loads in mountainous country.

On his second expedition Evans again appears to have had only packhorses, which he again failed to secure at night. It is surprising that by 1815 a safe method of securing horses had not been developed, for by then they had been used in explorations for at least fifteen years. On the night of 14 May his horses wandered. They had been tied together, 'but not secured in a proper manner', presumably by tying them to a tree. Consequently most of the following day was spent searching for the animals, which were eventually found with the ropes fortuitously wrapped around a tree. Later in the same year, during Governor Macquarie's tour of examination of the new settlement of Bathurst and its surrounds, the party's carthorses broke free one night and wandered twenty kilometres back along their tracks.

This mishap not only entailed a walk of forty kilometres for the hapless groom, but also seriously delayed their progress. As Macquarie commented, '... this will be a lesson to Joseph during the rest of our journey, to be more careful in tethering his horses ...'[79] Both experiences clearly illustrate the contemporary level of horsemanship, which dictated that horses were either tied up for the night or left grazing free. The disadvantage of the latter, in almost unlimited bush, has already been demonstrated. The disadvantage of the former is that horses working all day and subsisting only on grass require several hours of grazing per day to obtain sufficient nourishment to maintain their condition. By tying them up for the night and working them during the day, insufficient time is left for essential grazing.

A book outlining bush life in the early settlement, entitled *Settlers and Convicts; or Recollection of Sixteen Years Labour in the Australian Backwoods*, written by 'an immigrant mechanic' and ascribed by Manning Clark to Alexander Harris, is a useful source of information on the techniques used to secure horses in the bush at that time. By the late 1820s it was standard practice to hobble horses at night and as a result it was not a great problem to find them in the morning. Even with hobbles, however, horses can still move freely, covering up to thirteen kilometres at night and can even canter, if they so desire. In fact, on Francis Gregory's 1861 expedition of the north-west of Western Australia, six of his horses actually galloped in their hobbles into the camp from where they had been grazing. They had a clear incentive, for hard behind were eighteen armed Aborigines who had already attempted to spear them.[80] Fortunately, by the late 1820s the wandering of stock was less of a problem, for, as Harris indicates, bushmen had become proficient in tracking their horses.

> When turned out for the night the horses seldom stray far; they are hungry and tired, and like to make the most of their time on any patch of good grass they come to. But if a young horse does happen to walk off, he is easily tracked by the experienced eye of the bushman and hobbled as he is, is easily overtaken.[81]

According to Naval Surgeon Peter Cunningham, who spent two years wandering inland New South Wales in the 1820s, bullocks were even more prone than horses to wander at night:

> A strong tether and a pair of strong fetters for their forelegs are essential, as the bullocks require to be tethered or fettered every night when let loose on the road, and even some considerable time after you are upon your farm, until they take a liking to the

place — the trouble occasioned by their straying being often excessive.[82]

Finally, although the hobbling of stock at night soon became standard practice, bells were slow to come into use. In the forest country of New South Wales and Queensland, bells saved a considerable amount of time, especially when there were several horses whose tracks had crisscrossed as they grazed throughout the night, or where rocky or hard ground made it almost impossible to track the horses. Leichhardt belled one horse on his first expedition, but the clapper broke near the future settlement of Burketown in the Gulf country, in August 1845. In memory of this incident he named the place Camp of the Broken Bell.[83] The later refinement of bells and their usage will be examined in subsequent chapters.

The increasing use of horses and bullocks by exploring parties not only increased their mobility, but also enabled them to carry a wider range of equipment and a greater quantity of provisions. Equally important was the growing ability of bushmen, if not to live off the land, at least to supplement the standard issue, derived from the British naval tradition, of biscuits, flour, rice, tinned soup, salt pork, sugar and tea.

Access to potable water was to remain a problem. At the very beginning of exploration in 1788, Phillip noted that water could not be relied on and that supplies had to be carried. Because of a failure to appreciate that water in Australia was not to be taken for granted, Tench and his expedition members suffered severely from thirst during his July 1791 excursion:

> ... we passed a miserable night, from want of a drop of water to quench our thirst; for as we believed that we were going to a river, we thought it needless to march with full canteens.[84]

Water shortages in Australia are due to the limited and intermittent nature of the rainfall and the sandy beds of watercourses, which lead to discontinuous flows. By 1791 the seasonal nature of the flow of most Australian streams had been deduced and was described thus:

> They ... complain of a very great scarcity of water. What they have met with is generally contained in stagnant pools, which seem to be reservoirs for rain water. Sometimes there is a continuation of them for a little distance; and after very heavy rains they frequently communicate with each other and then send out a stream through some of the adjacent vallies, which ceases to run shortly after the rain has ceased to fall.[85]

Water problems aside, in 1788, Phillip's second expedition was reduced to six days' duration because of a shortage of provisions. Despite seeing kangaroos frequently near the settlement at Sydney Cove and infrequently further inland, as well as a variety of duck, swan and quail around the lakes, his expedition members were unable to procure game. Obviously the Aborigines fared better, despite the inferiority of their weapons, and Phillip was '... surprised to find temporary huts made by the natives far inland, where they must depend solely on animals for food'.[86] He could scarcely believe that the inland country, apparently so poorly provided with game, could support them.

> I intend going [to the Blue Mountains] ... if it is possible and which will explain what is at present a mystery to me, how people who have not the least idea of cultivation can maintain themselves in the interior parts of this country.[87]

It is scarcely surprising that Phillip did not know that the Aborigines procured food by both hunting and gathering, with the latter activity providing the greater return. Also, as a naval officer he failed to understand the extent to which amateurish hunting skills and shortcomings of bushmanship impeded these first attempts at supplementation. Unfortunately, such deficiencies were not rapidly overcome. In 1792, for example, Tench maintained that white men still found it very difficult to shoot wildfowl, despite the abundance of ducks, geese and swans. They were also incapable of stalking game — particularly kangaroos — relying on kangaroo dogs, or remaining awake all night:

> ... near covers, into which the kanguroos were wont to retire at night and (watching) ... with great caution and vigilance when the game, in the morning, sallied forth to feed.[88]

Consequently, even though three convicts were licensed to carry firearms and directed to hunt kangaroos to supplement the colony's dwindling supplies of food, the early settlers had very limited success in capturing game. Curiously it was comparatively easy to hunt kangaroos in Van Diemen's Land, possibly because they were more plentiful. In fact, Lieutenant-Governor Collins commented in August 1806 that, without kangaroos, the colony would have gone hungry.[89]

The first clear indication of a developing ability to procure game comes from Barrallier's 1802 expedition, which covered 220 kilometres over seven weeks, the longest sustained exploration trip to date. It was achieved partly because the party was proficient enough to supplement the rations by shooting thirteen kangaroos, one of which weighed a hundred pounds gutted, four possums, some ducks and a twelve-pound eel. Furthermore, they were analysing and refining their hunting techniques. For example, when Barrallier noticed that his men were having considerable trouble getting close to the kangaroos, he suggested that they take off their red military jackets. After removing this discordant tonal variation against the Australian bush, the hunters had greater success. Nevertheless, Barrallier failed to take full advantage of the available food resources. Only once did he mention attempting to preserve some meat for future use. Indeed, the problem of preservation was not resolved until sun- and smoke-drying and salting techniques were developed. Although Barrallier was aware of the diversity of food eaten by the local Aborigines, his expedition members were not as capable of procuring it, nor would they eat snakes, lizards, wild dogs and so on.[90]

The relative lack of success in obtaining game during this period was also due to the inaccuracy of the available firearms. Leichhardt, some forty years later, obliquely commented on this problem when he criticised Australian shooters generally and his expedition members in particular, for their shortcomings at bringing down game. Leichhardt may have been a trifle unfair, for projectiles from smooth-barrelled muskets lack the aerial stability imparted to bullets spinning from a rifle barrel. As rifling did not become a common feature of British military weapons until the advent of breech-loading in the 1860s, the weapons available to early Australian explorers could only have been smooth-barrelled. In addition, the projectiles of smooth-barrelled muskets have to be smaller than the bore in order to allow for loading through fouled barrels. In contrast, the projectiles of breech-loading rifles are actually fractionally larger than the barrel. This tighter fit, in conjunction with the stability imparted by rifling, leads to considerably greater accuracy.

It is also likely that, in most cases, the weapons available to early Australian explorers were old and worn. Caley noted in a letter to Sir Joseph Banks in 1800 that most of the weapons available were obsolescent muskets.[91]

Other factors affecting the accuracy of muskets were the rudimentary sights then available and the inefficient powder, which necessitated a trajectory of 1.5 metres in 200 metres. The considerable variation in trajectory which had to be allowed when aiming over differing distances had to be based on experience. Problems also occurred with the composition of the powder used, for, with the inevitable jolting which occurred in field expeditions, the more volatile elements were differentially distributed in powder kegs and shooters' powder horns. As a result, the powder burning rates and trajectories were inconsistent.

Smooth-barrelled muskets were fifty per cent as accurate as rifles between 100 and 200 metres, on targets two metres by six metres. At 400 metres, smooth-barrelled muskets were only twenty per cent as accurate.[92] These factors may well have led to the exhortation not to fire 'till you see the whites of their eyes' and the inherent inaccuracy of smooth-barrelled muskets was such that, even up to the middle of the nineteenth century:

> ... firing at ranges much over 100 yards was usually a waste of shot and powder. Even at this range the musket was unreliable; its only effective use was to pour volleys into massed troops at very short range.[93]

One can understand, therefore, the problems that early bushmen faced in getting close enough in the parkland and plains country of inland Australia to shoot kangaroos and emus.

Nevertheless, despite such inescapable problems associated with shooting game, hunting skills improved. On 5 December 1815, for example, Evans noted that, although his expedition had lost a considerable amount of flour due to wet weather, he was not perturbed over a potential shortage of food for '...a Kangaroo can be procured at any time, there are also Emus, [and] we killed some Ducks this day.'[94]

In addition, fish were readily procured from the Lachlan River. 'If we want a fish it is caught immediately; they seem to bite at any time.' Significantly, Evans went on to note that '... had I brought a quantity of salt we could cure some 100lbs of them.'[95] Explorers were now learning to preserve meat in the field, extending the possible duration of their expeditions. No longer were they absolutely limited by the carrying capacity available at the beginning of the journey.

A further component of the overall development of hunting skills was the gradual introduction of hunting dogs. Tench mentions that greyhounds were being used in the early 1790s for hunting kangaroos and that the dogs quickly learnt from experience how to catch their prey by the foreleg to avoid being ripped. According to Tench the 'rough wiry greyhound suffers least in the conflict and is most prized by the hunters.'[96] He was probably referring to the long-haired Irish wolfhound, which is still used for hunting kangaroos, for it is bigger, heavier and more robust than the greyhound.

Blaxland and his companions took five dogs with them in 1813. Their breed is not mentioned but, as they were used for catching kangaroos, they were most probably greyhounds or wolfhounds, the predecessors of contemporary kangaroo dogs. These dogs were not only more successful than earlier explorers' dogs in obtaining a supply of game, but also, on one occasion at least, they disturbed a party of Aborigines creeping up on the camp late in the night. As a result of both experiences, dogs were to play an increasingly important part in subsequent inland exploration.

Although explorers became progressively more skilled in hunting with inadequate firearms, for almost four decades they also had to overcome problems relating to shortages and poor quality of equipment. Deficiencies were apparent from the beginning, with the first excursions in 1788 experiencing considerable difficulty with Sydney's autumn and winter weather. Indeed, Phillip was led to complain that even his tent at the settlement was 'neither wind nor waterproof.' Sleeping on the wet ground during these earliest expeditions affected the Governor's health, necessitating several weeks' rest when he returned.[97] Presumably his men also suffered from the absence of groundsheets and were continuously bedraggled because they had not been issued with waterproof coats. Instead, they wore heavy woollen three-quarter length greatcoats, which soon became sodden.

Although waterproof coats would appear to be essential, they were generally disregarded by explorers for over forty years. If they were aware of George Caley's 1802 comment that, without waterproofs, travelling through wet thickets was as bad as 'being up to the neck in water' and that one's clothing was consequently soon ruined,[98] they chose to ignore it. Even twenty-seven years after settlement, on Evans' expedition over the Blue Mountains, none of the expedition members appear to have had waterproofs. Evans noted on 8 December that he and his companions hoped the day would be fine '... as neither of us have been thoroughly dry these last 3 days and Nights ...'[99] He was to claim, eleven years later, that such experiences had ruined his health:

> ... having been for weeks together in the interior on foot, exposed to all of the vicissitudes of the Weather, subjected to chance for even a Supply of Food, with no covering but a blanket, for days without being perfectly dry ... which have had at last the effect of breaking up your Memorialist's Constitution and inflicting on him a permanent chronic rheumatism ...[100]

The reluctance of explorers to carry waterproofs is difficult to understand, particularly as the authorities soon became aware of their importance. For instance, the list of articles required for the abortive settlement at Port Phillip in 1803 includes: 'Some waterproof for gamekillers.'[101] By mid-century, however, the importance of waterproofs was at last recognised. Leichhardt notes in 1845 that:

> ... some of us were provided with Ponchos, made of light strong calico, saturated with oil, which proved very useful to us by keeping out the wet and made us independent of the weather.[102]

Cold nights were also a problem. Tench notes, for example, that on his 1791 expedition, he and his men each carried a heavy eighteen-kilogram load which included a knapsack with food for ten days, a gun, a canteen, a cooking kettle, a hatchet and one blanket.[103] Although a single blanket was scarcely adequate covering on April nights in inland New South Wales, it was probably impossible to increase the issue, for blankets were difficult to procure in the early days of the settlement. As late as 1801 Caley wrote to Banks requesting several items, including heavy blankets, for 'I cannot get any here ...'[104]

For at least a quarter of a century, Australian explorers were not only ill-equipped against the cold and damp, but also poorly shod. Hunter was the first to comment on the unsuitability of his shoes, the soles of which came loose after a walking expedition. 'The last march having tore all but the soals from my feet, and they were tied on with spun-yarn.'[105] The colonial youth and his companions, whom Hunter noted as having travelled for twenty-five days on one exploration, suffered even worse from inadequate footwear. When their shoes fell to pieces, they were obliged to cut their clothes up for rags to bind their feet

The situation was no better on Barrallier expedition, its leader noting that its members' 'boots were all torn and our feet full of wounds.'[106] Since the party consisted of regular soldiers, the standard British Army field issues at that time must have been of poor quality.

In 1815, when Evans' men's boots fell to pieces, they were forced to make moccasins, which they called 'pampoosers', from the skins of kangaroos killed by their dogs. Unfortunately such footwear wore out in a few hours, especially if the grass was wet from rain or dew. Two years later, when Evans was second-in-command on Surveyor-General John Oxley's exploration of the Lachlan and Macquarie Rivers, he does not appear to have advised of the necessity for better footwear or for carrying more spares, for the botanist Allan Cunningham commented that, during that expedition, the men were forced to make shoes from the skins of the horses which had died from overwork.[107]

Footwear was not the only article of clothing which proved inadequate in the Australian bush. Caley commented occasionally that extended field trips were severe on clothing. 'I have wrote home for a fustian jacket and some shoes, for the woods tear everything to pieces.'[108] It was not till 1826 that boots and clothes appear to have been manufactured specifically for the hard wear which would be encountered in extended outdoor work. Governor Darling's 1827 report to Under-Secretary Hay noted that convicts were now manufacturing clothing from cloth woven in the colony and making shoes. Furthermore, they had made:

> ... 94 pairs of boots for the Mounted Police and Mr. Cunningham's exploring Party and ... upwards of One Hundred Suits of Clothing ... for the Sydney and Mounted Police.[109]

Nevertheless, it took many years for explorers to become aware of the accelerated rate of wear and tear on boots and garments in the bush and to make provision accordingly. As late as 1844, for instance, John Gilbert commented that, through inexperience, several members of Leichhardt's expedition did not bring sufficient clothing.[110]

Phillip's problems in 1788 from exposure, which arose from limited carrying capacity, may have discouraged later explorers such as Barrallier from using tents. As a result, Barrallier's men were frequently drenched in very heavy thunderstorms. In attempting to provide shelter, their earlier procedure was to '... cut some trees to make a hut large enough for the whole of my party', which would have been inefficient and probably ineffective.[111] In contrast, a hut made by Aborigines for Barrallier was sophisticated enough to allow for a fire to be lit within it. The expedition members were slow to acquire hut-building skills and it took several weeks' practice before Barrallier could state that the Aborigines were not '... absolutely necessary to me in making the huts for myself, my people, and the provisions at night.'[112] Although by the end of November the white men could erect huts capable of withstanding the heaviest downpour, the process must be seen as inefficient relative to carrying and erecting lightweight canvas flies and digging a drip trench around the bottom. It is unclear why tents were not carried, for there were plenty in the colony. Perhaps those available were military tents and too heavy to carry on foot, but lightweight flies could have been cut, for canvas was readily available.[113] Presumably the British military personnel involved in early explorations were not inventive enough to contemplate a structure other than that fabricated to withstand European conditions.

Evans' failure to carry tents on both his 1813 and 1815 expeditions is difficult to understand, especially as the expedition had packhorses available. He noted on Wednesday 24 November 1813, for example, that they had to shelter in a hut made of green boughs, which was quite inadequate against the rains which they encountered. Although it appears that Evans and his men had learnt — probably from other explorers or Aborigines — how to construct bark huts, he could not do so in this country for 'the trees will not bark' (ie. the bark will not split off freely in large sheets).[114] On his second expedition Evans again did not use tents, perhaps because of confidence in his ability to make bark shelters. Nevertheless, on one occasion his party had a night of rain so heavy that their fire was extinguished, his papers were damaged and they were 'completely washed up.' However, he was not particularly perturbed by the likelihood of being rained out on the following night, for this time he had 'taken every precaution to prevent it', presumably by constructing a bark hut.[115]

The early explorers' problems with food, clothing and equipment were exacerbated by their lack of fitness and, in many cases, their failure to become acclimatised before setting out. Many of the earliest explorers were military officers, who had led sedentary lives for most of their careers and who were unfit for the rigours of traversing rugged country while carrying provisions and equipment. Among the lower ranks the situation was even worse.

High temperatures were a commonly perceived problem. When Hunter accompanied Phillip to the Hawkesbury River in 1788, he complained of the heat during a long stage which they covered on foot. Similar comments were made in the early days of the Swan River Settlement and by John Gilbert at Port Essington in the early 1840s. In all cases, complaints were made about the heat in the cooler part of the year, which suggests that many men were badly out of condition and that acclimatisation took longer than might be expected.

Although the colony had been established for fourteen years by the time of Barrallier's expedition to the Blue Mountains, he and his men were not accustomed to Australian temperatures. The party frequently halted for three or four hours in the middle of the day, often spending the time bathing to cool themselves down. One entry describes the heat as 'excessive', yet on that particular day the maximum was only 82°F. On another occasion a temperature of 82.5°F was described as 'suffocating'. It may be that heat acclimatisation is as much psychological as physiological and that an understanding of high temperatures would only come with later exploration further to the north and inland.[116]

It is also clear that early explorers lacked physical toughness. As Caley discovered, camping out over extended periods is particularly hard and often deleterious to the system. Tench also commented on this point, particularly with reference to the Aborigines' lifespan.

> Longevity, I think, is seldom attained by them. Unceasing agitation wears out the animal frame and it is unfriendly to length of days. We have seen them grey with age, but not old; perhaps never beyond sixty years.[117]

Among the early white explorers, Wiliam Wentworth was badly affected by his experiences on the Blue Mountains expedition. In a petition four years later to the Earl of Bathurst, in which he sought compensation, Wentworth noted that he had subsequently suffered from a lung inflammation which he had not been able to overcome and which severely curtailed the physical activities he could undertake.

Much later, and in contrast, volunteers for Surveyor George Goyder's expedition in the 1860s in the region surrounding Darwin were carefully selected and subjected to training and toughening. Not until expeditions consisted principally of fit young men, most them raised, if not born in Australia, would lack of physical resilience and durability cease to be a problem.[118]

Finally, besides the deficiencies of equipment, bush skills and physical durability, early bushmen also tended to be psychologically maladjusted. In many cases they were ill-at-ease in the bush, if not alienated by it. In fact it was so strange and forbidding an environment that new words had to be constructed, or existing words adapted, to give the explorers the means of describing it. King indicated the necessity for psychological accommodation in a report in 1805, when he defined or redefined such terms as 'bush', 'scrub', 'creek', 'lagoon' and 'forest land'.[119] As well, the silence and the generally uniform and unbroken nature of the bush often affected these earliest explorers.

Tench and his peers, perhaps because of their lack of bushmanship and difficulties in making their way through it, saw the relatively benign country inland from Sydney as almost malevolent. Psychologically they had not made the adjustment necessary to accommodate the different frame of reference through which they would have to view this continent:

> Before us lay the trackless immeasurable desert, in awful silence ... we continued to march all day through a country untrodden before by an European foot. Save that a melancholy crow now and then flew croaking overhead ... the picture of solitude was complete.[120]

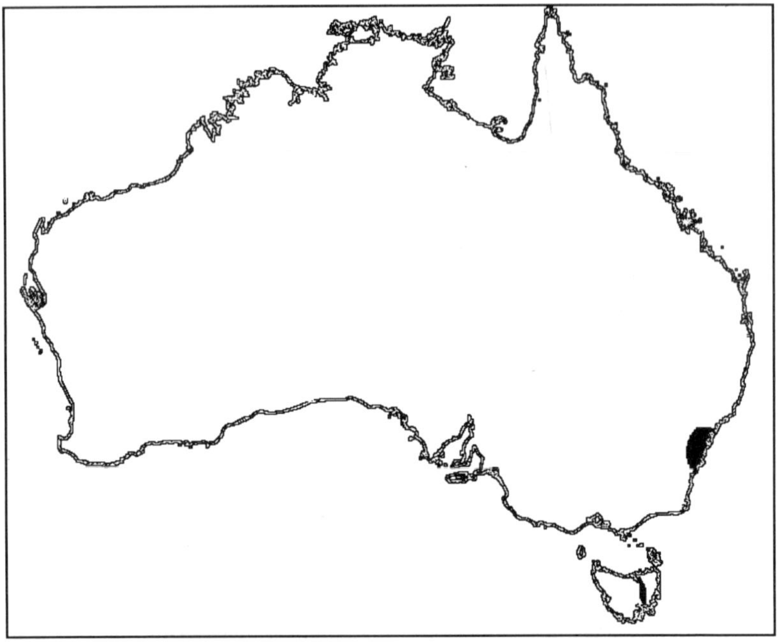

The area of Australia explored by Europeans between 1788 and 1815.

Caley was similarly affected. After one three-week expedition in coastal New South Wales in 1804, he commented that:

> The roughness of the country I found beyond description. I cannot give you a more expressive idea than travelling over the tops of the houses in a town.[121]

Furthermore, most early explorers were slow to adjust to extended absence from human society. Being part of a self-contained expedition slowly and timidly traversing the unknown terrain of an immense land mass was a psychologically and physically draining experience, which differed in every respect from making an overland journey in Britain. In the words of Caley:

> Travelling here is very disagreeable, by having one's victuals and bedding, together with other necessaries to carry, which becomes burthensome unless there is a large party. The low living ... tends to relax the constitution ...[122]

The psychological distance between these men and later professionals such as John McDouall Stuart, Ernest Giles and John Forrest, was immense.

3

Feeling the Way — Developments to the Early 1830s

The period from 1815 to the early 1830s saw considerable changes occurring in the approach to scientific research and in the overall ethos of the British scientific establishment. In part, this new order was reflected in the approach to field research and exploration in Australia. Banks' gradual decline in health and scientific stature prior to his death can be seen as symbolic of these changes, for he was very much a representative of the old scientific order.

The Industrial Revolution was having wide-ranging effects on British life, including the cultural and intellectual climate.[1] New-found wealth and middle-class comfort, coupled with improvements in transport and communication, allowed a larger proportion of the population to engage in intellectual pursuits. Scientific knowledge was pursued and colleges and universities were founded at an accelerated rate. Self-improvement through formal study and informal membership of scientific and philosophical societies and attendance at specialist lectures became fashionable, and an intelligentsia which respected intellectual achievement rather than social standing began to develop.

It was also a period of intense questioning and change in the areas of politics, religion, law and social values. It is possible that change in the scientific societies would have occurred irrespective of the exponential increase of scientific data being gathered, analysed and disseminated. At all events, specialist societies were being hived off from the Royal Society, or were forming spontaneously in response to perceived needs. The Astronomical Society was formed in 1820 for '... the [Linnean Society] could not cope with the increasing flood of investigation and this made the rise of new societies inevitable.'[2] Banks believed that the new societies would be 'the ruin of the Royal Society',[3] for him and his contemporaries, scientific societies, scientific research, wealth, power, status and social influence were indivisible. Perhaps he saw the growth of specialist societies, with their often more professional and less wealthy practitioners, as a rebuttal of his values and beliefs. The day of the wealthy amateur was drawing to a close. Wollaston, who was elected President of the Royal Society in 1820, was seen by some members as an unsuitable candidate, for he had made a considerable amount of money from his research into platinum malleability. This involvement contrasted with the traditional ideal of a 'disinterested search for truth'.[4]

The growing influence of the younger and more professional scientists within the major scientific societies forced the Royal Society to become more professional in its operations. More papers were read at each meeting, indexing of the Philosophical Transactions was more comprehensive, the library was catalogued, additional staff were hired to cope with these changes and membership became less conditional on the eclectic, if not dilettante, approach so favoured by Banks and his contemporaries.[5]

In the Linnean Society increasing membership, a growing library and a large increase in museum samples meant that paid staff were now required. A similar outlook was apparent in the British Museum, where in 1817 a revision of the natural history collection was begun on more scientific lines. The mineral collection was augmented until it was the equal of any in Europe and the curator of the botanical section was granted an annual fee with which to purchase samples of newly-discovered species.

By the 1820s British scientific societies were becoming involved in geographical exploration. The Royal Society, for example, initially fostered polar exploration[6] and by the late 1820s, through bequest funds, was able to provide financial support for the purchase of instruments and materials. The Linnean Society, which had seen this aspect of its charter as a professional responsibility from the beginning, provided a reference library and a resource museum of botanical and zoological specimens and endeavoured to provide instruments for research purposes.

In 1825, in order to promote excellence in scientific research, the Royal Society adopted the idea of making a prestigious annual award for outstanding work. This initiative was part of an attempt to improve the standards of British research which, although slowly becoming more professional, was inferior to much of that being carried out in Europe at the time. Addressing this problem in his *Reflections on the Decline of Science in England*, Charles Babbich attacked the Royal Society for being neither exclusively scientific nor a government instrumentality.[7] He was representative of a group who saw scientific investigation as a governmental responsibility. Research was becoming more sophisticated and increasingly expensive equipment was often required, placing the activity beyond the reach of less affluent, though more professional researchers. In this context, Herschel also commented that British scientists were unable to compete with their European counterparts who were often government-funded.

> ... it is idle for us to attempt competition with our Continental neighbours whether French or German in matters of science generally. Our day is fast going by ... [and] we are rapidly dropping behind in the race.[8]

Part of this decline in the standing of British scientific research was due to the relatively unfavourable light in which the British Government viewed and encouraged science. The authorities saw pure research as being of less value than applied science, but were prepared to fund neither. Accordingly, the government turned to the Royal Society for advice on a range of subjects. These matters were primarily pragmatically oriented and included an assessment of such issues as the merits and demerits of coal tar compared to pitch for caulking ships' timbers, and whether the former was responsible for an increase in illnesses amongst seamen. Scientific questions pertaining to the increasing number of voyages of exploration, longitude determination techniques, geomagnetic studies and the means of improving the life of the copper sheathing used on ships to prevent attacks by marine organisms were also handled by the Royal Society on behalf of the government.

Australian scientific research in the 1820s appeared superficially to be developing in a similar fashion to that occurring in Britain. There were, however, qualitative and quantitative differences. Factors which influenced scientific development and research in Australia included greater government involvement and funding, which led to a gradual increase in professional staff and better-equipped explorations. In contrast to Britain, there was little re-orienting of research away from the purely pragmatic and commercial. Finally, the climate congenial to scientific questioning and scientific research, which developed in Britain in this period, was not reproduced in Australia.

Apart from the Philosophical Society of Australasia, which was formed in 1821 and disbanded in 1822, there were no scientific societies until the Tasmanian Society of Natural History, established in 1837. The Philosophical Society was fortunate in having Governor Brisbane as President, and papers on astronomy, meteorology and geology were read at the meetings. Unfortunately there was insufficient interest to sustain it, which historian Ann Moyal attributes to a paucity of intellectual interest in the colony and consequent lack of sympathy with pure research:

> In a convict-emancipist society there were few educated citizens to entertain the study of natural history and fewer still who deemed expenditure on scientific investigation as a proper commitment.[9]

The British Government's strongly commercial outlook on science was reflected in its initial attitude towards Australian exploration and scientific research. This orientation can also be related to the fact that the colony continued to run at a loss. Governor Darling reported in 1828 that gross imports were £362,324 whilst exports totalled £76,314 — a deficit of £286,010. More importantly, Darling noted of the deficit that there appeared 'no adequate means of Making Returns.'[10] Consequently there was a continued emphasis on applied research. For example, the Royal Society-inspired measurement in 1826 of an arc of the meridian in New South Wales by Rumker was carried out, at least in part, because it '... would be useful in laying a foundation for a correct Survey of our Colonies.'[11] The importance of such a survey is easy to understand in the context of the increasingly rapid pastoral occupation of the lands west of the Great Divide. At that time Brisbane, who had been replaced by Darling in the previous year, also pointed out to the Earl of Bathurst, when attempting to sell his astronomical apparatus to the British Government, that astronomy was of 'great importance ... in advancing the interests of Navigation.'[12] His point was taken, for he was paid £1,614 for his telescope and other equipment and, in 1827, the authorities forwarded 'their general Catalogue of the principal fixed Stars' with instructions that it was 'for the use of the Observatory at Parramatta.'[13]

It is hardly surprising, therefore, that the instructions given to the leaders of exploration in this period were pragmatic in outlook. In Oxley's case, for example, he was not only to describe accurately:

> ... the general Appearance of the Country, its Surface, Soil, animals, vegetables and minerals, everything that relates to the Population, the Peculiar Manner, Customs, Language, Government and Domestic Economy of the Individual Natives, or the Tribes of them which he may meet with.[14]

but also to assess its economic potential. All fauna and flora were to be noted, specifically those '... that are applicable to any useful purposes, whether in Medicine, Dyeing, ... Woods, adapted to Cabinet Work ...

Household Furniture ... and Shipbuilding.' Samples had to be identified and indexed, especially 'Precious Metals or Stones'. Also, specimens of the most remarkable animals, vegetables or minerals had to be preserved, or drawings made. Finally, and perhaps most tellingly, '... a Circumstancial Account of Such Articles, if any, as might be advantageously imported into Great Britain ...'[15] had to be made.

By 1830, a gradual change of emphasis is discernible in the British Government's instructions to exploration leaders. Sturt's 1828 instructions, for example, contained no explicit demands to analyse the country in economic terms. Sturt was to '... endeavour to determine the fate of the Macquarie River and to follow it to its mouth if possible.' It should not be assumed, however, that these instructions indicated a dispassionate desire for scientific knowledge alone. The British Government was certainly aware of the value of a large inland river as an efficient and cheap means of transport and communication in the development of the hinterland. It was also interested in an analysis of the country '... so as to enable His Majesty's Government to judge of the means which the Interior affords for more extensive Settlements.'[16]

Perhaps the best example of this change in attitude towards scientific research can be found in Darling's assessment of Sturt's expedition to the mouth of the Murray in 1828. Despite nothing of commercial value being found, the Governor was still satisfied, for '... a question of this importance, which has for some years past excited much curiosity and anxiety, has been thus put at rest.'[17] This was more the appraisal of a scientist than of an accountant and manifested an outlook which gradually became more influential as the century progressed.

Notwithstanding the minimal development of a scientific ethos, due to the intense pragmatism underlying colonial field research and exploration, discernible progress in scientific professionalism can be identified within Australia during this period, as more and more qualified scientists were employed to carry out essential investigations. The day of the untrained amateur was coming to an end, as exemplified by the experience of the convict Hutchison. In 1813 Macquarie provided Hutchison, who claimed expertise in the chemistry of dyeing, with sophisticated scientific equipment to carry out research on Australian plants. The results were inconsequential, for Hutchison did not have the necessary background to cope with either the theoretical or practical requirements of the task. According to Macquarie, 'his Knowledge and Talents have been much overrated ... [and] as to Scientific Principles, I apprehend he will be found very deficient.'[18] The Governor pointed out to Bathurst that trained specialists were now required in a variety of disciplines. For example: 'I beg to observe to Your Lordship that an active, Clever Scientific Mineralogist of respectable Character would be a most Valuable Acquisition to this Colony ...'[19]

John Oxley was appointed Surveyor-General of New South Wales in 1812, in preference to George Evans, because of his superior training. Oxley's better qualifications were demonstrated in various ways, including his requests for equipment of a more sophisticated and extensive nature than that used by his predecessors.[20]

Finally, when Surveyor-General Mitchell undertook the first trigonometrical survey of New South Wales in 1828, the Colonial Office sent out two expert geodesists to take charge of the operation. According to Bathurst , these men had '... the advantage of that liberal Education which is so essential in the higher duties of the Department ...' and one of them had taken '... a very high degree in Mathematics at the University of Oxford.'[21]

The importance of establishing a Museum of Natural History was realised by the late 1820s, when Bathurst instructed Darling that £200 per year was to be spent in procuring samples and establishing such an institution. In order to obtain the desired standard of collection and display, Bathurst further instructed that a zoologist be sent to New South Wales to oversee the museum. Thus, some forty years after the establishment of the colony, steps were at last being taken to integrate locally the natural history information available in New South Wales, in order to prevent repetition of research and to develop an orderly local collection.

Generally speaking, however, scientific data was still being forwarded to Britain for incorporation and analysis, because the general level of expertise in Australia remained inadequate for the task. Indeed, in sciences such as botany and geology, major theoretical readjustments were being made and all new samples were required for evaluation against known samples and contemporaneous theories. As the largest collections of samples were in Europe and reference texts were more readily available there, the decision to forward samples for analysis was scientifically realistic.

With the rise of professionalism in British science and increasing numbers of specialists working in Australia, British scientific societies were becoming more interested in Australian research. In 1829 Under-Secretary Twiss wrote to Darling requesting that he obtain the information necessary to answer sixteen questions posed by the Royal College of Physicians concerning the health of the white settlers and Aborigines. Several of the questions revealed a considerable ignorance of the size of

Australia and its range of edaphic and climatic conditions. To have asked 'What is the nature of the soil?' and 'What is the medium height of the thermometer in the summer and winter months?'[22] raises doubts about the physicians' purported growing professionalism. Nevertheless, the request was treated seriously, data also being supplied on medical substances obtained in the colony and on prevalent diseases.

Government funding of the equipment, men and means of transport necessary for exploration and associated scientific research in Australia continued during this period. The authorities realised that large-scale exploration was too costly for private citizens and that the prospect of privately sponsored scientific research was negligible. Government support was thus more significant in Australia than it was for comparable activities in Britain.

By 1830 sufficient knowledge had been obtained to provide an Australian overview, a framework, and field research was now, in part at least, a form of hypothesis testing. Bathurst's instruction to Macquarie concerning Evans' discovery of the Macquarie River is a good example of this approach. Bathurst pointed out that the finding of a large westward-flowing stream arising from the watershed of the Great Dividing Range was surprising, given the '... fruitless Attempt made by Captain Flinders to discover, on the West Coast of New Holland, the Embouchure of any considerable River.'[23] As a result, Bathurst wished for an exploration to be made to resolve the course of the Macquarie and instructed the Governor accordingly.

After Oxley's failures to penetrate the Macquarie Swamps, speculation about the nature and direction of inland drainage increased with the discovery of other large rivers to the north, such as the Namoi, Gwydir and Macintyre, which flowed west or south-west off the Great Dividing Range. Cunningham, for example, believed that such streams drained into an inland sea, supporting his argument with reports from Aborigines of very large fish being caught in the interior and with reference to the migratory patterns of birds.[24] Although Sturt was to end speculation about the Murray-Darling drainage system in 1828, the myth of the inland sea was to persist for several decades.[25]

Meanwhile, increasing professionalism was directly affecting conduct of field research and exploration. As early as 1815 Bathurst drew attention to the deficiencies in Evans' journals:

> Although Mr. Evans is entitled to great praise for the perseverance with which he overcame the Natural Obstacles opposed to the Progress of his Discoveries, and the Activity with which he afterwards pursued his course to the Westward, yet he does not appear from the Style of his Journal to be qualified by

> his Education for the task of giving the Information respecting this New Country, which it is so desirable to obtain.[26]

Bathurst therefore insisted that the leaders of future explorations had to be men better educated than Evans:

> I hope therefore that in the further prosecution of these discoveries you will associate with him (Evans) some person of more scientific Observation and of more General Knowledge. It appears to me that such persons will be found either among the Officers of the Regiment now stationed in the Colony or among the Medical Officers ... if anyone can be found in the Colony possessing any competent Knowledge of Botany or Mineralogy.[27]

As a consequence, Surveyor-General John Oxley was appointed to lead the expedition to trace the course of the Macquarie. Oxley's navigational skills provide an index of the growing professionalism of Australian explorers. As a result of his training and the quality of his equipment, he was able to take astronomical and other readings which permitted the compilation of detailed and accurate maps of the region.[28] In a contemporary reappraisal of the Coonabarabran section of Oxley's 1818 route, shire engineer J Whitehead has estimated that Oxley's latitude readings were accurate to within a kilometre, while his longitude readings were consistently eight minutes and thirty seconds to the west, which represents an error of approximately sixteen miles.[29] Although substantial, this longitudinal discrepancy reflects more upon the limited accuracy of chronometers available in the colony at the time than upon Oxley's expertise.

On Oxley's 1817 expedition, scientific observation was the responsibility of Kew botanist Allan Cunningham, Colonial Botanist Charles Fraser and mineralogist William Parr. Cunningham's previous field experience in Brazil stood him in good stead, for he took care, for example, to equip himself with moderate-sized saddlebags and specimen cases '... well canvassed over and painted, for the reception and protection of those treasures that the interior of this country may afford me.'[30] In addition, he sent forward to the expedition's depot a specimen press and an adequate amount of drying paper.

The specimens gathered by the two botanists were extensive, being 'upwards of Five Hundred Plants totally different from those hitherto Collected or Known in this country ...'[31] Dried samples of all these plants and seeds of 150 of them were forwarded by Macquarie to Bathurst.

Despite the results achieved by the botanists, Cunningham for one came to appreciate that the aims of field exploration were not necessarily compatible with those of scientific research. He encountered problems with drying his specimens, with water damage to his samples when a horse fell into a marsh and with finding time to re-paper, classify and annotate the material. Since the primary aim of the expedition was to cover new ground, the requirements of the scientists attached to the expedition were secondary. The increasing mobility of explorers was inimical to patient, methodical and extensive sampling and surveying. As field research grew more sophisticated, this conflict of interests became more of a problem, to the point in Burke and Wills' expedition where the naturalist and illustrator Becker died from exhaustion before the expedition reached Cooper Creek on the journey north.

Unfortunately, by Oxley's second expedition, scientific research appears to have been greatly reduced in scope and importance. Nevertheless, although Fraser was the only scientist appointed, his results were better than those obtained previously by both himself and Cunningham. Towards the end of the journey Oxley noted that '... our cargo now principally consists of plants,'[32] for approximately seven hundred previously unknown specimens were gathered and later forwarded to England.

By the time of Sturt's exploration of the Murray-Darling river systems, scientific observation still remained in the background. Although there is no direct evidence that trained scientists accompanied the expedition, mention is made of a Fraser collecting numerous specimens. This may have been the Colonial Botanist recently returned from his voyage to the Swan River with Captain James Stirling.[33]

Sturt was intelligent and highly literate, but no scientific observer. Although his climatic data was valuable, his mapping activities appear to have been subordinate to the overall aims of the expedition. Indeed, he freely admitted '... that in respect of longitude observation he was only self-taught, that he went into the interior to explore, not to survey.'[34]

In 1828, in keeping with the prevailing policy, Governor Darling stressed in his instructions to Sturt that the Government Stores would supply all of the equipment which he requested for his expedition:

> You are to consider it an important duty to attend to the providing of all the supplies and to take care not only that every article is of the best quality that can be procured, but also that no article be wanting with which you may desire to be provided.[35]

Scientific equipment was, however, given a low priority by Sturt, who requisitioned surveying and weather recording equipment only. There was no paper for drying specimens, no specimen jars and no preserving spirits.

Consequently when on one occasion Sturt killed a snake of '... bright yellow colour; I had not ... the means of preserving it.'[36]

Equipment alone was not, however, the sole prerequisite for scientific success, as Oxley had earlier discovered. Field exploration was not a simple equation of packhorses, qualified personnel and scientific equipment. Even before Oxley's first expedition had left the Lachlan, a horse threw its load and broke the barometer, making it impossible for him to '... ascertain the height of the country with tolerable accuracy ...'[37] As well, the artificial horizon later leaked most of its mercury. This setback did not surprise Oxley, who had already concluded that it was impossible to carry delicate instruments safely through scrub country, because of the repeated buffeting the saddlebags received.

Such a problem would later be partially overcome with better quality pack animals, better stockmen and the provision of spare pieces of vital or delicate equipment.[38] Meanwhile, Oxley experienced similar problems on his second expedition. On one occasion a horse rolled down the bank and into the river, nearly drowning under its load before it could be pulled clear. Oxley commented that '... my baggage was on him and was entirely spoilt; the chart case and charts were materially damaged and our spare thermometer broken.'[39] Furthermore, since the barometer broken on the first expedition had not yet been repaired, they were still unable to measure altitude.

It is possible that Oxley's difficulties carrying scientific equipment were due more to his overloading of the horses than to any inherent difficulty in getting such equipment through the bush. Experienced packhorses, left to their own pace, rarely damage saddlebags. Once they adjust to their new effective width, they tend to clear obstructions by a minimal but consistent amount. By contrast, fatigued horses staggering, lurching and continually falling, are less concerned with clearing trees with the saddlebags than with staying on their feet.

As scientific research in Australia between 1815 and 1830 became considerably more professional, so also did the art of bushmanship. Skills developed before the crossing of the Blue Mountains provided the impetus for mounting markedly larger scale expeditions of a more ambitious and demanding nature. Prior to Oxley's expedition, the transmission of bush expertise was haphazard and discontinuous; there was still much to be learned. Evans' appointment as second-in-command to Oxley made the process more automatic. Bathurst's decision to make Evans' practical bush skills available to Oxley is a significant turning point in Australian exploration history, for it appears to be the first instance of a planned expedition deliberately and in a sequential fashion drawing on the available pool of experienced bushmen. There is clear evidence that the appointment resulted in a continuity of learning — sometimes from mistakes and sometimes as new conditions were presented. Obviously Evans played a major role in keeping Oxley's expedition organised and functional for an extended period of time. In his 1825 memorial, for example, Evans pointed out how he had '... always [been] ... employed in advance [of the main body].'[40]

For the same reasons, Darling attached the Australian-born Hamilton Hume to Sturt's first expedition, for the Governor was aware of Sturt's lack of bush experience. Hume had acquired his considerable bush skills from carrying out a previous reconnaissance further to the south. He was the first native-born Australian to be given a position of authority in a major inland exploration. This appointment was of particular significance, as it demonstrated Darling's convictions about the value and necessity of local experience and bushmanship, especially now that exploration was being carried out in increasingly more difficult country:

> ... I have attached Mr. Hume to the Expedition, who (has) made an Excursion to the Southward in the Neighbourhood of Western Port during Sir Thomas Brisbane's Administration. He is an enterprising Man, whose knowledge of the Country generally and experience in conducting an Establishment of the nature, now employed, cannot fail to promote the success of the Expedition.[41]

Hume justified this judgement very early in the expedition after the bullocks strayed overnight, earning Sturt's gratitude for their prompt tracing and return:

> I found Mr. Hume of the most essential service in tracking the animals, and to his perseverance we are indebted for their speedy recovery.[42]

Sturt also learnt to appreciate his associate's reconnoitring skills:

> Mr. Hume's experience rendered it unnecessary for me to give him other than general directions.[43]

In Sturt's subsequent Murray River expedition, continuity of experienced personnel was again an important factor. Including Sturt, there were five people from the first expedition and, although Hume did not accompany them, the knowledge accumulated from the earlier expedition must have been of considerable value.

As Oxley's and Sturt's expeditions were intended to be of between three and six months' duration and to venture well away from settled areas, the provision of tradesmen and supplies was given considerable emphasis. But although Oxley's first party was quite generously equipped, there were surprising inadequacies. On the positive side, his party included a farrier, a harness-maker, a boat builder and twelve others. Macquarie ensured that they would be well nourished:

> In order to give every facility to the objects of the expedition now fitting out, and to afford you the means of prolonging your absence from headquarters, and consequently extending the range of your discoveries, I have deemed it advisable to furnish yourself and party with a sufficient supply of good wholesome provisions for five months.[44]

In addition, a tent was carried; perhaps because of Evans' earlier experience, or possibly because of the greater availability of packhorses. The shelter provided was invaluable, for on several occasions the expedition encountered heavy rains which would otherwise have ruined their supplies.

On the other hand, expedition members did not wear waterproofs or even carry lightweight oiled ponchos. Perhaps the ill-effects of continued exposure to rain were not appreciated until members of the first generation of major explorers were growing older and, like Evans, were crippled by chronic rheumatism. It was not until the 1840s that waterproofs were commonly used.[45]

Glaring deficiencies are also apparent in the list of equipment supplied to Oxley. Only four muskets and four pistols were provided for the entire expedition. Worse, only a hundred rounds of ball cartridge and six pounds of powder were supplied. As the expedition was expected to be in the field for up to five months it had, therefore, the capacity to fire, on average, just over five shots per week. One extended battle with Aborigines would have exhausted the bulk of their ammunition. Sturt's allocation of 350 balls on an expedition of similar duration in 1828 was much less parsimonious. Perhaps more importantly, horseshoes were not seen as particularly necessary, for provision was made only for 'some spare horseshoes and nails for 13 horses.'[46] Taken as a whole, the list of equipment was neither extensive nor thoughtful and demonstrated how much was yet to be learnt of the requirements for larger scale and more extended exploration.

By comparison with Oxley, Sturt, eleven years later, was well provided with equipment and supplies. For each man there were ten pounds of flour, six pounds of bacon (or ten pounds of fresh meat, where available), two pounds of sugar, a quarter-pound of tea, a quarter-pound of tobacco and two ounces of soap per man, per week. Hard dry biscuits, salt and pepper and tins of preserved meat were also provided.

In light of a later bushman's maxim never to carry anything in pack saddle bags which can break, spill, or leak,[47] Sturt was well equipped. Bags specifically made to carry flour and salt were provided and tin cases were supplied for the sugar and tea. Such methods of storage and carriage were still being used 150 years later, although flour was later carried in rectangular twenty-litre drums, with large press-in lids.

Although Sturt took care to ensure the safe transport of provisions, he unfortunately burdened his packhorses with a heavy and unwieldy array of iron cooking utensils, including boilers, kettles and camp ovens, which were standard military issue.[48] It would be some time before the ubiquitous lightweight tin-plated billy can came to fill the role of kettle, boiler and saucepan, leaving only a cast-iron camp oven to be taken for roasting and stewing meat and sometimes for making damper.

Only five muskets were taken and there is no mention of light shot, despite Sturt's plan to follow the Macquarie, where waterflow could be expected. This is a rather surprising omission, given Governor Darling's instructions to maximise the chances of success by '... observing every possible economy in the expenditure of provisions and preventing waste of every kind.'[49] On Sturt's second expedition each member had a firearm, either because of the increased number of pack animals or simply because a greater number of firearms were now considered desirable.

Provision for clothing and shelter on Sturt's first expedition was inadequate in some aspects, although spare garments were carried and sixteen blankets were taken for twelve men. Surprisingly, the party was not provided with waterproof ground sheets. Thus, although two tents were taken, it appears that the men were still required to sleep on the bare and often wet ground.

The horses were allotted two spare sets of shoes each, sufficient for the five-month expedition. On the other hand, the necessity for carrying spares of critical tools and instruments still does not appear to have been learnt by this stage. The farrier had only one set of tools and would have been totally unable to cope should the rasp or pincers have been lost.

Possibly the most innovative aspect of Sturt's provisioning was the supply of vinegar and lime juice, which constituted a milestone of sophistication in the history of land exploration. That it took forty years to realise the necessity of taking a supply of vitamin C in order to counter the debilitating effects of vegetable-deficient diets is extremely surprising, given that the British authorities knew, even before the First Settlement in 1788, of the cause and the severe effects of scurvy. Surgeon Perry had commended the Lords of the Admiralty in 1771 for instructing Cook to guard against 'sea scurvy, and the very great probability of that distemper raging at some time or other in the course of a long voyage', by carrying in the *Endeavour*:

> Sour Krout, mustard, vinegar, wheat, inspissated orange and lemon juices, saloup, portable soup, sugar, melasses, (and) vegetables (at all times when they could be possibly got).[50]

In the year before Sturt's expedition, a severe outbreak of scurvy occurred at the Raffles Bay settlement in the present Northern Territory, because the medical officer, it appears, had not been consulted about provisioning:

> ... these cases of Scurvy are very bad, their limbs terribly swoln, hard as sticks and black, unable to assist themselves without crutches, eleven or twelve pairs of which are unhappily in use ... The lime juice appears to be the only means of arresting its progress; unhappily we had a very scanty supply of this so essential article ...[51]

It may be that anti-scorbutics only came to be considered practicable and necessary on inland Australian exploration as the provision of pack animals improved and expeditions penetrated more deeply into the interior.

Although Leichhardt had neither the funds nor the pack animals to allow him to carry a specific remedy for scurvy on his 1844–5 expedition, he was aware of the problem. Fortunately his botanical expertise allowed him to experiment with native fruits so that, despite being in the field for fifteen months with a highly vitamin-deficient ration, his men were not affected by scurvy. The small native limes which Leichhardt used early in his trip to make a pleasant, thirst-quenching drink were still used for that purpose in 1992 by residents of the Taroom area of southern Queensland.[52]

Notwithstanding the substantial improvements in equipment and experience prior to 1830, the value and necessity of mobility was still not appreciated. Although Oxley indicates in his journals that he was aware of the value of mobility, he did not necessarily pursue it. On his first expedition he had fourteen horses, one of which was specifically for him to ride. No other member was allocated a horse, although, as George Evans did almost all reconnoitring, it appears that he was usually mounted. At the point well to the south of the Lachlan, where Oxley was forced to turn back to the north due to water shortages and a failing food supply, he decided to reconnoitre as far as possible with two mounted companions, believing that this lightly equipped and mobile group would cover in three days as much as the main expedition would cover in seven. Although Oxley appeared to be becoming aware of the optimal mode of travelling in inland Australia, paradoxically, he failed to apply this knowledge to his second expedition, which was again unmounted, with the packhorses again being brutally overloaded.

Sturt's expeditions were better equipped than Oxley's with riding and pack animals. Eight pack bullocks, seven packhorses and six riding horses were provided. The ratio of twenty-one horses and bullocks to twelve men, which was the most favourable of the major expeditions so far, perhaps reflected the lower prices which such animals now commanded. According to Sturt they were now cheaper in Australia than in England.[53] Nevertheless, the expedition was still deficient in riding horses.

The decision to use pack-bullocks, which appears to have been Governor Darling's, was questionable, for their mobility is less than half that of horses. Leichhardt experienced the same problem sixteen years later, when he took approximately five months to cover Queensland's Gulf region, whereas Augustus Gregory subsequently traversed much of the same country in three months with an all-horse team. Sturt soon realised the bullocks' shortcomings, commenting early in the expedition that the heat affected them severely and that 'our cattle suffered so much, and moved so slowly.'[54]

Although the advantages offered by riding horses must have been apparent to Sturt on his extended and rapid reconnaissances, neither his second expedition nor his third, into the unforgiving central desert region, was fully mounted. Problems of limited mobility, exposure to fatigue and debilitation and a reduction in safety through reduced ability to retreat rapidly were not overcome till later. In Sturt's case, even if all of his expedition members had been mounted, it would have been to no great advantage because they would have had to wait for the bullock wagon. It was not until Gregory's time that all-horse teams were effectively employed in major exploration.

Looking back from the safety of 160 years later and in the absence of any necessity to drive animals beyond the limits of their endurance, it is easy to condemn Oxley for the treatment of his horses. Nevertheless, his horsemanship on both expeditions was inexcusable, particularly his cruel and dangerous overloading of the packhorses. Once his expedition left the Lachlan in 1817, the stores were divided up and sufficient rations taken for the estimated exploration in front of them. At the time the daily military ration was one-and-a-half pounds of flour and approximately three-quarters of a pound of salted pork. Using these amounts as a base, the gross requirements for the party could have been calculated and its weight established. It would then have been possible to determine the required number of packhorses. Such a procedure was not followed and an arbitrary number of horses seems to have been taken, which, from the available evidence, constituted only half the number adequate for the task.[55]

Oxley notes that the horses were very heavily laden and that, after only four days' travel away from the Lachlan, they were all exhausted. Within eighteen days three horses had died or had been shot because of exhaustion-induced paralysis of the hindquarters. Allan Cunningham also commented upon the horses' plight: 'The horses groaned beneath the weight of their loads, which was not less than 300 pounds [136 kilograms] weight each.'[56]

Such exhaustion is inconceivable under normal circumstances. Gregory, for example, took packhorses from the Victoria River through much more difficult country across the top of the Barkly Tableland and down through Central Queensland in 1856, with minimal problems.

From the above experiences and from the commonly-applied figure, evolved over the years from packing horses through inland Australia, of a maximum load of about seventy kilograms, it can be concluded that Oxley and, more culpably, Evans, can be accused of ignorance, if not cruelty.[57] As horses were still a valuable commodity, and as Bathurst's intent conveyed to Macquarie was for the expedition to be conducted as cheaply as possible, ignorance is, at first sight, the more likely explanation. At all events, Oxley's horses were unfortunate experimental subjects in the early days of large-scale and extended exploration in Australia.

Besides being excessive, each horse's load appears to have been poorly distributed, for Oxley mentions that on marshy country the animals were continually falling.[58] Although such behaviour could simply indicate exhaustion or overloading, when coupled with his comment that barrels of pork and flour were carried by the horses, it is evidence of an extremely unbalanced load. Load balancing is a critical factor in keeping packhorses in good health, for unbalanced loads lead to galling of their withers and girths, from the girth straps having to be pulled up tighter than is desirable to ensure that the saddle and load do not slip. Oxley reported that most of his surviving horses were, in fact, badly galled on their backs. With pork barrels weighing between ninety and 130 kilograms[59] it is inconceivable that the horses could have carried two barrels of pork in order to balance their loads. Somehow therefore, a single barrel was strapped onto one side of the pack-saddle, leading not only to extreme overloading, but also to severe imbalance and frequent falls. As a consequence, the expedition was continually forced to make short daily stages to coincide with areas of good feed and adequate water and, on frequent occasions, to spell the horses for a day or so, all of which unnecessarily reduced its mobility.

Any initial opinion that Oxley's treatment of his horses might have stemmed from ignorance and not cruelty, must be dispelled, however, by his conduct on the second expedition, when he loaded the horses with even heavier, if better balanced, burdens and literally broke their hearts.[60] Oxley was well aware of the inhumane demands he was making upon his animals:

> The horses were, however, very heavily laden, carrying at least 350 pounds each; a weight which I was fearful the description of country we had to pass over would render still more burthensome. We had, however, relinquished everything that was not indispensable, and the saddle-horses were equally laden with the others.[61]

The results were predictable and, given the saturated, marshy country they were attempting to traverse, worse than on the first expedition. After only two days the horses were exhausted and '... failed much during the day, and several of them were severely wrung with their burthens ...'[62] A fortnight later, in one terribly marshy section, the horses' exhaustion and unbalanced loads saw them continually falling. Oxley commented that they covered only six miles for the day and '... for the last half mile, the horses were not on their legs for twenty yards altogether.'[63] Galling, combined with exhaustion, accelerates incapacitation and debilitation. On one occasion Oxley reported that, after the horses were unsaddled, they all lay down:

> ... like dogs about us. ... The backs of the greater part of them were, not withstanding every care, dreadfully galled, so that they could, when first saddled, scarcely stand under their burdens.
>
> Our horses too were so extremely weak and crippled, that the short distance that we are enabled to travel is accomplished in pain and difficulty.[64]

Perhaps the worst example of Oxley's callousness and lack of horsemanship occurred when the party was attempting to cross the Great Dividing Range, at a point where two horses had already died and several others were incapable of carrying supplies. The expedition members were packing their supplies up the range in a series of reduced loads when, about 100 yards from the tent, the abdominal wall of a powerfully built mare:

> ... literally burst with the violent exertion which the ascent

> required. In this shocking state, with her entrails on the ground, she arrived at the tent, when, to put an end to her agonies, she was shot.[65]

Should Gregory, Sturt, Stuart or Forrest have treated their horses in a similar manner to Oxley, in far less forgiving country, they would quite possibly have perished. These later explorers were well aware that bushmanship is not simply a matter of pressing forward irrespective of the costs. It entails getting through, by protecting and husbanding the stock and by avoiding undue risks. Such was not the case with Oxley. Indeed, when approximately three hundred kilometres from Sydney and when the horses were failing, instead of husbanding their strength and nursing them along over each stage he commented that in order to achieve his goal he would, if necessary, press on till all the horses were dead.[66] How Oxley thought he would then transport the stores and equipment essential to return to the Lachlan River depot is anyone's guess.

By contrast, Sturt's treatment of his pack and riding horses was humane and professional. Despite the heat, poor food and often salty water, none of them died. Sturt, no doubt receptive to bushman Hume's advice, did not overtax them through gross overloading and although they did gall, it was from continual sweating caused by the tremendous heat and not from excessive or unbalanced loads. On one occasion when Sturt reconnoitred three hundred kilometres north and east from the Macquarie in a week, the horses coped comfortably. Compared to Oxley's exhausted and footsore animals, this performance represented a considerable advance in bushmanship. When the effects of heat and poor food began to be felt and '... it was evident our animals would soon fail, since they trembled exceedingly, and had the look of total exhaustion.'[67] Sturt and Hume immediately took the only sensible course and returned.

Sturt was also aware of the importance of hobbling both horses and bullocks, and included fourteen sets of spare hobbles in his equipment. Although Oxley had also had hobbles, he appeared unable to use them effectively. At one point on the first expedition, on the south-eastern leg away from the Lachlan, his horses strayed overnight. As a result he was forced to send his men out searching for them on foot — an operation which took five days and with every hour the horses could have been moving beyond the reach of unmounted persons. Because the men had trouble tracking the animals, they had to rely on stumbling across them, which also clearly indicates that the horses were not belled.[68] This whole episode was particularly serious, for the expedition members could have been stranded well away from the depot, in an almost waterless area.

Oxley notes that the horses strayed despite being spencilled. Spencilling is hobbling or fettering horses, milking cows or oxen with a leather strap or short-noosed rope — a practice being used in England as early as 1610.[69] The spencil could be used on front or rear legs, or on offside or nearside legs, a configuration called a side-line in Australia. Given that Oxley's location between the Lachlan and Murrumbidgee was deficient in water and the danger posed by the horses' straying was extreme, he would have been best served by tethering a night-horse to a tree so that he would have been guaranteed a mount in the morning, if necessary, to recover his team of horses. This practice, which does not appear to have been employed during this period, later became common, no doubt as the result of many similar experiences.

Finding water rapidly became an essential bush skill in exploration in inland Australia, particularly once explorers began to move away from the major rivers. Oxley's group was the first major expedition which had a large number of stock to be watered daily, but which had deliberately, possibly through ignorance, struck away from known watercourses. It was Cunningham who pointed out the problems inherent in their early lack of concern over water supplies:

> We had hitherto been tolerably supplied with water, nor was it till this morning that we learnt to appreciate the value of good water, which like other great blessings are only estimated by the loss of them. All the water we could procure, which we brought from distant corrupted holes, was very foul and muddy and filled with animalcules, to destroy which we boiled and strained the water.[70]

Oxley's men painstakingly learnt how to identify from the flora and topography those locations where water would most likely be found, which was an important skill once they left the Lachlan. Cunningham notes that they very quickly learned that the presence of *Acacia pendula* (myall scrub) could be taken as an infallible sign that water would be close handy.[71]

On one occasion, when they became seriously short of water to the south of the Lachlan, Oxley turned the expedition back to the north-west because he perceived that the almost imperceptible slope, and therefore the drainage, of the country was in that direction. He then headed for Peel's Range and followed its foothills, where water run-off is more concentrated.[72] At one stage his men used an adze to dig a well at a spot which:

> ... seemed most likely to have received the drainings of the hills
> ... and in a few hours were rewarded by obtaining near a quart of

> thick muddy water per man, which by boiling, skimming, and straining ... (allowed them to eat their bread and salt pork for tea and breakfast).[73]

By the end of this extremely dry stage, Oxley and his expedition members had also learnt how to follow dry watercourses, to climb rocky outcrops in search of gnamma holes and to look for Aboriginal axe-marks on trees as indicators of areas where water would be found.

In addition to the techniques for discovering water a small keg was carried on one of the packhorses. Without its contents the expedition would have gone hungry at the many waterless camps for, without water, their salted pork and dry bread were virtually inedible. According to Cunningham:

> We had for some time seen the necessity of carrying water with us rather than trust to the contingency of falling in with any holes at those places where necessity herself might oblige us to halt.[74]

The size of the keg — fourteen litres for fifteen men — indicates that its use was probably not planned in advance, but was rather a fortuitous afterthought. Nevertheless, Oxley's appears to have been the first major expedition to deliberately carry a supply of water on a pack animal.

Once on the extensive flat areas adjoining the Lachlan, Oxley soon learnt the importance of reconnoitring. According to Cunningham, he usually took advantage of any rise from which he could see the layout of the country ahead, determine possible short-cuts, locate any swampy areas to be avoided and, after he had left the Lachlan behind, identify possible sources of water.[75]

Leichhardt also employed this technique, taking his two Aborigines with him, sending the first one back to bring up the expedition when water was found, while he advanced further. Later, if necessary, he would send the second man and finally return himself. This method was considerably more efficient and flexible.[76]

On Oxley's second expedition it was the over-abundance, rather than the shortage, of water that constituted a serious problem. Consequently the expedition members soon became adept at identifying the '... apparently dry brush ... or forest [which was] ... found [to be] a certain fore-runner of quicksands and bogs.'[77] Overall, the explorer's water-finding and water-avoiding techniques represent a significant development in Australian bushmanship.

Sturt and his 1828 expedition members appear to have coped well with the trying conditions which they encountered, especially once they had left the Macquarie River and were in poorly-watered areas. Their developing bush skills enabled them to find '... a small puddle of water, to which (they)

... had been led by a pigeon,'[78] adjusting their expectations so they could drink water '... so mixed with slime as to hang in strings between the fingers ...'[79] and deducing the location of water from signs of the presence of Aborigines. Furthermore, supplies were now regularly carried on a bullock '... so uncertain were we of finding water at the end of the day's journey.'[80] Within Sturt's equipment list is an entry for three water beakers,[81] indicating that some individual riders were now carrying supplies of water for consumption during the day.

Sturt and Hume also developed a system of reconnoitring for water supplies, to which the main body of the expedition could then move. Although the party was adept at using the known indicators and techniques, risks were not taken. Even while reconnoitring on horseback, a small supply was carried in a bucket on one of the packhorses and the slow-moving, unmounted main body of the expedition was held in safety until the highly mobile mounted advance party found water. Sturt was always aware of the danger of water supplies drying up and cutting off his retreat. Consequently he had to evaluate their long-term sustainability, for '... every day increased the probable difficulty of our return.'[82]

Due to the arid nature of much of the country traversed on both Oxley's and Sturt's first expeditions, game was often not available. Nevertheless, Oxley's dogs appear to have caught a good number of kangaroos and emus, despite being initially confused or frightened by the birds and refusing to chase them. Both animals were welcome additions to the expedition's otherwise plain fare of salted pork and flour. Although ducks, swans and brolgas were plentiful, they were rarely taken because the expedition carried no shot. This discrepancy was remedied on later expeditions, such as Leichhardt's, where waterfowl became an important part of the diet.

Leichhardt and other later explorers with botanical training used their knowledge to identify those plants which were safe to eat, thereby avoiding the ever-present problem of scurvy. They were following the tradition of Oxley who, a quarter of a century previously, had Cunningham to advise him of the plants that were safe to eat, as well as two men specialising in the procuring of game, assisted by 'those most invaluable, faithful animals and bush companions, our dogs.'[83] Even in food-gathering, the development of bushmanship was an incremental and collective process.

In the early explorations on the eastern side of the Blue Mountains, Aborigines were seen as a major threat, but once large-scale expeditions began to follow the courses of the big inland rivers, explorers had to develop techniques for ensuring their safety in the presence of the larger numbers of Aboriginal people they encountered.

Such a need was not immediately apparent to Oxley who, on his first expedition along the Lachlan River, allowed several dangerous practices to develop. His group tended to straggle over as much as two miles on their daily stages. Worse, particularly along the higher country adjoining the rivers, several of the members were often unarmed even though Aborigines were present. Although on this expedition Oxley was not threatened by the native people, whose usual reaction was one of terror and flight, the potential for armed encounter remained. It was on the second journey, when his expedition had regained the coast and was working southwards, that one member alone in the bush was speared by a number of Aborigines who had professed friendship on the previous evening. It is significant that the assailants had had previous contact with whites, for experience later demonstrated that such men were generally more antagonistic than those who had had little or no contact. After this event Oxley was forced to re-evaluate his approach, resolving '... for the future, never to suffer them to come near us at all.'[84]

Sturt appears to have been consistently and conspicuously successful in his relationships with Aborigines. In 1827 and 1828, when moving along the very large waterways of inland south-eastern Australia, with their guaranteed water and food resources, he was constantly exposed to large numbers of Aborigines. Word of Sturt's approach was frequently passed ahead from group to group and in many cases the Aborigines were waiting for the white men. Because at times their camp was visited by large Aboriginal parties, armed night pickets were considered essential to protect the expedition members and prevent pilfering. On other occasions the party was threatened by spear-wielding groups who waded out onto sandbars, making it necessary for the expedition members to be continually armed and vigilant. If at any time Sturt had misjudged these people and forced a bloody confrontation, he would almost certainly have been faced with a succession of armed and aggressive groups along his whole route. That he managed not only to stay calm but also to gain the confidence of these people is a tribute to his level-headedness. Indeed, he soon learned to walk unarmed towards them, waving a branch as an indication of peaceful intent. Nevertheless, Sturt did not trust the Aborigines, for he believed that their disposition:

> ... to commit personal violence was evident from [their] ... repeated acts of treachery; and we should doubtless have suffered from it on some occasion or other, had we not been constantly on the alert.[85]

On one occasion on the Murray the Aborigines sent eight women along the river '... who tried to allure us by the most unequivocal manifestations of love,'[86] while the men hid nearby in the bushes. Although the explorers avoided the trap, Sturt was '... really provoked at their barefaced treachery, and should most undoubtedly have attacked them, had they not precipitately retreated.'[87] As a result of such experiences, Sturt asserted that in establishing relationships with Aborigines it was essential:

> .... not to alarm their natural timidity; to exercise patience in your intercourse with them; to treat them kindly; and to watch them with suspicion, especially at night. Never permit your men to steal away from the camp, but keep them as compact as possible; and at every station so arrange your drays and provisions that they may serve as a defence in case of your being attacked.[88]

Sturt's carefully developed skills in communicating with numerically superior Aboriginal groups, his efforts to promote a friendly and trustworthy image and his care to keep them at a distance should have been beneficial to subsequent explorers. As will be seen later, however, Mitchell and Grey violated most of Sturt's principles.

Considerable psychological readjustment was necessary for explorers to be able to accept the country on its own terms, rather than perceive it as a harsh, desolate alternative to Britain. Such readjustment embraced a wide range of aspects, including the realisation that assistance was not available in case of emergencies, that water supplies could not be counted on and that available game was often not particularly appetising. In this light, when some members of Oxley's party cooked and ate a large carpet snake and later a dingo, their leader correctly noted that they were becoming resourceful![89] Such resourcefulness also saw Cunningham suggesting that the men boil the leaves of one of the most common native plants, *Rhagodia dilatata*, and use it as a green vegetable. He reported that they later made several 'excellent meals' of this plant and that it was an 'excellent substitute for spinach.'[90]

In some respects at least, Oxley's expedition was a watershed, in that the gradual accretion of skills and knowledge over the previous twenty-five years at last began to pay dividends. While absent from Bathurst for over 120 days, Oxley covered over 1900 kilometres,[91] by far the longest expedition to date. Although the use of boats and a significantly greater number of packhorses were important elements, such exploration could not have been undertaken without applying the skills and experience acquired over the previous quarter of a century. Thereafter, successively larger and more difficult explorations could be both contemplated and successfully completed.

Nevertheless, Oxley still felt ill-at-ease and alienated by the Australian environment, for he had not made the adjustment necessary to cope with the immense areas of almost featureless bush, the intermittent nature of the watercourses and the silence. Depressed by the apparent barrenness, he was certain that west of a certain meridian:

> ...the interior of this country ... is uninhabittable, deprived as it is of wood, water and grass [and that the Aborigines lived a very precarious life and were forced to dig] ... with immense labour, little wells at the bottom of the hills to procure and preserve a necessary of life which is evidently not to be obtained by any other method.[92]

Such a sense of alienation appears to have been a common feature of the writings of early British explorers. Even upon the completion of Oxley's second major expedition, in which he successfully traversed almost three thousand kilometres of previously unknown country and despite having Evans' expertise to draw upon, Oxley was still overawed and subdued by the bush. The time of psychological readjustment, though near, was yet to come:

> The highlands ... were lost in the immense levels, which bound the interior abyss of this singular country; the gulf in which both water and mountain seem to be as nothing.[93]
> ... even the noise (of the Aborigines' clubs) upon the trees is a relief from the otherwise utter loneliness of feeling we cannot help experiencing in these desolate wilds.[94]

In Sturt can be seen the first signs of an acceptance of the Australian bush on its own terms. During much of his first expedition, the explorer and his men were exposed on occasions to conditions so severe that they could only work in the early morning or evening, with temperatures as high as 129°F in the shade by two o'clock in the afternoon. Indeed, on occasions, 'the heat had become intolerable long ere the sun had gained the meridian.'[95] In addition, south-eastern Australia was in the midst of a prolonged drought. Those plants and trees which survived were under stress, large areas were bare of game, the Aborigines had fled and the soil was broken down to a fine dust.

> So long had the drought continued, that the vegetable kingdom was almost annihilated and minor vegetation had disappeared ... the largest forest trees were drooping and many were dead.[96]

Despite the heat, dust, hard food, inadequate water and continuous travelling, the expedition coped well. In the process Sturt became aware that psychological adjustment was more important than physiological factors, pointing out that, 'I feel persuaded the tone of mind has a great deal to do with success, because it influences the conduct of the individual.'[97]

Despite Sturt's sombre analysis of the region to the north of the Macquarie ('there is no life upon its surface, if I may so express myself; but the stillness of death reigns in its brushes and over its plains'[98]), he was neither frightened nor repelled by inland Australia. He appears to have made the psychological leap necessary to discard his British environmental values, in order to see and appreciate what the local countryside offered.

> In a climate, therefore, so soft that man scarcely requires a dwelling, and so enchanting that few have left it but with regret, the spirits must necessarily be acted upon — and the heart feel lighter ... nor have I ever been happier than when roving through the woods ... (and yet) I went to New South Wales as I have already remarked, highly prejudiced against it.[99]

Sturt's ready adaptation to the Australian environment was due not only to his own temperament, but also to the contemporary situation. By the late 1820s, exploration and bushmanship were well advanced in eastern Australia and a considerable pool of information and expertise was being continually expanded and disseminated. Given this hard-earned knowledge, it could be expected that experienced men from New South Wales would have been employed in the exploration of new areas in Australia, such as the Swan River Colony. Yet, with the exception of Fraser's visit in 1827, such was not the case. Although the patterns of inquiry and the development of bushmanship were similar to those of the eastern colonies, the available expertise was not directly employed to facilitate exploration and discovery in Western Australia.

In April 1827, shortly after Major Lockyer and his men set out from Albany with four days' provisions, towards the Porongorup Range thirty-five kilometres to the north, they were caught in a rainstorm. As neither tents nor waterproofs were being carried, the supplies and firearms were placed in a large hollow tree. Soon the party was 'all wet to the skin' and the rain then became even heavier, with thunderstorms setting in. Bark strips were procured and, after some trouble, a hut was built for the night.[100] By the next morning one man was ill from a severe chill, two were lame from their lack of fitness and Lockyer was reluctantly forced to return to the settlement at King George Sound.

Several points of interest to this study can be found in Lockyer's journal. Perhaps the most important was that, in contrast to Phillip in New South Wales, Lockyer found the landscape quite easy to traverse ('walking is not at all difficult through the country'[101]) and did not feel at all threatened or alienated by the bush. This tone, which appears constant in many of the earlier Western Australian explorers' journals, is markedly at variance with the experience of the early eastern explorers.

In addition, Western Australian Aborigines were in most cases helpful and non-threatening, at least in the early days of settlement. Those instances of Aborigines attempting to attack the colonists at King George Sound can be traced to the earlier bad treatment they had received from sealers. This pattern of helpfulness and cordiality to explorers was repeated over much of south-western Australia, before problems began to occur due to Aboriginal food shortages. In his report to the Geographical Society on 1 January 1830, Governor Stirling commented that:

> ... the natives ... indeed were found to be so harmless that single individuals even, who had traversed the country and particularly among the mountains, had never met with any insult nor injury.[102]

Employing Aboriginal guides was a feature of early exploration in Western Australia, particularly in the Albany region. As in the eastern colonies, however, once beyond their customary territory, such men were soon found to be of little assistance. Dr T B Wilson, leader of the first major exploration of the Albany region, reported that his Aboriginal guide Mokare was unable to return to Albany after only five days, for he was then well outside his tribal area and unfamiliar with the terrain.[103]

As with subsequent Western Australian expeditions, the rationale underlying the exploration of the hinterland of King George Sound was inevitably pragmatic. Lockyer had been ordered by Secretary of State for the Colonies Macleay to ascertain its topography, especially the major rivers, and the '... nature and quality of the soil, its fertility and its purposes ... [for settlers].' As well it was deemed very desirable that:

> ... no time should be lost in ascertaining as far as practicable the natural Productions of the Country, in order that their utility for supplying the immediate wants of the Settlement or for the purposes of Commerce may be known.[104]

To assist in these aims John Browne, a gardener, was sent to collect and forward botanical samples and Lockyer was instructed to facilitate this work by acceding to all of Browne's requests. In 1829 the botanist Baxter was sent to Albany with government instructions for him to be supplied with accommodation, a convict servant and field hand and a military ration. As Lieutenant Sleeman of the colony noted, this assistance enabled Baxter to '... proceed with more expedition in collecting and preserving the most valuable Seeds and Plants in this neighbourhood.'[105] Baxter's samples were sent to the Botanical Garden in Sydney for analysis and then forwarded to England.

At approximately the same time as Major Lockyer's exploration in the Albany region, Lieutenant James Stirling was exploring the Swan River and its immediate surrounds. Although his was predominantly a waterborne expedition, some evidence can be discerned from expedition members' journals regarding their level of bushmanship. Again, as occurred initially in the eastern colonies, the heat was a problem and the rowing schedule included a break each day from 11.00 a.m. to 3.00 p.m. Heat aside, Stirling and his men seem to have adapted well to the alien conditions. They were surrounded completely by unbroken bush, often unknown wildlife and, at least in the initial stages, were camping on the river bank. Part of their competence and assurance may have been due to the presence of Fraser, a veteran of both of Oxley's large-scale, extended inland expeditions and of other excursions.

Stirling was enthusiastic over what he saw, describing the country as 'rich and romantic'. A number of parties 'sallied forth in various directions' and within minutes of landing for the evening they had a '... blazing fire, with roasting swans before it (which) ... shed cheerfulness on our resting place.'[106] The contrast between the tone of this report and that of the eastern colonists' earlier exploration journals is marked. In his enthusiastic appraisal of the country Stirling was possibly influenced by the greener foliage of the Western Australian bush relative to the grey-green colour of the bush of the eastern colonies, believing that it signified more fertile soil. Less excusable were Fraser's assessment of the sands of the Swan Coastal Plain as suitable for growing garden vegetables and light crops, for his appraisal fitted poorly with botanist Robert Brown's more sober subsequent assessment from Britain. Brown quickly realised that the plant species forwarded indicated a very poor type of soil, a description which tallies with Perth's notoriously sterile coastal sands.

> If an opinion were to be formed of the nature of the country merely from the inspection of these collections, it certainly would be extremely unfavourable as to the fertility of the soil.[107]

Notwithstanding their rapport with the Western Australian bush, Stirling and his men had problems similar to those encountered by their earliest eastern counterparts, in their inability to procure terrestrial game:

> ... kangaroos were seen, and indeed the latter animal had been observed in the course of the day's progress, but we were not sufficiently acquainted with that species of hunting to make prize of any of them.[108]

Following the favourable reports of Stirling and Fraser, the Swan River Colony was established in mid-1829. Exploration which commenced almost immediately was accelerated when that area between the ocean and the Darling Ranges and for fifty miles southwards was opened to settlers. Initially the expeditions were on foot, of a few days' duration and frequently attempted with little forethought. In August 1829, for example, Jane Currie lamented the bedraggled state of her naval officer husband after a twenty-mile reconnaissance to the south:

> Dearest returned at 10 o'clock oh so miserably wet, having passed the night on an open plain of 3 miles without even a tree for shelter, and not the smallest comfort, owing to the man carrying his luggage remaining behind in the bush.[109]

Exploration of the Swan and Canning Rivers was waterborne, not only for ease of travel, but also because Stirling and his Surveyor-General J S Roe wished to mark along the river-banks the narrow frontages of the first settlers' ribbon grants. The exploring parties were generally well equipped, with tents, adequate food supplies and a considerable amount of navigational equipment. Local explorations frequently took place almost in a picnic atmosphere. On one occasion Dr Wilson and Captain Barker were examining the Canning River when they came across the Commander of the brig *Thompson* who invited them for lunch in the tent which he had set up on one of the islands immediately above the site of the future Riverton Bridge:

> We entered his tent, which was well stored with a profusion of corn'd beef, cold fowls, Scotch ale, and London porter, and we partook willingly of his cheerfully proffered hospitality — wishing him and his successors to enjoy health, prosperity, happiness, and all other blessings that are usually bestowed, in liberal abundance, on the givers of good fares.[110]

The speed with which the early Western Australian explorers embarked upon larger scale and extended exploration is quite surprising, especially seeing that almost all of them were military or naval personnel, or expatriate

British civilians. Their rapid acquisition of bushmanship and ready psychological adjustment appear to be based on several factors, possibly the most important of which was the relatively benign nature of the topography of the south-west. There were no forbidding and almost impenetrable ranges. Captain Thomas Bannister commented that on his 1831 expedition from Perth to Albany, after passing '... over a hill of moderate height, we were generally surprised to find that we had crossed the higher range of the Darling mountains.'[111]

The southern forests were also considerably more open in those days and therefore easier to traverse. Their park-like nature was largely due to firing initiated both by the Aborigines and by lightning strikes. Once European livestock began grazing this forest country and the Aboriginal people were driven from their hunting grounds, there was a considerable thickening of the understorey at the expense of the native grasses. This phenomenon is also noticeable in southern and central Queensland, along the route taken by Leichhardt.[112]

These factors, coupled with the initially friendly and cooperative Aborigines, appears to have engendered confidence and accelerated the process of exploration. Before the first six months had elapsed, Lieutenant Preston and eleven men took provisions for eight days and attempted to cross the Darling Range. In October 1829, Wilson's party, in their exploration of the Canning River, clearly demonstrated that they had learnt how to cope with wet weather, for they erected a:

> ... convenient shelter ... to defend us from the rain: and a large half burned tree being rekindled opposite the entrance, soon diffused a genial warmth, and an air of comfort, well known to those fond of a bush life. We sat down, with hearty appetites, to an excellent meal, and enjoyed ourselves much, laughing heartily at the misfortune that befel the Governor and his party, who, Mr. Drummond informed us, had lost themselves ... last evening ... and were consequently compelled to remain in the bush all night, suffering from hunger, and exposed to cold, and heavy rain.[113]

The contrast between that experience and the first week of Barrallier's expedition, more than twelve years after the settlement of New South Wales, requires little comment.

As a consequence Stirling, in his report to the Royal Geographical Society on 1 January 1830, noted that, within six months, the colonists had gained knowledge of the country for 110 kilometres to the north and 140 kilometres to the south and that, although the Darling Range had not been crossed, the plain had been explored for forty kilometres from the coast.[114]

Within two years explorations had been carried out to Albany (400 kilometres), to the east of York (160 kilometres) and along much of the south-western coastline. Compared to the early exploration of New South Wales, this was a considerable achievement and a favourable reflection on the development of bushmanship in Western Australia.

Even in those first six months, the earliest explorers had no qualms about heading off across unknown country, despite being minimally equipped. Unperturbed about having to find their way back, they were obviously quite proficient at developing a sense of location and direction, although in many cases carrying only hand compasses or possessing no navigational equipment at all. In one instance, in October 1829, Wilson and his party walked southwards from the Canning River for twelve hours and were able to find their way back, in a direct line, to their setting off point '... by having had an eye, either on the compass or on the sun ...'[115]

Wilson, who is mentioned as having visited every point of Australia from Raffles Bay in the north to King George Sound in the south, undertook the first substantial land-based exploration in Western Australia. Following his two minor explorations of the Swan and Canning Rivers, he and three others, including the Aborigine Mokare, set off from Albany in December 1829, intending to travel to the north for some days then gradually curve around to the west and south-west and finally return to Albany. The character of this expedition is in stark, if not ludicrous, contrast with that of comparable early efforts in New South Wales. Indeed, Wilson's degree of unconcern is totally different from the attitude shown by Oxley in 1818.

The expedition members took a week's provisions in three kitbags and a musket and two fowling pieces. Tents were carried and each man took one blanket and an additional pair of shoes. Two kangaroo dogs were also taken, the technique of training and using these animals apparently having been imported from the eastern colony. As the journey extended over twelve days, Wilson and his men shot a proportion of the game, while the dogs caught several kangaroos. Initially the dogs and the hunters could not get close enough to the kangaroos and at one stage Mokare even stripped and attempted to stalk them, but they were gone before he was within musket range. Despite the notorious deficiencies of the muskets, within a few days both men and dogs were procuring some extremely large specimens.

The most extraordinary feature of the expedition is the light-hearted manner in which it was undertaken. The tone of the diary is almost jovial, Wilson obviously enjoying himself considerably. He was not alienated by the country, nor were his plans tentative. He and his expedition members appear to have been far more relaxed in their general attitude than the earliest explorers in New South Wales. In addition, they took care not to burden themselves with unnecessary gear. Whereas, for example, the eastern explorers took heavy iron pots for cooking, Wilson merely makes note after the first camp, of '... an empty preserved-meat canister serving the double purpose of tea-kettle and tea-pot.'[116]

Perhaps the best indication of their relaxed and confident attitude can be seen in the fact that of the three kitbags used to carry provisions, one was entirely filled with brandy, rum and gin. It was, therefore, scarcely surprising that after stopping on the first day because of the heat, the expedition members decided to 'partake of some refreshment', the consequence of which was that a few miles later one of the party '... fell suddenly down, the heat of the day having overpowered him.'[117]

Later in the expedition, when enthusiasm was flagging, Wilson allowed a double ration of spirits and the party members '... were now in high glee, and talked with the utmost sangfroid of going to Swan River ...'[118]

More importantly, Wilson put into practice what he had learnt from his earlier expeditions along the Canning and Swan Rivers about the importance of keeping warm and dry at night. He and his expedition members always built their camp to the windward of a large fallen tree, which was then set alight. A low semicircular windbreak of branches and bushes was then erected and a smaller cooking fire lit. After tea the men then lay near the large fire, with their feet towards it. It was fortunate that guard watches were not really necessary for, the men and dogs having gorged themselves on game, '... not much watchfulness could be expected from either party.'[119]

Wilson and his party covered approximately three hundred kilometres of new country, procured their own rations for the concluding few days, did not at any stage feel threatened by their inability to see landmarks, or by the unbroken bush, and enjoyed themselves considerably. Indeed Wilson concluded his report with the comment that they had not '... experienced any privation worthy of notice.'[120] Furthermore, Wilson was able to provide an overview of the soil types, vegetation, water supplies and topography of the region, though well aware that a reconnaissance of that type was basically incompatible with serious scientific research:

> I have not entered into any detail regarding the mineralogical or botanical features of the country, as, even were I capable of doing so, the knowledge gained during such a rapid journey must be very imperfect, and of no public utility.[121]

Not all early Western Australian exploration ventures were so light-hearted or trouble-free. Thomas Bannister's exploration from Perth to Albany in 1830 demonstrated a lack of professionalism similar to that shown several decades earlier in New South Wales. It was initially to be an expedition of some four hundred kilometres and stores were taken for approximately four weeks. However, because H W H Smythe of the Surveyor-General's Department, who was a member of the party, failed to take with him the Naval Almanac necessary for longitude calculations, he was soon unable to place the expedition's daily position. As a consequence they drifted well to the west, missing the clearer country along the future Albany Highway route through Kojonup, Cranbrook and Mount Barker, and appear to have traversed the very dense and tall forest country in the Frankland River and Walpole areas. The expedition made poor progress through this timber, where the understorey alone was up to six metres high.

In the absence of proper pack-saddles, the supplies were apparently tied onto riding saddles and the loads not only frequently came off, but also continually made the saddles move. As a result, the horses soon galled along their backs and six days were lost through having to rest them. This experience produced a strong recommendation from Bannister that, in future government explorations, the horses be properly equipped.

> I would beg to recommend the necessity of having some description of pack-saddle for such expeditions, with a breast strap to prevent the load shifting back in ascending steep places and a crupper to prevent its pressing forward in descending. Our horses' backs were more injured in consequence of the constant shifting of the load than from the positive weight, but at this season of the year you are obliged to carry waters which of course adds much to your loads, the only remedy is to be prepared with proper pack saddles.[122]

As a consequence of losing time through the state of their horses and the dense scrub along their route, for the last nineteen days of the expedition supplies were almost exhausted and the men were reduced to one meal a day. As a result Smythe suffered repeated fainting fits before they finally reached the south coast, well to the west of Albany. There they were able to subsist only by catching fish and finding oysters and abalone, which further slowed their rate of progress. Unlike contemporary explorations, Bannister's expedition members do not appear to have shot much game. In the heavily timbered country described they would probably have been hard pressed to have got close enough to do so. When the expedition finally reached Albany its members were exhausted, had no supplies left and had lost two horses.

Although Bannister's experiences were similar in many ways to those of Barrallier and other early explorers in New South Wales and notwithstanding the amateurishness of some of the early short excursions from Perth, the more rapid evolution of bushmanship and associated exploration techniques in Western Australia was largely independent of similar developments in the eastern colonies. For a start, horses were more readily available. They were first employed in Ensign Dale's expedition in August 1830, when he crossed the Darling Range to the east and then proceeded further inland to the Avon Valley. Dale and three others took two packhorses laden with three weeks' supply of food and equipment. Less than six months after settlement there were 850 people and fifty-seven horses in Western Australia, or a ratio of approximately 15:1. Such a ratio was not achieved in New South Wales until 1806. Dale's journey again indicated that local information can only be gained by experience. To set out in August, at the end of the wettest season of the year, and to find on occasions that, due to the boggy ground, the horses had to be unloaded and the saddle-bags carried by expedition members, cannot be deemed a fault.

On a more general issue, Dale was aware of the necessity of securing horses at night in forest country. He used the military technique of picquetting, by which the horses are secured by their lead ropes to stakes driven into the ground. The common adoption of this quite unsatisfactory procedure in Western Australia helps explain why his and subsequent explorers' horses failed so rapidly and frequently. In fact they were suffering from malnutrition, being unable to complete the grazing essential to maintain their condition. Dale's experience of 1830 was all too typical:

> ... one of our horses became so completely exhausted that he sank to the ground in which situation we were obliged to leave him till the following morning.[123]

Early Western Australian explorers' horses may also have been small and not particularly robust. The *Perth Gazette* of 23 March 1833[124] carried an advertisement offering a reward of £5 for a mare which had strayed. Although a four-year-old, she was only thirteen hands high which, by today's standards, would warrant her being classified as a pony. As many of the colony's stock were imported direct from the Cape, where horses are known to be small, it is reasonable to assume that this mare was representative of the stature of the horses available in Western Australia at that time. Their inability to carry loads for any period of time is therefore understandable.

On the other hand, a significant factor which facilitated the progress of explorers in south Western Australia was that they were not intimidated by the bush and were eager to learn from the Aboriginal people in order to further their exploration. In his 1829 expedition up the Canning River, Wilson commented that a group of Aborigines they had met '... shewed us various roots which they used for food, and also the manner of digging for them ...'[125] This eagerness to embrace Aboriginal bush skills, in contrast to the early eastern explorers' inability to learn from their native guides, is not readily explained. Perhaps the greater urge to explore the surrounding country and the more rapid development of bushmanship were due to the predominance of free settlers looking for fertile land. New South Wales had been established primarily as a convict depot and not until 1800, when the colony was coming to be viewed by Banks and others in economic terms, did exploration begin to accelerate.

Procuring game in forest country of the south-west of Western Australia also appears to have been a considerably easier task than it was for the earlier eastern colonists. Kangaroo dogs were employed from the beginning in the Albany hinterland, where Captain Barker also mentioned in 1830 that he sent some Aborigines and half his party to spear wallabies and shoot ducks. In the same year, while visiting Flinders Bay, Governor Stirling commented that '... (we) rejoined our friends at the encampment loaded with ducks, cockatoos and other game, the produce of our sportmen's exertions.'[126]

Equipment was an another element showing developmental variations between Western Australian and New South Wales. Discounting minor excursions such as Wilson's 1829 examination of the Canning, upon which he and his men took '... a bottle of water and a little bread, cheese and brandy ...' for a twelve-hour ramble to the south of the river,[127] excursions were generally well prepared. In 1830 John Wall Hardey and his associates in their exploration a hundred miles to the east of Perth took ten to fourteen days' provisions consisting of flour, biscuit, pork, rice, sugar, tea, spirits and further unspecified stores.[128] Thus, within one year, Western Australian explorers were carrying rations comparable to those taken by Caley and Barrallier, who had had twelve to fifteen years of eastern exploration experience on which to draw. As it is virtually certain that Hardey had never even heard of Caley or Barrallier, his preparedness was more than likely due to his solid Lincolnshire yeoman commonsense, than to any lessons he learned from others.

Perhaps because of the ready availability of packhorses, Western Australian explorers carried tent flies for shelter. Hardey notes that he took '... the lining of a tent to keep off the heavy dews in the night, and to refresh ourselves under in the heat of the day.'[129] The rate at which the idea of carrying light tent flies was accepted in Western Australia is quite surprising, given that the eastern explorers appear to have taken until Oxley's time to carry, as a matter of routine, even the much more bulky and inconvenient tents, when a fly would have been as effective in most cases. What is important is that the Western Australian explorers were experimental and flexible enough not to feel bound to burden themselves with a complete tent.

Despite these examples, which tend to indicate an accelerated rate of development of bushmanship amongst Western Australian explorers, some elements appear comparable with those in the eastern colonies. Probably the most important of these was the ongoing problem of clothing. Although Sturt in 1828 and Wilson in 1829 were both taking spare items, shoes, shirts and trousers remained inadequate for the conditions encountered. Hardey's description of the shortcomings of their clothing on his 1830 expedition east of the Darling Range is particularly illustrative of the problem:

> Had you seen the party arrive you would certainly have either laughed or cried, I don't know which; some were in a pitiable plight, having worn out their shoes — a good crop of toes to be seen before, and a famous round heel behind; others with their trowsers worn off half-way up the leg, and a knee peeping out ...[130]

Scientific observation in Western Australia up to the end of 1830 does not appear to have enjoyed the same rate of development as bushmanship, a situation which can be ascribed almost solely to the newness of the colony and the lack of qualified persons. As very little was known of the colony's geography, information was urgently required so that the areas best suited for grazing and cultivation could be developed. Consequently early Western Australian exploration was almost exclusively concerned with gaining an overview of the country, which involved covering the ground as quickly as possible. Dale's comment in 1830 that he had '... collected a few specimens of rocks and taken a few bearings of the country around us ...'[131] was hardly the stuff of painstaking scientific research. Hardey's lack of scientific expertise was comparable but irrelevant, since his aim was to find grazing country:

> I frankly confess that I am a novice in botany, and botanical phrases, or I would have given you the proper names of each of these grasses ...[132]

The similarities between Hardey's comments and Phillip's lament that he had no botanical knowledge are apparent, while the collecting of mineral and botanical samples also appears to have received lip service at best.

Although early Western Australian scientific research was no better than that exhibited in the first years of New South Wales, there was a desire to integrate knowledge gained and to generalise from it. This trend is exemplified in Stirling's report in May 1830 to the Royal Geographical Society, on his coastal explorations of the Cape Leeuwin area. Based on the ranges he had seen, and other reports, he surmised that:

> ... there are three distinct parallel ranges of primitive mountains traversing the Territory of Western Australia from north to south. The highest and easternmost of these has its southern termination near to King George Sound. The second terminates at Cape Chatham, and is that of which General Darling's range behind Cockburn Sound forms a portion. Cape Leeuwin, is the southern termination of the third range.[133]

That the above hypothesis was incorrect is immaterial. What is important is the desire to come to an understanding of the Western Australian environment. In his report, Stirling appears to have attempted to present useful information by providing an overview of the results of several discrete though partially overlapping expeditions. This careful analysis and synthesis of the data gathered by persons of differing knowledge presumably provided a model for A C Gregory's later comprehensive and thoughtful summaries of his expeditions, both in Western Australia and elsewhere.

By the end of the 1820s exploration and bushmanship had developed remarkably and much larger scale expeditions were being undertaken into far more demanding country. This growing expertise arose not only from the process of exploration, but also from the overall progression of bushmanship through the experiences of everyday bush people such as surveyors, drovers, stockmen and shepherds. Even the bushrangers and the mounted police who pursued them contributed both directly and indirectly to this development. Within a short time the men of the Veterans Company, who had formed the Mounted Police Corps in New South Wales, were found to be unequal to their task.

> The men of the Veteran Companies, having proved unfit for the duties of the Mounted Police, being in general unequal to the exposure and fatigue, which are unavoidable in that Service, have been returned to Head Quarters ...[134]

Clearly these failings would have demonstrated to the authorities that living out-of-doors for extended periods in Australia is demanding, and a vital component of bushmanship is physical and psychological toughness.[135]

According to Peter Cunningham, settlers now saw the country as well-stocked with game which was relatively easy to obtain:

> Your muskets will furnish you with birds of various kinds; — and with a brace of good grayhounds you will never lack kangaroos and emus ...[136]

Cunningham outlined methods which had been developed for procuring the different species, which included shooting nocturnal animals by using a 'bright or chalked barrel' in order to aim better at night. He also described techniques for making the meat from native animals more palatable, such as soaking possums in water for some hours to take away the strong odour of gum leaves on which they fed. Tastes were changing to accommodate Australian game, as the following quotation illustrates.

> The bandicoot tastes somewhat like a sucking pig, and makes a delicious dish with a well prepared pudding in its belly.[137]

By the mid-1820s horses were cheaper and more readily available for exploration purposes. Colonial horses were also proving to be hardier than their parent stock, although British disdain for colonial-bred products, which was derived from the notion of degeneration, had earlier branded them as inferior.[138] Alexander Harris, for one, was amazed at the capacity of grass-fed Australian horses for repeated hard work:

> Most horses live on grass in this way for months together, and it is almost incredible what work they can perform. For instance, I have known a stockman ride his horse 60 or 70 miles a day, and with little abatement continue this for five or six days together; the horse all the time feeding only on grass and stabling in the bush.[139]

Yet, despite the colonial horse's durability and its contribution towards extending exploration in Australia, its limitations in arid regions were already being realised. When Ballantyne proposed in 1827 to cross Australia from west to east in order to ascertain the geography of the central region, he wished to import fourteen camels for the expedition. As he pointed out of earlier explorations:

> To the extent [they] went, [horses] were so far satisfactory, but, if not so much as anticipated, the cause ought partly to be attributed to the want of camels, animals well known to be the

> best adapted for travelling in such a country as Australasia. ... neither horses nor mules seeming adequate.[140]

Nevertheless, horses were now being used more effectively. Saddlebags made of canvas and later of leather, and containing a change of clothes and some food, were now slung across riding horses' loins and, with a rolled blanket strapped across the withers in front of the saddle, mobility was maximised. By this arrangement a single rider was independent for some days, not even requiring a packhorse. Bulky tents were not favoured, explorers preferring to string up light tent flies, with a drip trench dug around the bottom. In this light, Cunningham's observation on the usage of canvas sheets in hot weather is pertinent.

> ... white-painted tarpaulings ... may be converted into most excellent tents, by stretching them over ridge poles, supported upon two forked posts, closing up one end of the tent by sheets of bark, and covering the whole with loose sheets of this also, to keep the tent cool within.[141]

Finally, as a yardstick of the increasing scope and sophistication of Australian exploration, it is fruitful to consider the costs of individual expeditions. Hovell noted that his and Hume's 1824 expedition in the south-east of New South Wales cost approximately £280 for stores and equipment,[142] while Sturt's first expedition along the Macquarie cost £205 for stores only and his second along the Murray £266. Compared to larger expeditions such as those carried out later by Mitchell and Gregory, such costs were modest.

Unfortunately, British condescension towards things and people colonial persisted. Government-funded explorations were exclusively commanded by British-born persons, although Hume's appointment as Second-in-Command to Sturt was an important development towards recognition of the value in the Australian bush of physical and psychological experience and endurance. Nevertheless, even a bushman of Hume's experience had to demean himself in a petition to Earl Bathurst by virtually apologising for his place of birth:

> Presuming myself (altho' an Australian) capable from experience of undertaking such an expedition ...[143]

Despite this progress, there was still much to be learnt. In Sturt's second expedition in 1828, for example, when he and his men endured excessive heat, inadequate diet, worry and the physical rigours of an extended period of exploration, their health suffered severely. Conditions were so hard on the homeward trip along the Murray and Murrumbidgee that one man went temporarily insane. Sturt's health subsequently declined to the extent that, after his return, he was completely blind for four months. Although his vision returned after a course of treatment with ascorbic acid, his general health remained precarious. That later explorers such as Giles, Forrest and Colonel Peter Warburton managed to cope with even harder country was probably due to their more robust constitutions, their more appropriate equipment and their superior bushmanship skills, which had not been available to Sturt.

4

THE 1830S AND THE FAILURE TO BENEFIT FROM EXPERIENCE

The expeditions of the 1830s, although successively larger and more sophisticated, contributed little to the overall development of bushmanship and scientific research. They were primarily concerned with solving the question of the south-eastern and central drainage patterns, exploring the forest country in the south-west of Western Australia and examining the Western District of Victoria. The decade also witnessed Lieutenant George Grey's abortive efforts in the north of Western Australia and Edward John Eyre's first tentative excursions into the hinterland of Adelaide.

In 1827 Major Thomas Mitchell, who had gained surveying experience in the Peninsula War, was appointed Assistant Surveyor-General to John Oxley and arrived in Sydney later that year. Commencing work in 1828, Mitchell began the immense task of making a general triangulation of New South Wales, as a prerequisite to more specific title surveys. On Oxley's death in 1828, Mitchell became Surveyor-General and carried out considerable field work in the south-east of the colony. During three expeditions in 1831, 1835 and 1836, he attempted to define in greater detail the nature of the south-eastern drainage system. His efforts were characterised by such a slow-moving, ineffectual approach that he rarely achieved his goals. Furthermore, in most cases settlers were usually close behind or even ahead of him, as with the Henty brothers at Portland Bay in the Western District of Victoria. Because of careless management, his men were continually strung out, which on two occasions led to their being attacked by Aborigines, several of whom were killed in both instances.

Like Mitchell, Lieutenant George Grey had a military background. During his service in Ireland he became disenchanted with military duties and developed an interest in colonisation as a means of ameliorating the situation of the British poor. Towards this end he obtained permission from the Colonial Office to mount an expedition in the north of Western Australia, ostensibly to discover the outfall of the supposed great north-westward flowing river. After landing at Hanover Bay in the far north of the Kimberleys and carrying out several small-scale training excursions, he and his party set off overland in January 1838 for the Swan River Settlement. Lack of experience, poor equipment, unsatisfactory horses, extremely rugged terrain, monsoonal downpours and Aboriginal attacks forced Grey to return to Hanover Bay after several weeks' desperate struggle. In the following year he was forced to make an overland march to Perth from Shark Bay, after losing his stores and his whaleboats while landing there.

John Septimus Roe was largely responsible for the successful exploration of the south-western corner of Western Australia. After extensive experience in coastal surveys of New South Wales he was appointed Surveyor-General of Western Australia in 1829. Between 1830 and 1848 he participated in sixteen explorations, beginning with small-scale journeys but rapidly developing in scope to encompass trips from Perth to Albany and return via the settlement of York. In 1839 he also led a party north to find and bring back the survivors of Grey's second expedition. What is particularly important about Roe's work as Surveyor-General is that men such as the Gregory and Forrest brothers, who worked, trained and learnt under him later went on to undertake some of the most difficult, important and professional explorations in Australian history.

Finally, in 1839 the young South Australian squatter Edward John Eyre, after progressively developing his bushcraft over a six-year period, decided to carry out a series of explorations of the Adelaide hinterland, at his own expense, for the benefit of the 'Colony at large'.[1]

If the 1830s were relatively unremarkable in the history of Australian exploration, the same cannot be said of changes in British science. The trends which had emerged after 1813, including a growing scientific awareness and interest amongst the newly affluent and the increasing professionalism of scientific societies, became considerably more pronounced in the 1830s. As well as being a decade of political and social reform, the 1830s marked the commencement of an era in which '... the altered realities of wealth, leisure and communication (which involved) ... turnpike roads, canals, steamships and — from 1830 — passenger railways ...' allowed a considerably greater proportion of the population to indulge their interests in science. The result was a '... flowering of regionally coordinated organisations and peripatetic associations ...'[2] related to science.

Growing dissatisfaction with the conservative Royal Society and concern over the relative decline of British science led in 1831 to the formation of the British Association for the Advancement of Science, initially a loose gathering of scientists with the rather ill-defined goal of '... unrestrained communication of scientific opinions and discoveries.'[3] Its founders envisaged that the Association would draw regional scientists into collaboration with those of the major cities and in this regard it was highly successful. The Association further popularised science by allowing interested lay persons to attend its broad-ranging annual conferences. Not surprisingly, it became an extremely influential body, which soon realised its power to lobby the government for assistance with large-scale research projects. Examples include the systematic tidal observations made in 1834 and 1835 along the British and Irish coasts, when five hundred coastguard stations were instructed by the authorities to cooperate for a fortnight in the taking of essential measurements.[4] The Association also saw research funding as essential for progress, making grants available to its members after 1831.

An indication of increasing scientific specialisation in Britain in the 1830s was the establishment of the Royal Geographical Society, whose activities included the printing of research findings, the establishment of a substantial library and map collection and communication with other geographical societies and individual geographers. Importantly, the Royal Geographical Society now attempted to formalise field research techniques, outlining desirable equipment and giving detailed instructions. The society encouraged exploration through direct grants, logistical assistance, expert advice and the provision of contacts. It also encouraged and popularised field research by awarding gold medals for meritorious achievement.

The exponential increase in data generated by scientific research in the 1830s not only heralded an increase in the professionalism of the scientific societies, but also spelt the end of the polymath. Herschel, for one, lamented that specialisation was now inescapable. 'Such is science now-a-days,' he wrote. 'No man can now hope to know more than one part of one science.'[5]

Data-gathering was now seen as subservient to, and the basis of, hypothesising and hypothesis testing. As the physicist and theoretician William Whewell argued:

> ... the mere gathering of raw facts may be compared to the gathering of cotton from the tree. The separate filaments must be drawn into a connected thread, and the threads woven into an ample web, before it can form the drapery of science.[6]

The contrast between this emphasis and that which prevailed in Australia, where even the gathering of raw data was uncoordinated and indiscriminate, is apparent. This rapidly developing and pronounced sense of professionalism was expressed in a number of ways, including a call by the younger Fellows of the Royal Society for the exclusion from ordinary Fellowship of all but practising scientists.[7] As well, the British Museum was radically reorganised along more modern lines, with its natural history collection subdivided into the distinct Departments of Zoology, Mineralogy and Botany. In 1837 the British Museum sent 500 copies of instructions on the collection and preservation of natural history specimens to the Colonial Office, for distribution to various colonial administrators, in order that samples forwarded to the Museum would be of a satisfactory standard.

By the end of the 1830s the ethos of British science had changed markedly from that prevailing in the 1820s. Research methodology had been formalised, scientists were now aware of their professional standing and personal areas of specialisation and limited funding was available. Perhaps most importantly of all, the British government was increasingly being persuaded to assist in research projects.

In contrast to the previous decade or so, the changes in the British scientific world between 1830 and 1840 had little immediate impact upon exploration and discovery in Australia. For one thing, specialised professional involvement was a rarity in New South Wales. In 1827 a mineral surveyor and a botanist were the only professional scientists on the government payroll. On Mitchell's first expedition there were no scientific staff. On his second expedition he took Richard Cunningham, who had succeeded Fraser as Government Botanist in 1832, and a qualified assistant surveyor.[8] The list of men involved in his third expedition includes only the research assistants: 'John Roach, collector of birds', and 'John Richardson, collector of Plants'.[9] Grey's 1838 expedition was similarly ill-provided with scientific staff, including only the amateur 'Mr. Walker, a surgeon and naturalist'.[10]

Mitchell, Grey and Roe were not scientifically qualified. In fact Mitchell made explicit reference to his lack of proficiency in botany, palaeontology and zoology. Indeed, as this comment suggests, the low quality of his botanical observations was comparable to that of Evans:

> This was a fortunate day for us, in regard to plants. Besides several curious kinds of grass, a splendid blue Brunonia was found.[11]

The footnotes to his journal were later provided by British scientists.[12] Although Mitchell collected few botanical or zoological specimens, he did execute a series of highly professional line drawings of fossil remains, from which, together with his samples, the palaeontologist Professor Owen was able to provide a substantial appendix to the explorer's journal. Generally, however, Mitchell's lack of scientific expertise, together with the almost total absence of professional men on his expeditions, made his field research findings no better than those achieved by Oxley some eighteen years previously.

Grey's scientific findings were similarly sparse, despite his official instructions to collect specimens of natural history. Not only did the serious problems Grey encountered during his expedition almost preclude any possibility of field research, but also the absence of scientists and the explorer's meagre scientific knowledge meant even the small amount of work carried out was of a poor standard. Grey's journals are dotted with drawings and descriptions of botanical and zoological specimens, but his prose, though detailed, rarely transcends the pseudo-scientific. His writings suffer from his lack of a scientific vocabulary and a theoretical background, as his description of a sea creature caught on the journey to Australia demonstrates:

> Presently a little head peered out, then the body expanded itself, and finally two little things like wings were spread forth, formed of a fine membrane; they moved these very rapidly, and swam with great velocity.[13]

A lack of professional staff was not the only unsatisfactory aspect of Australian field research during this decade. Despite the Royal Geographical Society's support for Grey's expedition and some evidence that field research in Australia during the 1830s was less pragmatically based than that of the preceding decades, this work was in fact still severely limited in quality because of its intensely economic orientation. It appears that the selective and pragmatic approach of local field researchers was a function of economic factors, with the generation of financial returns being seen as of primary importance, in contrast to the comprehensive and usually non-fiscally oriented approach of pure research. Even enthusiastic amateur James Drummond, who achieved world-wide recognition for his contribution to botanical science, was driven by the precarious condition of the Western Australian economy to collect and sell specimens to British nurserymen on a professional basis for much of his adult life.[14] He and his contemporaries did anything but exemplify the burgeoning dispassionate search for truth which was so evident in British scientific research at that time. Grey proclaimed his intention to solve the unknown geography of the Kimberley region, pointing out that as a result of Dampier and King's work it was hoped that a 'great river, or water inlet, might be found to open out at some point on its western or north western side; which had then been only partially surveyed from seaward.'[15] Yet in retrospect he conceded the fact that his sponsors had actually sent him to look for 'Commercial Advantages'. To that end, several pages of his journal were devoted to outlining the crops, particularly cotton, which he thought were suited to the climate of the North West and which would:

> .... give employment to British vessels alone, and the industry of our manufacturers would be called into operation, by an entirely new market for cotton goods being thrown open to them ... [ie. via an entrepot trading post to sell manufactured cotton goods in the Indian Archipelago].[16]

Mitchell also claimed a scholarly rationale for his explorations in search of the mythical great river and inland sea:

> The principal object of my plan was the exploration of Australia, so that whether the report of the river proved true or false, the results of the expedition would be, at least, useful, in affording so much additional information; equally important geographically, whether positive or negative.[17]

Again, the reality was, in fact, dominated by financial considerations, for Mitchell's official journeying in search of the great river was commercially motivated. This fact was unequivocally spelled out by Governor Gipps in his 1840 analysis of Mitchell's journeying:

> The expectation of finding the large River, or an Inland Sea, sufficiently near to be of any use to our Settlers, has altogether vanished; and consequently the desire to penetrate into the Interior is less ardent than it was.[18]

Gipps then went on to make explicit his view of the importance of exploration:

> The long and expensive journies of Sir Thomas Mitchell in the years 1835 and 1836, though highly interesting, led to no discoveries which could be turned to profit, with the exception perhaps of the fertile land of Australia Felix, which would surely have been reached by the ordinary advance of our Graziers, even though he had never visited it.[19]

As a consequence of the official outlook and of the economically disappointing results obtained during the 1830s, by the end of the decade

Gipps, in a letter to Lord Russell, denied the possibility of, or belief in, dispassionate field research in Australia for several years to come. In fact, he was quite condescending towards the idea of pure research:

> Your Lordship will have observed that I have not spoken of any New Expedition, undertaken either by the Government or by Individuals for the mere purpose of Discovery, and indeed none such have been attempted.[20]

At least Roe and Stirling, who were working in the south-west of Western Australia, were totally honest about their goals. A return was desired, as Stirling's amateurishly optimistic 1835 description of a series of salt lakes north of Cranbrook indicates:

> I have little doubt that these lakes might be drained and made fresh, and that much of this sort of land admits of profitable cultivation. The spontaneous and vigorous growth of the wild flax upon it gives reason to hope that, at least, that plant might be raised to advantage.[21]

As late as 1840, therefore, due both to the critical shortage of expert personnel and the continuing preoccupation with resource identification, field research in Australia was neither scientifically planned nor systematically directed. Apart from Brown's work in the *Investigator* and Cunningham's achievements under Oxley, expectations in the natural sciences were generally low and research outcomes minimal. Only when scientific societies became directly involved in the planning and carrying out of field research during major explorations did any degree of sophistication become evident. In the case of Grey's 1838 expedition, the Royal Geographical Society's role was too peripheral to be effective.

There were, nevertheless, some successful developments in Australian field research during the 1830s, including further progress in the scientific hypothesising which now underlay most of the major field explorations. A considerable amount was now known about the existence of major rivers and the ultimate drainage of south-eastern Australia. Consequently explorations during this period were, in part at least, concerned with filling in details of the theoretical structures. Mitchell's first exploration was carried out in order to determine whether a large river flowed to the north and north-west towards the Gulf of Carpentaria, contrary to Cunningham's earlier discovery of a series of rivers flowing to the west and south-west.[22] When Mitchell eventually reached the Darling via Cunningham's Gwydir River, he could conclude the drainage was definitely in accordance with the deductions made from Sturt's and Cunningham's earlier field research and was prepared to hypothesise further about the overall drainage pattern of this region:

> ... there was no necessity for extending [the exploration] further, as I could not suppose that it was any other than the Darling. Into this river we had traced the Gwyder; the junction of the Nammoy [Namoi], also, could not be far distant; and even that of the Castlereagh was only about 70 miles to the south west, which was the direction of the supposed general course of the Darling. It was probable, that the streams we had now explored, formed the chief sources of that river ...[23]

Similarly, Grey's work in the Kimberleys intended, as a secondary consideration at least, to prove or disprove the existence of the great river and its accompanying inland sea. This notion, which had been current for some thirty to forty years, was based on European preconceptions that a continent of this size must be either discharging a considerable volume of water, via a single river such as the Rhine in Europe or the Mississippi in North America, or storing it internally.[24]

Even though Australian interest in natural science was slow to develop, there was an increasing awareness of the necessity for improving the standard of education, in New South Wales at least. By 1840 the colony had been in existence for fifty-two years and had a population of over 100,000. Notwithstanding its convict origins, it can be argued that, in part at least, the lack of an intelligentsia was due to the inadequacies of the colonial educational system. In 1818 Macquarie, who had a typical Scottish respect for learning, expressed his misgivings about the situation to Samuel Marsden:

> ... in addition to the several public Endowments for disseminating the first principles of Common Education in the Towns of Sydney, Parramatta, Windsor, Liverpool and Newcastle (and there being) ... several inferior School Establishments, at Richmond, Castlereagh, Pitt Town, Wilberforce and etc. ... where the rudiments of Education are given in a tolerably fair and extensive degree, (and) ... Various Classical Schools (which exist) ... for the higher Attainment of Learning ... Our Schools ... are still inadequate to the great Work of rendering Education co-extensive with the Population in that Measure and degree that I am anxious to render it.[25]

Seven years later Governor Darling found scant improvement. Of 4,724 children in the colony in 1825, 2,698 were 'in a state of receiving no education.'[26] The underlying causes included the scarcity of persons even minimally qualified to act as teachers, the extremely scattered population

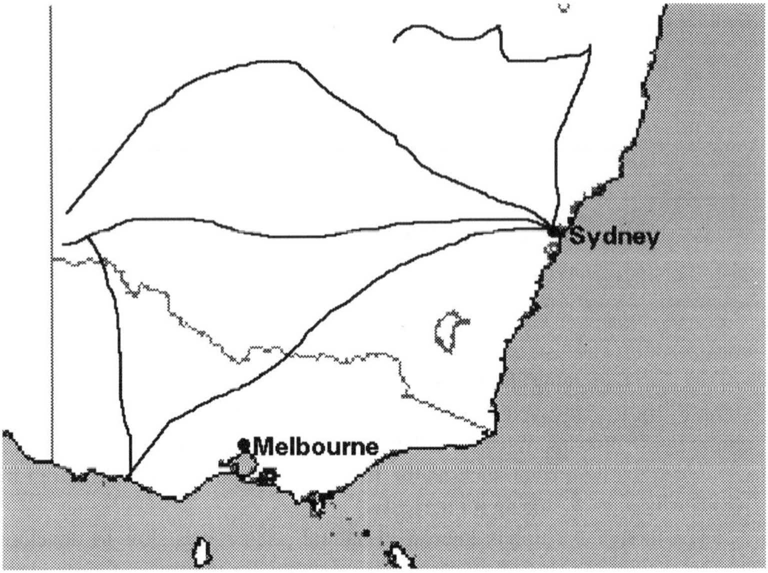

Major Thomas Mitchell's explorations in south-eastern Australia, 1831–1836.

and the need for children to help work their parents' properties. Darling doubted that the situation would improve, for the parents did not value education above their immediate labour requirements.

> Whenever I have visited the people personally, I have invariably found a great desire in the parents that the children should attend; but, when the Schoolmaster complains of irregularity, every excuse is made and very frequently a threat to withdraw the Child altogether.[27]

Nevertheless, despite Lawrence Halloran's claim in 1827 that '... in this country, during the first 30 years of its existence, the education of Youth was confined (with a single exception on a small scale) to the Acquirement of merely the inferior Branches of Elementary Instruction,'[28] there was a growing appreciation during the 1830s of the necessity and desirability of a more comprehensive educational system. Lord Bathurst was contemplating the establishment of a university in New South Wales and plans for boarding schools and denominational educational systems were submitted to the Local Government.[29] The Presbyterians planned to provide instruction in mathematics and the physical and biological sciences, believing that this approach would bring 'direct and incalculable benefits ... to the colony of New South Wales.' Although their system would not produce scientists, its products would be competent to provide to '... men of eminence in the Departments of Philosophy and Science in the Mother Country ... valuable specimens and valuable information ... from the Australian Colonies.'[30]

In 1832 the British Government granted two Sydney town lots to the Committee of the Australian Library, not for building purposes, but for sale in order to raise money for the establishment of a library and museum. Later, Lord Glenelg persuaded the authorities to donate £4,000 for the same purpose.[31] The opening of the library, as a 'Public Institution of great importance to the Colony',[32] was a turning point in intellectual and scientific development in early Australia.

By March 1833 the Sydney Mechanics Institute was established, along similar lines to those in Britain. Governor Bourke thought it a meritorious project, which was '... already somewhat successful in promoting a taste for mental cultivation among persons in the middle ranks ...'[33] Established under his patronage, for 'the diffusion of scientific and useful knowledge', it made rapid progress. Within less than two years it had acquired over six hundred texts and a number of models and apparatus had been collected for lecture purposes. Yet despite such encouraging progress, involvement in popular science and scientific societies was a slowly developing feature of colonial life. Although the progress made in education during the 1830s would provide a firm basis for later scientific development, the day of the Australian-trained scientist was yet to come.

At a time when both church and state were introducing progressive educational changes appropriate to Australia's cultural and economic environment, two of the country's most prominent explorers chose a military style of operation quite unsuited to conditions in the interior of the continent. Mitchell and Grey appear to have taken over where Evans and Oxley left off, pursuing beyond the limits of its usefulness an exploration style which had been of doubtful relevance in the first place. Their approach, featuring unmounted men and, in Mitchell's case, slow-moving pack and draught oxen, was not appropriate to the increasingly difficult country being traversed. To continue with this style of exploration in a larger format did not increase its effectiveness. Beyond a certain point, it was necessary to abandon it.

The most serious disadvantage of Grey's and Mitchell's dysfunctional approach to exploration was lack of mobility. This problem attained ludicrous proportions in Mitchell's 1845 expedition, in which he penetrated a short distance beyond the Tropic of Capricorn, on the Belyando River in Central Queensland. He took with him, through rough and unknown country, boats, wagons, packhorses, 250 sheep and over a hundred bullocks.

Favouring wheeled transport over pack animals from the beginning, for his first expedition Mitchell had a number of light carts constructed, which could be drawn by one or two horses, depending on the nature of the going, and which were also light enough to be manhandled across difficult, narrow passes. He also had three bullock drays. Draught bullocks and drays were selected because Mitchell's field surveying experience had convinced him that they were well suited to the supposedly level nature of inland Australia, could be loaded more rapidly than a team of pack animals, would be less liable to the problem of galling and would obviate the loss of saddlebags.[34]

Mitchell's inexperience was soon apparent, for the drays he designed proved to be highly unsuited for exploration purposes. He does not seem to have understood that inland Australia is not uniformly level or smooth, nor that, in order to reach the inland regions from Bathurst, mountain ranges and rivers had to be crossed. All too often the country was too steep, too rough or too thickly wooded for these cumbersome vehicles. Consequently, Mitchell frequently had to find alternative routes around ranges and to have his men chop tracks through miles of scrub, all of which impeded progress. Not surprisingly the carts and drays suffered. On 5 December 1831, only fifteen days after setting off from Sydney, a cart was abandoned after its axle broke and the load was transferred to the bullocks. The extreme dryness of the season meant that the dray wheels frequently shrank until the spokes became loose and wore so badly as to require a halt while repairs were made. Worse, as the wooden wheels shrank, the steel tyres became loose and had to be wedged, or even taken off, cut, shortened, re-welded and heated to cherry-red in order to replace them on the wooden wheels. This task, difficult enough in a wheelwright's shop, was formidable in outback Australia. Once damp conditions returned the situation was reversed.

> ... we began to experience the effects of moisture on the felloes of the wheels. The heat and contraction had lately obliged us to tighten and wedge them to such a degree, that now, when the ground had become wet, the expansion of the whole broke the tirering of the wheel. Having no forge, we could only attempt the necessary repairs with a common fire ...[35]

During his three expeditions Mitchell was repeatedly forced to hook double teams, and sometimes all of his bullocks, onto one vehicle at a time to pull the wagons up creek and river beds, over range country and out of bogs. Even traversing steep-sided creeks was a major problem, for the wagons had to be unyoked, slowly lowered, floated across in tarpaulins, then pulled up the other side. The process was extremely time-consuming, difficult and fraught with problems.

> In one place, where a narrow point of ground projected across, a passage seemed just possible; and after we had made it better with spades, we attempted to take a light cart over. The acclivity was still, however, rather too much, and over went the cart, carrying the shaft bullock with it, and depositing all my instruments, and etc. under it in the bed of the stream. ... By means of a block and tackle attached to a large tree, the remaining carts and the boat carriage were safely lowered to the bed of the stream. To draw them up the opposite bank was practicable only by uniting the strength of several teams ...[36]

On his third expedition in 1836, when Mitchell was traversing northern Victoria, the country was extremely wet, the heavily laden drays frequently bogged and his straining oxen often exhausted to the point of collapse and, occasionally, death.

> The drays sunk to the axles, the whole of the soil in our way having become so liquid, that it rolled in waves around the struggling bullocks[37].
>
> ... the surface under the pressure of the cattle was immediately converted into white and liquid mud. It was necessary to take the loads from the carts, and carry them by hand half a mile; and then to remove the empty vehicles by the same means. After all this had been accomplished, the boat carriage, [a four wheeled wagon] still remained immovably fixed up to the axle-tree in mud, in a situation where the block and tackle used in hoisting out the boats could not be applied ... by joining all the chains we possessed, and applying the united strength of all the bullocks; [they managed to free the wagon]. [38]

So ill-suited were oxen and heavily laden drays to these conditions that Eyre noted two years later, when overlanding cattle from Port Phillip to Adelaide, that he occasionally followed Mitchell's still clearly-visible wheel ruts.[39]

Mitchell was also to discover that dry conditions were equally difficult for his bullocks. In particular the leading teams, whose task it was to compress the powdery soil of river flood plains into wheel ruts, were soon exhausted.

> The labour which this kind of ground cost the poor bullocks, drawing heavy carts, reduced them to so great a state of weakness, that six never returned from the Darling. The work was so heavy for the two first teams on our advancing into these regions, that one team was rendered quite unserviceable by leading; but on returning we found the beaten track much easier for the whole party.[40]

Exacerbating such problems was Mitchell's insistence, on his second and third expeditions, on taking boats carried by drays, though he scarcely even wetted their keels. Of his second expedition Mitchell later commented that he had hauled his boats for over 2,500 kilometres 'without finding a river, where I could use them.'[41] Nevertheless, he refused to leave the virtually unused craft behind, and during the third expedition, while the bullocks floundered and strained in their often pitiable attempts to free the bogged boat dray, he stated:

Major Mitchell's boat finally gets used.

> Although the boats and their carriage had been of late a great hindrance to us, I was very unwilling to abandon such useful appendages to an exploring party, having already drawn them over-land nearly 3,000 miles.[42]

In fact, so unproductive were Mitchell's boats that it is perhaps not unfair to state that the best use he made of them occurred on the fourth expedition, when the banks of the Macquarie River were so boggy and dangerous that the cattle could not be driven to water. The great number of bullocks involved meant that watering them individually from buckets was out of the question, so a boat was used as a trough.

The second factor impeding Mitchell's rate of progress was his choice of bullocks for pack and draught purposes, for bullocks do not have the same rate of travel as horses. On his second expedition Mitchell boasted that his team had covered '... over 600 miles, [960 kilometres] even in a *direct* distance'[43] in approximately sixty-three days, at an effective rate of under sixteen kilometres per day. In contrast, approximately six years before Mitchell's journey, on his expedition south to Albany, John Septimus Roe was able to cover over three hundred kilometres 'in less than 15 days', which included one day of rest.[44] Francis Gregory, on his 1851 exploration of the Murchison and Gascoyne regions, covered over three thousand kilometres at better than thirty kilometres per day, in a performance on which he did not even bother to comment. Also worth noting in this context was the feat, at approximately the same time, of George Fletcher Moore, one of the fledgling bushmen of Western Australia, who covered sixty kilometres in one day on horseback.[45]

The limited mobility of Mitchell's bullocks was a particularly serious problem when water was drying up and long stages had to be covered quickly. Further problems also occurred when heavy rain was imminent while the party was on clayey, marshy country which would rapidly become impassable to wagons. Bullocks, when laden, also appear to be worse affected by heat than horses and require watering more frequently. Yet on his fourth and final expedition, Mitchell continued using bullocks, while commenting in his journal on several occasions that he rued ever taking them in preference to horses.

Given that Mitchell was involved in four expeditions, the latter two on an extremely large scale and of up to twelve months' duration, it is also difficult to understand why he persisted in having his staff unmounted. By 1844 there were more than fifty thousand horses in Australia,[46] so scarcity would not have been a problem. Possibly he saw little point in having his men mounted in a situation where his draught bullocks and drays limited progress to a snail's pace, even under the most favourable circumstances.

Yet another factor which appears to have retarded Mitchell's mobility was the increasingly large scale of his expeditions. An index of their magnitude can be gauged from Sturt's earlier total cost estimates of £205 and £265 in 1828 and 1829 respectively, in contrast to Mitchell's cost of approximately £940 for equipment alone on his second expedition. On this occasion the explorer had twenty-four men, seven carts, the heavy carriage carrying the two boats, seven packhorses and a team of oxen. On the third expedition he took twenty-five men. With so many people a disproportionate number were involved primarily in maintaining the operation. Amongst the staff on the third expedition, for example, were a shoemaker and a storekeeper. Such supernumeraries also required supplies and equipment, which entailed more drays and oxen, which then required more men to care for them and so on.

Compounding this problem was the fact that the British Government was now committed to equipping expeditions more thoroughly. In the preamble to the journal of his third expedition Mitchell noted that, despite the high prices for horses and bullocks as a consequence of the prolonged drought, '... no expense was spared by the government in providing the animals required.'[47] Roe was given similar support in his 1835 expedition from Perth to Albany, being informed that it was the Governor's wish that '... the Expedition should be equipped with everything which you may deem essential to its efficiency and comfort.'[48]

The final factor inhibiting the mobility of both Grey and Mitchell was their practice of droving stock for slaughter, to supplement their rations. On his second expedition Mitchell took fifteen sheep from Buree '... to try whether this kind of livestock was available [viable] on such expeditions.'[49] Satisfied with the success of this first experiment, on his next expedition Mitchell took 100 sheep and five fat oxen.[50] He commented that, when they killed the last sheep after 1700 kilometres, it was more than a kilogram heavier than any of its predecessors. In south-eastern Australia at least, droving stock for slaughter was a feasible proposition, provided one was in no great hurry. 'It appears thus how well a wandering and migratory life agrees with sheep in this hemisphere, as of old in the other,' wrote Mitchell.[51] On his expedition in Western Australia's north-west George Grey disembarked thirty-one sheep and nineteen goats at Hanover Bay, but the humid tropical climate and intensely wet conditions did not suit these animals and most died or were quite unthrifty.[52]

The droving of stock gradually became a feature of exploration, with Leichhardt, Eyre and Sturt also taking sheep and cattle. Later, however, once explorers such as Stuart, Warburton and Giles began their assaults on the central desert region using highly mobile horse or camel teams, slow-moving herds of stock were no longer practicable.

With these larger expeditions and their considerable numbers of livestock, the difficulty of finding adequate water and feed increased exponentially. Both Eyre and Sturt commented on this problem during their large-scale expeditions in the early 1840s, with Sturt pointing out that his expedition's daily water consumption rate was in the vicinity of 5000 litres.[53] Obviously such quantities of water were difficult to find in arid areas, especially during the dry season. Furthermore, with larger numbers of stock, the possibility of their dispersing overnight into a number of very small groups was magnified. With small numbers of stock an experienced stockman can intuitively tell where they are, but larger numbers invariably become more scattered. Mitchell suffered severely from this problem, particularly on his fourth expedition which was accompanied by over a hundred oxen and 250 killer wethers.[54]

Mitchell steadfastly refused to learn from experience. On his final expedition, the worst aspects of his first three ventures were magnified to an almost ludicrous degree. It seems that Mitchell was locked into such a large scale, formal and slow-moving style of exploration because of his martial background. Despite his manifest interest in its natural history, he never came to terms with the nature of inland Australia and never broke out of his military frame of mind. He even took three men to act as servants to himself and others on the second expedition and a professional trumpeter on the third expedition.[55] In addition, Mitchell especially outfitted the men on that occasion with '... grey trowsers and a red woollen shirt, the latter article, when crossed by white braces, giving the men somewhat of a military appearance.'[56]

Even in Mitchell's everyday demeanour and mode of operation can be found evidence of a rigid, unnecessarily autocratic and martial approach. Small examples abound, such as selecting convicts to accompany him, for he believed that such men, with their eyes on a conditional pardon once the expedition was completed, would be obliging and conscientious in their work. He also set a fixed time for encamping each day and refused to allow the men to eat until the travelling and setting up of camp had been completed. Another pointless exercise in authority concerned Mitchell's belief that the men, when thirsty, would not be able to control themselves and would drink to excess. He consequently forbade the men from drinking till he gave permission.

> ... I had frequently an opportunity of observing, that the worst

> characters have the least control over their appetites, in cases of extreme privation. It was a standing order, which I insisted on being observed, that no man should quit the line of route to drink, without my permission.[57]

The certainty that these men would then still drink as much as they wanted appears to have eluded Mitchell.

On one occasion Mitchell decided to establish a depot camp on the Darling while he pushed forward by boat. He had trees felled and rolled to the site, branches lopped and a stockade and cattle yard erected. The whole was to form a secure fortress, a 'place of defence',[58] for the protection of the men and stock left at the depot. In a land relatively sparsely peopled by small groups of nomadic Aboriginal people, he named this incongruous structure 'Fort Bourke'.

The clearest example of Mitchell's military view of inland exploration can be found in his plan of encampment. Its orientation depended upon the direction of the moon, of which Mitchell took night sightings from his tent door. Since no firelight was allowed to interfere with these sightings, Mitchell first determined the site for his tent and the position of its mouth. The heavy wagon, light carts and boat wagon were then positioned in a specific layout relative to Mitchell's tent, in order to act as a redoubt in case of attack by Aborigines. The other tents and their fires were placed further out in a set pattern so that the respective fires would illuminate all the wagons and prevent Aborigines from creeping up undetected.[59]

It must be emphasised also, that Mitchell saw his goals and means in surveying, rather than exploring, terms. For this reason he rarely took the easiest route. He was constrained by his search for peaks with the good lookouts required for his triangulation surveys, which he considered to be an essential component of his work.

> I availed myself of trigonometrical measurements ... in which case such a survey engaged my whole attention, and my route was often directed according to the position of good points.[60]

Mitchell also appears to have had a surveyor's straight-line mentality, for he often had his men cutting a passage directly through patches of thick scrub rather than circumnavigating them. When Leichhardt encountered similar obstacles in the brigalow country to the north of Dalby in southern Queensland, he skirted around them, or followed river banks or dry river beds. Mitchell lacked the psychological flexibility so essential to cope with the diversity of topographic, botanic, and climatic conditions he encountered. Fortunately, few later explorers copied his approach.

Mitchell was not the only explorer of the decade to suffer from poor mobility. Roe and the other Western Australian explorers and surveyors of the 1830s were also not well equipped overall with pack, riding and draught animals. On Stirling and Roe's expedition to Albany in 1835, only the Governor and his retinue were mounted and the private soldiers had to walk.[61] Two years earlier, Surveyor Hillman had blamed the perfunctory nature of his map of the route to Albany on his lack of pack animals.

> I am sorry to say I cannot give a more correct sketch of this journey for not being supplied with horses it was quite out of my power to take any other Instruments besides my pocket compass, our provisions for ten days proving as much as we could well carry ...[62]

Bullock and horse teams are also frequently mentioned in Western Australian field exploration and surveying journals from 1835 onwards, but problems occurred with breakages and in getting the drays through the forest country and over the rocky Darling Range. Such delays, combined with the bullocks' inherently slow rate of travel, inevitably slowed progress. In October 1835 Hillman led a party to explore from Perth south to the Williams River and thence in an arc to the east and north-east to the Avon River. Daily distances of four and a half kilometres, six kilometres, seven kilometres and so on[63] reflect inherent problems with bullock teams.

The major explorers of this period suffered from other shortcomings which, collectively, inhibited the application of learned bushcraft skills to exploration. Perhaps the most important of these secondary factors was the breaking of the continuity which was so important to the earlier development of bushmanship. Mitchell, who did not draw heavily on the skills of experienced bushmen as had Oxley and Sturt, was in many ways a regressive influence. Consistently choosing convicts to accompany him, he was not concerned by the almost total absence of experience among this group of former sail makers, cashiered soldiers, London grooms, coachmen and so on.[64] Even if they accompanied him on subsequent expeditions, they were employed as overseers, bullock drivers and personal servants, rather than being involved in carrying out the critical reconnoitring so vital to successful explorations. Mitchell lacked the valuable expertise which Hume, for example, had brought to Sturt's exploration. In fact Mitchell's men were so lacking in bush skills that a permanent worry was for the safety of his stock handlers while they looked for stock which had strayed overnight.

> ... there is also the risk of losing the men sent in pursuit, who, even after coming on the objects of their search, may be unable afterwards to find the camp, especially when there may be no water-course to lead them to it.[65]

The importance of bushmanship in the exploration of inland Australia was exemplified when Richard Cunningham, the botanist accompanying Mitchell's party, became lost in the Bogan River area in 1835. Although several members of the expedition managed to trace his movements for some distance on different occasions, they always lost the tracks. Twelve days were spent searching and waiting, until Mitchell realised that no more could be done and that he had probably perished. If competent bushmen had been included in the expedition, it is likely that Cunningham would have been saved.

Possibly as a means of overcoming the practical deficiencies so apparent in his expedition members, Mitchell made far greater use of Aboriginal guides than his immediate predecessors, gaining considerable value from their assistance. The Aborigines were required not merely to advise but also to guide Mitchell's expeditions. He seems to have valued their company, for he refers on frequent occasions to the ways in which their bush skills facilitated his passage. For example, with Aborigines leading his expedition, his men were:

> ... perfectly safe from the danger of sudden collision with a tribe. Their caution, in approaching waterholes was most remarkable; for they always cooyed from a great distance ...[66]

Mitchell used the Aborigines' knowledge to determine the location and quality of water and feed. His guides could frequently make themselves understood with local tribal groups, whom they would often persuade to accompany the expedition for limited distances in order to share the benefit of their knowledge. On his third expedition, in Victoria, Mitchell commented that the Aboriginal guide Piper and two Aboriginal boys who had attached themselves to the party along the way more or less dictated the route. The three of them reconnoitred ahead in a broad semi-circle, examining the country and ascertaining the best route for the heavy boat wagons. They also tracked lost cattle and horses, consulted with local Aborigines, hunted game and caught fish. Thus Mitchell admitted:

> The whole management of the chase now devolved on him and the two boys, his humble servants; and this native party usually explored the woods with our dogs, for several miles in front of the column.[67]

Yet despite Mitchell's reliance on and close affinity with his Aboriginal guides, he underestimated the dangers represented by the Aboriginal people overall. For one thing, he failed to profit from Sturt's acute observations, committing the cardinal sin of repeatedly splitting up his expedition whilst under way and allowing his men to straggle over extended distances.

On one occasion in 1835, a small unarmed party left without a sentry to pull bogged cattle from the banks of the Darling, were lucky to be saved from a party of Aborigines who were stalking them.[68] He was also worried about his men having to muster stock which had strayed overnight, for he felt '... the death of some of these men (was) certain.'[69] For this failing Mitchell paid dearly on several occasions. On his first expedition to the basins of the Namoi and Gwydir Rivers in 1831, he had arranged for three men to follow up with bullocks and a dray to resupply the main body. When this small party was ambushed, two of its members murdered and the critically required provisions looted and spoiled, Mitchell was forced to turn back.[70] On the same expedition, while he was reconnoitring with a small group away from the main body, the Aborigines became increasingly threatening, causing Mitchell to later comment:

> I had then thought it unsafe to divide my party, it was already divided now, and the cunning foe was between the two portions; a more desperate situation, therefore, than this half of my party was then in, can scarcely be imagined. To attempt to concilliate these people had last year proved hopeless.[71]

Nevertheless, he failed to abandon the practice, precipitating skirmishes with Aborigines on both the second and third expeditions. On both occasions the Aborigines sensed their immediate numerical strength, having infiltrated the expedition's extended line of march. The second incident, in which at least seven Aborigines were killed, was later the subject of a governmental inquiry.[72]

Mitchell's unfortunate encounters with Aborigines can also be attributed to his poor mobility, which not only made his party vulnerable to attack but also antagonised the local inhabitants. Leichhardt was later to argue the advantages of light, highly mobile expeditions which, in moving quickly through a tribal district, neither fouled waterholes nor trampled and destroyed feed and consequently rarely upset the tribal owners.

As a result of his unfortunate experiences, Mitchell eventually reassessed his strategy for establishing relations with Aborigines. Not surprisingly, his ideas became congruent with Sturt's. He now believed that it was dangerous to attempt to give gifts or propitiate these people, for they were not only capable of duplicity, but also construed such behaviour as weakness.

> We met frequently with instances of natives, receiving from us all they could want on one day, yet approaching us on the next, with the most unequivocal demonstrations of enmity and hostility. Indeed, it seemed impossible, in any manner, to conciliate these people, when united in a body.[73] ... I am now of the opinion, that to discourage at once the approach of such natives, would tend more to the safety of an exploring party, than presenting them with gifts. These rovers of the wilds seem to consider such presents, as the offerings of fear and weakness; and I attribute much of their outrageous conduct to such mistaken notions, and their incorrigible covetousness ...[74]

Furthermore, Mitchell felt that Aborigines should always be kept at a distance in order to allow for a margin of safety and that members of an expedition should never be allowed to spread out and straggle along.

> To be in detached parties amongst a savage population, was perilous in proportion to the length of time we continued separate.[75]

Finally and perhaps melodramatically, Mitchell:

> ... was at length convinced, that no kindness had the slightest effect in altering the disposition and savage desire of these wild men to kill white strangers, on their first coming among them.[76]

Such a belief helps explain Mitchell's concern that Australia '... can never be explored with safety, except by very powerful parties ...'[77] More competent bushmen such as Roe, Stuart and the Gregory brothers did not have the same need for interaction with Aborigines and, as their mobility was considerably superior, they effectively negated Mitchell's assertion.

Bad as Mitchell's practical shortcomings were, they paled by comparison with those of Lieutenant George Grey. The rationale behind Grey's exploration is difficult to understand. Although extremely little was known of the topography, flora and fauna of the area he proposed to explore in northern and north-western Australia, none of the party, which included soldiers, sailors, shoemakers, stockkeepers and two surgeons, had any bush experience. Grey himself had not previously even set foot on Australia. Furthermore, no attempt was made to tap the expertise of those men experienced in exploration, bushmanship and horsemanship, who were available in Perth or the eastern colonies. Consequently, Grey and his men suffered appalling hardships. Perhaps the best summation of the problems caused by the lack of local knowledge and expertise can be seen in Grey's shocked appraisal in November 1837 of the country at Port King George IV, where he was soon to land:

> At the first streak of dawn, I leant over the vessel's side, to gaze upon those shores I had so longed to see. I had not anticipated that they would present any appearance of inviting fertility; but I was not altogether prepared to behold so arid and barren a surface, as that which now met my view.[78]

Given the extremely harsh conditions in the Kimberley region of Western Australia, the results were inevitable. Within an hour of a small landing party setting foot on Western Australia, serious problems arose. The first was related to their low level of physical fitness and their inability to cope with the extremely high summer temperature. Because they carried no water, the men were soon in grave difficulties.

> I soon found that we had landed under very unfavourable circumstances. The sun was intensely hot. The long and close confinement on board a small vessel, had unfitted us all for taking any violent or continued exercise, without some previous training, and the country, in which we had landed, was of a more rocky and precipitous character, than any I had ever before seen.[79]
>
> The trees were small, and their foliage so scant and slight, that they afforded no shelter whatever from the burning rays of the sun; which appeared to strike up again from the sandstone with redoubled heat, so that it was really painful to touch, or to stand upon a bare rock.
>
> A feeling of thirst and lassitude, such as I had never before experienced, soon began to overcome all of us; for such a state of things we had unfortunately landed quite unprepared, having only two pints of water with us, a portion of which it was necessary to give to the dogs; who apparently suffered from the heat, in an equal degree with ourselves.[80]

One of the dogs soon died and the second, a greyhound, had to be carried until the men, who were also suffering severely, could take him no further. 'For some time we dragged him along, but he was at last, from necessity, abandoned.'[81] The third dog disappeared, to be seen again two days later when, having suffered so badly, the poor brute was '... quite mad, and without recognising any of them ran wildly away into the woods.'[82]

Water was eventually found, which saved the men, who managed to return to the beach, where they threw themselves into the shallows. Already two of them were so seriously ill that they were unable to continue to the nominated rendezvous at Hanover Bay with the boat which had previously landed them. Grey decided to continue but had to cross a creek which, with treacherous currents associated with a tidal variation of approximately ten metres,[83] not to mention the possibility of salt-water crocodiles, sea snakes and sharks, presented an extremely dangerous challenge. Grey had hoped to keep his pistol above the water while crossing, but was forced to swim with both arms, wetting his powder and rendering the weapon useless. In addition, the strength of the tide was so severe that his cap was caught by the current and the throat strap nearly throttled him. On emerging exhausted from the water on the other side he found himself unarmed, in a locality where the Aborigines already knew of his whereabouts. Nevertheless, even if he had had the strength to swim back to join his companions, he could not have done so, for it was imperative for him to continue on to the rendezvous in order to save the others.

Despite this unpromising beginning, Grey made determined efforts to continue with his planned exploration. The whole party was landed and the ship was despatched to Timor to purchase horses, returning with twenty-four colts and stallions and two mares. Unfortunately the mob had '... two faults, which could not have been avoided and these were, that they were very small, and perfectly wild.'[84]

Being unhandled, the horses could not be let loose and, because there were too many to lead, they had to be tied in long lines and driven. Inevitably, 'being wholly unused to this kind of discipline, they strenuously resisted it, biting and kicking at one another with the greatest ferocity ...'[85] As a consequence the animals were continually falling over, becoming entangled around trees, lashing out with their hooves and terrorising the men who, almost without exception, had no experience with such aggressive, unbroken little ponies. Progress was appallingly slow, such that when night fell the exhausted men and horses were forced to halt well short of the main camp. Grey was already paying the penalty for his failure to use experienced Australian horsemen and their acclimatised and well-broken stock.

Grey's horses were so tiny that all the pack-saddles had to be reduced in size. Should these animals be comparable to those found in Timor and Indonesia 150 years later, they would have been hardy, but no more than thirteen and a half hands high. They were too small for riding and only when Grey was severely wounded by three spears were they used to carry him. The limited capacity of these horses not only meant that the expedition was forced to go unmounted, but also that Grey had to abandon much of the enormous quantity of equipment he had brought with him. He had boasted earlier that his party was well enough equipped to establish a colony if need be.[86]

These immediate problems aside, the extremely harsh environment of Hanover Bay would have daunted even the best mounted of expeditions. For one thing, the scrub was almost impenetrable.

> The thickness of the vegetation made it difficult to force a way through, and whenever, in attempting so to do, a tree was shaken, numbers of a large green sort of ant fell from the boughs on the unhappy trespasser, and making the best of their way to the back of his neck, gave warning by a series of most painful bites, that he was encroaching on their domain. Yet it was sometimes ludicrous to see one of the party momentarily stamping and roaring with pain ...[87]

Flies also caused Grey and his men considerable distress, making it impossible to sleep after sunrise and difficult to eat and talk. More seriously, the flies caused intense irritation to the corners of the men's eyes.

The deeply dissected country in this region meant that pathways had to be cut along cliff edges in order to bring the ponies from the point of disembarkation to the camp and to ascend and descend ridges. Once over the coastal ranges, the party frequently encountered marshes. With the commencement of the wet season, such areas soon became impassable bogs of tall grass and swamp, leaving the expedition no alternative but to painstakingly retrace its steps and try again. Such efforts, coupled with an inadequate diet, intense heat and often unremitting rain and high humidity, brought considerable suffering.

> At dawn, this morning, the men were at work forming the road; the poor fellows were however, so much enfeebled from constant fatigue, and very inefficient nutriment, whilst exposed to the great heat of a tropical climate, that they were unable to exert the same energy as formerly.[88]

A further blow to Grey's hopes occurred in February 1838 when he and his men were taken totally by surprise in an Aboriginal attack.

> ... immediately numbers of other natives burst upon my sight; each tree, each rock seemed to give forth its black denizen, as if by enchantment.
>
> A moment before, the most solemn silence pervaded these woods, we deemed that not a human being moved within miles of us, and now they rang with savage and ferocious yells, and

> fierce armed men crowded round us on every side, bent on our destruction.[89]

When Grey, who by now had received three spear wounds, shot his closest assailant in the back, the attackers 'noiselessly disappeared'.[90] The explorer was gravely injured, a wound in his hip rendering him immobile and requiring him to be lifted on and off a pony, the riding of which alone must have been agonising. Coupled with the incessant rain, temperatures of up to 136°F in his tent, a diet of damper and tea and a lack of ground sheets, Grey's condition deteriorated, for he also suffered severely both from rheumatism in his left hip and knee and from sores resulting from lying on rocky ground. Nevertheless, he pressed on to explore the lands on the southern side of King George basin as far as the Prince Regent River.

It was to be almost two months before Grey's declining health forced him to admit defeat and order a return to Hanover Bay where, luckily, he had ordered his boats to wait. On reflection, he acknowledged that everything had been completed 'in a hurried and unsatisfactory manner.'[91] This fact, coupled with '... unforseen difficulties, ... scanty means ... the remote unknown region, and the impossibility of our receiving further aid from any quarter' had made it impossible to continue. He was forced to abandon his plan to re-provision at Hanover Bay then proceed overland with four men to the Swan River. The whole party re-embarked at Hanover Bay, releasing their remaining horses with the hope that they would become '... a new race upon the land, ... the progenitors of a numerous herd.'[92] In summing up the unfortunate venture, Grey was forced to acknowledge the inadequacies of his own planning and preparation:

> Our whole residence in this country had been marked by toils and sufferings. Heat, wounds, hunger, thirst, and many other things had combined to harass us.
>
> I could not but reflect how different our position and the condition of the ponies would have been had we known as much of the country at first starting as we did at present ...[93]

In the following year Grey made an equally ill-fated attempt to explore the coastline from the Shark Bay region to the Swan River Settlement. His boats were badly damaged while attempting to come ashore in a heavy surf and the bulk of the supplies were damaged, forcing Grey and his men to struggle for survival as they walked approximately 800 kilometres southwards. One member died en route and the remainder were in a very poor state when met by their rescuers.[94]

These problems aside, and despite their increasing reliance on animals for pack and draught purposes and meat supplies, both Mitchell's and Grey's expeditions were deficient in stock husbandry skills. Mitchell appears to have at first ignored the fact that working animals require several hours' grazing each day to maintain their condition. Initially he had the bullocks hobbled and tethered each night, thus denying them almost all chance of grazing. Impatience arising from being delayed in the mornings while searching for stock later saw Mitchell adopt the practice of building temporary stock yards with ropes each night to confine the bullocks. This practice precluded all possibility of grazing and watering at night, such activities therefore having to consume precious daylight hours. Furthermore, on one occasion on Mitchell's second expedition the bullocks had travelled too slowly to reach water before nightfall. Rather than take the risk of the animals wandering back to their last camp in search of water, he left them yoked in pairs all night, so effectively denying the poor beasts any grazing.[95] Because Mitchell was ignorant of the practical measures necessary to maintain his working animals over an extended period, their consequent decline in condition would later affect his mobility.

Grey's practice of tethering his horses at night undoubtedly contributed to their rapid loss of condition. He does make one mention of 'knee haltering' his ponies one day in daylight 'amidst very good feed, of which they now stood much in need,'[96] but generally appears to have lacked the skills necessary to hobble them out at night. Although explorers such as Roe and Moore in the south-west of Western Australia tethered their horses, at least they were aware of the necessity for the stock to graze. Roe frequently set up camp early when good feed was available and generally sited his camps according to the availability of pasturage. He also regularly changed his horses' tethering points so that they could graze a full circumference on their tethering ropes. Alternatively, he tied the horses to a fixed tethering point for the night but, in the hours between the daily halt and nightfall, had the horses out grazing on the best feed available while tied to light logs. In this way they could slowly drag their logs behind them while moving to fresh grass, as required, but could not make off freely.[97] This practice unfortunatcly involved the risk of the horses taking fright and bolting and being seriously injured by the wildly swinging log.

Grazing aside, Grey had other severe problems with his stock. The hot, humid conditions did not suit his sheep, most of whom soon died. As well, within a short time after landing, his horses lost condition so fast that an increasing proportion were soon able to carry only light loads, or no loads at all:

> ... the poor beasts were so much weakened since yesterday, that

> we were obliged to diminish their loads considerably. They all appeared to be gradually declining in health, strength, and condition, but from what cause, except exposure, I could not tell.[98]

Their rapid deterioration was not entirely due to their having to clamber over ranges and struggle through two-metre high wet grass and heavy swamps and bogs and endure extremely heavy rain. By the end of the expedition only eleven of the twenty-six were still alive. When a post-mortem was carried out on one of the ponies, its intestines were found to contain a hatful of sand. Grey attributed this intake to the area of poorly grassed, loose sandy soil which the horses had been grazed on when first landed.[99] This illness, nowadays termed sanding, was later to become a severe problem in the poor coastal plain soils of south-western Australia. The horses ingest sand which accumulates in the bottoms of their intestinal loops and impedes the passage of food, so reducing absorptive capacity and leading to a gradual loss of condition. In the worst cases the sand completely blocks the intestine, leading to colic and death. Treatment consists of paraffin oil administered by a nasal tube to the stomach. The oil breaks up the compacted sand and simultaneously lubricates the intestine and bowel, thus facilitating voiding of the sand.[100] Unfortunately Grey had neither oil nor tube, not to mention the expertise necessary to carry out the procedures. More importantly, given knowledge of the problem, he probably would not have grazed his stock under these conditions.

Grey's ponies also suffered badly from a lack of shoes, which in turn severely impeded the expedition's progress.

> Had our ponies been provided with shoes we could have travelled here with great speed and facility, but the higher land was invariably covered with sharp pebbles, over which the unshod ponies could only move with pain and difficulty.[101]

Badly footsore horses are less able and often unwilling to graze adequately. Francis Gregory demonstrated this fact quite clearly in his North-West Expedition, when he was forced to keep pushing his horses on, even though, due to the rugged nature of the ranges immediately east of Nickol Bay, '... some of which now walked upon stones as they would over red-hot coals.'[102] One of the worst affected horses had already been left behind, 'the hoof being fairly worn through.'[103] When Gregory returned through the area eighteen days later, he commented that:

> [I had] hoped to find him improved by the rest; but, on approaching the spot, the presence of crows and a wild dog gave

> indications of a different fate; we found him partly devoured within a few yards of where we left him, inflammation of the feet having most probably produced mortification.[104]

The lack of continuity of expertise in the caring for and maintaining of working stock was a significant limiting factor for both Mitchell and Grey. Stock husbandry skills are not learnt rapidly and keeping a large number of stock alive and fit on extended journeys is a particularly worrisome task.

In attempting to ascertain why Mitchell and Grey largely failed to build on the expertise accumulated by their predecessors, one is continually driven back to the hypothesis that they were attempting to refine an inherently unworkable approach. In addition, they were removed from the ongoing development of a sense of placement and direction. In this regard, both Mitchell and Grey were inferior to their predecessors and grossly inferior to their immediate successors Eyre and Leichhardt. The reason appears, in Mitchell's case especially, to be based on his preoccupation with surveying. His journals have consistent references to setting up observation points on peaks and carrying out triangulation surveys in order to connect his entire route. When in new country he worked on reverse triangulations from known peaks until he could place himself with what he claimed to be mathematical precision.[105]

But Mitchell failed to develop the complementary skill of being able to intuitively place himself, to know where he was, where he had come from and what route he had to take to attain a given destination. On his first expedition he noted, for example, that despite having Mount Fraser as an orienting feature before nightfall, he still travelled by compass in the dark to his campsite. 'I knew the bearing sufficiently well to be able to travel by compass nearly in their direction.'[106] Less than nine years later Leichhardt, whose orientation skills had become superb, would set out at night in the flat featureless scrub of the Gulf country to reconnoitre for water and, by a series of doglegs, make his unerring way back towards his camp in the dark.

Grey was similarly disposed to Mitchell. On 9 April 1838, for instance, during the return to Hanover Bay, he commented that he positioned himself by using cross bearings, 'which I was now able to do.'[107] Unfortunately in forest country where timber often prevents one from proceeding in a straight line and from gaining sight of peaks or other landmarks, explorers who do not have an intuitive appreciation of their position and are forced to rely on compass bearings, can rapidly get into difficulties. Further, because both Mitchell and Grey did not have experienced bushmen accompanying them, their survival was essential to the safety of their respective expeditions. Grey realised this fact after the Aboriginal attack near Hanover Bay.

> My wound began, by degrees, to get very stiff and painful, and I was, moreover, excessively weak and faint from loss of blood; indeed, I grew so dizzy that I could scarcely see, and neither of the others were capable of leading the party back to the tents ...[108]

A factor which further complicated Mitchell's approach to orientation was his pedantic insistence on the accurate measurement of distance. Besides being extremely time-consuming, this exercise was fundamentally unproductive because, unless distances are measured by chaining or perambulator, estimates can be extremely variable. John Bussell came to appreciate this problem on a relatively short journey in the Blackwood River area, in the south-west corner of Western Australia, in 1832. He was working on a series of doglegs, but was unable to make an accurate estimate of distances covered in order to calculate the correct course bearing for the final leg. He had failed to make allowance for differing rates of progress.

> My error in making the Blackwood about two miles west of the point I originally steered for arose probably from this cause. The first of our journey to the Vasse in which I made my casting was rated at the same average (speed) with the rest, whereas both on account of our heavy loads, bad travelling, and the being not yet used to our packs, it was most probably performed more slowly.[109]

Grey was aware of the problem of errors of estimations, but could offer no satisfactory means of overcoming it.

> [I have] always found the estimates of every one of the party, as to the daily distance travelled, very erroneous, and sometimes more than doubled. This, indeed, is a mistake well known to be of common occurrence, and very difficult to guard against in a new and wild country, [especially] when I consider the diminished strength of the men's pedestrian powers, and the weights they had to carry.[110]

Even Leichhardt was inconsistent in his estimation of distances. Field research carried out by the present author in 1991 indicates that in the earlier part of his journey to Port Essington a useful rule of thumb for Leichhardt's distances is that one of his estimated miles is approximately equal to one kilometre. Elsewhere, rugged and rocky country along the Lynd River in north Queensland, mountains, such as the Expedition Range north of Taroom, and dense brigalow scrub south of Chinchilla all slowed Leichhardt's rate of advance to the point where his estimates were at times double the actual distances travelled.

Grey and Mitchell were not alone amongst the explorers during this period in being unable intuitively to make a line across country. After Roe's journey from Perth to Albany in 1835 he decided to return to Perth via York, a settlement approximately 100 kilometres inland from the capital. At one point between Kojonup and Williams on the return journey, the Surveyor-General found that he had crossed his southward tracks and thus was at least fifty kilometres too far west.[111]

Unlike Grey and Mitchell, however, Roe achieved from the beginning a comfortable psychological accommodation to his environment. Grey, of course, was disadvantaged by being set down on one of the most difficult stretches of the Australian coastline, a land he had never so much as laid eyes on before. On the other hand Mitchell, who was prone to hyperbole, appeared to be at ease only in country which was well provided with surface water, such as his Australia Felix in the Western District of Victoria. Away from the rivers, he surmised, much of northern and central New South Wales '... would be deserts, inaccessible to, and uninhabitable by, either man or beast.'[112] Much of this country was later opened up as first class grazing and cropping land.

The same sense of alienation was not evident in Western Australia where, in contrast to the early experience in New South Wales, there was a ready accommodation. Explorers crisscrossing the forests of the south-west frequently found the scenery, botany, topography and climate intensely satisfying and congenial. Bussell, in his 1831 exploration of the Vasse River basin, came upon a particularly attractive area and was florid in his praise:

> Here was a spot that the creative fancy of a Greek would have peopled with Dryad and Naiad and all the beautiful phantoms, and wild imagery of his Sylvan Mythology.[113]

Stirling published a slim booklet of reports of exploration in Western Australia between 1829 and 1832, in which several of the contributors praised the climate and lifestyle. In particular, Surgeon James Wingate Johnston of HMS *Sulphur* wrote, '... I beg leave to state, as a climate with regard to health, I am not aware of any other that can be compared with it.'[114] Stirling also reported in January 1830 that the new settlers found the climate 'favourable to health in an uncommon degree.'[115]

Settlers and the native-born had made an immense adjustment, for Britain's climate and countryside were no longer the yardstick by which others were measured. The Australian bush was now being accepted on its own terms, so much so that odes were being written in praise of it.

Despite Mitchell's and Grey's minimal contributions to the development of bushmanship, exploration during the 1830s did produce some beneficial results. The hunting of game and the gathering of food were slowly becoming integral parts of extended explorations and the development of expertise in these activities continued throughout the decade. On Mitchell's first expedition, along the Namoi River where game was scarce, his men shot and boiled hawks and crows for the dogs. Mitchell had also brought lines and hooks and the party was 'tolerably successful' in catching fish.[116] Unfortunately this option was not available to most other explorers, who rarely had access to large expanses of water. Generally, however, Mitchell's men ate the rations they had brought with them, as well as the bullocks periodically slaughtered for that purpose. Grey's hunting skills were minimal. Although often desperate for fresh meat, he only succeeded on three occasions in getting close enough to a kangaroo to fire a shot at it. Part of Grey's problems also stemmed from the weather, for his powder was often damp and the percussion caps frequently failed to ignite.[117]

Mitchell and Grey appear to have been careful to ascertain the forms of food the Aborigines ate and how they obtained and prepared them. In particular they were impressed by the Aborigines' ability to gather food from a range of sources.[118] Grey noted that generally the Aborigines ate well, although at times certain areas were deficient in food and temporarily deserted. Mitchell described a people endowed with a variety of foods, in a 'land flowing with honey.'[119] Bush food, beyond the basic fare of kangaroo, possum and emu, was available and white bushmen were gradually acquiring the skills necessary to identify and gather it. Nevertheless, when Roe's expedition north from Albany to York in 1835 camped in the Hotham River district for Christmas Day, the dinner had, apart from the local game, a distinctively English flavour. The meal consisted of:

> ... soup, haunches of Kangaroo (inevitably roasted by Mr. Northcott's superior skill), cockatoos, plum pudding, made for the occasion, and a most undeniable can of punch.[120]

The far-ranging white men had more to learn, for unlike the Aborigines, who confined themselves to their own tribal areas, explorers and bushmen had to learn to cope with food-gathering in a diversity of environments.

This was a considerably more difficult task and it was understandable if the accumulation of knowledge and skills took some time. Most explorers were emphatic that, beyond their traditional ground, the majority of Aborigines could not survive easily. As Grey, writing of his desperate struggle southwards towards Perth in 1839, commented:

> ... to obtain a sufficiency of food, even for a native, requires in Australia a great degree of skill and knowledge of the productions of the country; but for a European, utterly unaccustomed to this species of labour, and totally unacquainted with the productions of the land, to obtain enough to support life for any period, whilst at the same time, he has to search for water, is quite impossible. Even Kaiber [his Aboriginal guide], from his ignorance of the roots, declared that he should starve in this country [south of Geraldton].[121]
>
> But in his own district a native is very differently situated; he knows exactly what it produces, [and] the proper time at which the several articles are in season, and the readiest means of procuring them.[122]
>
> It is, however, utterly impossible for a traveller or even for a strange native to judge whether a district affords an abundance of food, or the contrary; for in traversing extensive parts of Australia, I have found the sorts of food vary from latitude to latitude, so that the vegetable productions used by the Aborigines in one are totally different to those in another; if, therefore, a stranger has no-one to point out to him the vegetable productions, the soil beneath his feet may teem with food, whilst he starves. The same rule holds good with regard to animal productions ...[123]

An even more fundamental requirement for explorers was the ability to find water, a skill at which Mitchell was initially quite inept, so much so that events such as this were depressingly common:

> The extreme heat, and the fatigue of travelling, could not have been borne much longer. One man (Woods) had been left behind at his own request, being unable even to ride, from violent pains in his stomach; another was also so ill that he could not walk; the bullocks still drew, but with their tongues protruding most piteously. I sent a man on horseback back with a kettleful of water to Woods. The cattle being unyoked rushed to the stream ...[124]

In part this problem resulted from Mitchell's inexperience and failure to reconnoitre adequately. He does not appear to have learnt from Sturt's technique of refusing to move the main party forward until water supplies had been secured: 'We left each friendly waterhole, in the greatest uncertainty whether we should ever drink again ...'[125]

But it did not take Mitchell and his men long to become proficient at finding water. Mitchell was aware, and appears to have been the first explorer to point out, that the turbulence which occurs at the junctions of creeks or rivers often scours out deep holes in the riverbed, which frequently retain water well after the remainder of the watercourse is dry.[126] Like Oxley with *Acacia pendula* Mitchell thought that white-barked eucalypts were a good indicator of water. He was not quite correct, for while such gums are frequently found along watercourses and around waterholes, they are not necessarily signs of permanent water. As also with Oxley some thirty years earlier in similar country, Mitchell was introduced by his Aboriginal guide Barney to the water-filled gnamma holes on the ridges, beside which Aboriginal groups would camp when the Lachlan River ran dry.

> I learned, that the only water in these deserts was to be found in the crevices of rocks, on such hills as this; and I thus understood the cause of the smoke, I observed last year arising from so many summits, when I looked over the same region, from a hill on its northern limits. Perhaps within thirty miles around, there was no other water, and the bare top of a mountain, was certainly one of the last situations where I should thought of seeking for it.[127]

Four years previously Moore observed that a tree which the Western Australian Aborigines called 'wando' could be used to relieve '... the distress of thirst to some travellers ... on some of the most arid tracts of ground ...'[128] He reported that the tree was a eucalypt of yellowish colour with a rusty tinged bark and that not every tree contained water. Only those with a slight discolouration on the surface were worth tapping, 'when a liberal jet of water will frequently reward the search.'[129] Roe and Moore both commented that in Western Australia the screech of white cockatoos was a '... certain indication of the vicinity of water.'[130] Moore also noted that when on one occasion they were forced to camp waterless, during the night '... we heard shouting of natives and screaming of white cockatoos right ahead, both sure signs of water.'[131] A short reconnaissance the following morning justified his conclusion.

More often than not, bush water was contaminated with mineral and organic matter. Although boiling and straining partially overcame such problems, they were slow and painstaking processes. Early Western Australian explorers sought other solutions, including disguising the taste of salty and offensive smelling water by using it in soup.[132] When Roe was once forced to use some water which had been rendered nauseating because of the presence of a decomposing duck, he reported that soup 'well seasoned with pepper ...' was found to be the best disguise.[133] Roe also pointed out that boiling salty water was the worst possible technique, for the saltiness was increased by evaporation. Moore dealt with tainted water by using it in tea, purifying it with magnesia, or mixing it with alcohol.[134]

If Mitchell had made known a technique he had learnt from his Aboriginal guides for clearing water, Roe, Stirling and Moore would have been spared some of their often nauseating experimentation. During his first expedition the party encamped beside a waterhole which was hot and muddy:

> [Fortunately] the blacks knew well how to obtain a cool and clean draught, by first scratching a hole in the soft sand beside the pool, thus making a filter, in which the water rose cooled but muddy. They next threw into this some tufts of long grass, through which they sucked the cooler water thus purified also from the sand or gravel. I was very glad to follow the example, and I found the sweet fragrance of the grass an agreeable addition to the luxury of drinking.[135]

While Roe and his contemporaries were learning quickly to cope with the new environment in the south-west of Western Australia, further east Edward John Eyre was developing the bush skills which would be invaluable in his subsequent explorations in southern Australia.

Eyre's father was a British clergyman who, after providing for his son's education until his seventeenth year, could offer few other prospects. Consequently Eyre decided to emigrate to Australia, using the £400 gratuity from his father to establish himself as a settler. Arriving in Sydney in late 1832, he soon went into business, trading in sheep. From this point onwards he rapidly began to acquire bush experience and skills. Within twelve months he had decided to take up a property five hundred kilometres southwards on Molonglo Plains, near the future Australian Capital Territory. This transfer was a major undertaking, for no roads existed, most of the country was unsettled, there were no maps and Eyre was totally reliant on his own resources. Shortly afterwards he was made an offer to run 3,000 sheep on shares, eventually transferring the sheep to the Liverpool Plains district. The droving of his flock was a considerable problem, for the convicts assigned to him were quite apathetic and repeatedly let the sheep wander overnight. Drays were continually becoming bogged, their wheels frequently broke or fell off and the whole party straggled out over long distances. Eyre and his partner were forced to spend very long hours in the saddle rounding up stock, extricating bogged wagons, bringing up supplies and so on, all the while moving across '... a country quite unknown to us, almost unoccupied and very difficult for wheeled vehicles.'[136] Their clothes and equipment proved inadequate and soon wore out. Often:

> After a hard day's work and being wet thro' all the day we had to lay down in the open air at night, frequently in damp clothes and subject to the contingency of the weather which, if not rainy, was bitterly cold. The dews were also very heavy and penetrating. Often we were badly off for provisions, sometimes being for several days at a time without meat ... Each had to cook for himself after his day's work as well as keep watch over the sheep for half the night. Frequently owing to the rains it was impossible to bake even the indigestible bread called damper and the only alternative then was to mix flour and water into a paste and boil it, making what was technically called 'dough boys', neither a very wholesome nor agreeable way of cooking the staff of life, but still far from unwelcome after a hard day's work ...[137]

These were trying times but invaluable in the long term. Eyre was gaining experience in keeping teams of stock together and in tracking them when they strayed. He also learnt how to cope with problems and breakages, how to cajole and enthuse his men and how to husband his livestock's strength. In particular, he quickly learnt the necessity of providing his working stock with sufficient grazing. It was significant that on the occasions when Eyre did not accompany his team, his men either lost the oxen altogether through their wandering at night, or prevented them from grazing overnight, until 'yarding them without food, got them so reduced in strength and condition that they were fit for nothing and often died on the road.'[138]

Unlike Mitchell, Eyre soon came to appreciate the severe limitations of bullocks and accordingly shifted towards all-horse teams.

> In fact, whether travelling at a sheep station or a farm, I have ever found the working oxen one of the most fruitful sources of trouble and expense: they so often stray away, get lost, tumble into waterholes or die in some other way — or get lame, or become poor and unable to work — in short there is almost always something going wrong with them and in calculating probable expenses a wide margin requires to be left for these kinds of contingencies.[139]

By 1837 Eyre had overlanded sheep to the settlement at Port Phillip and then set about preparing to drove cattle to Adelaide. Such trips were of considerable value to the young man, who learnt very quickly to cope with unknown and changing conditions. At a point well into the north-west of Victoria in 1838, for example, he found his line of march impossible, for all water supplies had dried up. He reconnoitred extensively in advance for three days but found no water, being eventually forced to turn back when 175 kilometres distant from the camp. At this point Eyre made the useful discovery that jaded stock recuperate markedly when they realise they are on their way home. He soon realised, however, that he would have to punish his horses severely if he was to reach the camp and drove them until they could go no further. He then took the saddles off the horses and set them free and, with his men, began to walk the eighty-six kilometres back to their camp. Suffering severely from exertion and poor food they eventually reached their destination, where they took several days to recuperate. Meanwhile Eyre sent out a dray with kegs of water to try and save the abandoned horses. Although unsuccessful on this occasion, for the horses had all perished, this technique later formed an integral part of Eyre's exploration style. From this point onwards Eyre was ever mindful of the necessity of reconnoitring and securing water supplies before bringing up the main group.[140]

Once on the flood-plain of the Murray, Eyre and his men were harassed by Aborigines in a fashion similar to that experienced by Sturt. The Aborigines greatly outnumbered Eyre's party, whose leader cleverly demonstrated the effectiveness of his firearms by bringing down five crows with one shot. When the Aborigines later began to press continuously forward and became increasingly antagonistic, Eyre drew a line on the ground and threatened to shoot any Aborigine who stepped beyond it. The Aborigines gradually moved away and the next day they were considerably more amenable, to which Eyre responded by handing over gifts. Clearly it paid to take a hard line, as Eyre would again demonstrate in his later South Australian desert exploration.

> I believe, however, that under God's mercy we had escaped a most imminent peril and that had there been the least fear or indecision shewn the whole party would certainly have been murdered, as some other parties following down the Murray with stock subsequently were.[141]

By the time Eyre completed the overland journey to Adelaide he had been on the track for 268 days and had travelled 2497 kilometres. Within a month he organised a second droving trip, between Sydney and Adelaide. On this occasion he had fifteen men and was droving six hundred cattle and a thousand sheep. The party took two drays, two carts, ten horses and fourteen working oxen. This time they fared considerably better than on the first trip, for Eyre had developed and refined the skills necessary to manage a large group of men and livestock over long distances.[142]

Eyre was now twenty-three years old, strong and healthy, with almost six years of Australian bush experience behind him. Compared with all other explorers to this time he was uniquely qualified for his task when he set out on 1 May 1839, to explore the country to the north of Adelaide. In sixty days he and his men reached the Port Augusta region, made a limited reconnaissance to the west and north of this area and returned in an eastward arc until they met the Murray River. They then followed the Murray down to Lake Alexandrina, before returning to Adelaide.

Although Eyre's expedition was a limited excursion over relatively easy country, it had several features which warrant analysis. All the expedition members, bar one of the Aboriginal youths, were mounted, for Eyre had sufficient experience to appreciate the value of the mobility offered by having his men on horseback. Two horse-drawn drays were taken to carry provisions, equipment and water kegs sufficient for men and horses. Well aware of the importance of an assured supply, Eyre set up his depot camp at a waterhole south of Port Augusta, from which he conducted his exploration of the surrounding region. While on the move he continually reconnoitred for water, accompanied by a dray loaded with water kegs. At a certain distance out from the main camp the dray would either stop and wait for Eyre's return, or leave the water and return to the main group. This practice effectively increased Eyre's range. All of these factors formed the basis of his later style of exploration in central South Australia.

Notwithstanding Eyre's achievements, he was but one of a substantial number of proficient bushmen during the 1830s, for once people became aware of the lightly timbered and well grassed plain and forest country over the Great Dividing Range, squatters streamed inland, taking up runs and developing bush skills as they went. The government of the time took a pragmatic view of this activity for, as Gipps commented:

> All the power of Government, aided even by a Military force ten times greater than that which is maintained in the Colony, would not suffice to bring back within the limits of our 20 counties the Flocks and Herds, which now stray hundreds of miles beyond them ...[143]

By 1840, 7,088 horses, 371,699 horned cattle and 1,334,593 sheep were depastured on 694 licensed stations in New South Wales.[144] Staffing and running these large unfenced bush properties were 7,287 men and women. By the end of the 1830s, life in the remote bush was a common experience for these settlers. New techniques had to be developed to retain and control stock on the pastoral runs. More time was now spent in out-camps far away from the homestead facilities, forcing stockmen and shepherds to be more self-sufficient. Supplies and equipment were conveyed by packhorses and drays, living and cooking were primarily out-of-doors and livestock husbandry had to be achieved without the aid of fences or yards. The vastly expanded pool of knowledge which accompanied the squatting occupation of eastern Australia formed the basis of the immense leap in exploration achievements of the 1840s and 1850s.

5

Harder Country, Harder Men — The Quantum Leap in Bushmanship

The years between 1840 and 1860 saw considerable development in both scientific field research and bushmanship. The major explorers of this time rapidly traversed large areas which had previously been impassable due to the hard nature of the country and a lack of expertise. In order to understand the importance of these developments, a clear appreciation is essential of the often immensely difficult and uncompromising nature of the country being traversed.

In 1840 and 1841 Edward John Eyre attempted to travel over the ranges northwards from Adelaide to reach the centre of Australia and possibly the Gulf of Carpentaria. In the Lake Torrens area he reconnoitred in vain, attempting to find a way through. Because the landscape was flat with no defined drainage pattern, there was no possibility of water storage in creeks or gnamma holes. Even if rain fell, within a few hours the water became tainted by ground salt. Eyre appears to have described the country well in naming one peak 'Mount Hopeless', for from this point he ascertained that further movement forward was not feasible.[1] He further quoted Sturt, who stated that the local Aborigines saw the country as being '... all sand and rocks; that there is neither grass or water, or wood, and that it is awfully hot.'[2]

On realising the futility of his Central Australian venture, Eyre moved his focus westward, seeking a practicable stock route to King George Sound. He eventually traversed the southern coastline and arrived in Albany in 1841. Even before setting off, Eyre reflected that his proposed route was through scarcely more promising terrain, which must raise questions concerning his motivation.[3]

> ... by crossing to the westward, I should have to encounter a country which I knew to be all but destitute of water, and to consist, for a very great distance, of barren sandy ridges and low lands, covered by an almost impenetrable scrub, at a season, too,

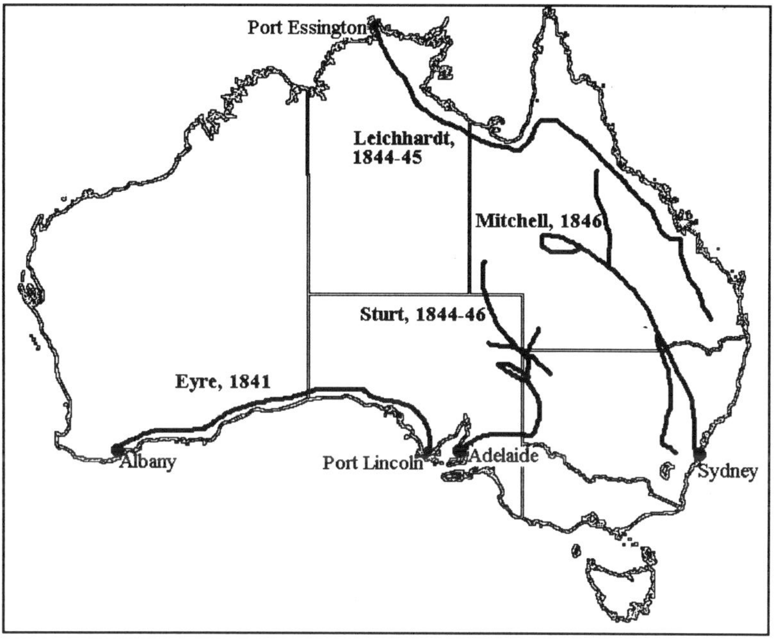

Major explorations during the 1840s.

> when but little rain could be expected, and the heat would, in all probability, be intense.[4]

Sturt made the next major exploration, when in August 1844 he moved northwards and westwards from the Darling River at Menindee, searching for the drainage divide. He was eventually forced to return after running into insoluble difficulties in the Simpson Desert. On one occasion his horses were so desperate for water that they begged for a drink.

> ... all the others, but particularly the grey horse I ride, clustered around me in a ring as if imploring for water. They licked my face, tried to pull my hat off, and did everything to attract my attention but poor animals I could only pat them. I had not the wherewith to supply their wants.[5]

Much of the reason for the horses' desperate need for water was the searing heat the expedition encountered daily. One day in November 1845, Sturt found his thermometer reading 125°F at 9.00 a.m. When he checked it at 2.00 p.m., in a shady spot in which it had been placed, the mercury had burst the end of the thermometer, for it was only graduated to 127°F. Such heat affected not only the men and horses, but also much of the equipment.

> You cannot indeed conceive the dreadful heat in this exposed and stony region. Every article we have went to ruin before it, the teeth of our combs fell off, the handles of our razors split, every box warped, and every nail was loosened. Our tyres fell off the wheels, and the drays rattled all over. The soles of the men's shoes were fairly burnt off, and citric acid melted in the bottle in which it was kept. The dogs would not stir from the water but remained on the bank, after having gone into it up to their necks, repeating their bathing as soon as they were dry.[6]

Two months previously, at the point where Sturt was forced to return, he and his assistant Browne had been confronted with waterless dunes stretching away out of sight.

> Ascending one of the sand ridges I saw a numberless succession of these terrific objects rising above each other to the east and west of me. Northwards they ran away before me for more than 15 miles, with the most undeviating straightness, as if those masses had been thrown up with the plumb and rule ... There was a species of mesembryanthemum that happened to be in blossom and so thickly does it bloom that it gave to the ground its own purple and sulphureous tint between long lines of fiery red, whilst the valleys (were) occupied by dark masses of Acacia trees ... The scene was awfully fearful ... It looked like the entrance into Hell. Mr. Browne stood horrified. 'Did man,' he exclaimed, 'ever see such a place?!'[7]

Less than two months after Sturt's expedition set off, Ludwig Leichhardt moved out from Jimbour House Station on the Darling Downs, on his way to Port Essington in the Northern Territory. He kept to the valleys of the major rivers for most of the way until he reached the Mitchell River on the Cape York Peninsula. There he turned and followed the coast to the Roper River in the Northern Territory, at which point he moved to the north-west and, fourteen months after his departure, reached his goal. The worst aspect of Leichhardt's journey was not aridity, but the tremendously rugged country he and his party encountered in the future Kakadu National Park. In the south-western corner of Arnhem Land he described an especially bad section which, in conjunction with the exhausted state of their horses and bullocks, caused some distress:

> ... I had a most disheartening, sickening view over a tremendously rocky country. A high land, composed of horizontal strata of

> sandstone, seemed to be literally hashed, leaving the remaining blocks in fantastic figures of every shape; and a green vegetation, crowding deceitfully within their fissures and gullies, and covering half of the difficulties which awaited us on our attempt to travel over it. The creek, in and along the bed of which we wound slowly down, was frequently covered with large loose boulders, between which our horses and cattle often slipped.[8]

Before Leichhardt had completed his first expedition, Mitchell also set out for Port Essington, on a more inland route. After spending over a year tracing the Belyando and Barcoo Rivers, the large and slow-moving expedition reached scarcely 120 kilometres beyond the Tropic before being forced by diminishing supplies to return to Sydney.

In 1847, Edmund Kennedy, second-in-command on Mitchell's 1845–6 expedition, refuted his former leader's claim that the Barcoo was part of the headwaters of the Victoria River, which discharges into the sea near the Western Australian border. In the following year he attempted to explore the eastern side of Cape York Peninsula, but suffered extreme hardships in the almost impenetrable rainforests and was eventually murdered by Aborigines.

Meanwhile, in Western Australia, John Septimus Roe was exploring the hinterland of Champion Bay and the country within a 160-kilometre radius of Esperance. His departmental protégés Augustus, Francis and Charles Gregory were soon to begin their own series of expeditions, based on techniques they had learnt from, or in conjunction with the Surveyor-General. By the late 1860s their explorations had encompassed the Shark Bay, Murchison, Gascoyne and Pilbara regions. Augustus Gregory had also been active in the far north. In 1855–56, his North Australian expedition examined the Victoria River to ascertain if it was a major river fed from an inland sea, then moved to the Roper River and overland to connect with Leichhardt's route at the Burdekin River and thence to the settled regions in southern Queensland. Two years later he was sent out in an unsuccessful attempt to determine the whereabouts of Leichhardt's ill-fated third expedition. His party travelled from Brisbane to the Alice River and, in a rapid sweep, moved down the Barcoo and Cooper Creek via the huge salt lakes of South Australia and thence to Adelaide. In doing so the expedition successfully traversed country almost totally lacking in water and feed:

> ... nothing could be more desolate than the aspect of the country; except the few trees which grew on the immediate bank of the river there was scarcely a tree left alive, while the plains were quite bare of vegetation, except a few salsolaceous bushes. At the distance of five miles low ridges of red drift sand showed the

desert character of all around; even the lower surfaces of the clouds assumed a lurid tinge from the reflection of the bare surface of red sand.

> Steering north-west, after toiling nearly thirty miles across this fearful waste of dry mud, we at length reached a small patch of grasson a sandy hummock, but only just in time to save the horses, as many could scarcely keep on their legs, and we had to remove their loads to those which were less exhausted.[9]

Finally, in the height of summer, some ten years after Sturt's 1844 expedition, Surveyor Robert Austin and his party were beaten to a standstill by a lack of water in similar country 300 kilometres inland from Geraldton in Western Australia. On this occasion their horses had not had a drink for two days and Austin had split the party into three reconnoitring groups to search for water. By 3.00 p.m. he returned to find that all the other groups had been unsuccessful and were back in the camp. The men had thrown their blankets over the sparse-leafed acacia scrub of the region and had stripped naked and buried themselves under the red dust in the shade. Worse:

> ... our horses (were) standing up with their heads under their masters' blankets, too thirsty to feed. ... I was of the opinion this country extended many miles without a chance of water, <u>and the men were drinking their own and the horses' urine</u> and a native I captured and kept to find water, as he knew the country, did the same, saying we should all die if I persisted in pushing on as there was no water in the direction we were going ... [10]

The successes, not to mention the survival, of the Gregory brothers and other explorers of the period in isolated and difficult terrain reflected both their bushmanship and the care with which their expeditions were planned and equipped. Similar progress was also being achieved in the range and quality of their scientific observations, in response to the growing involvement of British learned societies in the explorations. During this period, British scientific research was characterised by an increasing professionalism, as research methodology, the lobbying by scientific societies and the trend towards pure research were further developed and refined. Scientific societies were becoming intimately involved in world-wide exploration and field research. Projects received expert advice in the planning stages, logistical support, grants and lobbying assistance. Australian field research projects to receive Royal Geographical Society funds included Grey's 1838 Kimberley expedition and Augustus Gregory's

1855 North Australian expedition. Francis Gregory's north-west expedition was originally supported by the Royal Geographical Society, but funding and control were eventually taken over by the British Government.[11] Furthermore, scientific societies were now pooling their resources to work together on joint projects.[12]

The awarding of medals, instituted by some societies a decade or so previously, now became a general feature of the recognition of outstanding scientific research. Australian explorers to receive such awards during this period included Eyre[13] in 1843, Count Strzelecki in 1846, Sturt and Leichhardt in 1847 and Augustus Gregory in 1857. Researchers of merit were awarded fellowships and becoming a Fellow of the Royal Society was, in particular, a prestigious achievement.

Finally, the British Government was now placing much greater emphasis upon the training of scientists, responding to the advocacy of Prince Albert for a systematic approach to the teaching of science, similar to that adopted by Prussia. By the mid-1850s, as a result of the Prince's influence and the success of the 1851 Exhibition, the Exchequer was making an annual £1000 grant to the Royal Society and the Government had founded the Royal School of Mines and the Department of Science and Art. Grants were also being supplied for '... science, applied science and technical training.'[14]

During this time of steady progress in Britain, scientific research in Australia was at last beginning to burgeon in response to a growing appreciation of the value of education and intellectual pursuits. In 1848, a Board of National Education was established in New South Wales and a secular, government-funded school system introduced to function alongside the subsidised schools supervised by the denominational Board of Education.[15] The Government was at last attempting to overcome the inequalities and deficiencies of the existing sectarian system, under which, in 1844, approximately half of the colony's children received no formal education at all.[16] The University of Sydney was established in 1852 and the University of Melbourne in 1855. Being modelled on the University of London rather than on Cambridge or Oxford, both had a strong scientific emphasis.[17]

Concurrent with these academic developments was the establishment of scientific associations and museums. Populist zoological and acclimatisation societies were established in the 1850s, a Board of Science was created in 1858 to advise the Government of Victoria, and the Philosophical Society of New South Wales was revived and stabilised in 1856.[18] Other organisations included the Victorian Institute for the

Advancement of Science and the Victorian Philosophical Society, both formed in 1854, and the Adelaide Philosophical Society, established in 1853.[19] The National Museum of Victoria was established in 1858 under the guidance of Frederick McCoy,[20] while the Brisbane Museum opened in 1855.

Such substantial growth in intellectual activity arose, in large part, from the rapid increase in population following the gold discoveries in the 1850s. Between 1850 and 1861 the population of Australia, excluding Aborigines, almost trebled, from 405,000 to 1,168,000. According to Moyal, the population had now reached the threshold necessary to sustain scientific societies.

> ... the fifties brought notable changes to the community of science. The gold discoveries attracted many scientists to the colonies to be absorbed, when gold proved fickle, into governmental surveys and museums ... These infusions fortified the scattered communities of science ... [21]

A second factor positively affecting scientific research in Australia was the qualitative and quantitative improvement in professional staff. The authorities became aware of the necessity for trained scientists, particularly once promising mineral finds had been made. Many of those now being appointed by the Colonial Office were highly qualified and intelligent men, acutely aware of and interested in current scientific debates in Britain and the continent. Perhaps the most notable was the Danish-born Ferdinand Mueller who arrived in South Australia in 1847 and, after five years practising in that colony, was appointed Government Botanist in Victoria. Mueller carried out extensive field work, which led to his selection as botanist on Gregory's North Australian expedition. His work was of such an exemplary standard that he was elected a Fellow of the Linnean Society in 1859 and of the Royal Society in 1861. The King of Wurtemburg made him a hereditary baron in 1871 (thus making him 'von Mueller'), and the Queen of England made him a Knight Commander of St Michael and St George in 1879.[22] William McCoy, Foundation Professor of Natural Science at the University of Melbourne, was the first palaeontologist resident in Australia. Prior to his arrival, even W B Clark and Strzelecki had had to send specimens to Professor Owen in Britain.[23] Although John Gould, the entrepreneurial bird collector, publisher and salesman, who worked in Australia between 1830 and 1840, had neither professional qualifications nor an official appointment, he came with the strongest recommendation from the Colonial Office.

Despite the number of talented men now available in the Australian colonies, the standard of scientific staff attached to exploration parties remained unimpressive until Gregory's 1856 North Australian expedition. On his fourth expedition in 1844 Mitchell took only the amateur William Stephenson, who was described as a 'Surgeon and Collector in Natural History'.[24] Gipps' intentions in 1840 and 1841 to provide Eyre with the 'services of competent men of Science'[25] to provide expertise in those areas '... [in] which the author is conscious he is himself defective'[26] were not realised. Sturt's 1844 exploration of Central Australia included neither scientific researchers nor collectors. Even more surprisingly, Francis Gregory's north-west exploration, which was initiated and largely overseen by the Royal Geographical Society and which was intended to provide a professional appraisal of the cotton-growing capacity of the region, included no geologist or botanist, but only '... P. Walcott, (who) joined as a volunteer for the collection of specimens of natural history and botany.'[27] On the other hand Leichhardt, having spent several years in study and field research in Germany, Britain and France, was botanist, zoologist, geologist and palaeontologist to his expedition, as well as being its leader. He was also accompanied by the self-taught but knowledgeable and highly competent naturalist and collector, John Gilbert.

By 1855 the increasing specialisation and professionalism in British science meant that Gregory's North Australian expedition, which was conceived and overseen by the Royal Geographical Society, would employ qualified personnel to carry out field research of a professional standard. Eminent scientists such as Sir Roderick Murchison, Sir William Hooker and Sir Henry de la Beche outlined their requirements and listed the equipment they felt would be essential to carry out such tasks. Although the expedition's scientists were not those originally considered, botanist Mueller, naturalist Joseph Elsey and geologist James Wilson were highly competent.[28]

Where previously those who accompanied Australian expeditions had been relegated to collectors' roles, local expertise now equalled that of British experts in many cases. As a result, field research and interpretation came to be increasingly Australian-initiated and directed. In sciences such as botany and zoology, however, where the majority of samples were held in Britain, specimens were still sent overseas for analysis. Not surprisingly Mueller, for one, felt slighted as a result, because he was not selected to oversee the examination and cataloguing of Australian botanical specimens, which were sent to George Bentham at the Kew Botanical Gardens[29].

Because by 1860 all the Australian periphery other than the Kimberleys had been traversed, the major explorers were now able to make more comprehensive and integrated analyses, both of the country they traversed and of what lay ahead. From his own experiences and other available data, Eyre correctly deduced the nature of much of the still unexplored central desert region. He rejected Sturt's dream of an inland sea on three grounds: that the hot winds emanating from that region meant '... there is little probability that such winds can have been wafted over a large expanse of water', that all the Aborigines he had spoken to had no knowledge of any large body of water and that there was no ethnographic evidence of lake-side dwellers toward the centre of the continent.[30] It was highly likely, in fact, that much of the remaining unexplored country would consist of:

> ... basins of salt lakes or swamps, as Lake Torrens ... I think, also, that these alternate with sandy deserts, and that probably ... there are many isolated ranges, like the Gawler Range.[31]

On the other hand, the presence of extensive salt lakes, the flatness of the terrain and the presence of shells far inland led him to support Sturt's theory of the mode of origin of the continent.

> [That] ... Australia might formerly have been an Archipelago of islands, appears to me to have been a happy idea, and to afford the most rational and satisfactory way of accounting for many of the peculiarities observable upon its surface or in its structure.[32]

Similarly, Leichhardt's assessment of the disparate geographical, botanical and zoological forms found between the eastern and western coasts, plus the uniformly flat nature of much of the Gulf Country, led him to conclude that:

> ... this continent was originally divided into two large islands, or into an archipelago, which have been united by their progressive, and, perhaps, still continued, elevation.[33]

As public awareness of science increased and professional scientists became more numerous, it is not surprising that pure research was coming to be seen as valid, even in the field of exploration. Sturt's 1844 expedition to Central Australia, for instance, was principally aimed at ascertaining the existence or otherwise of a watershed at the twenty-eighth parallel, in order to help explain the inland drainage pattern. No specific commercial benefits were expected of similar undertakings, by Sturt or anyone else.

> If it is asked what practical good I should expect to result from such an undertaking, I would observe ... that in truth there is no knowing what the ultimate results would be.[34]

Again, in the case of Gregory's North Australian expedition some eleven years later, only the appointment of geologist Wilson within the scientific entourage was specifically pragmatic.[35] Nevertheless, the generally economic orientation of exploration remained, particularly in Western Australia, where a severe economic recession in the mid-1840s, the rapid grazing-out of the meagre native grasses and the increasing livestock population made it imperative to find additional grazing land.[36] Consequently, before Augustus Gregory set out on his 1848 exploration of the Shark Bay–Murchison River area, he was instructed to:

> ... bear in mind that the primary object of this expedition is the examination of a new tract of unknown country for practical purposes, by practical men — that, in fact, the discovery of new land of an available kind for pasture has become a thing to be desired, of paramount importance, and an object in the attainment of which the interests and perhaps the fate of this colony depend.[37]

Francis Gregory's north-west expedition was similarly predicated, but in this case the goal was arable land rather than native pastures.

> The important additions to geographical discovery, and the large extent of valuable pastoral country that had been found on the Gascoyne River and its tributaries, attracted the attention of a number of English capitalists interested in cotton manufactures, which were then in a very depressed condition in consequence of the civil war in America; it was proposed to establish a new colony on the north-west coast of Australia, having for its special object the cultivation of cotton.[38]

It is ironic then, that at the very time the research aspects of exploration were at last being recognised, the mobility of explorers was increasing at a rapid rate, exacerbating the longstanding antagonistic relationship between exploration on the one hand and patient sampling and research on the other. In the 1840s both Eyre and Leichhardt had remarked that the need to keep moving had precluded any meaningful field research. As Eyre commented:

> ... the dreadful nature of the country, and the difficulties and disasters to which this led, made it quite impossible either to make collections of any kind, or to examine the country beyond the immediate line of route ... [39]
>
> ... I have never been able to delay a moment in my route, or to deviate in any way from the line I was pursuing, to reconnoitre or examine what may haply be beyond.[40]

A decade later, during his North Australia Expedition, Gregory's attempts to accommodate his scientists[41] were largely prevented by the need for them to help tend the large team of horses, stand watches, cook, wash and, above all, cover long distances each day. This situation developed despite the project initially being envisaged as involving the establishment of a series of depots to allow for comprehensive lateral reconnoitring and analysis.[42] Elsey, for one, was soon to learn from the expedition leader the realities of the situation.

> ... He told me that his own experience led him to expect that there would be very few opportunities of collecting on the journey; especially insects and small class of animals; that the arrangement of the expedition was so different from that it first intended ... (that I could) count on the occasional services of one of the men, but as it is at present circumstances, with a double duty to perform, I fear I shall be little able to take advantage of the opportunities I may have to procure information regarding Natural History.
>
> I have ... to stuff and fit my saddle, to stuff, mend or alter pack saddles, look to hobbles, clean gun and revolver, and put up ammunition, and cut wads, and to put away, label and sort out my collections, and in short, to do everything that surgeon and naturalist to the North Australian Exploring Expedition, would fancy of leaving England he might expect to have done for him. But as there is no-one to do it for him, he must do it, and that quickly and well, or he is sadly in the lurch. It is certainly a great mistake to send out persons for the advancement of science, under the impression that they will be able to employ their time, when the fact is that they can only avail themselves of a rare hour of leisure.[43]

The preparing and carrying of specimens was an even more difficult task than before, for a better standard was now required by museums and dealers. Living specimens were, as always, a particular problem. Naturalist George Bennett, for example, noted in a letter to Richard Owen in 1833, that he had attempted to carry four platypus over three hundred kilometres to Sydney on horseback, for no bullock wagons were available. Though one platypus died en route and one escaped, that he managed to bring the other two back alive was a credit to his care and attention.[44]

Gilbert complained on several occasions of the problems facing zoological collectors. It was a time-consuming task to skin, dry and mount specimens, which were then frequently destroyed by mites, weevils, mould or damp. Hawks were also prone to snatch drying samples, unaware that they had been treated with arsenical soap. Ants were also a constant problem, as Gilbert informed Gould in 1840:

> You have no idea of the difficulty I find in keeping my collection free from the Ants, which so abound here, many of my specimens have been completely destroyed by them in a single night, so that as fast as they dry, I am obliged to paste them up in Boxes ... [45]

Finally, there were rarely sufficient pack animals available to convey the scientists' specimens. Reference has already been made to the scientifically significant and personally devastating effects of Leichhardt's loss of four horses in two days in 1845:

> This disastrous event staggered me, and for a moment I turned almost giddy; but there was no help. Unable to increase the load of my bullocks, I was obliged to leave that part of my botanical collection which had been carried by one of the horses. The fruit of many a day's work was consigned to the fire, and tears were in my eyes when I saw one of the most interesting results of my expedition vanish into smoke.[46]

In this regard the scientists on the North Australian expedition were more fortunately placed, as a supply ship would be available for:

> ... the general purposes of conveyance and cooperation, and be of great service in contributing to, and storing the geological, botanical and zoological collections.[47]

As Commander John Lort Stokes, RN, who had been engaged as a consultant to the expedition, pointed out, the ship was to provide '... a place of safety for the harvest of the collectors such as previous explorers have so much needed.'[48]

Equally serious was the problem of hot and thirsty horses and bullocks plunging into waterholes and swimming or rolling on dry land while fully laden. In 1845, Leichhardt could only express his frustration:

> One of them — that which carried the remainder of my botanical collection — watched his opportunity, and plunged into a deep pond, where he was quietly swimming about and enjoying himself, whilst I was almost crying with vexation at seeing all my plants thoroughly soaked.[49]

Even with an adequate number of well-behaved animals, the constant friction, together with the heat, dust and humidity associated with carriage on horseback over many months, often meant that samples were eventually of little value, as Elsey and Mueller discovered on the North Australian Expedition.[50]

The carriage of scientific instruments was also a problem which was not fully overcome until motorised wheeled transport was used. Even when the best available equipment was taken, many of the instruments became unserviceable through the buffeting which they received. Eyre, for example, lost both of his barometers when dampness softened the leather bags containing the mercury, allowing most of it to leak away.[51] Similarly, despite all the care that Augustus Gregory provided for his instruments during the North Australian expedition, his barometers became unreliable.

> The metallic barometer has a second time suddenly deviated from the aneroid barometer, and the form of the vacuum vessel has visibly altered, the construction being too slight to bear the motion of the pack horse, though one of the steadiest animals had been selected to carry the instruments, and they are always surrounded with blankets.[52]

The experiences of Eyre and Gregory exemplify the incompatibility of field research and exploration. Despite the insistence of scientists and scientific societies, the goodwill of expedition leaders and the availability of instruments, reliable packhorses and skilled bushmen, it would be a further quarter-century before the emphasis was changed and field work could be satisfactorily completed at a more appropriate pace.

The success of exploration in northern and inland Australia owed much to the continuing development of bush skills and to the attainment of a considerable degree of professionalism. Such progress was derived from continuity, the importance of which had previously, for the most part, been paid lip-service only. Eyre, who was probably the best-qualified explorer at the time of setting off on his first expedition, stressed the importance of prior learning.

> ... it may not be out of place to state, that the Expeditions of 1840–41 were not entered upon without a sufficient previous and practical experience in exploring.[53]

Sturt was more explicit than Eyre on the advantages of being qualified and well-read in the subject. From his previous explorations he knew that experience was the building block of facility.

> I would yet hope, that those who shall hereafter enter the field of Australian discovery, will profit from my experience, and be

> spared many of the inconveniences and sufferings to which I was unavoidably exposed.[54]

Consequently in 1843, when Sturt wrote to Lord Stanley outlining the rationale underlying his proposed central Australian exploration, he pointed out that:

> ... some years ago I expressed my opinion that no party from Europe would succeed in any effort to penetrate this continent from the Coast. I was aware from experience that altho' Men of Spirit enterprise and ability could be found, the necessary elements of an Expedition such as ought to be employed on so gigantic a work could no where be put together except in the Australian Colonies. The Men My Lord should be habituated to the Bush and confident in meandering about it, accustomed to and fearless of the Natives, uncomplaining under privations, and vigilant and steady in the performance of their duties ... for Australia has large tracts of barren land like Africa, between the more fertile portions of it in crossing which it requires precautions which experience can alone suggest.[55]

Accordingly, Sturt ensured that his 1844 expedition included a number of experienced or well-qualified men. The fact that, in the same year, Leichhardt took no experienced bushmen other than the ornithological collector John Gilbert, was more a matter of financial inadequacy than of choice.

The contribution of John Septimus Roe to the development of professionalism in exploration tactics and strategy is worthy of special note. The Western Australian Surveyor-General created a school of exploration perhaps unrivalled in Australian history. During his successively larger and more complex explorations he developed a range of successful techniques and also tutored the various members of his staff, including John and Alexander Forrest, Robert Austin and the Gregory brothers. In July 1847, in his exploration of the country between the Hutt River and Champion Bay he included Henry Gregory in the party, whilst on his large and difficult exploration of the Esperance hinterland in 1848–49, he was accompanied by Francis Gregory. When Augustus Gregory finally left Western Australia for Sydney prior to his North Australian expedition, Roe presented him with a boxed sextant and prismatic compass, accompanied by a letter which, in part, noted Gregory's '... unwearied zeal and ability ... uniformly displayed whilst filling the situation of an Assistant Surveyor and in the Survey Department of the Colony, during a period of nearly 13 years.'[56]

In their expeditions the Gregory brothers maintained the continuity of experience which was an essential component of the success of Roe and his pupils. On their first exploration of seven weeks to the north and east of Perth, Augustus, Francis and Henry Gregory worked together. On subsequent expeditions the four brothers worked in varying combinations. As well, during Francis' exploration of the Shark Bay region he took Roe's son James as Second-in-Command. The Gregorys also appreciated the importance of keeping together a team of experienced men. It was no accident that Phibbs, Bowman and Selby of the North Australian expedition were also members of Augustus Gregory's Leichhardt search party in 1858.

In his selection of scientific staff Gregory also chose men with field experience. Thomas Baines, who was artist to the North Australian expedition, had had field experience in South Africa. Geologist James Wilson was considered a good bushman on the basis of his eleven years' farming experience in inland South Australia[57] and botanist Mueller had carried out extensive field research in both South Australia and Victoria.

Of all the improvements involved in the considerable development of bushcraft during this period, the achievement of mobility was perhaps the most important. Determining the most efficient method of conveyance and choosing the most appropriate types of pack, draught or riding animals were frequently slow and painful processes, for explorers did not always draw on the experiences of their predecessors.

Eyre took an all-horse team and, although he still used drays, he was the first explorer consistently to cover very large distances in a series of lightly-laden and highly mobile reconnaissances. Eyre knew very clearly the degree of mobility inherent in small, lightly equipped and well-mounted groups. In this light, on one of his reconnaissances he pointed out that:

> ... I did not think it right to take more than a single native with me, as every addition to the number of a party, on such occasions only tends to increase the difficulty and anxiety of the task.[58]

By this technique, on one occasion he covered about three hundred kilometres in five and a half days.[59]

Despite the advantages offered by Eyre's approach, the shortcomings of his drays soon became apparent. All his draughthorses died from over-exertion and thirst while attempting to pull the drays through the sandy coastal country above the Great Australian Bight in 1841. Even getting to the Bight with the drays was a problem for, while travelling between Port

Augusta and Port Lincoln, his horses were forced to smash their way through mile after mile of scrub, which was both wearying and distressing to them.

Although Eyre carried out his 1840–41 exploration in advance of Mitchell and Sturt, those explorers did not learn from his or their own earlier efforts. In 1844 Sturt set out for the Murray River from Moorundi, north-east of Adelaide, with sixteen men, four riding horses, eight draughthorses, thirty-two bullocks, two hundred sheep, one spring cart, one horse dray and five bullock drays. Sturt believed that bullocks were better suited than horses to inland exploration. He acknowledged that they were slower, but saw this feature as:

> ... an advantage rather than otherwise. Horses are much more liable to accident than bullocks, and all the horses I consider necessary on such a journey as this are a sufficient number to feel the way.[60]

In order to reduce the total number of his stock, Sturt decided not to take packhorses. He knew that a team of bullocks could pull a dray carrying a load greater than they or an equal number of horses could carry on their backs. Nevertheless, the explorer was frequently placed in dangerous situations because of his lack of mobility when water supplies were rapidly drying. Ironically, much of Sturt's fast and far-reaching reconnoitring was done purely with horses. Altogether, from 14 August to 17 November 1845, he covered 3023 kilometres,[61] although stationary for fifteen days during that period. He still refused, however, to admit the shortcomings of his overall approach. In fact, when acting as an adviser to Gregory for the North Australian expedition, he continued to advocate the use of bullock drays. With his wealth of experience in dry, scrubby and rough country, Gregory flatly rejected the idea for he believed that:

> The employment of drays would retard the progress of the party, and though the number of animals required for the transport of a given weight would be less, the consumption of provisions would be increased, so as to nearly counter balance the advantage, while it would often compel the party to deviate from their line of route ... (to) cross steep ridges and gullies.[62]

Mitchell was the last of the large-scale explorers to depend on bullock wagons for transport. In 1845 he had 103 bullocks, seventeen horses, eight drays and three light carts to carry the provisions for his expedition of twenty-nine men, and 250 sheep for slaughtering. Mitchell, who claimed that he had been advised by 'experienced persons' that bullocks were more enduring than cart-horses,[63] came to rue ever accepting such an opinion.

Owing to the animals' high water requirements and slow rate of travel, the explorer was severely constrained as to where he could go. On one occasion he took eight days to travel the sixty kilometres between the Darling and the Narran Rivers, a stage which horse-drawn transport could have completed in one day. As things stood, the party had to unyoke the bullocks and bring them forward to water at the Narran on the second morning, and then to allow them time off to recruit. When taken back to the wagons they had to be double-yoked for they were now weakened, which necessitated double the number of trips, and so on. All the while stock were straying, both overnight and during the daytime, for often while the first group were being returned, further stock were straying and Mitchell's group was almost continuously divided and weakened. In addition, the expedition was held up by rain on the flat inland country, where the drays were continually bogging. In despair, Mitchell commented in his journal:

> The man who travels with bullocks must expect to be impeded by wet ground, as well as by the scarcity of water, in many situations where horses could pass without difficulty.[64]
>
> The patience necessary to any traveller depending on bullocks and bullock drivers, I then thought ought to exceed that of Job.[65]
>
> How bitterly I regretted the alteration of my original plan of equipment, which had reference to horses and light carts alone.[66]

Overall there was minimal rapid reconnoitring on Mitchell's expedition, during which a sequence of depots were established and increasingly smaller groups were hived off to proceed slowly forward. That Mitchell finally learnt from the serious errors of his last expedition can be seen from his design, in the following year, of Kennedy's expedition to ascertain the direction of the supposed Victoria River. On this occasion Mitchell decided to outfit his Second-in-Command with an all-horse team, which, he maintained, would help ensure rapid progress.

In the context of evolving mobility, Leichhardt's expedition is difficult to place, for he was badly affected by a shortage of funds, a factor which did not affect the other expeditions of this period. The expedition was equipped purely from Leichhardt's own meagre resources and from donations and he set off with eight pack-bullocks, eight bullocks for slaughter and seventeen riding horses for ten men. Although all of his men could be mounted once a proportion of the provisions had been consumed, the bullocks' slow rate of travel restricted progress to between sixteen and twenty kilometres per day, even when the going was good.[67] On the few occasions when more than twenty-two kilometres were covered, Leichhardt commonly found it necessary to give the bullocks the next day off to recruit.

On his subsequent expedition, when money was less of a problem, Leichhardt chose mules rather than bullocks. The mules' extremely hard feet, greater endurance, better tolerance of water shortages and faster rate of travel made them far superior as pack animals.

The arid conditions, the very long distances, the occasionally thick scrub and rugged country now being encountered told against drays and draught animals in general and against bullocks in particular. As a result the explorers were receptive to the style developed in Western Australia by Roe and transmitted to his protégés in the Department of Lands and Surveys. The technique appears to have had its genesis in 1848, when Roe set out from Perth, travelling up the Avon Valley then east and south of the Stirling Ranges to the Cape Riche area on the south coast. Along the way, despite the Surveyor-General's attempts to pick the easiest route in order to spare his horses:

> [the] best draft horse, 'Parker', burst an important blood vessel and dropt instantly dead in the shafts whilst exerting himself to extricate the cart from some soft ground. [Worse still] ... our largest and best looking horse, 'Colonel', lay stretched on his side, completely done-up ... [68]

Realising the futility of continuing in the same manner, Roe revised his approach, believing that '... our future progress would be effected with much greater rapidity and ease by pack horses alone, without any cart.'[69] The remainder of the expedition was therefore carried out in that way.

As a result of this decision, Roe was faced with the problem of reducing weight, particularly as his horses gradually worsened through long stages on the often waterless and usually grassless mallee country in the south-east of the colony. At the Cape Riche depot he replaced the heavy canvas tents with flies of lightweight calico and dungaree, '... and discarded every article we could possibly dispense with ...'[70] At one point he even contemplated abandoning his supply of dried beef because the horses appeared incapable of carrying it further. He made several further reassessments of his loads, learning all the time to distinguish between the essential and non-essential, and to determine a feasible load for packhorses. Francis Gregory, who accompanied him on this expedition, would have learnt much from the experience, for he and his brothers were also convinced of the necessity of minimising the weight their packhorses had to carry. Augustus Gregory even devised a system of carrying biscuits made from flour, dripping and dried beef, which gave a weight saving of approximately thirty-three per cent over carrying the ingredients separately.[71] Before setting off from the Victoria River depot on the North Australian expedition, Gregory had the salted pork boned out, which reduced its weight by seventeen per cent.[72]

The North Australian expedition was the only occasion when Gregory took livestock for slaughter. His decision to abandon the practice marked a turning point, for mobility had now increased to the stage where bullocks and wethers could no longer keep up with the pack and riding horses. Instead Gregory managed to ensure his meat supply without sacrificing mobility by slaughtering his horses and drying their meat as they became unserviceable. Accordingly, on the North Australian expedition seven months' supplies of tea, flour and sugar were taken, but only four months' supply of dried meat.[73]

Expeditions could only be mobile, however, if all members were adequately mounted, for walking, particularly over difficult terrain, is both slow and debilitating. Experiences during Leichhardt's first expedition gave ample evidence of this fact. At the beginning, when Leichhardt did not have enough horses to transport both supplies and men, he and his associates were forced to take turns at walking until the supplies were sufficiently depleted. They found the fatigue from walking during the middle of the day in November to be 'very severe'.[74] Later, when travelling along the Isaac River in mid-February 1845, Leichhardt had an argument with the Aboriginal assistant Charley, who knocked his leader down and broke several of his teeth. Charley was immediately dismissed, though Leichhardt knew that he would be forced to follow the expedition as he was too far away from his own country to be able to return to it in safety. Consequently the Aborigine, accompanied by his companion Harry Brown, was compelled to walk all day without water or food, in the most trying conditions. He soon capitulated and was reinstated, for, as Leichhardt pointed out:

> ... the day was very hot, and the heat of the rotten ground was intense. Our little terrier, which had so well borne former fatigues, died; and our remaining kangaroo-dog was only saved by Mr. Calvert's carrying him on his horse. It was a day well calculated to impress on the Blackfellows the difference between riding and walking ... and, before sunset, he arrived quite exhausted at our camping place, and begged me to pardon him ...[75]

Experience also convinced the Gregory brothers of the need to be fully mounted and to use packhorses for the transportation of supplies. In particular Augustus, on learning that Edmund Kennedy's horses and drays had covered the distance from the Namoi to the junction of the Alice and Barcoo Rivers in six weeks in 1847, commented that '... packhorses should, therefore, travel it in one month.'[76] Notwithstanding the success of Gregory's North Australian Expedition, which was outfitted with fifty-one horses, in 1858 when preparing to set out in search of Leichhardt, the explorer was criticised by Cowper, the Government Assessor, who claimed that too many horses had been requested for the project.[77]

Because fully mounted expeditions traversed the country far more quickly, fewer supplies (and therefore fewer horses and stockmen) were required for a given route. Expeditions became smaller, tighter and more efficient, water supplies were less of a problem and straying horses took proportionally less time to find in the mornings. Overall mobility therefore increased exponentially in this style of exploration, which could outpace Aborigines over an extended period of time.[78]

The final factor directly affecting mobility from the 1840s to the early 1860s was the gradual abandonment of the practice of dead reckoning. When Evans crossed the Blue Mountains in 1815, Macquarie's instructions that he chain-measure his entire route meant that he was able to cover only 454 kilometres in fifty days. Oxley's habit of measuring his daily distances also contributed to his slow rate of progress. Of all the Australian explorers, it was Mitchell who carried a preoccupation with precision to obsessive lengths. On the completion of his third expedition, he boasted that he had covered:

> ... upwards of 2,400 miles [which] was measured with the chain, and this measurement was connected with angular surveys, and observed latitudes ... [79]

It is unlikely that Mitchell would have agreed with Captain Frome who, when surveying the Lake Torrens area, which Eyre had sighted in 1839, pointed out the essential difference between exploration and surveying:

> ... it was not to be expected that Mr Eyre, whose principal and almost sole object was the discovery of a road into the interior, would, at the same time, have been able to lay down the position of his route with the same accuracy that might have been expected from a surveyor.[80]

Roe and Gregory were of the same mould, being more concerned with mobility and satisfied with approximate placement from celestial sightings. Ironically, in his capacity as Surveyor-General of Queensland after 1859,

Augustus Gregory was to comment that much of Mitchell's survey of the Darling Downs was too inaccurate to be of any value.[81]

Increased mobility demanded a high standard of horsemanship to keep the animals sound and fit during extended periods of work in difficult terrain. The skills necessary to husband the horses' strength included the ability to assess their condition, awareness of the tasks still to be completed, the capacity to locate feed and water and the intuitive identification of the warning signs which indicated that animals were close to their limits. On his 1848 expedition, Roe was quick to realise that the conditions they were encountering were too severe for the horses to cope with:

> ... when half way to the granite hill four of the horses gave convincing proofs of their inability to proceed another mile, by streaming out in those profuse cold sweats which are always the forerunner of a complete and fatal breakup. Thankful for the warning, the party was halted, the complaining horses unloaded, and arrangements immediately made for leaving behind everything that could possibly be dispensed with ... [82]

Similarly, Francis Gregory, when in dune country east of Nullagine during his 1861 North-West Expedition, was quick to recognise the symptoms of critical dehydration:

> I cannot omit to remark the singular effects of excessive thirst upon the eyes of the horses; they absolutely sunk into their heads until there was a hollow of sufficient depth to entirely bury the thumb in, and there was an appearance as though the whole of the head had shrunk with them, producing a very unpleasant and ghastly expression.[83]

Later, on the North Australian expedition, the inexperienced Mueller did not have the practical skills necessary to husband his horses' strength and, according to Gregory, knocked up four horses in seven months. Even though all the other experienced riders were heavier, not one of their horses knocked up during this period.[84]

Sturt learnt from experience that explorers' horses must be absolutely free from blemishes on the back and withers, which were symptoms of former galling. He had found that such marks not only indicated a predisposition towards galling, but were also weaker than the surrounding tissue and likely to break out again.

Native feed was augmented in a range of ways. Eyre, for example, had a supply of oats landed near Port Augusta at the head of the Gulf, for he knew that little or no decent grazing could be expected in this region. Roe copied this technique in 1848 when he left Cape Riche carrying provisions for ninety days, plus 300 pounds of corn for the horses.[85] Because such augmentation was not possible in inland explorations, Gregory, Leichhardt and Sturt had to use the available food to its best advantage. They therefore camped where the feed was good and gave their stock days off in order to recuperate.

Another method of gaining maximum benefit from available feed involved the establishing of depots, where the main body of the expedition stopped while reconnoitring was carried out with the stronger horses and bullocks. Provided spare riding and packhorses were available, this technique allowed the poorer and galled animals to recuperate. Leichhardt, who was always short of stock, was denied this luxury, particularly after his losses along the Roper River. He therefore made sure that on his subsequent expeditions he had an adequate number of spare horses.[86]

When Gregory reached the Victoria River region on his 1855 North Australian expedition, his ship was stuck fast on a mud bank for eight days. At each low tide the vessel keeled over for several hours, causing the horses to pile on one another. Though the locality was not ideal, Gregory landed the horses as soon as possible, for many were severely debilitated as a result of their experiences and all were losing condition rapidly as supplies of food and water ran low. Once ashore, he drift-grazed them slowly, at a rate of ten to sixteen kilometres per day, to the site of the intended depot, thus allowing them to recover as they went. It is a tribute to his horsemanship that horses which were so weak on landing as to require assistance to stand not only reached the depot, but also, in most cases, completed the expedition's full distance of over 3,500 kilometres.[87]

A good horseman needed to be able to assess how much further his animals could go without water. Eyre was concerned but not perturbed by making his horses go for up to four days without water, for as a horseman he was able to nurse them through such stages. On one occasion he recorded the crossing of:

> ... upwards of 100 miles of desert country, during the last three days, in which the horses had got nothing either to eat or drink. It is painful in the extreme, to be obliged to subject them to such hardship, but alas, in such country, what else can be done?[88]

According to Eyre, his skill at maintaining his horses was shown at its best when, on the three waterless sections along the cliffs above the Bight, he got them through stages of five, six and seven days without water. This alleged feat was, however, later subjected to severe questioning by Giles.[89]

Nevertheless Eyre was the first explorer to consistently and successfully expect his horses to endure long waterless stages.

Both Eyre and Sturt had learnt from experience that extremely thirsty stock will not graze and will thus rapidly lose condition. In situations where survival was finely balanced, inducing the stock to graze could be the difference between success and failure. Both men would walk their stock until they were tired, then gave them a limited amount of water from a supply that they carried on their drays. The stock would then graze and rest for some hours before they were again given water, reharnessed and set under way.[90] By using this technique Sturt was able to cover the last 185 kilometres of waterless country on his return journey from Central Australia in 1846 and reach the safety of the Darling River.

> We started last Sunday with a fearful hot wind blowing, but at midnight the wind shifted to the south and it became cool. By 3 o'clock on Monday morning we had advanced 24 miles ... I continued moving until 3 in the afternoon when I halted on the edge of the scrub to rest the cattle and to water them, but at first they would not drink. Having picked a little however, they were not so nice and we got the most of them to take a little. I then threw away the remainder of the water in the skins ... I foresaw indeed that all we had now to do was to perform the rest of our journey with all possible expedition. I therefore lightened the drays as much as I could, reserving only a few gallons of water to give any of the animals that might knock up ... We journeyed on all Monday, and we had during the day a sharp shower, the most providential thing that could have happened to us. It moistened the herbage and left a very little surface water which the cattle eagerly drank. At 3 o'clock on Tuesday morning I stopped until daylight and then again starting reaching Flood's Creek at midnight. Mr. Browne came up with the drays two hours after me. Thus, Dearest, we performed this long journey of 115 miles from 7.00 p.m. on Sunday to 2.00 a.m. of Wednesday, without losing an animal, travelling night and day we brought horses, bullocks and sheep in safety to our destination.[91]

Francis Gregory found on his North-West Expedition that his debilitated horses coped better if he matched his travelling and camping schedule to available water supplies. He therefore camped beside water during the hot part of the day, set off again in the late afternoon, camped for the night without water further along the track, then got under way again very early when the morning was still cool.[92]

Explorers also came to realise the necessity of abandoning all equipment in emergencies. On one reconnaissance, for example, Sturt reported leaving behind '... 75lb of flour, all my heavy stores, and one of the packsaddles.'[93] In 1861, after Francis Gregory's horses began to fail east of Nullagine, the explorer was forced to turn back, as there was no certainty of finding water in the mountain range which he could see away to the east. Setting out in the coolness at the 'first peep of dawn' and carrying with them only saddles, firearms and instruments, he and his associates made towards the depot thirty-two miles away. Once a horse knocked up it was left behind. Gregory sent Brown forward with the freshest horses to bring back water, whilst he and Harding continued on as best they could, quietly droving the remainder. Along the way, they could see the desperate nature of Brown's progress:

> By dark we had succeeded in reaching to within nine miles of the depot, finding unmistakable evidence towards evening of the condition to which the horses taken on by Mr. Brown were reduced, by the saddles, guns, hobbles, and even bridles, scattered along the line of march, which had been taken off to enable them to go on a few miles further.[94]

In addition to the more obvious facets of horsemanship, explorers came to acquire the small skills which, collectively, facilitated their animals' daily travel and preserved their strength. Mitchell, for example, had become aware by 1830 that bullocks pull best when warm. He therefore attempted to place his campsites in positions from which the stock would have relatively easy country to cover while they warmed up in the mornings. Eyre also favoured an easy beginning to the day.

> I generally preferred, if practicable, to lengthen the stage a little in the vicinity of watercourses or hills, in order to get the worst of the road over whilst the horses worked together and were warm, rather than leave a difficult country to be passed over the first thing in the morning, when, for want of exercise, the teams are chill and stiff, and require to be stimulated before they will work well in unison.[95]

In this vein of hard-learnt experience, the Victorian grazier Edward Curr recommended that long journeys should be broken into a series of varying distances, so that horses were not debilitated. As he pointed out, once underway, '... you will find it, beyond comparison, easier to save [the horses'] condition than to replace it.'[96]

Because explorers were now aware of the need to prevent galling and debilitation, they often travelled only short distances in the early stages, so as not to overtax animals still soft in condition. This gradual working-up period also allowed the riding horses' girths and the draught horses' and bullocks' necks to toughen up, so preventing galling. As Eyre commented, early in his 1841 expedition:

> ... I was anxious to move quietly on at first, that nothing might be done in a hurry ... Nothing is more common than to get the withers of horses wrung, or their shoulders and backs galled at the commencement of a journey, and nothing more difficult than to effect a cure of this mischief whilst the animals are in use. By the precaution which I adopted, I succeeded in preventing this, for the present.[97]

Part of the everyday care of working stock also entails cleaning those areas under the saddles and harness which have sweated badly. Unless this sweat is carefully removed, when dry it can lead to galling, for it abrades the skin when the harness is placed over it again. Leichhardt took especial care to keep his horses' backs carefully washed but, because he had no spare mounts, most of them eventually became badly galled. If water is not available to remove sweat marks, as is generally the case in inland Australia, careful brushing of the sweat after it has dried is equally satisfactory. Augustus Gregory, who appears to have been the first explorer to appreciate and practise this, included twelve brushes in the equipment for his North Australian Expedition.[98]

Should galling occur from continuous work in hot weather or failure to keep the neck and girth clean, the animal should ideally be rested and oil- or grease-based remedies applied in order to keep the wound supple as it dries, to prevent scar tissue forming and to keep flies away. Continuing to work an animal that has galled, especially in hot weather when it is continually sweating, usually causes the wound to worsen and enlarge until the animal eventually either loses condition badly or bucks when harnessed.

Augustus Gregory had learnt from Roe the importance of distributing the loads among his horses in order to husband the weaker ones. During his search for Leichhardt, when the horses were severely debilitated from an almost complete lack of food and water, he took the loads completely off the worst affected.[99] Earlier, on his North Australian expedition, some horses had been reduced to carrying as little as eighteen kilograms, or no loads at all.[100]

One aspect of horsemanship which came to assume growing importance in Western Australia was the identification of poisonous plants. Large

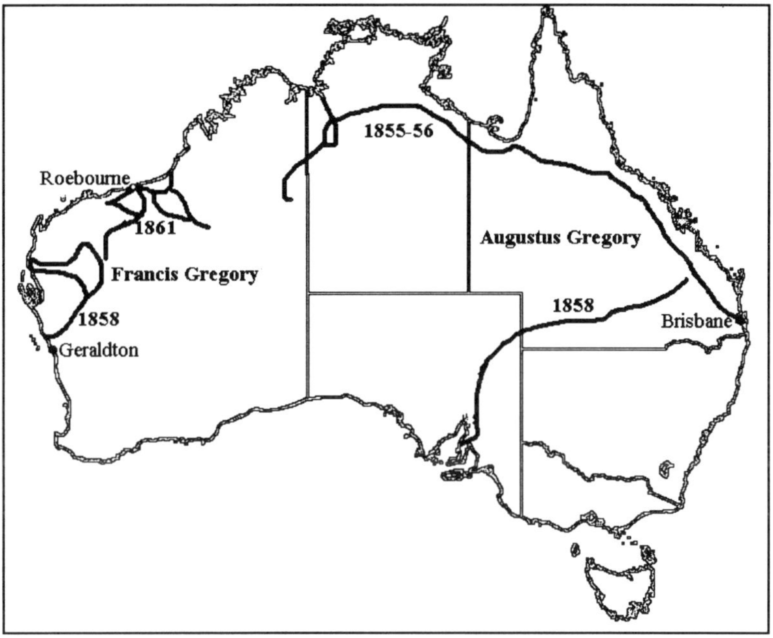

The explorations of the Gregory brothers.

areas of the south-west support native plants which contain lethal levels of sodium fluoroacetate. This chemical, which is commonly known as 1080, is used to bait foxes and rabbits for control purposes, though indigenous fauna are relatively immune to it. Problems with such plants date from the early 1830s, when Surveyor Hillman and several groups of settlers were working their way south from Perth to the Williams River district. In October 1835 one party lost eight out of ten bullocks in the country behind the Darling Scarp.[101] Roe noted other losses as well.

In 1848 Roe's own progress was interrupted by poison plants when, forty kilometres from Kojonup on his way home from his expedition to the south-east, several of his horses were badly affected. This experience discredited the prevailing belief that only ruminants were prone to poisoning in this way.[102] Six years later, Austin's Murchison expedition was devastated when all of his horses were poisoned.

> Ten of them died, and five others were so much injured that they lingered on almost useless and fell away one after another during the ensuing months.[103]

The expedition was forced to continue on foot, its members suffering very badly as a result.

Because the Gregory brothers were Western Australians, they were vigilant about poison and could recognise the local varieties. Although they did not lose stock during their early Western Australian expeditions, they commented on several occasions on the presence or absence of the *Gastrolobium* species.[104] When horses were lost on the North Australian expedition, Mueller examined their gut in order to ascertain which plants they had eaten, for Gregory wished to be able to avoid repetition. Unfortunately the plants had been digested to the extent that identification of individual specimens was not possible.[105]

When Leichhardt lost a horse at the junction of the Lynd and Mitchell Rivers in Queensland in 1845, its death was attributed to snakebite. He later assumed that the three horses found dead on a sand bar projecting out on the Roper River had been drowned by crocodiles. In fact it is probable that all four were poisoned.[106]

As the length of expeditions increased and the country being traversed became more difficult, it was essential that horses were well shod. This necessity was lost on Leichhardt, whose horses and bullocks often suffered appallingly from footsoreness. During his first expedition he took only one spare set of shoes for each animal[107] despite originally calculating that the expedition would last between five and seven months. Worse, he threw the spares away at the Staaten River. He was later to make frequent comments that his stock were badly footsore and that he had periodically had to halt to rest them for a few days.[108] In fact, after one particularly torrid day spent toiling over the hard basaltic outcrops which cover so much of the Lynd River basin, another expedition member commented that '... we could have been tracked for miles over the Rocks by the blood which came from the poor Animals' [feet].'[109] In the face of such neglect, the horses of more mobile explorers, who were repeatedly covering long distances each day, would have soon been immobilised.

In Central Australia, Sturt's horses also faced the problem of a sandy surface totally desiccated by the intense heat. Horses' hooves require some moisture to keep them in good condition, unless they are of the naturally very hard black type. Because mules have such hooves, they rarely need shoeing, which is one of their advantages. On one occasion when Sturt's horses were unshod, their hooves became so dry 'that splinters flew from them at every step.'[110] In November 1845, he was forced to abandon a horse which had fallen further and further behind. On examination it was found to have worn its feet down so badly that the sensitive frog had been torn from one hoof, '...

and you could see a large raw cavity up the heel.'[111] In fact, Sturt's horses would actually have been walking on their soles and the soft frog of the hooves. These soft structures are part of the shock-absorbing design of the entire hoof and lower leg and are not intended to directly carry weight. Not surprisingly, therefore, Sturt's horses were often intensely footsore, their rate of travel was reduced and their general level of debilitation increased.

When Eyre found that the ranges he was traversing while looking for water in the Lake Torrens region were severe on shoes, he had the horses re-shod twice, using three sets in less than two months.[112] Because this rate of wear is considerably greater than would normally be expected, Eyre had 'a large supply of horse shoes' made up at Port Lincoln when he was preparing to explore farther west.[113]

The Gregory brothers appear to have learned from Roe the necessity of keeping their horses well shod. At one stage on his 1848–49 expedition the Surveyor-General commented that his animals had lost so many of their shoes and were so sore and exhausted that he was beginning to doubt whether he could complete his journey. Worse, he had no spare nails even to tighten up the remaining loose shoes.[114] Twelve years later Francis Gregory demonstrated that he had benefited from his experience with Roe when he terminated the first, southerly section of his North-West Expedition, under similar circumstances.

> ... our provisions on a reduced allowance would admit of our remaining out forty days longer; but the lameness of many of the horses and lacerated condition of their fetlocks convinced me that, should we meet with any more difficulties or rough country before obtaining a fresh supply of shoes, much valuable time would be lost, and we should probably fail to get many of the horses back. I therefore deemed it more prudent to return at once ...[115]

Augustus Gregory kept a watchful eye on his horses' hooves during the North Australian exploration. On rocky country between the Roper and Albert Rivers he commented that '... the day seldom passes without having to replace the shoes of several of the horses.'[116] Fortunately he was well prepared, having been equipped with 600 sets of shoes at the outset and manufacturing more at the Victoria River depot.[117]

Horsemanship and mobility also benefited during this period from the development of more appropriate riding and pack saddles. Riding saddles used by explorers before the 1850s appear to have been of two types: the

Contemporary cartoon by Charlie Abbold, depicting the high spirits of Australian horses.

relatively flat, light, British hunting saddle and the heavier cavalry saddle. The latter were so lightly padded that they became notorious for causing galling. Curr, describing the arrival of a troop of mounted police at his Port Phillip property in the 1840s, noted sarcastically that

> ... their horses, with the exception of tether ropes round their necks, were turned out in a decidedly military way, with inconvenient bits, peculiar saddle cloths, awkward saddles, and sore backs.[118]

On the other hand, hunting saddles, because of their size and lightness, are uncomfortable for horse and rider during periods of extended use. Furthermore, nineteenth-century outback horses were often poorly handled, if at all and, on being mounted, frequently bucked badly, to the surprise of more than one British commentator. The Reverend William Haygarth, who spent eight years riding, camping and travelling through inland eastern Australia in the 1850s and 1860s, appears to have best captured such surprise.

> Australian horses have a vicious habit known as 'buck-jumping', or as it is more familiarly called, 'bucking'. This trick, in its

> aggravated form, is peculiar to the colts bred in the colony and in Van Diemen's Land, and is decidedly the most expeditious way that could be devised for emptying a saddle ... [119]

In such circumstances the hunting saddles provided scant assistance and the rider was either bucked off or the saddle moved forward over the withers until both it and the rider were thrown over the horse's shoulders. Edward Curr explains how colonial riders soon became better equipped in order to keep their seats.

> In breaking or rough riding, a crupper is always used, as without it the saddle cannot be made to remain on the back of the buck-jumping horse. In the case of a low-withered horse, the saddle is forced on the neck, if the wither be high, the girths are usually burst if no crupper be used. Neither is the crupper strap, in all districts, attached to the crupper-iron or staple, which, in the event of a severe struggle, is certain to be pulled out or broken; but, being passed between the saddle and saddle-cloth until it obtrudes before the pummel, it is then passed two or three times around a stick about 20 inches long, and as thick as the wrist, called the 'kid', and there buckled, which kid is strapped to two iron staples, with which the saddle is provided, behind the pummel. This kid comes across the horseman about six inches above the knees, and adds very much to the security of his seat... [120]

It appears that the Australian stock saddle rapidly evolved from this rudimentary form of knee pad. Certainly as early as 1873, a local commentator's description of a saddle could well have been of the article being used by stockmen over a century later.

> His saddle is peculiar. It is very strong and heavy, say 24 pounds. It has enormous knee pads, very high up and far forward; the cantle far back and high, the seat very broad, and the pommel very low ... It is admirably adapted for rough country ... [121]

Such saddles, which are considerably more comfortable for both horse and rider, were definitely being used by explorers at that time, for W H Tietkens commented during Giles' second expedition, when they were attacked by Aborigines near the Musgrave Ranges in Central Australia, that '... a spear hit the knee-pad of my saddle, nearly piercing it.'[122]

Pack-saddles also underwent considerable development during this period. Although information on the style of the earliest British pack-saddles is not available, it is almost certain that cavalry-type riding saddles were mainly used in the early days. These have a large tree with several buckles and attachment points on either side. The inclusion in Macquarie's list of equipment for Oxley's expedition of '... ropes for tying kegs etc onto the horses ...' tends to indicate that true pack-saddles were not being used before 1820.[123] The illustration of Eyre's arrival in Albany in July 1841, which was probably drawn by a spectator shortly after the event, also portrays saddles which are similar in shape to the military saddles of the period. Definite evidence that riding saddles were being replaced by Australian pack-saddles in the early 1860s can be found in William Landsborough's journal, which was written in the Gulf Country during his search for traces of the Burke and Wills expedition. On this occasion Landsborough commented that his party stopped very shortly after setting off from the Gregory River one morning '... to adjust a pack on a riding saddle. The other pack-saddles were constructed on Gregory's principle and required less adjusting.'[124]

The early ill-fitting and poorly lined pack-saddles almost invariably caused galling. Evans' saddles, for example, were not lined with serge. When Leichhardt decided to use bullocks instead of horses, he had the pack-saddles altered, but they were still of such a poor fit that his bullocks suffered severely from galling and for many weeks would buck, bolt and smash the saddles and packs against trees, in an effort to be free of them.[125] Roe was similarly affected on his 1848 expedition, for most of his pack-saddles had been made for ponies, not horses, and thus were too small to fit correctly.[126]

It may be that the general indifference of many early explorers to galling was due to ignorance of the extreme undesirability of the condition. In contrast, even as early as his exploration of the Murchison River region in the late 1840s, Augustus Gregory was aware of the necessity for well-fitting saddle padding and set time aside to restuff unsatisfactory saddles.[127] Certainly, it was after such knowledge had become widespread that the first pack-saddles specifically designed for Australian conditions were made by Augustus Gregory for his North Australian expedition. Gregory also insisted on good, hard-wearing saddle blankets to further protect the horses' backs and withers. The specifications for his pack-saddles would alter little over the ensuing 130 years or so.

> The pack saddle, made under the direction of Mr. Gregory consisted simply of two boards of Australian cedar, about 20 inches long to seven broad, inclined at such an angle as to sit fairly on the horse's ribs, and at such a distance from each other that the

> spine would remain uninjured between them. These were connected by two stout bows of iron, one and a half inches broad by one inch thick, arching well clear of the horse's back, and having on each side hooks firmly riveted into them for the suspension of the bags in which our provisions and etc., were stowed. The crupper was buckled around the aftermost bow, and the straps for the attachment of the breasting, breeching, and girths were screwed on the outside of the cedar planks ... A pair of pads, sufficiently large to prevent not only the saddle but also the packs chafing the horses, were attached to the boards by thongs passing through the holes bored in either end, so that upon occasion we could easily remove them to re-arrange the stuffing, and tie them again in their places. A thick felted saddle cloth was invaluable as an added protection ... The bags were of stout canvas, as wide as one breadth of the material ... no other fastening was used, so that if a horse fell in the rugged mountain paths, or in fording a rough swollen torrent, it was an advantage to him to shake off his bags at once ... Nothing whatever was allowed to be fastened to the bows above the suspension hooks; indeed there was a general order that the horse should carry nothing that was not contained in the side bags ...[128]

Modern pack-saddles differ from those designed by Gregory only in that the padding is integrally related to the wooden part of the tree by having its leather facing wrapped around the wooden planks. A particularly beneficial aspect of the design of such pack-saddles is that the horses' withers and backs are kept as cool and well aired as possible, reducing the likelihood of galling.

In addition, rectangular leather saddle bags have replaced the less durable canvas bags. Their attachment points are so placed as to lower both their position and the animal's centre of gravity to at least that specified by Gregory, substantially improving the horse's stability in rough going. A large leather surcingle is also now used to completely surround the horse and the leather saddle bags. The low centre of gravity of the unit makes it less likely that the horse will fall over, and therefore does away with Gregory's requirement that the bags should come free in such an eventuality. Although it is not known precisely when leather bags and surcingles came into everyday use, a drawing from Alexander Forrest's expedition in the King Leopold Ranges of the Kimberleys in 1878 demonstrates that they were certainly employed by that date.

The strength and durability of the colonial pack-saddle was amply demonstrated when Gregory's horses bolted after the schooner *Tom Thumb* fired a farewell salute at the Victoria River depot in 1855. When the horses

A modern pack-saddle, differing little from Gregory's design.

were finally rounded up, Gregory noted with some pride that:

> A few of the straps of the colonial-made pack-saddles had given way, but there was no other damage done to them; but the English-made saddle was shaken to pieces.[129]

Not surprisingly, Gregory[130] had a further thirty-one pack-saddles made to the same design for his Leichhardt expedition.

The increasing use of bells during this period also contributed in a minor way to the development of horsemanship. As we have seen, Oxley was delayed for five days because his horses were not belled when they wandered away and became lost south of the Lachlan River in 1817. Although, by the time of Leichhardt's expedition, bells were commonly employed, he could only afford to purchase one. As expeditions were now equipped with necessarily larger numbers of horses which, then as now, tended to keep to small groups and, in some cases to wander off alone, a considerable number of bells were required. Gregory, who was particularly aware of their value, took twenty bells with him on his North Australian expedition[131] and ten on the Leichhardt expedition.[132]

The hunting and gathering of food by explorers declined in importance after the mid-1840s. Because expeditions were now moving much faster, less time was available for hunting. Several commentators of this period also mentioned that, because kangaroos were not plentiful in the interior, hunting was a time-consuming procedure.

The use of increasing numbers of pack animals also reduced the need to procure a proportion of the ration in the field. Sturt carried seven tonnes of supplies and equipment in 1844 and, on Augustus Gregory's North Australia expedition, 1,450 kilograms of preserved beef, 3,500 kilograms of salted pork, 7,830 kilograms of flour, 1,985 kilograms of rice and 1,811 kilograms of sugar were taken.[133] Furthermore, at least until 1855, increasing numbers of livestock were being taken to be slaughtered along the way. Finally, because very large scale expeditions of up to twelve months' duration were being planned, to explore at considerable distances from settled areas, it simply was not satisfactory to plan food provision on the basis of a proportion being game. Five weeks after setting off from Jimbour House Station in October 1844, for example, Leichhardt, who had planned to obtain a considerable proportion of his supplies through hunting, was forced to send two members back in order to conserve his meagre supplies. As he noted:

> It had now become painfully evident to me that I had been too sanguine in my calculations, as to our finding a sufficiency of game to furnish my party with animal food, and that the want of it was impairing our strength.[134]

Augustus Gregory, the most experienced and successful explorer of the period, was emphatic on the same issue, noting that he had '... never found kangaroo or other game to more than compensate for the ordinary losses (of supplies) contingent on accidents of a trifling nature.'[135]

Of all the explorers, it was Ludwig Leichhardt who brought the skills of food-gathering to their highest level in Australian exploration history, partly due to his scientific training, but primarily because of his lack of funds. He had sufficient food for an estimated seven months, at relatively reduced rations,[136] but took fourteen and a half months to complete the expedition. Consequently his men had no flour or sugar for the final six months and no tea for approximately the final three months. For much of the expedition the men subsisted on dried bullock meat, game and native plants.

Leichhardt's botanical knowledge enabled him to identify those plants which should be safe and, through caution, to survive their tasting. On several occasions, however, he and Gilbert were purged violently, or burnt their lips and mouths severely, as a result of their experimentations.[137] Leichhardt's familiarity with plants and his quick mind also enabled him to ascertain how the various poisonous plants, which were found in various stages of preparation in Aborigines' camps, could be made edible. He learnt, for example, to soak then bake or boil pandanus fruit[138] and to soak cycad seeds.[139]

His willingness to experiment also meant that foodstuffs otherwise bland or uninteresting were made palatable.[140] Several different types of bean, such as those in kurrajong pods, were roasted and ground to make a coffee-like drink, and wild marjoram was gathered and used after the tea ran out.[141] Green succulent plants such as portulaca,[142] fat-hen (*Atriplex*) and sowthistle (*sonchus*) were used as vegetables,[143]and a variety of native limes, figs and apples provided the vitamin C so essential on such a long exploration.[144] It was through this willingness to experiment that Leichhardt and his men avoided the attacks of scurvy which broke the health of Sturt and Stuart, killed Poole, Sturt's assistant, and badly affected several of their men.[145]

During this period all expeditions were accompanied by hunting dogs. Leichhardt's kangaroo dog, Spring, for example, was particularly successful in bringing down kangaroos and emus in the more open country of the Cape York Peninsula and the Gulf. Unfortunately, as explorers began to traverse the considerably more difficult country in the interior, most of the dogs died from exhaustion, thirst or neglect, for the explorers simply did not have the skills or take the trouble to care for their animals. Forty-five days after setting off, three of Mitchell's dogs died on a hot January day in 1846 and Leichhardt lost Spring in similar circumstances in October 1845, after mislaying the native's calabash in which he had carried water for his last surviving dog.[146]

As explorations moved further into tropical regions, new dangers emerged, as Augustus Gregory discovered when one of his kangaroo dogs was taken by a crocodile during his North Australian expedition.[147]

The drying and preserving of meat also reached new standards of professionalism in this period. An important activity at one of Mitchell's depot camps during his 1844 expedition was the drying of mutton from the wethers taken along for slaughter.[148] Leichhardt's ability to dry meat was even more crucial, for he was slaughtering bullocks, not sheep. Fortunately each batch of dried beef showed little sign of deterioration over the month or so during which it was consumed. As he reported in late October 1844:

> This, our first experiment — on the favourable result of which the success of our expedition entirely depended — kept us, during the process, in a state of great excitement. It succeeded, however, to our great joy, and inspired us with confidence for the future ... in fact, good dry beef, without any further preparation, was much relished by all of us ...[149]

The process involved cutting the meat into strips and hanging them from branches of trees and shrubs around the camp. Depending on the weather, one to three days were spent continuously turning the meat to expose it to the sun and in keeping away the predatory kites.[150]

Leichhardt also dried kangaroo and emu meat, which '... served considerably to save our stock of dried beef, and to lengthen the lives of our bullocks.'[151] He even cut up and dried the meat of one of his horses which had slipped backwards on basalt rubble on a steep slope in the Valley of Lagoons in North Queensland and broken its hip. He had first to overcome the considerable aversion of his men to eating horse flesh.

> I immediately resolved upon going to the place where the accident had happened, and proposed to my companions, that we should try to make the best of the meat, as the animal was young and healthy, and the supply would greatly assist in saving our bullocks to the end of our long journey; and they declared themselves willing at all events to give a fair trial to the horse flesh. ... We, therefore, shot the horse, skinned and quartered it the same night; and ate its liver and kidneys, which were quite as good as those of a bullock.[152]

Not everyone agreed with Leichhardt about the wholesomeness of the horseflesh, with one member of the group later exclaiming: '... thank God our disgusting Horseflesh is nearly expended.'[153] The true bushmen who made up Augustus Gregory's North Australian expedition some ten years later had no qualms over his matter-of-fact comment that part of the overall ration was to be derived from unserviceable horses.

It was only towards the end of Leichhardt's expedition, in the humid December weather, that his meat-drying techniques failed and members of his party became ill after attempting to eat rancid beef. After some experimentation Leichhardt '... succeeded in saving a great part of our meat by smoking it.'[154] Both smoking and salting later became standard procedures in the Northern Territory.[155]

The diet of Leichhardt and his men was so quantitatively and qualitatively deficient that they came to reject almost all prevailing notions of correctness and propriety. Everything became grist to their mill. To help satisfy their craving for fats, they learnt to gently roast emus by suspending them at an angle on forked sticks, so that the oil ran slowly down and dripped into a container. Bullock's fat, which in the early stages had been thrown away or used to grease the harness, was now retained and eagerly consumed. As Leichhardt noted in February 1845, less than five months after setting off:

> In consequence of the additional fatigues of the day, I allowed some pieces of fat to be fried with our meat. Scarcely a fortnight ago, some of my companions had looked with disgust on the fat of our stews, and had jerked it contemptuously out of their plates; now, however, every one of us thought the addition of fat a peculiar favour, and no-one hesitated to drink the liquid fat, after having finished our meat. This relish continued to increase as our bullocks became poorer; and we became as eager to examine the condition of a slaughtered beast, as the natives, whose practice in that respect we had formerly ridiculed.[156]

Supping on stewed fat aside, Leichhardt and his men later learnt that, by boiling pieces of bullock hide in the stew of dried beef simmered overnight, its flavour was found to be '... preferable to the tasteless meat of our knocked up bullocks.'[157] The expedition's 1844 Christmas dinner consisted of suet pudding and stewed cockatoos.[158] Just before reaching the Isaac River near Peak Range in Southern Queensland, in February 1845, they were so famished that they found a broth made from crows to be both tasty and nourishing. On several occasions also, Leichhardt's men gorged themselves on flying fox, even staying a day extra, north of Snowdrop Creek in south-western Arnhem Land, in order that more could be procured. Francis Gregory and his men would later reject flying foxes, despite their being very fat, on the grounds that they '... emitted such an intolerable odour that it would require even an explorer to be hard pressed before he could make a supper of them, either roasted or boiled.'[159] Clearly Leichhardt was one explorer who was forced, on many occasions, to make a virtue of necessity.

> Oppressed by hunger, I swallowed the bones and the feet of the pigeon, to allay the cravings of my stomach. A sleeping lizard with a blunt tail and knobby scales, fell into our hands, and was of course roasted and greedily eaten.[160]

Upon making our camp, we cut part of their [emu] meat into slices, and dried it on green hide ropes; the bones, heads, and necks were stewed: formerly, we threw the heads, gizzards, and feet away, but necessity had taught us economy; and, upon trial, the feet of young emus was found to be as good and tender as cow heel.[161]

Iguanas, opossums, and birds of all kinds, had for some time past been most gladly consigned to our stewing pot, neither good, bad, nor indifferent being rejected ... It is remarkable how soon man becomes indifferent to the niceties of food; and, when all the artificial wants of society have dropped off, the bare necessities of life form the only object of his desires.[162]

Augustus Gregory, whose list of food for the North Australian expedition included such items as preserved potatoes, sago, arrowroot and colonial jam, appears epicurean in comparison.[163]

Because exploration was now penetrating increasingly arid and hostile regions, water supply became a critical issue. Mitchell's comment that 'we had been so accustomed to a higher temperature than 100°F that any degree under that felt refreshing'[164] may be somewhat facetious, but does give some idea of the conditions encountered. In the 1850s Francis Gregory suffered perhaps hotter conditions on his North-West Expedition, recording a temperature of 178°F from a thermometer placed in the sun in October. All the explorers of this period suffered badly at some stage from lack of water. Eyre's draught horses in 1840–41 and several of Mitchell's bullocks in 1844 died from thirst, prompting the latter to comment, 'I determined never to move the party again, until I could ascertain where the water was at which [we] should encamp.'[165]

In January 1844 Leichhardt and one of his men almost perished in the Peak Range area of south-eastern Queensland while searching for water. They had become disoriented due to heatstroke, when they fortuitously cut across the tracks of the main body of the expedition. The condition of the two men was so critical that they took several days to recuperate. Leichhardt's description of the events makes compelling reading:

In travelling over the hot plains our horses began to fail us; neither whip nor spur could accelerate their snail-like pace; they seemed to expect that every little shade of the scattered trees would prove a halting place; and it was not without the greatest difficulty that we could induce them to pass on. It was indeed distressingly hot: with open mouths we tried to catch occasional puffs of cooler air; our lips and tongue got parched, our voice

> became hoarse, and our speech unintelligible. Both of us, but particularly my poor companion, were in the most deplorable state. In order to ease my horse, I tried to walk; but, after a few paces, I found it impossible; I was too much exhausted ... [166]

The experiences of Leichhardt and others made explorers critically aware of the importance of linking expeditions to specific seasons, in order to capitalise on the availability of rain, surface water and green feed. When Eyre decided in 1840 to change the location of his exploration from the central to the western regions of South Australia, he was worried about the climatic conditions.

> ... the summer weather too, was rapidly approaching, and I dreaded the task of forcing a way through the low level scrubby waste, around Streaky and Smoky Bays, under a tropical sun.[167]

Even Mitchell recognised the dangers of dry season exploration:

> The difficulty of finding water may be, in a great degree, avoided, by awaiting a proper time for setting out on journeys to the interior. This would be when saturating rains had fallen, and filled the hollows of the surface; after which water may be found, even on the plains, where certain inequalities on a surface of clay may retain it for several months. Seasons of flood or of drought are so extremely irregular in Australia, that some caution is necessary as to the period of setting out.[168]

In similar vein Francis Gregory attributed many of the problems encountered on his North-West Expedition to his being delayed for two months by logistical problems:

> I am, however, unable to refrain from again expressing my opinion, that had not so many concurrent circumstances combined to retard the departure of the Expedition until so late in the season, and it had arrived on the coast at the time originally recommended by the Geographical Society, it would, in all probability, have resulted in the full accomplishment of the object they had in view.[169]

In arid areas where water supplies were problematic, extensive reconnoitring was systematically carried out before the main body advanced. Ranges were first examined for gnamma holes and for pools in the creeks which ran from them. Roe aptly captured the importance of inland watersheds when, on his 1847 expedition he recorded '... I looked anxiously, but in vain, across the downs for a range of mountains which might afford promise of some interior waters.'[170]

Roe also became acutely aware of the value of isolated granitic hills, where water could be found in gnamma holes, in pools close to the base or at shallow depths in the sediments surrounding the outcrop.[171] Furthermore, because of the shallow sub-surface water in such areas, there was a good chance that the immediate vicinity would support fair stands of grass. Several such sites saved Roe's horses near the Russell Range area of Western Australia in 1848, when they were failing badly in the surrounding poorly grassed mallee country.[172] In fact, Roe's warmth of feeling for granitic hills was clearly apparent.

> ... there was no mistaking the nature of the intervening country, which was desolate and cheerless in the extreme, presenting no more friendly granite hills at which we could hope to keep our horses alive ...[173]

The Gregory brothers also looked for granite outcrops, particularly in their explorations of the regions to the north-east of Perth and in the arid Murchison and Gascoyne areas. In 1846, Augustus Gregory, when east of Perth, noted:

> The extremely level character of the country between the ranges to the east and north, and the immense columns of red sand or dust which were raised by whirlwinds to a height of 200 to 500 feet, gave but little hope of finding water in that direction.
>
> ... all the hills within 20 miles were of a trap formation, and therefore gave no prospect of obtaining water, the soil being loose and the rock full of fissures; hitherto we seldom had found water except on or near granite rocks, which serve to collect the rain-water of even slight showers.[174]

In better watered areas, particularly in Queensland, the locating of watercourses in the flat, thickly wooded country was also a process which had to be learnt. Leichhardt provides a masterly description of all those water-finding skills which became part of the explorer's stock-in-trade:

> In looking for water, my search was first made in the neighbourhood of hills, ridges, and ranges, from which their extent and elevation were most likely to lead me to it, either in beds of creeks, or rivers, or in waterholes, parallel to them. In an open country, there are many indications which a practised eye will readily seize: a cluster of trees of a greener foliage, hollows with luxuriant grass, eagles circling in the air, crows, cockatoos, pigeons (especially before sunset), and the call of Grallina

> Australis and flocks of little finches, would always attract our attention. The margins of scrubs were generally provided with chains of holes ... In coming on creeks, it required some experience in the country, to know whether to travel up or down the bed: some being well provided with water immediately at the foot of the range, and others being entirely dry at their upper part, but forming large puddled holes, lower down, in a flat country. From daily experience, we acquired a sort of instinctive feeling as to the course we should adopt, and were seldom wrong in our decisions.[175]

Sturt, who traversed more arid country than most prior to 1860, was often forced to dig in watercourses. As his bullock teams and horses were using up to 5200 litres each day,[176] regular water supplies were critical. On occasions he dug out small dams in creek beds, to ensure that a supply of water would be available on his return.[177]

Explorers soon followed Eyre's lead in carrying water through the more difficult country. Frome took a light spring cart with '... the bottom filled entirely with kegs containing sufficient water for our horses for nearly three days ...'[178] On one occasion in December 1845, Sturt managed to cover 184 kilometres of waterless country by making water casks from the hides of three bullocks and carrying them on his drays.[179] Individual riders took to carrying water containers.

Although Leichhardt set out in 1844 with no water bags for his men, they soon equipped themselves with natives' calabashes, which held about two litres each.[180] He noted on one occasion that:

> Browne had taken the precaution to fill Charley's large calabash with water, so that we were enabled to make a refreshing cup of tea in the most scorching heat of the day.[181]

Such vessels were, however, inadequate and, as temperatures rose in the dry country to the west of the Albert River, the necessity of carrying more water became apparent. Accordingly Leichhardt had some wallaby skins softened and tied over the lids of the expedition's one-litre and nine-litre pots.[182] On Gregory's 1858 Leichhardt expedition, his nine men were equipped with large water bags and fourteen smaller indiarubber water holders.[183]

Not all explorers during this period developed a strong sense of orientation. Mitchell, for one, still had to use a compass in his daily work, even towards the end of his fourth expedition and on one occasion was disoriented by an unexpected magnetic variation.[184] On the other hand, by the late 1850s the Gregory brothers were able to carry out extensive reconnoitring away from the Victoria River into the northern extremities of the Great Sandy Desert, yet return, with facility and with limited use of instruments, to their setting-off point. Indeed, Leichhardt and Augustus and Francis Gregory moved across country like homing pigeons, to destinations over 3,000 kilometres distant.

The learning process in attaining this standard, however, was at times painful. Some of Leichhardt's men and many of Mitchell's convict stockmen became lost, mainly because they had had little or no bush experience before setting out. Without Leichhardt's Aboriginal stockman Charley, it is almost certain that several of his men would have perished, for in all cases, when found each was heading approximately 180 degrees in the wrong direction.[185] Mitchell's men were often so inept that they became disoriented whilst searching for their bullocks. On one occasion a shepherd and his entire flock of sheep became lost. When located by an Aborigine he was found to have been describing a series of circles.[186]

Riders soon discovered that some horses, if given their head, would return home of their own accord. In 1844, when attempting to push back to their camp through dense brigalow scrub at night in the Arcadia Valley, south of Rolleston in Queensland, Leichhardt's Aboriginal stockman Charley lost the track. According to the expedition leader, once given its head '... my good little horse, Jim Crow, guided us to the camp, which we reached about 11.00 o'clock'.[187]

Leichhardt and the Gregory brothers were able to ride with confidence through the night because they knew how to follow the stars. Leichhardt, for example, discovered Moonlight Creek, immediately west of the future settlement of Burketown, while reconnoitring after dark on 20 August, 1845. He had set off from the camp when the evening sky was clear, '... and followed the star Vega as it declined to the westward.'[188]

A final factor in the development of this overall sense of orientation was the ability to recall specific features in what, to the uninitiated, was featureless bush. Leichhardt, who developed this skill to perfection, was able to retrace his path through the Expedition Range, south of the future settlement of Rolleston in Queensland, on several occasions. Had he made a wrong choice among the maze of similar ridges and gullies, he would frequently have been confronted with sheer drops of up to 150 metres and with the need to then return to the proper track. Leichhardt attributed this skill to concentration and careful attention to detail, acknowledging, however, that in this respect, he was quite inferior to his Aboriginal assistants.

> I shall have to mention several other instances of the wonderful quickness and accuracy with which Brown as well as Charley were able to recognise localities which they had previously seen. The impressions on their retina seemed to be naturally more intense than on that of the European; and their recollections are remarkably exact, even to the most minute details. Trees peculiarly formed or grouped, broken branches, slight elevations of the ground — in fact, a hundred things, which we should remark only when paying great attention to a place — seem to form a kind of Daguerreotype impression on their minds, every part of which is readily recollected.[189]

The contribution by Aborigines to Australian exploration probably reached its zenith during the early 1840s, when white men's bush skills were, at times, still inadequate for the task. Eyre, for example, commented in 1844, that he:

> ... always made it a point, if possible, to be accompanied by one or more natives, and I have often found great advantage from it. Attached to an exploring party they are frequently invaluable, as their perceptive powers are very great, and enable them both to see and hear anything at a much greater distance than a European. In tracking stray animals, and keeping on indistinct paths, they display a degree of perseverance and skill that is really wonderful.[190]

Yet despite this praise, none of the explorers fully trusted the Aborigines who, since Barrallier's time, had been described as subhuman, vengeful, treacherous and cunning. Mitchell, notwithstanding his reliance on and friendship with these people, was the most outspoken of all in his assessment of their nature.

> I am quite aware that there have been individual instances of brutality amongst them, that can hardly be palliated even in savage life — that they have disgusting customs — that they are revengeful and addicted to theft ... Treachery and cunning are inherent in the breast of every savage. I question, indeed, if they are not considered by them as cardinal virtues ...[191]

As we have noted earlier, Mitchell was clearly aware of the danger of dividing exploration parties into small, relatively defenceless groups when there were Aborigines in the vicinity. In due course, he also came to realise that to attack Aborigines was not only dishonourable, but could also provoke later attacks of revenge on innocent parties. It now seemed that

Barrallier's earlier outline of the features of Aboriginal life and his advice on dealing with Aborigines were remarkably accurate.

The official instructions given to Augustus Gregory prior to his 1848 exploration of the Murchison River warned him to be wary of the Aboriginal people. Colonial Secretary Madden outlined in some detail how John Baxter had been murdered on Eyre's expedition and Richard Cunningham and two others on Mitchell's various journeys. He claimed that their deaths, together with the wounding of Grey and others, had been occasioned by '... the want of caution, (and) forgetfulness of the nature of barbarians.'[192]

Apart from the Kennedy expedition's fate in 1848, the worst incident involving Aborigines during this period occurred when John Gilbert was murdered immediately south of the Mitchell River in the Cape York Peninsula area in 1845, after the two Aboriginal members of Leichhardt's party had molested three women and assaulted an old man. Not surprisingly, after this event Leichhardt took far greater care to protect his party from surprise attacks.

> Since Mr. Gilbert's death, the arrangements of our camp have been changed. I now select an entirely open space, sufficiently distant from any scrub or thicket, even if we have to go a considerable distance for water. Our pack-saddles are piled in two parallel lines close together, facing that side from which a covered attack of the natives might be expected. We sleep behind this kind of bulwark, which of itself would have been a sufficient barrier against the spears of the natives. [Night watches were kept and] ... we generally tethered three horses, and kept one bridled; and, with these arrangements, we slept as securely and soundly as ever; for I felt sure that we had nothing to fear, as long as our tinkling bell horse, and perhaps a second horse, was moving near us. The natives considered our animals to be large dogs, and had frequently asked whether they would bite (which I affirmed, of course); so that they themselves furnished us with a protection, which otherwise I should not have thought of inventing.[193]

The Gregory brothers were always circumspect in the presence of Aborigines. In the Murchison basin in 1848, Messrs Bedart and C F Gregory reported that '... it was not considered prudent to remain geologising amongst the cliffs ...' because there were natives about, and that they had returned to camp.[194] Night watches were carefully planned and seriously observed. When Augustus Gregory perceived an Aborigine 'crawling up amongst the thick grass about ten yards from the back of the tents', he walked up and chased the man away with the barrel of his gun, not considering '... it prudent either to fire at or capture him.'[195] Some months later when taking the Governor to examine the site at which they had earlier found tin, the party was stoned by Aborigines, but no effort was made in retaliation for '... we did not see any method of resenting it, except by expressing our disapprobation in words.'[196] Their restraint may have been a mistake, for four days later on the return journey, the Aborigines came closer and gradually more antagonistic, throwing spears and even attempting to pull riders off their horses. The Governor immediately shot and killed one of the assailants and was soon afterwards speared through the leg. The Aborigines followed for several hours, continually throwing rocks, spears and clubs, while the Gregorys' party fired whenever anyone exposed himself through the thick scrub. After this incident, the Gregory brothers made a practice of always distancing themselves from Aborigines. Commenting on a later confrontation during the north-west expedition, Francis considered that:

> It was very evident that our forbearance was mistaken for weakness, and that mischief was preparing. I accordingly took hold of one of the most refractory and compelled him to march off at double-quick time.[197]

Thereafter the brothers would either charge the Aborigines on horseback[198] or fire their rifles at rocks and trees very close to their assailants, so terrifying them with fragments smashed by the projectiles[199] and, only if the situation became desperate would they fire light shot directly at them.[200]

The 1840s and 1850s were a time, not only of deteriorating relationships between explorers and the Aboriginal people whose lands they traversed, but also of massive advances in the scale, comprehensiveness, sophistication and cost of equipment. In part, this development may have been due to the realisation that, once well inland, there was no chance of replacing critical supplies and that particularly expensive and large scale expeditions could therefore be jeopardised through the failure of poor quality equipment or for want of relatively trivial items. Eyre certainly appreciated these problems, pointing out that Sturt's results had been deleteriously affected by inferior equipment, and requesting a comprehensive list of scientific equipment of the 'best construction' for his proposed Port Essington Expedition.[201]

The table below gives some indication of the difference of scale between Oxley's 1817 expedition and Augustus Gregory's North Australia expedition of 1855–6, both of which involved a similar number of participants.[202]

Item	Oxley	Gregory
Number of men	15	18
Ammunition	100 rounds	25,000 rounds
Firearms	4 muskets 4 pistols	17 shotguns, 4 rifles, 10 revolving pistols
Tin Plates	13	60
Spare shirts	24	240
Spare horseshoes	less than 2 sets for each horse	Over 12 sets for each horse plus more that were manufactured at the Victoria River depot.

The range of materials included by Gregory is also worthy of comment, for it included many items that had not been a feature of previous expeditions, including five sets of spare stirrup irons, six body brushes and six curry combs, mosquito netting, candles and waterproof cloth. Leather punches, bullet moulds and lead ladles were also included.[203] The food supplies, which included coffee, peas, tamarind, cooking oil, gin and wine,[204] were a considerable improvement over the basic rations of Oxley and Sturt.

The sophistication of Gregory's North Australian exploration can best be gauged by studying the list of scientific equipment taken to cater for position-fixing and mapping, Baines' painting and sketching, Elsey's botanical and biological collecting and Wilson's geological analysis and sampling. It included nests of specimen boxes, thirty-seven charts of Australia, oil colours, arsenical soap, chloroform, one skin of parchment, copper sulphate and corrosive sublimate.[205] Under such circumstances, research would only be hindered, not by the lack of equipment, but by the shortage of time.

Inevitably, increases in the scope and comprehensiveness of both expeditions and equipment incurred greater financial costs. Mitchell was granted £2,000 to finance his 1845 attempt to travel overland to Port Essington, while Augustus Gregory's North Australian expedition, originally budgeted at £5,000, was to cost £15,000 because of the extended hire of two supply vessels. Such money was well spent, largely because of the attention given to matters of detail. On Francis Gregory's 1858 Gascoyne expedition, for example, fifteen swivels were taken for the tethering ropes.[206] Although not essential, such devices prevent ropes from tying into knots and bunching up as the horses continually walk in circles around their tethering points. On the North Australian expedition, seventy-five kilograms of leather, 200 spare buckles, nine kilograms of sewing twine and four kilograms of beeswax were taken, to not only cope with expected breakages and wear and tear, but also to allow for the fabrication of new equipment if necessary. Clearly Gregory left nothing to chance. Each expedition member was well armed, with at least one long-barrelled firearm and, in most cases, a revolving pistol as well. Now that integral cartridges and the firearms specifically designed to use them were available, the explorers benefited from a much more reliable and greatly increased firepower and a consequently greater margin of safety.

Greater care was also being taken in planning the provisioning of expeditions. In 1840, for example, Eyre arranged for stores to be landed near Port Augusta and in a series of dumps further to the west.[207] He had also intended using this technique on his aborted expedition to Port Essington, with proposed supply dumps at Halifax Bay and in the Gulf region.[208] The Gregory brothers adapted this method for their North-West and North Australian Expeditions, requesting the ships' masters to hold certain positions until specific dates, in order to ensure the exploring parties were not stranded without adequate provisions.[209]

Although his Leichhardt expedition was located well inland, Gregory intended, nevertheless, to incorporate a provisioning point by having his team establish a depot at the junction of the Alice and Barcoo Rivers. Here the fittest and most competent men and the best livestock were to remain, whilst the remainder returned. This technique allowed Gregory a larger team to carry his supplies forward, the choice of those best suited to continue and maximum mobility when required.[210]

Horse-related expertise was equally important. As early as 1845 Augustus Gregory was calculating horse requirements on the basis of the weight of his equipment and provisions. By the late 1850s he and his brothers knew quite clearly what a horse could be expected to carry and what equipment was required for an extended period of time.[211] Gregory knew that, as supplies were consumed and gross weight declined, the horses' carrying capacity was in most cases also declining. Consequently he never entertained the idea of overloading the horses in the earlier parts of the journey, in anticipation that the gross weight would soon be reduced.

> A pack horse does not carry more than 150 pounds exclusive of packages and harness and even when the quantity is being reduced by the regular consumption of provisions, the casualties and reduction of strength from fatigue, reduce the means of transport to nearly an equal amount. Thus 3,300 pounds would require 22

> horses for its conveyance, each carrying 150 pounds.[212]

The difference between this approach and that of Oxley warrants no further comment.

Once in the field, loads were allocated by weighing the contents with a spring balance. On the North Australian Expedition saddlebags were then numbered, with specific numbers belonging to specific horses. Each man was allocated a group of horses and was responsible for their general care and their associated saddles and harness. Under this arrangement the men were able to be more particular over a limited number of horses which were their definite responsibility.[213] On the North-West Expedition, Francis Gregory assigned the men to work in groups of two, so that the heavy saddlebags were loaded on both sides simultaneously.[214] In this way the saddles and saddle blankets were not dragged to one side during the loading process, reducing the possibility of saddle blankets being creased and galling the horses.

For the immense task of controlling and caring for such large teams of horses, the Gregory brothers chose professional stockmen, well able to hobble out large numbers of horses, find them again the next morning and unhobble and drive them in through bush country.

Camps and exploration ran like clockwork. Watches were set and strictly observed. The first watch for the night cooked the bread for the following day and the last watch had breakfast ready by dawn. 'By this arrangement no time was lost, and everyone knew what was under his particular charge.'[215] These men were consummate professionals, with the capacity to handle problems as they arose. Near the end of Francis Gregory's North-West Expedition, when he and his men were over forty kilometres from known water, the horses exhausted and critically weak and the October temperatures very high, Gregory, doubting whether the horses could make the stage:

> ... set to work and soldered up a number of preserved meat-tins that had been carefully opened and kept for this purpose, putting a small spout to each; eight of these we found to contain something over four gallons, which, added to our water belts and the two remaining kegs, would provide for the conveyance of 12 gallons of water, which I hoped would prove sufficient to enable us to pass the dry tract of country in safety, as it would allow half a gallon to each horse and an ample supply for the party for two days.[216]

Such methodical behaviour in the face of a hostile environment not only does Gregory great credit but also tends to obscure the magnitude of his achievement.

Clearly, by the end of the 1850s explorers such as the Gregory brothers were at ease in the harsher regions of the Australian bush. The tone of the Gregorys' journal, even during Francis' critically close call on the North-West Expedition, when he and his reconnoitring party nearly lost all their horses, is consistently matter-of-fact. With time and experience, they had come to feel at ease with the country and to appreciate its inherent and unique beauty. Leichhardt frequently expressed his appreciation of inland Australia in descriptions that are poetic to say the least.

> The mornings and evenings were very beautiful, and are surpassed by no climate that I have ever lived in. It was delightful to watch the fading and changing tints of the western sky after sunset, and to contemplate, in the refreshing coolness of advancing night, the stars as they successively appeared, and entered on their nightly course.[217]
>
> I wish I could sufficiently describe the loveliness of the morning just before and after sunrise: the air so clear, so transparent; the sky slightly tinged with roseate hues, all nature so fresh, so calm, so cool. If water were plentiful, the downs of Peak Range would be inferior to no country in the world.[218]

The psychological distance between this stance and that of Oxley, Caley and Mitchell was immeasurable.

6

LEICHHARDT REVISITED

Among the contributions made by individual explorers to the quantum leap in knowledge and expertise during the 1840s and 1850s, those of Ludwig Leichhardt were highly significant for the progress of exploration. Yet attempts to assess their value are difficult, for he was a man who aroused considerable and conflicting passions among his supporters and critics. He is possibly the single most controversial figure in the history of Australian exploration. Books by Alec Chisholm and Colin Roderick, for example, could almost have been written about two different men, so divergent are their assessments of the man. A clear illustration of these differing points of view is provided in Roderick's introduction.

> Half a century ago every schoolboy in Australia held the gaunt figure of Ludwig Leichhardt in veneration. His *Overland Journey to Port Essington*was on the shelf of station libraries. Queensland schoolboys traced his 3000 mile journey from the Darling Downs to the Arafura Sea on the map. Their fathers used to speak of Leichhardt as the prince of explorers ...
>
> Any schoolboy could read Leichhardt's praises in the writings of other explorers. The most esteemed of them, Charles Sturt, was one of Leichhardt's admirers: to Sturt he was that 'bold and ardent traveller'. Even Sir Thomas Mitchell, jealous of his own reputation though he was, counted it a loss that Leichhardt was not one of his exploring party.
>
> It was with some doubt that one schoolboy brought up in that tradition later read a book by the Australian veteran journalist, A H Chisholm, *Strange New World*, which depicted Leichhardt as a bogus pretender who was lucky enough to blunder through the bush to his appointed goal.[1]

The doubt of Colin Roderick, the former schoolboy, is easy to understand when it is realised that Ernest Giles, one of the greatest explorers in Australian history, wrote of Leichhardt in the introduction to his Journal, that:

> ... on the list of explorers (is) Ludwig Leichhardt, a surgeon, a botanist and an eager seeker after fame in the Australian field of discovery, and (one) whose memory all must revere.[2]

Giles not only offered an unequivocal endorsement of Leichhardt's stature, but, more importantly, also provided a justification for his later failure and disappearance, pointing out that the task which he had attempted was beyond the prevailing levels of bushmanship.

> Of Leichhardt's sad fate in the interior of Australia no tidings have ever been heard. On this fatal journey, which occurred in 1848, he undertook the too gigantic task of crossing Australia from east to west, that is to say, from Moreton Bay to Swan River.[3]

If Chisholm knew of Giles' endorsement, he chose to ignore it. He begins his book by asserting that, notwithstanding the homage paid by the naming of over twenty botanical species, geographical features, many Queensland hotels, a Sydney suburb, pastoral stations, dingo extermination boards and even children, after Leichhardt,[4] he was, in fact:

> ... not only a poor explorer, but ... in some respects was an impostor and in general was unworthy to rank, either in ability or character, with many men who are partly or wholly forgotten.
>
> In suggesting that Leichhardt was to some extent an impostor I do not question the importance of his discoveries. I merely say that, contrary to historical acceptance, he was not a qualified doctor and not an accomplished scientist, and that as an explorer he was unreliable in his data and a basely unworthy leader and companion. His exploratory ideas were born of self-centred dreaming, and when he led his parties into Australian wilds, with a large sword dangling beside him, he reacted from his evasion of military service and imagined himself a general leading a band of private soldiers.[5]

His conclusion is even more insulting.

> Clearly, the man was largely irresponsible. He was incapable of assessing hazards and, more significant, he had no appreciation of what was owing to associates. Everything was subordinated to the blind urge of an unruly brain — a formless wanderlust.[6]
>
> His early neglect of his parents and the synthetic fervour he

> afterwards manifested towards them (from a distance); his wails regarding the imagined approach of illness and death; his continual self-pity and self-dramatizing; his conscienceless sponging during many years; his lofty attitude towards men whose offences frequently were no worse than his own; his 'playing at soldiers' in the bush; his petty jealousy, amazing obstinacy, and general clumsiness on expeditions, his alternate fits of 'brightest hope and deepest misery'; his inability to profit by hard experience; his startling gastronomic feats while condemning imaginary gormandizing in others; and, above all, his rank ingratitude towards his companions — all these taints give clear proof that his brain contained 'blind spots'.
>
> In short, Leichhardt was a misfit who became an explorer through youthful imaginings playing on a disorderly mind, and because the appeal of his personality enabled him to find benefactors. He is not a refreshing subject for contemplation. The best that can be said of him, on a personal basis, is that he was not wholly responsible for his actions he was 'born that way'.[7]

Although Roderick later attempts in his own work to counter this trenchant criticism in an effort to justify the earlier veneration of the 'prince of explorers', his argument is weakened by the quantity of previously-published material supporting Chisholm's appraisal. For example Ernest Favenc, who in 1888 assessed the first century of exploration, asserts of Leichhardt that:

> His route had been through a country so easy to penetrate and well-watered, that on one night only, had the party camped without water. The blacks, with the exception of the time when Mr. Gilbert was killed, were neither troublesome nor hostile, beyond occasionally threatening them. Game was fairly plentiful and, compared with the obstacles that beset Sturt, Eyre and Mitchell, the footsteps of the explorer had been through a garden of Eden.[8]

Furthermore, Favenc believed that Leichhardt was:

> ... singularly deficient in observation. In one place he writes that horses and bullocks never showed that instinctive faculty of detecting water so often mentioned by travellers and that they seemed to be guided entirely by their sight when in search of it — an assertion which seems incredible on the part of a man with any bush training at all. If Leichhardt had ever had to steady a thirsty mob of cattle during the pitch dark night, with a strong wind blowing from water, or even across the damp bed of a lagoon or river, miles and miles away, he would soon have found

> out by what sense cattle are guided in their search for water.
>
> Although one does not want to harshly criticise these obvious errors in the very rudiments of bushcraft, they serve to indicate how likely he would have been, if entrapped in dry country, to commit a mistake that would sacrifice his men.[9]

In the same vein, the widely travelled and experienced Queensland bushman and pastoralist Henry Russell, who saw Leichhardt in operation in the field, comments that:

> I run the risk of provoking the Apellean censure: *ne sutor supra crepidam*, when I tread upon the toes of popular and unqualified approbation by venturing to question Ludwig Leichhardt's fitness for the leadership of men (in the bush sense, with no doubting as to his scientific qualifications) in the undertaking to which he bound himself in 1844 and persisted in until he passed out of sight.[10]
>
> It is not for me to withhold or wish to withdraw respect and admiration of Ludwig Leichhardt as a brave man; one of great perseverance and high attainments; but ... I refuse to lay my private tribute in addition to the public record and reward of his public service.[11]

In order to substantiate his reluctance, Russell then outlines why he withheld his praise.

> ... he lacked, I think, in the practical adaptation of his talents to a struggle with a venture then formidable through unknown difficulties by land, and certain risks by man, which he almost ignored; common sense, and a sufficiency of self-denial in crises of sufferings.[12]

Finally, and perhaps more specifically, in 1922 Robert Logan Jack, in summarising Leichhardt's achievements, asserted that:

> The success of the 'Overland' expedition was due in a great measure more to the luck of an exceptionally favourable season that to the perfection of his plans. His other expeditions were no less ill-planned and they confronted him with obstacles which he was incompetent to overcome.
>
> Out in the field with his men, and faced with difficulties which foresight and resource on his part should have averted or minimised, he would not have been recognised as the suave and tactful courtier known to Sydney Society. The coarse bully lecturing his followers and comparing himself to a general

> leading an army had forgotten that he had taken advantage of a mistake of the registrar to evade the military service which was the law of his own land. He was callous to the sufferings of the fever-stricken members of the party, who were unable to keep up with his pace. He made agreements which he refused to fulfil. He carried secret stores of dainties on which he luxuriated while his followers were on the brink of starvation.[13]

Contributors to the discussion of Leichhardt have thus invariably fallen into one or other of two diametrically opposed camps, functioning not as jurors, but as legal counsel using a variety of not necessarily impartial techniques in order to present their case in the best possible light. For example Chisholm, in writing of the crossing of the Roper River Bar in October 1845, implies incompetence and bare survival by stating that the expedition 'scrambled over the rocky crossing'.[14] Yet the exploration Journal makes no reference to such behaviour,[15] and Chisholm was certainly not there to determine whether or not the crossing was badly carried out. Moreover, at this point the river bed is covered almost completely with a sheet of flat rock, over which the Roper usually trickles when not in flood. Crossing here would not, therefore, by any stretch of imagination, be a process of 'scrambling'.

Roderick is equally guilty of emotive prose in speaking of Gilbert's 'funk' when it appeared that the two Aboriginal members had abandoned the expedition immediately north of Peak Range in early 1845,[16] and of his 'wail' of concern when Leichhardt finally calculated their true longitude in January 1845 and found that they had actually covered only a small proportion of the total distance and that their supplies would therefore almost certainly be inadequate.[17] Of this event, Gilbert quite reasonably wrote in his diary that they were now less than a quarter of the way along their proposed route after four months, despite only having provisions for six to seven months. On the other hand, Roderick attempts to discount Leichhardt's laxity in not having taken longitude readings more frequently, by asserting that:

> Leichhardt had delayed working out his longitude, as other leaders of exploring parties had done and were to continue to do, for fear of dismaying their followers. When he revealed their position, which was accurately calculated, what he feared actually happened. Gilbert confided his trepidation to his diary.[18]

Inaccurate and erroneous assertions are apparent in the arguments of both sides. When writing of Leichhardt's decision to leave the Valley of Lagoons area in May 1845, for example, Chisholm is patently incorrect in asserting that '... he knew not which way to turn from the Burdekin Valley ...'[19] In fact, Leichhardt wrote that he had decided to leave the Burdekin for two reasons. The river appeared to be heading too far to the north and east, a point which he had verified as best he could by discussion with local Aborigines whom he had difficulty in understanding. More importantly, the nature of the pebbles and sand in its bed indicated that the expedition was now past the extremely rough basalt fields which had earlier prevented them from heading north-west. They were now free, therefore, to move along Anthill Creek in the desired direction.[20] In short, Leichhardt knew exactly the direction he wished to take and, as soon as conditions were favourable, he proceeded to implement his plans.

Roderick is also guilty of curiously inaccurate claims, such as the following:

> Latter-day writers have created the erroneous impression that Leichhardt made no record of the names he gave to each camp. They assert that we should never have known them if Gilbert had not entered them in his diary, since they do not appear in Leichhardt's published narrative. The fact is that they were distinctly named in Leichhardt's fieldbook and that Gilbert's record of them, as well as that of latitudes and longitudes, is derived from Leichhardt's entries there.[21]

Numerous readings of Leichhardt's Journal and Field Maps, as well as Gilbert's and Murphy's diaries, do not substantiate this claim. In fact of the 309 campsites, only 152 were given a name.[22] Furthermore, not all were named by Leichhardt and, without Gilbert's and Murphy's contributions, the total would have been even less. Jack's later highly inaccurate claims about Leichhardt's navigational and mapping shortcomings, which are of greater significance, are dealt with at length below.

Overall, point-scoring over Leichhardt appears to have been refined almost to an artform. For example, when criticising the explorer's general demeanour and leadership, Chisholm quite properly quotes Gilbert.

> The Dr for some time past has been in one of his frequent gloomy fits and is very sparing in his ideas or information on general subjects. It is certainly very much to be regretted that we have such a leader, who never of late appears to be at all disposed to be cheerful or even agreeably civil to his companions.[23]

In doing so, he provides Roderick with an excellent opportunity to strike back.

> No-one has gone further out of his way to besmirch the character and belittle the ability of Leichhardt than A. H. Chisholm, who practised the professional sneer with accomplished urbanity. His misrepresentation of Leichhardt places him in the company of Gilbert, Roper, Murphy and Phillips, for he allies himself with them unreservedly by accepting their aspersions without testing their veracity. In his *Strange New World* casuistry replaced logic and emotive appeal the process of reason.[24]

Clearly, much of the research and writing on Leichhardt over the last 150 years has been unsatisfactory, not only demonstrating selectivity and bias but also, and equally seriously, the application of intensely subjective criteria. Kathleen Fitzpatrick exemplifies this weakness in 1963, in her two-page article on Leichhardt in *Walkabout.* After outlining the explorer's background and achievements and briefly examining criticisms of him, she goes on to say:

> It is, however, the psychology of Leichhardt, rather than his professional competence, that has attracted the attention of 20th century commentators ...
>
> We shall know more of the psychology of Leichhardt, when Mr. Aurousseau, of Sydney, completes the important work on Leichhardt, on which he has been long engaged. Meanwhile, I would hazard the guess that what Leichhardt's companions most disliked him for was his lack of interest in them ... [25]

Almost all other writers have included similar, naively unsupportable criteria relating to leadership qualities, dietary proclivities, manners, fastidiousness and so on. Only Roderick attempts to evaluate Leichhardt's navigational skills in a more rigorous fashion than the others.

In view of the obvious inaccuracy of previous assessments, and in order to do justice to Leichhardt, a different approach is therefore required. Perhaps ironically, the first requirement of a new approach must be the abandonment of the belief that the truth can be determined and that some historians, at least, are impartial. One must therefore reject claims such as Roderick's, where he asserts that a detailed analysis of Chisholm's errors is not necessary, for they '... may be detected readily enough by comparison with the facts as related here.'[26] Jack's belief that he could arrive unequivocally at the truth, is equally unacceptable.

> ... I am unable to place the easy-going rule of saying nothing but pleasant things of the dead above the duty devolving on the historian to write the unvarnished truth.[27]

Indeed, as E H Carr points out, historical research and writing are inevitably subjective:

> The belief in a hard-core of historical facts existing objectively and independently of the interpretation of the historian is a preposterous fallacy, but one which is very hard to eradicate.[28]

Any attempt to judge Leichhardt fairly must incorporate this notion. Free in the understanding that any historical work can only be a distortion and incomplete at best, the researcher should be less eager to take sides and more committed to presenting material in a dispassionate manner. Furthermore, highly intangible claims, which can never be adequately resolved, should, as far as possible, be avoided in favour of criteria which can be assessed by reference to substantive data.

In the case of Leichhardt, comparison with the techniques, methods and achievements of his contemporaries must be seen as a valid measure, particularly in the light of the foregoing chapters of this work. Such an analysis will be, in effect, a case study, but one which will also demonstrate how the conceptual framework and background material provided can be used to accurately reassess judgements on the other major figures in the history of Australian exploration. The insights arising from such a re-evaluation of Leichhardt will hopefully make clear how much of the historiography of Australian exploration has been distorted and diminished through being based on insufficient evidence, the partisan sifting and distortion of highly subjective interpretations, a lack of field research and, most unforgivably, a lack of practical experience in and knowledge of the subject. What follows, therefore, are assessments of Leichhardt's scientific status, of his navigational, mapping and route selection performance and of his standing as a bushman.

LEICHHARDT'S SCIENTIFIC STANDING

Although Chisholm rightly points out that Leichhardt was not entitled to use the title Doctor and indeed that he had not actually completed a university degree, his qualifications for field research in Australia were, nevertheless, impressive. Roderick devotes 231 pages to providing details of Leichhardt's academic and practical training, in order to refute some of Chisholm's criticisms and to demonstrate that the explorer was both exceedingly well-read and scientifically proficient. By the completion of his academic studies — both formal and informal — Leichhardt was profoundly conversant with a very broad range of subjects which had direct application to his field research in Australia. These included botany (which embraced systematic, economic, forest and medical botany), physical geography, chemistry, agricultural science, physical anthropology, physiology, comparative zoology, palaeontology and mineralogy.[29] Furthermore, after extensive subsequent studies in the museum of the London Zoological Society, he enrolled at the prestigious Jardin des Plantes in Paris, in '... as many of the natural history courses, from Anatomy to Zoology, as [he] ... could fit into [his] ... days.'[30] Overall, as Roderick points out:

> Writers on Leichhardt have not taken cognisance of the unrivalled preparation for his career in Australia that these studies, and the field work that accompanied and followed them, afforded him.[31]

Amongst the lecturers at the Jardin des Plantes were the eminent botanist Adolphe Brongniart and his mineralogist and geologist father, Professor Alexandre Brongniart. While Leichhardt was studying with the latter, geology became 'a passion'[32] as the quality of his work in this field in Australia was to demonstrate. Associates of the Brongniarts included the entomologist Jean Victor Audouin, who '... impressed upon Leichhardt the basic importance of making one's own collection of insects'[33] — advice which Leichhardt followed while engaged in his preliminary field research in Australia, prior to setting out on the 1844–5 Port Essington expedition. Other eminent scientists with whom he came in contact included the physicists Gay-Lussac and Antoine Cesar Becquerel, whose area of interest was thermodynamics, the springboard for Leichhardt's later studies in meteorology.[34]

By 1840 Leichhardt had finalised his plans for carrying out field research in Australia, with the object of building a meritorious scientific reputation and so gaining an academic position in Prussia. He therefore set about cataloguing in a methodical fashion '... the Australian and tropical flora in the Jardin des Plantes ... and went systematically through the comprehensive mineralogical collection in the museum.'[35] Furthermore, during and after this period of academic studies, he was indefatigable in his frequent field trips, collecting, dissecting, mounting, preserving and cataloguing specimens.

Shortly after arriving in New South Wales in mid-February 1842, Leichhardt embarked on minor field excursions. These ventures rapidly grew in scope until by 1844 he had carried out field research from Sydney to the Darling Downs, to Brisbane and north to the Bunya Mountains and had covered approximately 4000 kilometres. Being single-handed, poorly equipped with horses, short of funds and unconcerned about his personal appearance, Leichhardt resembled in many ways the archetypal dedicated and unworldly scientist. A contemporary observer reported, of his coming into their campsite one evening in May 1844, that his horse was 'staggering under a load of what appeared to be roots of trees and tufts of grass.'[36]

Leichhardt's academic and practical scientific background was, in the contemporary Australian context at least, unique. Until the 1890s no other field scientist would be so broadly qualified. Indeed, with the exception of von Mueller and possibly Cunningham, Leichhardt was possibly the most highly qualified botanist attached to a major exploration party in the first hundred years after settlement. Furthermore, the quality of his geological research remained unequalled until the activities of the scientific expeditions some fifty years later. Above all, in contrast to contemporaries like Oxley, who was only expected to write clearly of the country encountered, and Mitchell, who was incapable of scientific classification, Leichhardt was a scientist of a different order.

The Port Essington expedition was a shoestring operation, for Leichhardt was almost without funds of his own and relied heavily on donations. Whereas he costed the operation at approximately £130,[37] Eyre, in his preliminary budgeting for his own attempt at the same goal, estimated that he would require a government grant of £5,000. This figure included the hire of a vessel which would establish two depots, one at Halifax Bay and one in the Gulf region. Furthermore, Eyre requested an extensive range of equipment, which he insisted had to be of the 'best construction' for, as he noted, so much of Sturt's work had been diminished in value because of faulty or broken instruments.[38]

A single example is sufficient to illustrate the difference between Eyre's essential requirements and the equipment with which Leichhardt had to cope. Less than three months into Leichhardt's first expedition, his compass glass had been broken and Gilbert's compass had been lost. The effects of the broken glass can be seen thereafter in Leichhardt's field maps, where his orientations and compass bearings are frequently somewhat inaccurate. In his list of required equipment, Eyre specified six compasses and six spare glasses. Of his scientific equipment, Leichhardt later wrote:

> The only instruments which I carried, were a Sextant and Artificial Horizon, a Chronometer, a hand Kater's Compass, a small Thermometer and Arrowsmith's Map of the Continent of New Holland.[39]

He could not even afford to equip himself with suitable sample containers. Compared with Allan Cunningham's specially prepared, white-painted, canvas-covered sample boxes, and with the nests of boxes, sieves and wide-mouthed specimen bottles available to Augustus Gregory's scientists, Leichhardt's containers were so poor that, as we have seen, he was forced to wrap them in greenhide. Because the containers were not waterproof, almost all of the explorers' specimens were ruined when they were submerged while on the backs of pack animals.[40]

Although Leichhardt was better equipped on his subsequent expeditions, he was still working with very small quantities, such as two bottles of ink, one journal and one drawing book.[41] Compared with Augustus Gregory's supply of stationery on the North Australian Expedition, which included mapping parchment and drawing, tracing, ruled, feint, blotting and brown paper, plus nineteen reams of botanical paper, Leichhardt's provisions were clearly inadequate.

Leichhardt's 1844–5 expedition lacked both scientific personnel and (with the exception of Gilbert, who was murdered en route) trained amateurs. Mitchell had Allan Cunningham and Charles Fraser to collect botanical specimens, Sturt had D Brock as a collector on his 1844 expedition and Stuart would later have Waterhouse to collect and preserve natural history specimens on his final expedition. Leichhardt was totally reliant on his usually hard-pressed and quite untrained expedition members, who usually collected only the more showy specimens,[42] which were frequently incomplete and therefore of reduced scientific value. The responsibilities of collecting devolved in the main on the explorer himself, whose workload was already considerable. As a consequence he had to admit that his scientific achievements were, on occasion, less than optimum.

> Mind however well, my friend, I was not the easy traveller, who has everything at hand and can pay all his attention to botany. I was everything, leader of the party, bullock driver, having to load and unload 3 bullocks sometimes several times during the day. All the cares of such a position were upon me, all the anxieties during difficulties and dangers. The arrangement of our camps, the serving out of our provisions, the killing of our bullocks, the mending of the harness, the carrying on of my log, the daibook of my route, determining the latitude and longitude and the nightly watches — You will easily imagine, that even allowing I did my best, a man entirely given to one occupation could have done much more. This refers however almost entirely to the sketching of my plants and to the putting down more

explicit notes on the different especes we found.[43]

Accordingly, on Leichhardt's 1848 expedition, where finance was not such a severe problem, he proposed taking two men '... whom I thought to be useful to me in collecting birds ...'[44] and also hoped to take '... Peter Glynn ... as he is an excellent bird stuffer ...'[45]

Leichhardt was also never adequately equipped with pack animals. Not only did the loss of animals mean the abandonment of botanical and geological collections,[46] but also, even should no major accidents of this nature occur, the explorer realised that on such extended expeditions he would always be constrained. 'I cannot go on ad infinitum in collecting, for my means of carriage are very limited.'[47] Even on the 1846 expedition, with its sixteen mules and fourteen horses, he knew that the proposed length of time in the field, the distance to be travelled and the amount of food required meant that he would have to limit himself to half a ream of botanical paper and therefore to collecting little other than seeds.[48]

Overall, it was lack of funding which drastically inhibited the scientific achievements of the 1844–5 expedition. We have already noted that Leichhardt's abandoned botanical specimens would probably have constituted the greatest single collection in Australian exploration history. That he failed in this respect does not detract from his achievement in gathering such a collection without competent support staff, whilst simultaneously confronting the stress and problems inherent in such a large, extended and under-equipped expedition.

Chisholm also criticises Leichhardt for being a dilettante, claiming that, as a student, the explorer flitted from one subject to another, without mastering any, and:

> ... at the same time he developed the carelessness that caused him to use wrong dates, mis-spell names, muddle his latitudes and longitudes, and otherwise leave his records in disorder.[49]

More specifically he notes:

> Hitherto it has been supposed that the Burdekin was first seen by white men on 28 March (1845); for under that date Leichhardt states in his book that the Suttor River was found to wind round the base of Mount McConnel and, within four or five miles, join a large river flowing from the north-west.
>
> The truth is, Leichhardt at that stage was following the confusing practice, which he frequently adopted, of noting the events of several days under one back date; and thus (although

not pressed for time while the party was at a standstill) he allowed the date 28 March to cover five days.

No member of the expedition saw the Burdekin on 28 March, nor on any other day in that month. It was discovered by one of the Aborigines of the party on 1 April.[50]

Furthermore, in referring to Leichhardt's poor record of publications, Chisholm claims that:

> Leichhardt's failure to accomplish anything material in the way of scientific writings was a point that puzzled (the German scientist) Neumayer. In his enthusiasm over the success of the first great journey (and having only the leader's narrative for judgement) he did not realise what a scatter-brained scientist Leichhardt really was.[51]

To answer these accusations it is necessary to consider Leichhardt's background, which Roderick covers comprehensively. As a non-British newcomer with minimal connections and very little money, he was in a poor position to carry out unimpeded research and publication, especially as the colonists were particularly pragmatic in outlook at that time. Indeed, Leichhardt referred to this mentality on several occasions, pointing out that '... for artists there's little opportunity and no more for scientists.'[52] In short, he summarised his unenviable position with the acerbic comment that:

> Since an individual of limited means can achieve his purpose only partially or slowly, and the wealthy people of Sydney are so exclusively concerned with making money, it is not astonishing that so little is yet known about the rich world of marine life.[53]

Notwithstanding these problems, Leichhardt was soon conducting botanical excursions and providing lectures, in an effort to raise awareness and interest in the subject.[54] He also hypothesised, from the nature of the hot, dry inland winds,[55] that there could not be an inland sea,[56] nor 'surfaces clad with vegetation'. Clearly these deductions were based, in part, on the earlier training in physics which Leichhardt had received in Europe and, as Marcel Aurousseau points out:

> ... it brought him to the notice of German geographers and it established him as the first of the Australian explorers to take (to) the field with a sound hypothesis concerning the character of the interior of the continent. He was convinced that it was arid.[57]

Furthermore, Leichhardt examined the geology of Sydney and its hinterland, writing in October 1842 that:

> I have come to think that Newcastle, on account of the regularity of stratification here, and because of its very characteristic coal-seams, is the centre from which geologists will have to work outwards, in their study of geological relations in New Holland.[58]

By June 1844 he had completed a geological map of the Glendon district, no copy of which has survived.[59] Of Leichhardt's geological surveys and hypotheses, Professor W H Bryan wrote over a century later that:

> I am a great admirer of Leichhardt's most valuable pioneering work in the geological field and I, personally, have had the experience of finding that my interpretation of Mt. Tarampa, an interesting volcanic neck, had been anticipated by him many years ago.[60]

In 1844 Leichhardt also completed his *Contributions to the Geology of New England* which, for a variety of reasons, was never satisfactorily published.[61] Nevertheless, of this monograph, Dr F W Whitehouse, formerly of the University of Queensland, wrote in the 1920s that it was:

> ... a pioneering work, extraordinarily accurate in detail, showing Leichhardt as a geologist of considerable merit and a very accurate observer ... A few little things that we are finding out now in S.E. Queensland that no-one seemed to know of before are set down by Ludwig as a matter of course.[62]

In a later assessment, Whitehouse wrote to Aurousseau in 1958, stating that he believed Leichhardt to be:

> ... one of our greatest explorers and one of our very few scientific explorers. In my own travels I have passed over most of the tracks that Leichhardt pioneered; and I have been vastly impressed by his insight and his almost invariably correct interpretation of the geological evidences he saw in those times, when there were little means of correlating them.[63]

Roderick argues that the paucity of Leichhardt's published works was due to his untimely death. As a result, his Journal, which was heavily edited by Captain P P King before publication, is the best source from which to ascertain the merits of his scientific writings. There are three features of this work which deserve comment. Firstly, despite Mitchell's assertion in 1846 that '... a more useless mass of rubbish was never bound up in a book,'[64] it is, for the most part, a relatively unadorned, factual account of daily events, with relevant scientific comments. In Leichhardt's own words:

> It's a simple account of our journey, and just as simple a description of the country and the things we saw. The traveller who just tells the truth earns the thanks of scholars at home. He cannot enlarge Nature, so he can't describe the insignificant mountain ranges of Australia as if they were the giant mountain chains of America. I've never striven for effect and it was hardly worth my while to attempt the description of a kangaroo or emu hunt in the glowing terms of a poetical huntsman.[65]

This comment, beautifully understated in its irony and written in February 1848 would, doubtless, have been in response to Mitchell's assertions. The Major himself adopted a highly rhetorical style, drawing heavily on literary and classical allusions, which frequently gave inaccurate and misleading descriptions of the country in question. According to Paul Carter, this approach was to some extent excusable, for Mitchell, as Surveyor-General, would have had governmental interests at heart in painting the most favourable picture possible.[66] Similar charges could never be levelled against Leichhardt, whose depictions of the country which he traversed were found, during field research carried out by the present author in 1991, to be generally fair, factual and balanced.

Secondly, Leichhardt was the first major Australian explorer capable of recording accurate scientific data. Not only did he have the breadth of knowledge and experience necessary to cope in the field with the classificatory and descriptive demands of botany, geology, geography and zoology, but he was also capable, on his return to Sydney, of using specialised reference texts to catalogue unknown specimens. Indeed, while working at the MacArthur residence at Camden, where he had been invited in order to concentrate on the writing-up of his Journal uninterrupted by social demands, Leichhardt commented that after six weeks '... the necessity of referring to my collection and to several books compelled me to return to Sydney ...'[67] Like most other early field researchers in New South Wales, Leichhardt suffered from the lack of a resource museum and the inadequacy of available reference texts. In a letter to the French botanist, Gaetano Durando, in June 1842, he pointed out that, while Robert Brown's *Prodomus florae Noviae Hollandiae insulae Van Diemen* was extremely useful, particularly for researchers such as himself, he lacked texts on several major botanical families and commented that any such works which Durando might forward would be greatly appreciated. Eventually, although quite capable of identifying and cataloguing botanical specimens, Leichhardt was forced to admit, in 1847, that such work was better done by others:

> It is the business of the savant with his library, with his large collections and botanical gardens to work out the materials of the traveller and to prepare for the latter a ready, digestible food, which will keep his knowledge 'au courant' and will render him more adapted to make *judicious collections.*[68]

Finally, although Chisholm's comment that Leichhardt frequently combined several days' observations under the one date is correct, his assertion that this practice led to inaccuracies requires qualification. After several readings of the Journal in preparation for the field work carried out in 1991 and 1993, the present author did not find it difficult to establish the days on which particular events occurred. Unlike the well-funded explorers, Leichhardt had no second-in-command to relieve him, no qualified person apart from Gilbert to carry out the vital reconnaissances and a huge workload in overseeing the collection, preparation and cataloguing of specimens. It is therefore understandable why, once back in the camp after several days spent reconnoitring and with the prospect of breaking camp on the following day, he dealt with several days in the one journal entry. Furthermore, when the Journal is read in conjunction with the Field Maps, almost no uncertainty remains. For example, Chisholm argues that by placing the naming of the Mitchell River under the entry of 16 June, Leichhardt:

> ... offended against accuracy (for) ... Gilbert, who was meticulous in regard to geographical titles, has no reference at all to the naming of the new river, so that it becomes clear that Leichhardt did not 'take the liberty' of honouring his rival explorer until at least some weeks later.[69]

Yet Leichhardt's field maps reveal that the day on which he mentioned camping alongside the future Highbury Lagoon was also the day on which he tentatively decided to name the new river the Mitchell, should it subsequently not prove to be the Nassau or Staaten Rivers. As the expedition camped alongside Highbury Lagoon on 16 June, Leichhardt's placement of this naming under the entry for that day was correct, while Chisholm, who relied on Gilbert, is wrong. Those errors and carelessness which do occasionally occur in Leichhardt's Journal are understandable, given the small number of men in the expedition and his onerous workload.

Leichhardt's scientific writings were the most erudite and professional in Australian field research until Baldwin Spencer's account, in four volumes, of the Horn Scientific Expedition in 1896. In 1847, in recognition of his achievements in field research, he was awarded both the Royal Geographical Society's Patrons Medal[70] and the Grand Prix de la Société de Géographie.[71] Clearly, Leichhardt was a scientist and field researcher of the highest order, whose results, despite the handicaps under which he laboured, both merited and received the approbation of his contemporaries.

Navigation, Mapping and Route Selection

In his appraisal of Leichhardt's Port Essington expedition, Jack asserts that the explorer lacked competence in position-fixing.

> It may be said here that I have made painful and conscientious attempts to follow Leichhardt round the southern end of the Gulf by the aid of his diary and Arrowsmith's illustrative map and I warn those who may essay the task in future that 'that way madness lies'. Leichhardt did not give sufficient data for the identification of his positions on the modern map, whereas Arrowsmith, with only the coast-line to guide him, must have had even a harder task than was mine. I have come to the deliberate conclusion that all charting of this portion of Leichhardt's journey is worthless. His latitudes *must* be wrong. Perhaps his sextant was out of order. He must have been very careless about distances and bearings.[72]

Chisholm shares this view, particularly with reference to Leichhardt's longitude readings. For example, he is particularly critical of the fact that the expedition had been in progress for almost four months before the first satisfactory longitude measurement was made.[73] Concerning latitude readings, Chisholm asserts that, when approaching the latitude of the Gulf while travelling along the Burdekin and Lynd Rivers:

> ... Leichhardt had now made one of his worst blunders. Being unable to determine latitude or longitude with any preciseness, he was not aware that he was practically on a level with the base of the Gulf and should have struck due west.[74]

To an explorer, charged with producing an accurate record of his travels, the above accusations would be serious; to a field scientist they would spell professional ruin. It is therefore essential that these questions be resolved, especially when Roderick argues that:

> To represent his course of action as that of an aimless wanderer who did not know where he was or where he was going is far from the truth, as the entries in his fieldbook testify.[75]

As noted earlier, in a similar task John Whitehead, Shire Engineer of Coonabarabran, undertook in 1970 to retrace Oxley's 1818 route through that district and determine the accuracy of that explorer's longitude readings. In the preamble to his report, Whitehead outlines the early nineteenth century methods of determining latitude and longitude. Considering firstly the establishment of latitude, Whitehead writes:

> Latitude theoretically is the angle at [the] centre of the Earth between the Equator and the observer's position and can be measured by observing the angle that the sun stands above the horizon, suitable allowance being made for the sun's declination at certain times of the year.
>
> The measuring of latitude in 1818 was very accurate and it is safe to say it was as accurate as present day methods using similar equipment, ie. the navigational sextant or the theodolite. Nautical tables were available showing sun and star declination at that time, and throughout the journal it must be assumed that all [Oxley's] latitude observations are accurate in position to at least a half mile from the observed position.[76]

Verification of this level of accuracy can be found in Captain John Lort Stokes' comment that, after one hundred observations at Port Essington in the late 1830s, the mean latitude was fifteen seconds, or slightly more than a quarter of a mile, south of Captain Stanley's original determination of that point.[77] Establishing longitude was not such an easy task, though, as Whitehead clearly outlines.

> The longitude of a place is the 'difference in arc measure between its local time and that at the reference meridian at the same instant of time'; observation of the difference of time between two places determines their difference of longitude.
>
> Nowadays all longitudes have their base on Greenwich in London. This was also the case in 1818, for British Sailors, but at that time not all Countries adopted Greenwich as the Standard Meridian.[78]

Longitude can be determined by three methods: by comparing local solar time with Greenwich Mean Time; by celestial observations alone; or by measurement and triangulation from base points of known longitude. Mitchell used the third method which, while not explaining his inaccuracy,[79] helps account for his slow rate of travel and often unsatisfactory selection of routes. By contrast, by using the first method:

> To find one's actual position, it is only necessary to take the time of apparent noon at your location by observing the highest point reached by the sun with a theodolite and noting the Greenwich

time when this occurs ... In actual longitude measurement one hour of time represents fifteen degrees of longitude.[80]

Clearly, this particular technique requires accurate and well-cared-for timepieces, for '... an error of four seconds in time means an error of one minute of angle (or arc) which is one nautical mile along the Equator.'[81] Because his cheap chronometer had stopped, Leichhardt was forced to use the method of celestial observation. Unfortunately this technique relies on satisfactory sightings which, as Leichhardt found, can be a problem in the tropics. In fact the technique was not then sufficiently rigorous to guarantee any position in Australia, as Lort Stokes pointed out in the early 1840s, 'I much question whether any portion of the continent is accurately determined with reference to Greenwich.'[82]

Stokes' reservations have since been shown to be well founded, as research has demonstrated that in the nineteenth century measuring longitude by lunar distance gave an average error thirty times greater than that achieved by prevailing latitude measurement techniques.[83]

Given that longitude determination in the field was so far from exact, the quality of Leichhardt's results can only be judged in comparison with those of the other major contemporary explorers, most of whom had access to techniques of potentially greater accuracy and the best equipment available.

John Whitehead found Oxley's longitudes in the Warrumbungles region to be consistently discrepant by 8'30", no doubt because of a faulty chronometer.[84] Mitchell, when following Oxley's route of 1831, found his longitudes along the Macquarie River to be up to 30' different from those calculated by his predecessor. Not surprisingly, Mitchell assumed that Oxley's figures were in error.[85] In the 1820s, when Allan Cunningham was working northwards from Bathurst in the New England Ranges, he detected a 2'23" variation in longitude between the reading determined by triangulation and measurement and that arrived at by celestial observations.[86] By the late 1830s and early 1840s, when Stokes was engaged in his several circumnavigations and mapping of the Australian coastline, he frequently observed discrepancies of several miles between his readings and those indicated on the Admiralty Charts. One example of relevance to Leichhardt, was Stokes' placement of '... Cape [Danger] 27¼ miles east of Port Essington, instead of 20, as it is laid down in the Chart. This discovery is of vital importance to ships proceeding to Port Essington ...'[87] This error, which is greater than Leichhardt's average discrepancy over his last ten sightings, was the work of professional position-fixers using the best possible equipment not subject to the physical stresses of terrestrial exploration.

Later examples include Favenc's citing of Burke and Wills mistaking of the mouth of the Flinders River for that of the Albert in north-west Queensland. This error of over eighty kilometres prompted Favenc to comment that 'Leichhardt did not err so widely as Burke and Wills.'[88] Favenc also notes that when Captain Frome, the Surveyor-General of South Australia, attempted to map Lake Torrens, he found that Eyre had placed it fifty kilometres too far to the east.[89] It seems that longitudinal errors were common among South Australian explorers and Surveyors-General alike. According to Mona Webster, for instance, Babbage's and Stuart's maps of the Chambers Creek area disagreed so markedly that a government survey party under G W Goyder was sent in the late 1850s to resolve the problem.[90] Stuart was later embroiled in a more serious controversy regarding the location of the point where his expedition finally broke through to the Timor Sea. Through an error in measuring longitude he believed that the site was close to the Adelaide River, when in fact it was near the Mary River. Webster records that, as a result:

> His descriptions of the country along the Mary were taken as applying to the Adelaide and, when the settlement of Northern Australia was undertaken by the South Australian government, confusion resulted and grave doubts were cast upon the veracity of Stuart's journals. The mystery was only solved by the explorations and surveys of David Lindsay between 1879 and 1883.[91]

Finally, when in 1896 the members of the Calvert Scientific Exploring Expedition were in a critical situation in the Great Sandy Desert, south of the Fitzroy River in Western Australia, they were relying heavily on being able to locate Joanna Springs, which had been found and named by Warburton over twenty years previously. Unfortunately the springs could not be found, for as Wells pointed out:

> We all knew the finding of Joanna Springs was very doubtful, as Warburton was so much out in his reckoning when he reached the Oakover (River) that he said the position of this spot must be uncertain ...[92]

Consequently the expedition struggled desperately to survive, being reduced to travelling at night in order to reach the Fitzroy. Clearly position-fixing continued to be an exercise of dubious accuracy for decades after the disappearance of Leichhardt.

A major element of the field work carried out in connection with this book was to locate the sites of Leichhardt's latitude and longitude readings and to compare the modern coordinates of such sites with the results of the explorer's own observations. The methodology employed involved detailed studies of the maps and diaries of Leichhardt and other expedition members, the reconciliation of Leichhardt's recorded sites with probable corresponding locations on maps of the modern 1:100,000 Australian Topographic Map Series and field observations at such sites using Magellan Global Positioning Sattelite (GPS) equipment.

The re-measurement of latitude at positively identified sites where Leichhardt made similar observations demonstrates that, on average, he was 1'04", or approximately two kilometres discrepant from the GPS figure. In most instances his measurement placed him slightly south of his true latitude. The GPS findings tend to vindicate Leichhardt's assessment of the accuracy of his latitude readings. In October 1847 he pointed out to F N Isaac of the Darling Downs, that his figures and Mitchell's were almost identical, especially in the vicinity of the Maranoa River: '... my latitudes agree beautifully and I felt great satisfaction in finding that my map agreed so well with that of the Surveyor-General.'[93]

Leichhardt's longitude measurements could not be verified with the same precision. Not only did he make fewer longitude observations, but the majority of them were also made westward from Normanton, where in 1991 the exact location of campsites was rarely possible.[94] Nevertheless, based on the available evidence, Leichhardt's longitude readings were, on average, 18'57", or approximately thirty-four kilometres discrepant from those made using GPS equipment, or calculated from the relevant topographic map. Although this is not a particularly satisfactory result, even in comparative terms, the measurements warrant a closer study. The accuracy of Leichhardt's observations improved with practice, for the average error of his last ten observations on the Port Essington expedition was about 5'50", or approximately ten and a half kilometres.[95] This clear evidence of improvement in Leichhardt's observation technique negates Roderick's argument that the error was relatively constant and probably attributable to a mechanical fault in the explorer's equipment. Indeed, while seventeen of the first nineteen sightings were in error to the west, the last six observations were in error to the east, suggesting the delicate instruments had been damaged in transit through the frequently thick scrub — a problem which plagued many explorers, both in Australia and elsewhere.

In short, since Leichhardt's readings consistently placed him within approximately two kilometres of latitude and, for the final third of the expedition at least, within approximately ten kilometres of longitude of his true location, both Chisholm's and Jack's assertions as to his navigational incompetence can be rejected.

But Robert Jack also maintains that Leichhardt's maps, especially of the area between the Staaten River and Normanton, provided insufficient detail to allow him, seventy-five years later, to follow the route with any precision. The same documents also gave rise to claims that Leichhardt had confused the stream which Gregory later named the Leichhardt, with the Albert River and that he had failed to chart the Albert on his maps.

In rebuttal of Jack's first assertion, extensive personal academic and field research has demonstrated that, by and large, Leichhardt's route can be followed with a considerable degree of accuracy. Of the explorer's 309 campsites, the position of seventy-nine can be established exactly, a further thirty-five can be established within a probable 400-metre range and ninety-three within a probable range of 400 to 800 yards.[96] That the section from the Mitchell River turning point to Port Essington cannot be traced with the same precision as the preceding section is not denied, but with highly magnified copies of Leichhardt's field maps, the diaries of Leichhardt, Gilbert, Murphy and Phillip, modern large-scale topographic maps and a satellite-based system of establishing coordinates in the field, it can be shown that Leichhardt established the overall route for the second section with considerable accuracy.

Jack's criticism of Leichhardt's mapping was based on inadequate evidence. Firstly, it is extremely doubtful that he would have had access to Leichhardt's field maps, given that photocopiers, microfilms and facsimile machines were not available in the 1920s. That he was a Queensland Government official makes it even more unlikely that he would have seen the originals, which are stored in the Mitchell Library in Sydney. Further, if Roderick is to be believed, '... it should be added that Jack never consulted Leichhardt's fieldbook.'[97] Secondly, Jack did not have access to accurate large-scale topographic maps compiled from aerial photographs. Indeed, on one occasion, he qualified his campsite placements with the proviso that he was 'assuming the correctness of the modern map ...'[98] Finally, since Jack was therefore unable to arrive at an average latitude error for Leichhardt, he was in no position to accept or reject the explorer's posited campsite positions.

The claim that Leichhardt confused rivers or overlooked them altogether can, as a result of the present author's 1991 and 1993 field research, be totally rejected. There is irrefutable evidence that he included every major river he crossed. Furthermore, given that Leichhardt was often, for the sake of easier progress, travelling up to two kilometres away from rivers and thus had to infer their course, his configurations are, for the most part, surprisingly accurate.

A simultaneous reading of both Leichhardt's Journal and Field Maps indicates that he recorded, but did not specifically name, the Leichhardt River. Not only did Leichhardt capture it very accurately in his Field Map, but also commented on it in his Journal and, in a letter written in 1846 to Captain P P King, stated that:

> ... I crossed another considerable Saltwater [river] between both [the Albert and the Flinders Rivers] which does not appear to have any connection with either.[99]

There are several possible reasons why Leichhardt tentatively named this stream the Albert. (It was subsequently named the Leichhardt by Augustus Gregory during his North Australia Expedition.) Given the lack of accuracy of longitudinal reckoning at that time and the fact that he was working from map information dating from the time of Tasman, when establishment of longitude would have been even more questionable, he would have been hard-pressed to determine exactly where the rivers should have been and where exactly he was. Furthermore, such rivers, which do not run at right angles to the coast and which were rarely traced inland by the early Dutch navigators, were depicted by them with considerable inaccuracy. Chisholm acknowledges these problems, pointing out that:

> Both Flinders and Stokes had found difficulty in identifying the inlets of the early Dutchman, and now Leichhardt, working farther inland, found greater difficulty in identifying either the Dutch or English discoveries. He could do no more than make guesses in many instances.[100]

Furthermore, most northern rivers are not clearly visible from the ocean, their mouths often being diffuse systems of mangrove-lined distributaries and sandbars, and the ships carrying out the original mapping were frequently forced to keep well offshore in shoaling waters. Consequently there was a limited correlation between rivers existing and rivers mapped. The notion that Leichhardt had only to keep counting the rivers as he crossed them and to tick them off against those shown on Arrowsmith's map in order to determine his position, is a gross over-simplification of the problem.

In a general critique of Leichhardt's mapping standards, Chisholm claims that his failure to observe the true Albert River demonstrates that he was an incompetent scientist and cartographer. Once again it is an assertion based on a false premise. A careful review in the field of all available evidence demonstrated unequivocally that Leichhardt first reached and recorded the Albert at the point where he described it as a small river approximately forty metres in width. He crossed the Albert further upstream, at a point where it was much narrower and densely lined with Melaleucas and other waterloving species. This watercourse was named Beames Brook in honour of a Sydney grocer who had assisted the expedition by the provision of stores.[101] He then proceeded four or five kilometres westward where he forded and recorded the Nicholson River. Thus, the Albert was not overlooked, but correctly recorded at this position as a brook.[102]

The final cartographic aspect of Leichhardt's Port Essington expedition, and that which aroused considerable controversy, concerns his choice of route after leaving the Burdekin River immediately north of the Valley of Lagoons. At this point the expedition was at a latitude where it would have been prudent, given the critical shortage of food and clothing, to pick up the valley of a river flowing to the south-eastern corner of the Gulf. Leichhardt chose instead to follow the Lynd River north-north-westward to its junction with the Mitchell, which he then followed for approximately ten days before retracing his steps along the western side of Cape York Peninsula. During this time not only were more of their critically meagre supplies consumed, but also Gilbert was killed. Chisholm regards this detour as Leichhardt's greatest mistake, arguing that, at the Valley of Lagoons:

> ... had he reconnoitred more effectively at this stage — he would have come upon the head of a westerly river (which he was to meet much lower down some six weeks later and name the Gilbert) and would have been taken direct to the Gulf. On the other hand, through following the Lynd north-west he was to be taken hundreds of miles out of his course and forced to describe a vast semicircle. Moreover, through this digression the party was to lose many weeks of precious time and undergo its most tragic experience.[103]

Roderick answers these charges by pointing out that Leichhardt found no water in his reconnaissance west of the Burdekin and thus '... the only course was to make for the ranges he had seen to the north-west and to keep on a line that might assure the cavalcade of water.'[104] It was along this geographic divide that they found the Lynd River. Once on the Lynd, their options were severely circumscribed due to the rugged nature of the terrain, which more or less locked them into following its course. Roderick quotes Gilbert's description of this country to support his argument.

> ... unless seen, no idea can be formed of the difficulty of finding a passage for tender-footed bullocks through such a mass of broken rocks; through the most rugged part of all runs the river,

> the whole bed of which is either immense blocks or pavements of the granitic rock tumbled over, or standing up in places in the most extraordinary confusion, while all the hills around are composed of separate blocks of stones, standing one upon the other in the most grotesque forms, as if piled up by man.[105]

Leichhardt could not afford to waste too much time on possibly fruitless westerly reconnoitring in such forbidding country, especially when the party was so short of food and supplies and had the option of following an assured water supply and a relatively clear, though far from easy, route beside the watercourse. The Reverend W B Clarke, a contemporary, close friend and later strong apologist and defender of Leichhardt, also argues forcefully that following the Lynd was the only course. To have attempted to break clear of the Lynd basin by swinging to the west would, he argued, have further stressed Leichhardt's animals:

> ... which had been long without shoes (and thus) might be unable to travel over the sharp rocks at the top of the mountains; whereas, if he could descend to the river whose sources were on his left, though the passage down was exceedingly rough, he should eventually arrive at open country.[106]

Leichhardt explained his actions by pointing out that, from available geographical evidence, he expected the Lynd to turn to flow to the head of the Gulf, or to join a larger river which carried the waters of the Peninsula to the south-west or south-south-west and thus lead them to the desired location on the Gulf.[107] Once on the Mitchell River, the explorer then wished to resolve the question of its point of discharge and whether it was the Nassau, which discharges into the Gulf some seventy kilometres south of the Mitchell. Surprisingly, Gilbert did not strongly oppose this scheme, although he was certainly aware that they would be retracing their steps.

In an attempt to evaluate the claims and counter-claims regarding Leichhardt's movements, both before and after leaving the Burdekin, map and field analysis were employed. A study of a small-scale map of the region indicates that, from a location approximately 190 kilometres west of Charters Towers, the Great Dividing Range curves back towards the eastern coast in a series of ranges running from south-west to north-east and that the right bank tributaries of the Burdekin in this region, such as Lolworth Creek and Basalt River are accordingly constrained. Because below the Valley of Lagoons the Burdekin Valley was pointing upstream in the general direction Leichhardt wished to go, there was no point in following either of these two smaller watercourses upstream to their source east of Mount Stewart.

The first river to provide a possible alternative route to the Burdekin was the Clarke, which joins it at 19°12'S, 145°30'E, some seventy kilometres south-east of the Valley of Lagoons. However, because the Clarke also rose too far south of the Gulf and was smaller than the Burdekin, it did not constitute a satisfactory option.

Over the 120 or so kilometres of country separating the Clarke and the Lynd, Leichhardt failed to find a major watercourse flowing to the west. For the first thirty kilometres, the drainage from the Montgomery Range to their west, came from the wrong direction. To the north of this range, the headwaters of the Dry River, which runs from the west and north-west to the Burdekin, are separated by a narrow divide from Spring Creek, which is a tributary of the Einasleigh, which in time joins the Gilbert. Leichhardt chose, however, to move further northwards up the Burdekin Valley as far as Expedition Creek, beside which the expedition camped. Again, had he followed this valley to its head, near Mount McBride, he would have been only about fifteen kilometres from the headwaters of creeks like the Elizabeth and the Cassidy, which feed the Einasleigh. That Leichhardt failed to perceive the narrowness of the divide above Dry River and Expedition Creek is hardly surprising, for this area is quite hilly and in 1991 was still thickly covered with forest ten to fifteen metres high. Visibility was often no more than 200 metres and overviews of the country ahead rarely possible. For the explorer to miss such a small opportunity, particularly when it was not known to exist, is understandable.

Once past Mount McBride, however, the expedition was locked into the Lynd River system. In the early stages, the north-westerly direction of travel would have been satisfactory for almost seventy kilometres, to the junction of the Tate River, at latitude 17°20'S. Seven kilometres below this point, however, the Lynd swung to the north-north-west and north, which was ninety degrees off Leichhardt's desired course.

It is hard to understand why, at this stage, Leichhardt did not reconnoitre over the narrow, twenty-metre-high divide to the west, which for almost 160 kilometres downstream separates, by no more than five kilometres, the Lynd and Mitchell from the westward-flowing tributaries of the Staaten. On the other hand, such a reconnaissance might well have been misleading, since, for their first thirty kilometres at least, the Staaten's tributaries flow more or less parallel to the Lynd.

In summary, the limited field research done in the Burdekin and Lynd River areas has indicated that Leichhardt has been unfairly criticised in regard to becoming locked into the Lynd River system. Field observations carried out to date also tend to vindicate his pursuing the Lynd until at least in the region of 17°10'S, but cannot explain why, from this point, he did not attempt to strike westwards to the Gulf.

LEICHHARDT THE BUSHMAN

Although criticisms of Leichhardt as scientist and explorer are wide-ranging and profound, they do not match the intensity of claims concerning his alleged lack of bushmanship. Chisholm leads the attack with a broadside:

> It is clear, however, that Leichhardt merely blundered through. He went ahead for the most part in a bull-at-a-gate manner. His brain, it would seem, was unable to function to any extent over more than a brief period at any one time and so he rarely profited by hard experience. His native hue of resolution was never sicklied o'er with the pale cast of thought; it was, as his fate emphasises, simply a fanatical determination.[108]

More specifically, Chisholm then cites the impressions of the wealthy New South Wales grazier, A W Scott.

> But to make a sound bushman of him, Scott discovered, was a hopeless task. His poor eyesight prevented him from using a gun; he had little sense of direction, no real self-reliance, no resource. He lost his horse through carelessness; he lost papers and specimens through failing to guard a campfire; and between whiles he got into trouble with various creatures, ranging from ants to bulls.[109]

In his 1888 memoirs and reminiscences of early life in Queensland, H W Russell makes a similar observation, recalling that Leichhardt and his local guide had once passed by the Russell homestead without noticing it.

> 'But how did you manage to miss it, Doctor?'.
>
> 'Well! I was looking all over the ground and up the trees and through the air for what I could see, my friend: but I did not see your cottage.' 'That wouldn't do for Port Essington, Doctor: You'd have to keep your eyes open for something else than butterflies, beetles, berries and Botany bundles.'[110]

Russell further comments that his bush mentor, William Orton, was dismissive of Leichhardt's bushmanship and of the likelihood of his ever developing such skills.

> He crawls along with his compass and thingummies; why, we two, sir, and Jemmy to get honey and use his eyes, could do it in

> half the time he'll take about it: 'tis my belief, if Doctor Leichhardt do it at all, 'twill be more by good luck than good management. Why, sir, he hasn't got the knack of some of us, why, it comes to some like mothers milk! can't tell how or why, but it does. Some of my mates on the Big River were no better at the year's end in the bush than they were in the beginning. Regular crawlers. Mark my words, sir, Doctor Leichhardt hasn't got it in him and never will get it. I don't mean to be disrespectful; and I don't mean to say he can't and won't get there: he's a brave gentleman, I don't want to be told that: but how he will get there in his way, I can't guess, and don't like thinking about: he's no bushman, and I say again sir, if you go you'll be sorry for it. Then again, what does he know about the darkies? I know them better than he: and I can't say that I should care to be in a mess with them, when he won't carry even a gun: and if he did, can't use one.[111]

In addition, Favenc states that he could not understand how Leichhardt, who was so '... destitute of tact and readiness of resource ever achieved the journey to Port Essington, favoured even as he was on that occasion by circumstances and seasons.'[112]

Besides drawing attention to Leichhardt's inexperience and lack of bushmanship, Chisholm also criticises the poor quality of his companions. He attributes the selection of unpromising and inexperienced men for the Port Essington expedition to Leichhardt's worry that he might be incapable of controlling 'men of any spirit' and thus not a '... single selection was made on a basis of experience and ability.' The expedition was consequently composed of '... the most dubious band of explorers in Australian annals.'[113]

Chisholm goes on to criticise Leichhardt's arrangements for the proposed 1846 expedition to the Swan River settlement.

> Quite oblivious to the lessons afforded by his first journey, here he was on the Darling Downs, in December of 1846, preparing to attempt a crossing of the driest part of the continent in the hottest period of the year. The idea was, firstly, to risk the summer rains and pests of the tropics by making north as far as Peak Range, and then to strike fairly across Australia and so down the west coast to Perth.
>
> The whole adventure was expected to occupy two and a half years. His food supplies were inadequate for even half that period; his equipment was relatively trivial, and, as a crowning example of blind foolishness, he carried next to nothing in the way of drugs or medicines.[114]

In short, Scott, Russell and Favenc all argue that Leichhardt was seriously deficient in the essential skills of bushmanship, while Chisholm further asserts that the explorer also failed to learn from what Favenc called 'the long training and teaching of experience.'[115] Therefore, in assessing criticisms of Leichhardt as a bushman, it is necessary both to consider the experience he had gained prior to setting off on the Port Essington expedition and to identify any evidence of subsequent learning.

According to Roderick, in the thirty-two months Leichhardt spent in Australia prior to the Port Essington expedition, he devoted a considerable amount of time to field research. Beginning with unmounted half-day and day excursions from Sydney, he progressed to using graziers' properties as bases from which to carry out more extensive projects. Initially he frequently stayed in out-station huts but, after acquiring horses, ventured further, to the point where he came to be at ease camping in hollow trees, in which he also stored his food and specimens. On one occasion his paper for pressing botanical specimens caught fire and shortly after this incident a spark from the campfire set alight the dry brushes which he was using for bedding.[116] Leichhardt appears to have learnt from these incidents, for they were never repeated. Another early problem was his failure to secure his horses at night, which frequently entailed days spent in retrieving them. As we have seen, increasing proficiency brought greater confidence, with Leichhardt eventually travelling through the New England Ranges to the Darling Downs and back to Sydney. Thus, as the explorer noted in July 1843, in a letter to his grazier friend Helenus Scott of the Bunya Mountains, he had '... seen a great part of the colony and I am now almost at its northern extremity.'[117] Ten months later he wrote to Walker Scott of Sydney, excusing himself for leaving his posessions for so long, as he had '... never thought that my journey to Glendon and to Bengalla would extend to a line of short of 2,500 miles.'[118] Nevertheless, even such a wealth of experience, which certainly exceeded that of Sturt, Mitchell and possibly even Roe at similar stages in their careers, fails to satisfy Chisholm.

> True, the aspiring explorer had just completed an overland journey of more than two thousand miles and, although he had suffered all manner of misadventures, it was possible he had learnt at least something of bush life. But to travel through the partly settled areas between Sydney and Brisbane was one matter and to attack the unknown regions north of Brisbane was quite another proposition.[119]

Leichhardt, however, had a more favourable opinion of his own competence, noting in a letter to his mother in August 1843:

> The transported convicts, whom they call 'old hands' [have] ... lived where they are for a long time and have gained considerable experience. It's wonderful to see how many things a man like that can turn his hand to. He's a shepherd, stockman, builder, sawyer, timber cutter, carpenter and blacksmith; he can treat sick horses and sheep; he can bake bread, cook and sew — in short, he can do everything that's called for if you live in the bush. Besides all this, he has remarkable endurance, can walk for long distances or ride hundreds of miles in one stage — Life in the bush is very instructive. A man discovers his own powers and I've had a great deal of this kind of experience myself, which means that I'm a fairly good bushman by now.[120]

That he could, at least to some measure, 'do everything that's called for if you live in the bush' is demonstrated by his treatment for ophthalmia, a condition which had affected explorers since the time of Sturt's first expedition. On that occasion, while travelling across large dry floodplains, several of Sturt's men were badly infected, apparently from the thick dust arising from the fine dry soil and the heat, flies and generally unsanitary conditions. It is surprising that inland explorers had remained immune for so long for, in a report to the Royal College of Physicians in 1830, Governor Darling stated that the first cases in New South Wales had been noted in April 1794. He pointed out that the disease was so virulent that, '... when it got into a House, scarcely any person escaped it.' As well, he noted that if left untreated, it could lead to blindness. [121]

Eyre also suffered, reporting that in the vicinity of Lake Torrens:

> The flies were also incessant in their persecuting attacks. What with flies and dust and heat and disposition, I scarcely ever remember to have spent a more disagreeable day in my life. My eyes were swollen and very sore and altogether I was scarcely able to attend to any other thing, or employ myself in any profitable way.[122]

Mitchell's men were affected as well,[123] with the disease on one occasion bringing the entire expedition to a halt when the second-in-command, Kennedy, who was responsible for the ground survey, was afflicted by 'purulent ophthalmia during the day and was quite blind and had to be led in.'[124]

Despite the severity of the infection, no explorer before Leichhardt was capable of treating it successfully. Russell paid tribute to Leichhardt's skill in this matter, recollecting that at his property on one occasion in the early 1840s there were:

> ... three men here and one with a wife and two children; and not one of the poor things could have seen you pass. I can't leave this; and it is a misery to be here — specially at night — and listen to their groaning with pain from 'sandy-blight'. If it had attacked me too, we shouldn't have had a pair of eyes amongst us. So I have to do everything for all! 'What is that?' broke in Leichhardt, 'the sandy-blight? eh? It is Egyptian ophthalmia: I will cure it: a little waterplease: I will look to them'. He opened a little case: took from it some nitrate of silver: made a solution: a few drops under the lids upon each blood-blotch of an eye, and a most marvelous immediate relief and — within twenty four hours — a complete cure was the effect.[125]

Leichhardt always carried silver nitrate on his subsequent explorations, reporting during his second expedition that '... I (have) had several attacks of blight which however yielded readily to a strong solution of Nitrate of Silver.'[126]

Even if Chisholm is right in classifying the members of the Port Essington expedition as a 'most dubious band of explorers', this fact may simply point to the severe limitations of choice open to Leichhardt at that time. Indeed the explorer had already made clear the type of men he was looking for, whilst simultaneously criticising Mitchell's selection policy. Speaking of Henry Russell and his associates, who he hoped would accompany him to Port Essington, Leichhardt wrote:

> ... I know that if I start with these men, whom I know to be excellent bushman, excellent shots and without fear, I am sure to succeed. ... Every one of us has lived weeks and weeks together in the bush, frequently surrounded by hostile blacks, whose character we know and intercourse with whom we shall always try to avoid. Believe me that one experienced and courageous bushman is worth more than the eight soldiers Sir Thomas intends to take with him. They will be an immense burthen and of no use.[127]

That Leichhardt's awareness of the desirable did not necessarily translate into the actual was almost certainly due to a shortage of money. Furthermore, because he was not expected to succeed on his first expedition, he was unable to attract capable volunteers. By the time of his second expedition, however, with a sound reputation behind him, he could be more discriminating, selecting surveyor John Mann, botanical collector Daniel Bunce and self-appointed veterinarian Henry Turnbull. Irish journeyman saddler James Perry, German tanner Henry Boecking and Aborigine Harry Brown from the first expedition were also members of the party. A second native, Wommai, and Hovendon Hely, who had no specific qualifications, were selected as well. On the final expedition Leichhardt again took Wommai and also selected Arthur Hentig, who had had several years' experience in station work, and two other men who were accustomed to physical work.

The record of Leichhardt's mobility and stock husbandry refutes Chisholm's assertion that the explorer failed to learn from experience. In his earlier field work carried out in the New England Ranges and the Darling Downs, Leichhardt became competent in the handling of riding and packhorses. He therefore initially planned to use both types of animal on the Port Essington expedition.[128] Chisholm's claim that Leichhardt had envisaged using packhorses only is difficult to reconcile with the explorer's unequivocal statement that he intended taking 'thirteen horses, six for riding and seven to carry our provisions.'[129] Nevertheless, whatever the truth of the matter, he was apparently persuaded to use pack-bullocks[130] by John Campbell, a Darling Downs grazier. Such animals were reputed to have a 110-kilogram load-carrying capacity and their edibility reduced the amount of food that needed to be carried. Furthermore, the fact that bullocks were almost certainly cheaper than horses would have appealed to Leichhardt, who was in financial difficulties. The explorer was able to accumulate sixteen bullocks, as gifts and by purchase, but had to adapt packhorse saddles for their use. It is not surprising that this makeshift gear never fitted properly, severely galling the bullocks for weeks and causing them considerable pain and discomfort. In addition, Leichhardt and his men, being inexperienced with such animals, found that it took:

> ... a long time before we were reconciled to the dangerous vicinity of their horns. By means, however, of iron nose-rings with ropes attached, we obtained a tolerable command over their movements; and, at last, by dint of habit, soon became familiar with, and even got attached to, our blunt and often refractory *compagnons de voyage*.[131]

As a result of problems encountered on the first expedition, the 1846 expedition saw some important innovations. Firstly mules, purchased mainly from the Australian Agricultural Company, were selected as pack animals. Experience had shown Leichhardt that their load-carrying capacity was considerably greater than that of horses and bullocks. The wisdom of his choice was demonstrated when one, Don Pedro, escaped after being loaded, and roamed free on the Darling Downs for nearly a day before being found. Notwithstanding his exertions, to Leichhardt's admiration, on his return the beast '... trotted with the greatest of ease into the stockyard.'[132]

In addition, the mules' hard black hooves made them less prone to footsoreness. While proceeding northwards through the New England Ranges to the setting-off point on the Darling Downs, Leichhardt was thus able to comment that:

> The mules are all in excellent condition and generally admired. They showed their superiority even now in coming along, as none of them were footsore through constantly travelling over the hard and rocky road of New England whilst all of my horses were footsore and some nearly knocked-up, when arriving at Canning Downs ...[133]

Leichhardt had also equipped his expedition with eight horses for the expedition members and six spares in case of galling,[134] 270 goats, thirty-six bullocks and between eighty and a hundred wethers, which were to be killed as required. He was well aware of the possibility of consequent stockhandling problems.

> There is even the chance of increased difficulties, as we take four different kinds of animals, goats, bullocks, horses and mules, every one of which has its peculiar habits and requires attention ...[135]

The failure of the 1846 expedition was due, not to difficulties with livestock, but to wet season flooding and the onset of a severely debilitating tropical disease. Nevertheless, Leichhardt chose to take only pack mules, riding horses and rations bullocks on the 1848 expedition. Unlike Mitchell, he had learnt the advantage of a fully mounted team which was not encumbered by sheep or goats. Indeed, while returning from the aborted second expedition without his killing stock, which had been lost or abandoned, he took only thirty days to cover the distance which on the outward trip took approximately eight weeks. Leichhardt attributed this accelerated rate of travel '... from Peak Range to the last station on the Condamine, (to their being) unencumbered by cattle or sheep, which latter were a heavy drawback to us.'[136]

Thus Leichhardt had not only reached the same conclusions concerning pack animals as those reached by Gregory on his earliest exploration in 1846, but also, on the question of droving sheep as killing stock, had anticipated him by almost ten years.

Even on the Port Essington expedition, encumbered by the unsatisfactory pack bullocks, Leichhardt's adaptability soon enabled him to increase his rate of travel beyond that of Mitchell or Sturt. It is nevertheless true that the daily distances covered in the first few months were generally short, for the bullocks were frequently badly footsore from travelling over broken range country and across numerous gullies. Furthermore, the scrub and undergrowth along the early stages of their route were frequently extremely dense. In addition, the bullocks often threw their loads to relieve the pain from the galls caused by their ill-fitting pack-saddles. Even on good days, travel was normally restricted to about four hours. Later, however, once the expedition came to the lower reaches of the Lynd and the Mitchell, where the country was relatively flat, grassy and sparsely timbered, the daily travelling rate improved considerably. Chisholm acknowledges this fact, pointing out that even on the Burdekin River, the daily average was nearly sixteen kilometres, and that '... in the circumstances, the covering of such distances in such a period was a stout achievement.'[137]

In 1848, as he was about to leave the settled area behind him, Leichhardt was confident enough of his fully mounted third expedition, with its pack mules and rations bullocks, to predict that it would travel 'at the rate of 10 to 15 miles a day.'[138] Such a rate, although less than that of later explorers such as Roe and Gregory, with their all-horse teams, was a considerable improvement over that of most of his peers.

Leichhardt was also highly efficient at reconnoitring. Frequently he would move well in advance of the main party. On one occasion between the Nicholson River and Moonlight Creek, he was in the saddle from 10 p.m. until 6 p.m. the following day, with a rest of only one hour.[139] Perhaps the most striking appraisal of his proficiency both at reconnoitring for water and husbanding his stock can be made by comparing his activities with those of the horse-mounted reconnaissance patrols in the inaccessible regions of northern Australia during 1942 and 1943, when invasion by Japan appeared imminent. On one occasion two such patrols left simultaneously, one from Borroloola and one from the Roper River base, intending to meet up at the Limmen Bight River. Despite having well-fed horses, adequate provisions, spare mounts and, most importantly of all, local Aboriginal guides, these patrols were fortunate to survive. One member of the Roper River patrol suffered so badly from thirst he began hallucinating and had to be knocked unconscious for his own safety. The Borroloola patrol lost thirteen horses and mules out of twenty-five, with the men and the surviving beasts suffering dreadfully.[140] Yet Leichhardt traversed this region at almost the same time of year with no particular difficulty, notwithstanding that at this stage of his expedition he and his men had only dried beef, local game and edible plants to eat, and powdered roasted acacia beans to produce a beverage. Furthermore, by then he had almost no spare riding horses and his horses and bullocks had been travelling almost continuously for twelve months.

In the matter of horsemanship, there is evidence that Leichhardt was both an intelligent observer and a practical man, willing to experiment to overcome problems. During the Port Essington expedition he learnt the importance of washing horses' backs to prevent galling and of taking advantage of any available native feed. Horses and bullocks had to be hobbled and at least one night horse tethered near the camp. Perhaps most importantly of all, Leichhardt came to agree with Stuart and Sturt that constitution and endurance are not purely physiological factors; '... it is in a great degree the spirit, which carries man and beast through difficulties.'[141]

Leichhardt's conduct of his subsequent expeditions clearly reflected the application of what he had learnt in 1844–5. For example, as a direct result of the problems with the pack-saddles on the first expedition, he not only investigated the requirements of mules, as he had learnt from Captain P King that they required a 'peculiar sort of pack saddle', but also instructed his saddler to provide for individual differences. He maintained that, by:

> ... more careful measurement and fitting to their backs, (he would be able) to avoid sore backs, I should be most willing, to have it done as I know too well of what great importance good harness is.[142]

Experience had also taught him that the serge linings of pack saddles had only a limited life. He therefore arranged for his pack saddles to be lined with leather and thus be capable of standing 'a two years scrubbing'.[143]

Galling, however, remained a problem on the second expedition. Leichhardt freely admitted that, although the mules carried their loads 'through bog and scrubs and over mountains with wonderful strength. We could not prevent their getting sore backs.'[144] He blamed the condition on the mules' habit of grazing as they went, for:

> ... if allowed to feed, they try to run ahead to obtain a few moments to take a bite and consequently they break their steady step which is the principal cause of their sore backs.[145]

In an effort to prevent a recurrence of the problem during the third expedition, the saddler was instructed to make 'strong leather head-halters' for each animal, which would enable Leichhardt to '... rein them up and to prevent them from feeding during the journey ...'[146] While this practice would reduce the mules' ability to maintain their footing in rough country if they were reined up too short, it would not be difficult, by judicious experimentation, to establish the correct rein length for each animal. Thus Leichhardt could achieve his aim without endangering the animals in any way.

Leichhardt, like Mitchell and Eyre, also came to realise the necessity of not overtaxing his stock early in the expedition if they were in soft condition. To this end he contemplated putting the mules into work for three months before the start of his third expedition, so that they would be 'well worked' and in harder condition on the setting-off date. By doing so he would have obviated the need to reduce the daily mileages in the earlier part of the expedition, as Eyre had done in 1840.

In 1846, however, Leichhardt's mules were neither well-worked nor well-disciplined. In attempting to take the 'flashness' out of one of them the explorer was unseated several times and badly kicked in the arm. As some of these mules had been little handled and were difficult to catch without the danger of being kicked, he circled their necks with greenhide ropes, which trailed behind on the ground. He was not completely happy with the arrangement, noting that '... this is a dangerous practice, but we saw no other means of getting hold of the cunning rogues ...'[147] His reservations were unjustified, as the same technique is still being employed a century and a half later. Equally unjustified is Chisholm's accusation that Leichhardt was afraid of the mules and thrashed them irrationally. Indeed it appears that the mule problem was solved with skill, not cruelty, for Leichhardt was able to write shortly before setting off in 1848 that, 'The mules, though skittish, are by far more quiet than they were a year ago and we know better now how to manage them.'[148]

Although care of their kangaroo dogs was an additional important aspect of stockmanship for Leichhardt and his peers, Chisholm quotes Gilbert's criticism of Leichhardt for under-feeding them.

> The Dr is not a hunter and in his constant endeavours to save as much of the dried beef as possible has always taken this part from the dogs and allowanced them afterwards to perhaps half a pound per day for two or three days only. Then they had to go without until they killed again. This system, of course, ruined the dogs; it kept them in low condition and they were incapable of sustaining a length of run sufficient to catch their game.[149]

Unfortunately, game was so scarce that it would have been necessary to deprive the men of good meat in order to satisfy the appetites of the expedition's seven dogs. On the other hand, once six of them had died, the remaining animal survived on dried offal for almost a year. Furthermore, even before the completion of the first expedition, Leichhardt had determined the ideal type of explorer's dog and the means of sustaining it.

> This heat, should there be a want of water during a long stage and perhaps a run after game in addition, would inevitably kill a soft dog. It is, therefore, of the greatest importance to have a good traveller, with hard feet: a cross of the kangaroo dog with the bloodhound would be, perhaps, the best. He should be light and satisfied with little food in case of scarcity; although the dried tripe of our bullocks gave ample and good food to one dog. It is necessary to carry water for them; and to a little calabash, which we obtained from the natives of the Isaacs, we have been frequently indebted for the life of Spring.[150]

Both Favenc and Chisholm also criticise Leichhardt for the quantity of supplies and equipment taken on his three expeditions. Although Favenc is more restrained than Chisholm, he still describes of the lack of medicines on the second expedition as a 'strange omission' and the materials for the third expedition as being 'utterly inadequate'.[151] Certainly Leichhardt's supplies of foodstuffs and equipment were radically different from those of his peers, but the underlying reasons need to be examined. Firstly, in 1844, due to colonial politics and a probable personality clash, Gipps and Mitchell were at loggerheads over the Surveyor-General's proposed expedition to Port Essington. In order to thwart Mitchell, the Governor asserted on several occasions that there was no money to finance the venture. Consequently, when Leichhardt, convinced that the Mitchell expedition (and his position of natural historian in it) would not eventuate, decided to assemble his own exploring party, Gipps was unable to proffer financial assistance, supplies and equipment from the Government Stores, or logistical support in the form of resupply ships and depot bases.[152] In addition Leichhardt, who had sailed for Australia with only £200 in his pocket and had had almost no paid employment since arriving,[153] was in a poor financial position. He was therefore heavily dependent on donations of goods, equipment and livestock in order to equip his first expedition and his overall cash outlay was necessarily restricted to £130.[154] Under such circumstances, Chisholm's question as to why Leichhardt did not augment his supplies when more men volunteered to join the expedition does not require an answer. By contrast, when the explorer returned from the Port

Essington expedition in January 1846, he found that Mitchell had been outfitted for the same journey at almost eight times the cost.[155]

After the success of his first expedition, the rewards from an admiring public enabled Leichhardt more adequately to outfit his second venture. Nevertheless his budget was still forty-two per cent below Mitchell's, although he anticipated being in the field for almost twice as long as the Surveyor-General.[156]

It is clear that Leichhardt's selection of supplies and equipment for his second and third expeditions was based upon experience. He could now estimate his consumption rate, his length of time in the field and the likely extent of his breakages and losses. Above all, he was well aware that:

> The difficulty of my own journeys lies in the length of time I have to spend away from the settled districts of the colony, far from any possible source of help. I am obliged to keep the number of my companions and the quantity of my provisions as low as possible.[157]

Because of his deliberately Spartan approach, Leichhardt realised that he must proceed cautiously. In a letter to Mitchell, in July 1844, he wrote:

> What you can bear down by the force of your equipment, I can only by patience and by perseverence — I shall not do it so brilliantly, but I shall show by my unremitting efforts, how great my desire is, to investigate the nature of this continent, to which I have consecrated my life.[158]

Leichhardt has been particularly criticised over the small quantity of foodstuffs taken, compared with Sturt's and Gregory's huge weights of meat and flour. According to the explorer himself, however, he took only a token amount of flour on his second and third expeditions, because he had found '... during my last journey, that an entirely animal food agreed well with our constitution, though there was of course a constant longing for bread or damper.'[159] He also reduced the quantity of oatmeal which, in any case, deteriorated rapidly under tropical conditions.

Leichhardt's bullock herd did away with the need to set off with large quantities of dried meat. It seems, however, that in 1844 he committed himself irrevocably to the procedure of slaughtering and preserving in the field, without any local evidence of its likely success. Although similar techniques had long been practised in both South Africa and South America, it was remiss of Leichhardt to leave such a critical factor to chance.[160]

Chisholm also seizes on a comment of Gilbert's to criticise Leichhardt for the first expedition's inadequate supply of clothing. Bearing in mind, however, that the men's clothes greatly outlasted the expedition's initially estimated five months' duration, it is hard to sustain Chisholm's charge. Furthermore, as a result of the knowledge gained on the first expedition, Leichhardt was able to inform Daniel Bunce before the 1846 expedition that:

> I think that three pairs of strong moleskin trousers, three red flannel shirts, three cotton shirts, three pairs of shoes, stockings ad libitum, towels, one strong cabbage-tree hat, some combs, tooth-brushes, a housewife, scissors and a blanket will be sufficient for every man.[161]

Although Leichhardt's 1846 and 1848 supply requirements appear parsimonious, they cannot be dismissed as inadequate. He had, after all, successfully carried out the longest exploration in Australia to that date. It is, therefore, appropriate to conclude the analysis of this controversial subject with Leichhardt's succinct but highly pertinent assessment in 1848 of his experience-based knowledge.

> ... 2 blacks and 8 whites will be going with me [on the third expedition], all volunteers, all willing to live on dried beef and tea for the next 3 years, for my supplies of flour and sugar are not worth talking about — they'll hardly last for more than 6-8 months. My last expedition, however, was quite enough to show that this diet will be adequate in maintaining our health and strength.[162]

In assessing Leichhardt as a bushman, Favenc and Chisholm both make much of his alleged lack of a sense of direction, prompting Aurousseau to note that, 'A later generation (than Leichhardt's), however, has spread the belief, now widely held in Australia, that he was a very bad bushman indeed.'[163]

At the beginning of his field work, Leichhardt certainly had problems finding his way in the apparently featureless Australian bush. In November 1842, for example, he wrote of his difficulties even in the settled districts:

> It is difficult to find the way in the bush, as the people in this part of the country are not careful in marking the trees, to show that the footpath leads to an inhabited place and as many great swamps exist here, which are the favourite places for cattle, which form in filing one behind the other tracks exactly resembling to the footpaths made by man. Thus I lost my way hundred times and I had only my compass to guide me. My dear boy, you have no idea how sweet a cup of tea with brown sugar and a piece of damper tastes after such a day's journey in the

bush.[164]

An incident during the Port Essington expedition, in January 1845, in which Chisholm alleges that Leichhardt and Brown were lost for four days immediately north of the future Bedford Weir on the McKenzie River in southern Queensland, has frequently been misinterpreted. Because very heavy rain had washed out their tracks, the two men were unable to retrace their path back through the dense and featureless scrub to the main camp on the McKenzie. Nevertheless, Leichhardt was definitely not lost. In this locality the McKenzie runs from west to east and the often clearly visible Peak Ranges lie approximately forty kilometres to the north. Thus Leichhardt — who was capable of finding his course by stars, the sun and his compass — always had the option of travelling south until reaching the McKenzie and following it upstream until he found the camp. In fact, after some days' fruitless searching for their tracks, the explorer decided to return to the Peak Ranges, which they had seen some days earlier and, by using them as an orienting feature, retrace his steps. At this stage Brown recognised an area through which they had passed some days earlier and the men were able to re-orientate themselves and return to the main camp. Nevertheless, it must be stressed that at all times Leichhardt had an overview of the thirty-kilometres square piece of country in which he was located and a choice of means of finding his way back to the camp.

Leichhardt's reconnoitring skills were soon of a high order. On several occasions during the Port Essington expedition, he crossed and recrossed the Expedition Range, merely observing that it was important to note one's route carefully. In May 1845, when the main party was camped in the Valley of Lagoons, he covered a further fifty kilometres or so along Anthill Creek to Separation Creek, returning by a different route through well timbered country. Reference has already been made to perhaps the clearest demonstration of his bushmanship when, on one night in August 1845, he and Charley set out from the expedition's campsite twenty-two kilometres west of the Nicholson River. Searching for water, they headed west as far as Moonlight Creek, then separated and, avoiding natives' campfires as they went, followed it downstream for some miles before regrouping. Together they then rode across country, on a line determined by Leichhardt, heading for the tracks previously made by the main party, and followed them back to the campsite. By comparison, Stuart, while reconnoitring in 1862 in a similar landscape in the region of the Daly and Newcastle Waters, always worked by a compass, claiming that it would be fearful country to be lost in.[165] Leichhardt's bushmanship was recognised by his contemporaries, as Aurousseau reports.

> It was one of Bigge's men named Johnstone whom Steel Rudd questioned, many years afterwards, about Leichhardt's qualifications as a bushman. 'Bad bushman!' repeated Johnstone with a look of astonishment — 'When he'd be away all day in the gorges and scrub by himself and come home to the station in the dark? He couldn't do that if he was a bad bushmen, could he?'[166]

The final and possibly most telling refutation of Chisholm's claim that Leichhardt was a single-minded fanatic, incapable of learning from experience, relates to the explorer's usage of bush foods. Their diet, which included native plants, successfully protected his men from scurvy, while beverages resembling tea and coffee were made from roasted native beans. The meat from native game was dried, water containers with wallaby skin lids improvised and so on. Even Chisholm has to acknowledge Leichhardt's evolving capacity to live off the land. Writing of the events of November 1844, when the expedition was in the Palm Tree Creek area immediately north of Taroom, he states:

> The travellers were becoming mildly resourceful. They had dried the flesh of kangaroos and eels, as well as beef; they had learned to eat reptiles; they had discovered food of sorts in the pith of bottle-trees and palm-trees; they had contrived to make, from the leaf-stalk of a plant, 'a strong cordage which when made up very much resembles the coir rope of India'; and they had obtained, from the skins of emus, oil for the locks of their firearms and a salve for Leichhardt's rheumatism.
>
> Mother Necessity was at work. Thousands of years earlier she had taught, by trial and error, the ancestral blacks who had first wandered into this region and now she was teaching the first white men of the area.[167]

Leichhardt's attainments as a practising field scientist and bushman demonstrate both the relevance of his qualifications and his capacity to learn. He was also aware of the immense value of continuity in the overall development of bushmanship and of his own contribution to it. In 1846 he commented: '[In] the exploration of Australia ... I see expeditions, like Banquo's progeny, one behind the other in long long succession ...'[168]

Prophetic though these words were, Leichhardt, whose achievements clearly outstripped those of his predecessors, did not live to see the successes of those who followed him. Furthermore, although he does not deserve the title 'prince of explorers', which should fairly be reserved for the Gregory and Forrest brothers, Giles and Stuart, he nevertheless merits a prestigious position in the history of Australian exploration. Like Eyre, he was a transitional figure who played a vital role in the process whereby the old military-style, large-scale, slow-moving expeditions gave way to extremely lightly laden, intensely mobile and wide-ranging parties consisting of a handful of highly proficient bushmen.

Given both Leichhardt's secondary role and his single though significant achievement in the annals of Australian exploration, it is useful to identify those factors which prompted both his greatest champions and his most outstanding critics to adopt their extreme and opposing positions.

Certainly the most obvious is xenophobia. The writings of Chisholm, Jack, Gilbert and Leichhardt himself all demonstrate that the explorer's Prussian nationality was a potent factor underlying both his own difficulties and the subsequent opinions of his critics. As early as September 1842, Leichhardt wrote to Sir William Hooker of the Royal Botanic Gardens, informing him that he would like to name a new species of fungus after Lynd, his benefactor:

> ... as he is one of the *very few*, who also take an interest in scientific pursuits here and as he was the almost only one not biassed by national prejudice, who would support me and receive me in his house, when even the venerable Alexander M'Cleay acted against me.[169]

Chisholm also identifies a measure of ethnic prejudice in Gilbert who, in September 1844, informed the naturalist Dr George Bennett that he wished to accompany Leichhardt on the Port Essington expedition, not only for the opportunities thereby offered him in his role of Gould's collector, but also because:

> I felt a little jealous of a foreigner being the first to make known the hidden treasures of this vast and interesting country, which has been for so many years the particular province of our own countrymen.[170]

Even Leichhardt's twentieth century critics are xenophobic. Jack, writing shortly after World War I, claims that, 'In the middle of the 19th century he was a living proof that the Prussian spirit, as the world came to know it in 1914–18, was no new thing.'[171] Forty years later, Aurousseau was to write that, although Jack was no doubt 'an honourable man', his critique of Leichhardt was almost certainly 'strongly affected by the anti-German feeling of the time.'[172]

Notwithstanding his disclaimers to the contrary, Chisholm is more vehemently anti-German than Jack. In referring to the occasion when Charlie knocked Leichhardt down over a disagreement at the Isaac River camp, he asserts that '... apologists are unable to explain why he did not "fell Charlie to the ground", as an Englishman would have done ...'[173] Furthermore, in endeavouring to explain the public's adulation of Leichhardt ahead of 'Sturt and Mitchell (sound explorers both)', Chisholm is not convincing:

> The Britishers did their jobs according to schedule and the public accepted their successes as normal developments. The eccentric German, on the other hand, was not expected to succeed, and when he did make a sudden re-appearance in Sydney, months behind time, there was a strong and extravagant reaction from the attitude of 'I told you so!' His very blundering had caused him to become a public idol.[174]

Finally, by placing his writing in the context of the events of 1941, Chisholm virtually gives the game away:

> It is to be added that no pleasure is felt in submitting this indictment of Leichhardt. 'Debunking' is at best an unpleasant process, and in such a period as the present, when the British Empire is at war with Germany, there may be a temptation to suppose that a writer's judgement on such a subject is warped by national prejudice.[175]

The second factor deleteriously affecting assessments of Leichhardt is a prepensity for armchair geography on the part of his critics. Personal experience has shown that extensive physical coverage of the route in question is an essential prerequisite to any valid study and assessment of an explorer's achievements. After an intensive examination of both primary and secondary bibliographic sources, and spending more than eight months following Leichhardt's route, cautiously walking and riding over the sometimes frightening ridges of Expedition Range, traversing the gullies along the Burdekin, nursing his horses over the frequently brutally sharp shale country of central Queensland and across boggy billabongs, the present writer claims an authority grounded firmly in both library and field research. There is no evidence that either Chisholm or Roderick was physically acquainted with any substantial sections of Leichhardt's route. As we have seen above also, Jack claims to have been unable to reconcile Leichhardt's data with field evidence. If Chisholm had been acquainted with the countryside, for example, he would have rejected Gilbert's wildly exaggerated claim that where the expedition came upon the Mitchell River, sections of it were up to two kilometres wide.[176] Roderick's field experience was restricted to covering part of the route by vehicle, on the few occasions where roads allowed access. Observations of this sort are of negligible value in the assessment of Leichhardt's achievements.

Clearly, because they are not supported by field experience along Leichhardt's route, the armchair interpretations and assessments of all previous major researchers on Leichhardt are open to serious question.

Although Ludwig Leichhardt led an intensely busy and productive life, he experienced little happiness, for he confessed to being a driven man.

> Alas, it is with my science and with travelling, as it is with the desire of making money. The more you have, the more you wish to have. It is not like the social pleasures of life, which are only pleasant in moderation: as one toils up to a range of blue mountains, others confine again the horizon, one toils on again, to obtain an illimited view and comes never to an end ...[177]

It is unquestionable that Leichhardt's theoretical and practical experience in both Europe and Australia qualified him uniquely for his final proposed expedition to the Swan River Settlement. Indeed, as he wrote:

> ... I consider Exploration of this Continent my great task, which has been allotted to me and which my previous studies have rendered me capable of executing satisfactorily.[178]

Nevertheless, despite an almost obsessive commitment to the field, he regretted the long and continuing separation from family and friends. In December, 1846, he wrote:

> I hope that my dear mother (whose birthday I celebrated in silence on the 9th of November on a lonely ride across one of the broad plains of the Darling Downs) is still enjoying good health. Often, when my mind suddenly sweeps me away from the scene of a life here so different from yours, and I feel that I am back at home, I find myself wondering what mother thinks her poor wandering Ludwig is like now, and imagining how she must want to see him just once more before she dies. Tears run down my cheeks, and I turn in prayer for her, for myself, and for us all, to the Heavenly Father, who has so far kept us in his loving care.[179]

Yet Leichhardt was able to reduce the pangs of separation by drawing solace from his explorations of inland Australia. Spiritually he was at home in the bush and nowhere else. When writing of his proposed third expedition, he promised that:

> When this journey is over I shall return to Europe and shall go to see you all. But I would find it hard to remain in Germany, or even in Europe, now. I would have to return to the scene of my wanderings, to the clear, sunny skies of Australlia.[180]

Perhaps, therefore, his most fitting epitaph, which he would understand and appreciate, is to say that, in the annals of Australian field exploration and research, Leichhardt — scientist, navigator and bushman — was this country's truest polymath.

7

EXPLORING THE CENTRAL DESERT REGION

Between 1860 and 1890 signs of the first maturation of Australian science became evident. According to Moyal:

> ... *Flora Australiensis* was the last of the major systematic works carried out by extraterritorial experts on Australian botanical science, though similar growing pains were still to be experienced in other disciplines ... the days of ... deferential dependence on British leadership were over.[1]

Colonial scientists were becoming less willing to defer to those British scientists who lacked local expertise. They and the research institutions for which they worked were gradually assuming their rightful position as world authorities in studies of Australian natural science. As a consequence, and through the rapid growth of general and specialised scientific societies, the control of field research passed almost exclusively into colonial hands by 1890. Whereas earlier goals had been formulated and forwarded by British authorities, and later by their Australian representatives, after the 1860s field research plans were increasingly developed by Australian scientific societies. Nevertheless, despite the considerable improvement in scientific standards within Australia, there was little formal field research associated with exploration between 1860 and 1890.

The most prominent explorers of the period were John McDouall Stuart, Peter Egerton-Warburton the Forrest brothers and Ernest Giles, while the most conspicuously unsuccessful was Robert O'Hara Burke. After two preparatory expeditions in southern and central South Australia, Stuart made three assaults on the centre of the continent and finally succeeded in crossing Australia, reaching the coast in the vicinity of the Mary River in the Northern Territory in 1862. Egerton-Warburton crossed from Alice Springs to De Grey Station, north of Roebourne in Western Australia, in

1873–4. He had originally intended to make for Perth but conditions encountered in the Great Sandy Desert continually forced him northwards of his goal.

John and Alexander Forrest made several expeditions in Western Australia during the 1860s and 1870s. They first searched for signs of Leichhardt, some hundreds of kilometres to the east of Perth, then in 1870 travelled from Perth to Adelaide via Esperance. Their last joint expedition was eastward from the Murchison and the headwaters of the Gascoyne in 1874 to the Overland Telegraph Line. Ernest Giles made several attempts to break through to Western Australia in the Lake Amadeus and Gibson Desert region before successfully completing the task in 1875. On his westerly expedition Giles travelled through the Great Victoria Desert, but on his return to South Australia he traversed the country eastward from the headwaters of the Gascoyne River, linking up with the point in the Gibson Desert from whence he had been driven back during his second expedition. Finally, Alexander Forrest completed the peripheral exploration of Australia when he explored from Roebourne, through the Kimberleys and across to the Telegraph Line. In doing so he opened up huge areas of grazing country in the Ord and Fitzroy basins.

We have seen how field research associated with the first seventy years of Australian territorial exploration appears to have ebbed and flowed, in response to the difficulty of the country explorers were attempting and to the proficiency of the participants. The journeys of the 1860s and 1870s, across far more taxing country where explorers were vitally concerned with survival, would provide little scope for scientific activity. Only after the bushmanship skills essential for survival in the arid interior had been developed could expeditions burden themselves with the problems associated with research. It would be twenty years before the proliferation of scientific expeditions in the 1890s would provide an appropriate climax to nineteenth-century field research development in Australia.

Consequently, the purported aims of Burke and Wills' ill-fated expedition, which was supposedly concerned with methodical field research, were quite atypical of those of the majority of previous explorations. In fact, during the planning of the expedition, considerable controversy arose over whether the emphasis should be on rapid and highly mobile geographic exploration, or patient, slow-moving, methodical observation.[2] Although three observers and field researchers were selected and given very comprehensive instructions, they lacked competence and field support and were also required to carry out the same general duties as all other expedition members.

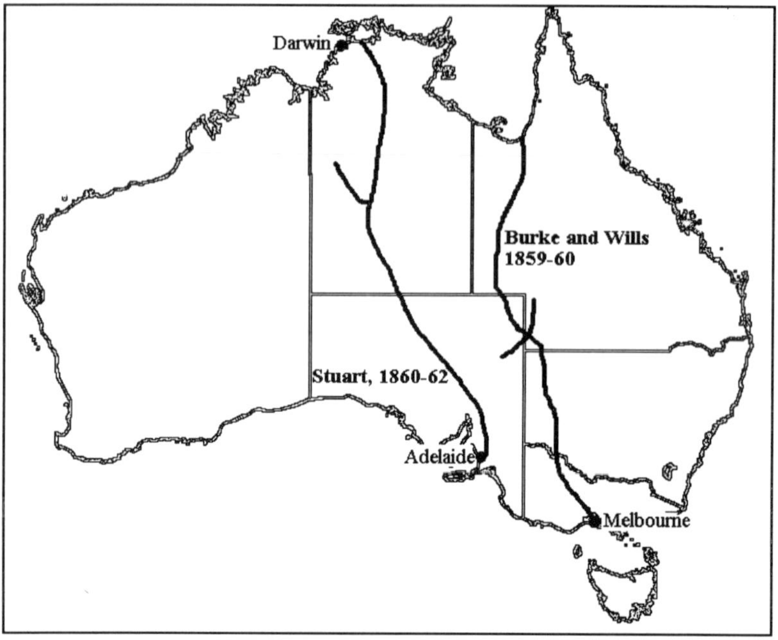

Crossing the continent.

Initially, however, the expedition appeared to be structured on the basis of scientific observation. Wills was required to carry out surveying, astronomical and meteorological observations, Becker was assigned geological, mineralogical, map-making, sketching and zoological tasks and Beckler botanical field work. Unfortunately all three lacked formal qualifications. The eclectic Becker was described by Governor Denison as a 'dabbler'. Beckler was a medical practitioner with an interest in botany, but had had limited field experience.[3] Wills' only qualification was a period of employment under Neumayer in the Melbourne Observatory. Worse still, this so-called scientific expedition had as its leader a man with no affinity for science. As Wills pointed out:

> The Exploring Expedition is postponed for six months, for want of a suitable leader, as none of the candidates who offered their services were thought qualified in a scientific point of view (oddly enough, Mr Burke, who was afterwards chosen, with many requisites of a high order, was deficient in this, which, indeed, he never for a moment pretended to possess).[4]

Despite these quasi-scientific trappings, Burke, who was obsessed with the idea of maximum mobility, soon informed all members of the expedition, scientists included, that they were to limit their personal effects to fourteen kilograms each. Furthermore, the scientists were expected to leave most of their equipment behind and work as stock-handlers, cooks and general rouseabouts. Thus little time was available for scientific observations or writing. Becker, for one, commented that he often had to work until midnight, which allowed him only four hours' sleep. Burke was quite unsympathetic, noting that:

> ... You should have seen old B--'s face ... Loading four camels and then marching 20 miles is no joke. The first two days of it nearly cooked poor B--, and I think he will not be able to stand it much longer.[5]

Wills, who had to take a range of observations and also write up his field notes, coped with these tasks as best he could while riding his camel.

Before the expedition reached Cooper Creek, Becker had died and Beckler had resigned. Henceforth only Wills carried out any scientific observation and reporting, for Burke did not even keep a diary.[6] All pretence of scientific status had been abandoned:

> ... this great expedition, starting with so much display from Melbourne, with a steady, declared and scientific object, would dwindle down into a flying light corps, making a sudden dash across the continent and back again with no permanent results ... No successor [had been] appointed to Dr Beckler. The last named gentleman brought back many of the scientific instruments entrusted to his charge, alleging that if he had not done so, Mr Burke, who was unscientific and impatient of the time lost in making and registering observations, threatened to throw them into the next creek.[7]

Giles, the Forrest brothers, Warburton and Stuart were never forced to forego unrealistic objectives or ignore impracticable constraints, for theirs were highly mobile and professional explorations from the start. As a result they were rarely accompanied by scientists. The presence of botanist F G Waterhouse on Stuart's final expedition and of geologist Hill in Alexander Forrest's exploration of the Kimberleys, were exceptions. Giles, John Forrest and Warburton had no scientific staff. There is thus little historical evidence to support the assertion made by Moyal that:

> ... from the mid century, the major expeditions combined the

> enterprise of collecting and reporting scientific data with the geographic objectives of marking overland routes.[8]

Furthermore, those scientists attached to expeditions were, without exception, poorly qualified. Waterhouse, who accompanied Stuart at the insistence of the South Australian Government, was a surveyor with an amateur interest in collecting natural history specimens. Alexander Forrest's geologist Hill was equally unimpressive. In his telegram to the Western Australian Government announcing the success of his 1879 Kimberley expedition, Forrest wrote:

> Have nothing to report. Hill says the country not gold bearing. Have seen myself plenty of country similar to the goldfields here. Do not think he is much of a geologist.[9]

As a result, the scientific collections and observations of Stuart, Giles, Warburton and John Forrest were meagre, to say the least. The relevant appendix to Forrest's journal of the Central Australian Expedition, for example, amounted to only three pages. He also admitted, on one occasion, that:

> ... as to minerals I am not sufficiently conversant with the science to offer an opinion, except that I should think it was worthwhile sending geologists to examine (the country) thoroughly.[10]

Giles' collecting on the fourth expedition was limited to the preservation of some insects in methylated spirits, on a few occasions only.[11]

The emphasis on extreme mobility during the initial penetration of the arid interior also meant that field researchers during this period worked under considerable difficulties. Although Waterhouse was given a packhorse for his equipment and samples, he was prevented by Stuart's written prohibition on any man leaving the main body of the expedition or the campsite without permission, from making good use of the considerable amount of time available while Stuart was reconnoitring. Those of his specimens which were not eaten by ants or broken up in transit had to be sacrificed when the horses were failing rapidly on the return journey, forcing Stuart to eliminate every extraneous item, including '... boots and clothes, leaving us only what we stood in.'[12] Auld, who was a member of the expedition, later commented that Waterhouse had not been treated well by Stuart and that the emphasis of such explorations worked against field researchers.

> ... I am afraid that the general public have no idea of the difficulties which a naturalist has to contend with on an expedition like this.[13]

The overall lack of emphasis upon field research during this period can also be attributed to the strong and constant pragmatism which still underlay most exploration. The increasing involvement by colonial governments and private sponsors might well have influenced this trend. Stuart's later work, for example, was predicated, in part, on finding a functional route across the continent for the Overland Telegraph in order to retain the switching station in South Australia. As well, the explorer's sponsors Chambers and Finke undeniably benefited from his earlier discoveries of useful pastoral country.

John Forrest, on his 1874 expedition, was instructed to obtain information on the hinterland of the Murchison and Gascoyne Rivers, for it was assumed the area would be 'neither barren nor badly watered' and thus the results would hopefully be 'most fortunate for our sheep farmers.'[14] Such orders echoed those of his first expedition in 1869 when, while searching for Leichhardt's remains, he was also required to render himself '... as extensively useful and valuable to this colony as circumstances may admit.'[15] The commercial realities of Alexander Forrest's exploration in the Kimberleys in 1878 were also quite unequivocal.

> It is supposed this exploration will be the means of opening up a large tract of country suitable not only for pastoral pursuits but for the cultivation of all Tropical products, probably intersected by rivers which on examination may be found navigable for some distance inland and if so would lead to its immediate settlement — moreover there are some grounds for believing that auriferous country will be found and much valuable information added.[16]

Even the Burke and Wills expedition which, ostensibly, was carried out for the most altruistic and noble of reasons, was financed by the government of Victoria, not only for purposes of prestige, but also because it foresaw trade benefits should settlements be established close to the northern mining towns.[17] Furthermore, it was common knowledge that the portion of New South Wales lying east of the Western Australian border, north of the South Australian border and extending to Longitude 141° east would soon be partitioned and Victoria hoped to receive some benefits for its efforts.[18] Consequently Victoria's claim that in supporting exploration beyond its borders, it was acting '... beyond the mere selfish interests of our colony [and instead for the] ... claims of science, of humanity, and of Australian settlement',[19] was only partly true at best. Indeed the government prayed that:

> ... the colony which has 'borne the heat and burden of the day', may not be overlooked when apportionment of Burke's Land comes under consideration of Her Majesty's advisors in England.[20]

Accompanying this pragmatic emphasis, which had been present since the earliest explorations in Australia, was evidence, however, of a developing interest in geographic knowledge for its own sake. Sufficient was now known of inland Australia to deduce that there was little likelihood of economic return from its exploration. As Charles Eden points out in his introduction to Warburton's journal:

> ... an ample supply of data exists, however, enabling us to predicate with some degree of certainty as to the probable physical and geographical characteristics of the regions yet untraversed by civilized man; and there is little to justify any expectation that these will be found to differ in character from the inhospitable wilderness, from the confines of which so many enterprising travellers have been obliged to turn their steps, and on the borders of which not a few have perished. It may, I think, be reasonably assumed, that the whole interior region west of the 140th degree of east longitude and north of the 30th degree of south latitude, is of the most unpromising kind; that it is without rivers, without mountains, forming an inhospitable and dreary desert, similar to that traversed by Stuart, Sturt, Burke, Wills and Mr Forrest; and I cannot forbear expressing my conviction that, beyond the desirability of simply determining the fact and all knowledge, even of a negative character is desirable — that there is little to tempt or repay an explorer in the desolate region included within the limits above mentioned.[21]

The shrewd pastoralist and business magnate, Sir Thomas Elder, exemplified this change of interest. Although Elder was obviously interested in possible mineral and pastoral discoveries, he nonetheless had a very strong interest in geographic knowledge. He had earlier imported 125 camels at a cost of approximately £25,000, and sent them to his inland South Australian property, Beltana. These animals were intended to form the nucleus of a stud which would supply camels for exploration and commercial purposes. In addition Elder, who was well placed to materially support exploration, provided saddlery and equipment for Giles and, in conjunction with Hughes, funded all the costs of Warburton's expedition.[22] As Eden notes in his introduction to Egerton-Warburton's journal, Elder's benevolence was especially praiseworthy for, even should he have so desired, this wealthy patron could scarcely have hoped to recoup his expenditure on explorations.

> Neither should the liberality of Messrs Elder and Hughes here pass unnoticed. Not the slightest personal benefit could accrue to either of these gentlemen whether their expedition was successful or the reverse. A pure public spirit animated them both, and such was Mr Elder's attachment to the cause of science, that while bearing half the present outlay, he wrote to Baron von Mueller of Melbourne ... offering to supply camels for the use of any further expeditions that Victoria or the more eastern settlements might think fit to organise for the examination of the unknown country lying between them and the Trans-Australian Telegraph.[23]

In all, a strong desire now existed to know the exact nature of the Central Australian region. Furthermore, this growing interest in knowledge for knowledge's sake was reflected in the several awards made by British scientific societies in recognition of the achievements of the major explorers. Giles received the Patron's Gold Medal of the Royal Geographical Society and also a Knighthood of the Crown of Italy.[24] Stuart, John Forrest, Francis Gregory and Warburton also all received the Royal Geographical Society Patrons' Medal during this period.[25] Even the South Australian and Western Australian governments at least paid lip service to the quest for scientific information, with John Forrest, for example, being instructed to obtain and preserve botanical, geological and zoological specimens in the 'interests of science'[26] during his 1869 expedition in search of Leichhardt. This emphasis is quite distinct from the earliest instructions given to Hunter and others, when natural history specimens were to be collected merely for appraisal of their commercial worth. Even at a time when exploration was necessarily preoccupied with mobility rather than science, a climate conducive to field research not necessarily tied to economic return was gradually developing, preparing the way for the major scientific expeditions of the 1890s.

To appreciate why mobility came to be valued above field research in the 1860s and 1870s, it is useful to examine the contemporary descriptions of the country involved. Despite the difficulties experienced by explorers like Sturt, Eyre and Augustus Gregory in the 1840s and 1850s, the lands which they traversed were generally less formidable than those attempted by later, better prepared explorers. Giles' comments on Sturt's appraisal of the country north-west of the Darling, for example, illustrate how rapidly and comprehensively bushmanship developed after the 1860s.

> So far as my opinion, formed in my wanderings over the greater portions of the country explored by Sturt, goes, his estimate of the regions he visited has scarcely been borne out according to the views of the present day. ... A great portion, if not all the country, explored by that expedition is now highly-prized pastoral land and a gold field was discovered almost in sight of a depot formed by Sturt, at a spot where he was imprisoned at a waterhole for six months without moving his camp. He described the whole region as a desert and he seems to have been haunted by the notion that he had got into and was surrounded by a wilderness the like of which no human being had ever seen or heard of before. His whole narrative is a tale of suffering and woe ...[27]

Ernest Favenc attributed the negative response of Sturt and his men to their being physically and mentally exhausted. Giles thought that Sturt had appraised the range lands of the interior against the yardstick of Australia's most fertile arable country.

> Sturts views are only to be accounted for by the fact that what we now call excellent sheep and cattle country appeared to him like a desert, because his comparison were made with the best alluvial lands he had left near the coast.[28]

In fact, the truly barren and desolate country was finally to be traversed, with considerable difficulty, by the last generation of explorers of Australia. In 1862, overcome by the long-term effects of scurvy and an inadequate diet, Stuart became crippled while returning from his successful south-to-north crossing of the continent. He was too ill to eat the native portulaca plants, his legs turned black, the skin hung from the roof his mouth, his tongue became swollen and he was incapable of walking. He had to be carried on a specially made horse-mounted stretcher for the last 650 kilometres and Auld commented that on several occasions they lifted their leader down at the end of the day believing he was dead. He and Billiatt sometimes had to open Stuart's mouth and pour a gruel of flour and water down his throat, for he was incapable of swallowing or ingesting any other food.[29]

Similarly, in 1873 in the east Pilbara, Warburton and his men were tormented almost incessantly by flies, poor food, intense heat, lack of water and ants. Sleep was almost impossible, for the ants were awake and foraging twenty-four hours a day. Often, in desperation, the men forced themselves to sit in the scorching sun to get some relief. Flies were a constant torment in daylight hours. After one of Warburton's camels was galled by an incorrectly fitting saddle, its hump became fly-blown. The maggots were scooped out daily with a pint pot, until the animal sickened and had to be left to die. According to Warburton:

> The number of flies in Australia and the rapidity with which they breed, are quite horrible. Nothing in the shape of meat can be left exposed for a moment, otherwise a swarm of flies descend and seem to emit living maggots on the flesh. They assail the ears, nostrils and eyes of the traveller, who is unable to stir without a veil ...[30]

During Giles' second expedition, when he was in salt lake country west of the Macdonnell Ranges, his horses became bogged. The explorer was powerless to free them.

> All I could do was to crack my whip to prevent the horses from ceasing to exert themselves, and although it was but a few moments that they were in this danger, to me it seemed an eternity. They staggered at last out of the quagmire, heads, backs, saddles, everything covered with blue mud, their mouths were filled with salt mud also, and they were completely exhausted when they reached firm ground. We let them rest in the shade of some quandong trees.[31]

Perhaps the most telling example of the nature of this country was the incident involving the loss of Gibson in 1874, in the area which Giles later named the Gibson Desert. Gibson and Giles were out reconnoitring when the young man's horse died. The explorer therefore mounted Gibson on the remaining horse and sent him back to camp to fetch a replacement. Gibson was never seen again, for he moved away from their outward tracks and was lost in the almost waterless desert to the south. Because of Gibson's fatal error, Giles was forced to walk for 190 kilometres in searing heat. For the last hundred kilometres he had had only a litre of water and eventually staggered into the camp late one night, 'looking like death'.[32] Notwithstanding the severe privations he had endured, he and his assistant Tietkens set out again some thirty-six hours later in a vain attempt to rescue Gibson. The sufferings they then underwent were so gruelling that Tietkens later recalled:

> ... lying down and begging Giles to push on and leave me for I was so weak I did not wish to live: death would have come to me as a welcome visitor. [33]

On his third expedition in 1875, Giles was caught in waterless country west of Lake Torrens. After two of his horses died from thirst, the third became so desperate and confused that it staggered to the campfire and lowered its muzzle to the flames, believing in some fashion that they represented water. Although Giles, from pity, gave the horse a couple of litres of their dangerously meagre supply of water, it almost immediately sank to the ground and died.[34]

Alexander Forrest experienced similar privations while attempting to cross the King Leopold Ranges in 1879. After struggling desperately for fourteen days and losing ten horses from exhaustion and debilitation, he and his party found themselves back at the point at which they had commenced their assault on the uplands. They then proceeded in the valley of the Margaret and over the divide into the Ord River basin. Towards the end of the expedition, with Forrest's younger brother severely affected by sunstroke, the Aboriginal Tommy Pierre dying from exhaustion and fever, insufficient horses for all men to be mounted, almost no supplies left and the prospect of waterless conditions ahead, Forrest was forced to make a 220-kilometre dash for the Overland Telegraph Line where he found assistance at a linesmen's camp and returned to the main party with food and horses.

On those frequent occasions when the country was without either feed or water, explorers had to drive their exhausted horses to their deaths. Giles lost four animals in one day in such circumstances near the aptly named Mount Destruction, on the borders of the Gibson Desert. He had struggled towards a range only to find that it contained no surface water and he and his party had enormous difficulties regaining the previous water supply point. In the process one horse fell and three others had to be abandoned. On reaching water he and Tietkens immediately returned to the horses which had fallen, yet found them all dead, even though only a few hours had passed since they had been left behind.

> On reaching ... the poor little ghost ... we found him stark and stiff, his hide all shrivelled and wrinkled, mouth wide open and lips drawn back to an extraordinary extent. Pushing on we arrived where Diamond and Pratt had fallen. They also were quite dead, and must have died immediately after they fell; they presented the same appearance as the little cob ... The distance they had to travel was not great — less than ninety miles — and they were only two nights without water; but the heat was

> intense, the country frightful, and to get over the distance as soon as possible, we may have travelled rather fast. The horses had not been well off for either grass or water at starting, and they were mostly footsore; but in the best of cases, and under the most favourable start from a water, the ephemeral thread of a horse's life may be snapped in a moment, in the height of an Australian summer ...[35]

This was appallingly hard country, as perhaps best described by Giles himself.

> ... in such a region as this, where that detestable vegetation, the *triodia* and high and rolling sandhills exist for such enormous distances. The very sight of the country, in all its hideous terrors clad, is sufficient to daunt a man and kill a horse.[36]

Should feed have been available the horses would, in great part, have tolerated their trials more easily. Unfortunately so much of the sandy country of the central and western deserts was covered with spinifex (*triodia* or *plectrachne*) which are almost inedible and valueless spiky grass-like plants which grow from six inches to three feet high. Compounding their lack of nutritional value was their effect on the legs of the horses who, as Giles reported, soon came to fear and hate exposure to their spikes.

> Close to the foot of the hills the country is open, but covered with large stones, between the interstices of which grow huge bunches of the hideous spinifex, which both we and the horses dread like a pestilence. We have encountered this scourge for over 200 miles. All around the coronets of most of the horses, in consequence of their being so continually punctured with the spines of this terrible grass, it has caused a swelling, or tough enlargement of the flesh and skin, giving them the appearance of having ringbones. Many of them have the flesh quite raw and bleeding; they are also very tenderfooted from traversing so much stony ground, as we have lately had to pass over.[37]

From pity for the suffering that his horses were having to endure in traversing spinifex country, Giles sometimes allowed them to choose their own path, although this approach was not without severe problems.

> Bordering upon the open stony *triodia* ground abovementioned is a bed of scrubs, composed chiefly of mulga, though there are various other trees, shrubs and plants amongst it. It is so dense and thick that in it we cannot see a third of the horses at once;

> they, of course, continually endeavour to make into it to avoid the stones and triodia; for, generally speaking, the pungent *triodia* and the Mulga acacia appear to be antagonistic members of the vegetable kingdom. The ground in the scrubs is generally soft and on that account also the horses seek it. Out of kindness, I have occasionally allowed them to travel in the scrubs, when our direct course should have been on the open, until some dire mishap forces us out again; for, the scrubs being so dense, the horses are compelled to crash through them, tearing the coverings of their loads and frequently forcing sticks in between their backs or sides and their saddles, sometimes staking themself severely. Then we hear a frantic crashing through the scrubs, and the sounds of the pounding of horsehoofs are the first notice we receive that some calamity has occurred. So soon as we ourselves can force our way through, and collect the horses the best way we can, yelling and howling to one another to say how many each may have got, we discover one or two missing. Then they have to be tracked; portions of loads are picked up here and there, and, in the course of an hour or more, the horse or horses are found, repacked, and on we push again, mostly for the open, though rough and stony spinifex ground, where at least we can see what is going on. These scrubs are really dreadful, and one's skin and clothes get torn and ripped in all directions.[38]

Given the above, it is hardly surprising, therefore, that W H L Ranken should write in the early 1870s:

> The physical geography of one-half of this continent cannot be described, for the country cannot be explored; and for this reason — that half of the map is a blank — in all probability, half the country is a blank. Of all that portion of Australia which lies west of the 135th meridian we know only that no one can penetrate it; that no river whatever drains it on the south ...[39]

And yet despite this justifiably pessimistic evaluation, the central and western deserts were conquered, though only after major changes in the techniques of exploration and terrible privations by men and beasts. The final unknown portions of Australia were covered during the 1870s when Warburton and Giles all broke through on an east-west axis and John Forrest and Giles on a west-east axis, while Alexander Forrest completed the section between Roebourne and Darwin. In all cases these explorers had the physical advantage of working across the unknown towards the known. In 1873, for example, when Warburton's party was almost completely debilitated in the vicinity of Shay Gap, he threw his best men and camels into a dash for the De Grey Station which he correctly believed was only about 160 kilometres distant. In the following year, when John Forrest was brought almost to a standstill by waterless conditions on his expedition to the Overland Telegraph Line, he knew he had only a limited distance to cover before reaching a known watering point in the Musgrave Ranges. Physical advantages aside, the psychological benefits of identifying one's destination in advance were immeasurable. Although the terrain to be covered was dreadfully hard, the distances to be travelled and the places where help was available were known. Thus, while the jubilation of John Forrest's party on sighting the Overland Telegraph Line on 27 September 1874, is understandable, Forrest himself was not surprised that they had attained their goal on that day.

Continuity was now quite indispensable to ongoing exploration, for the central and western deserts were unforgiving. Expedition leaders who were, for the most part, highly experienced, chose men of proven competence to accompany them through these regions. Stuart, who had accompanied Sturt on his 1844 expedition, had also worked for several years carrying out inland surveys for the South Australian Department of Lands and Surveys. He then undertook explorations in central South Australia before attempting to cross to the northern coast. His men were generally similarly well-experienced. On his first attempt to cross Australia, and on his fourth and fifth expeditions, he took Kekwick, who had also accompanied him on his previous large-scale reconnoitring and surveying exploration of the Chambers Creek area. Benjamin Head was also selected for, although only eighteen years of age, he had been previously involved with Babbage's survey and exploration of the Lake Torrens region in 1858.[40]

Frank W Thring, a member of the fourth expedition, was described by Stuart on the final expedition as his most experienced bushman. On the collapse of Stuart's health after reaching the northern coast, most of the arduous reconnoitring for water and the guiding of the expedition back to Adelaide fell to Thring. The twenty-year-old colonial-born Stephen King, who had spent his life in the bush was, according to Stuart, the second-best bushman, sufficiently experienced and competent to allow Stuart and Thring some respite from the almost incessant reconnoitring on the fifth expedition.

The Forrest brothers, with their rural upbringing, their surveying background and the help of the highly skilled and experienced Windich and Pierre, coped relatively easily with the demands of exploration. Warburton drew on his experience of thirteen years as Commander of the

South Australian Police Force and of several extended explorations, to carry him through his gruelling journey across the Great Sandy Desert. He was assisted by his son Richard, who was regarded as a 'first class bushman'.[41] Ernest Giles developed his bush skills over the ten years and more he spent reconnoitring in the northern and north-western sections of the Darling River basin and, later, in three expeditions in the arid western region of South Australia. Giles was ably assisted by Tietkens, who accompanied him on several occasions.

Probably the most important tangible change in the approach to exploration by 1880 was the replacement of horses by camels. Whereas in the 1840s and 1850s skilfully managed all-horse teams had come into their own, they were to reach their limits when pitted against the western deserts in the 1870s. In the previous decade a number of changes had been made to husband the horses and to improve their usefulness. After his third expedition, for instance, Stuart resolved to increase both the size of his party and the number of horses per man. A mere three men and thirteen horses on his third expedition were clearly inadequate: '... if I did not put my hands to almost everything that is required, I should never get on. My party is too small. It is killing work.'[42]

On his final expedition the explorer took ten men and seventy-one horses, providing the mobility necessary to carry out the extensive reconnoitring south of Daly Waters that finally allowed him to break through to the northern coastline. Having a team of this size also allowed Stuart to keep the loads light, for he knew that the horses would be sorely taxed by the length of the expedition and the severe conditions. Because Stuart took a minimal amount of food and equipment with him, provisions were frequently in short supply. When on one occasion a litter of wild pups was found, Auld commented that these '... innocents were slaughtered and were boiled and were eaten and were delicious!'[43]

Not long afterwards, a damper which had been set out to cool was stolen by a dingo. On the following night the animal was shot by the guard as it crept into the camp, presumably looking for a second damper. So poorly fed were the expedition members that, when the interloper was cooked and eaten, Auld claimed '... some of the men's palates were so sensitive that they solemnly declared they detected the lost damper as they ate. We had imaginative men in our party.'[44] Stuart's equipment was also meagre, prompting him on one occasion, after one of his horses died from poisoning, to instruct his men to retrieve the shoes and its hide, which was to be used for hobble straps.[45]

In order to gain maximum benefit from the feed available, Stuart and

Giles often let their horses graze unhobbled at night.[46] Although this action directly contradicted the earlier hard-learnt tenet of restraining horses overnight, it was essential in the circumstances. Nevertheless, adopting this practice was a calculated gamble, in which Giles, Forrest and Stuart were all caught out. Furthermore, in order to give his horses time for grazing and recuperation, Stuart attempted to get under way as early as possible each morning, in order that the work would be completed '... before the extreme heat of the day came on',[47] and aimed at travelling only six to eight hours per day. Yet despite such intentions, he and the other desert explorers were frequently forced to drive their horses to the limits of their endurance, pushing them in high temperatures and heavy going for up to a hundred hours without water. Under these conditions it became critical for the explorers to be able to judge exactly how the horses were coping and what could be further expected of them. Stuart appears to have been more careful in this respect than Giles. According to Auld:

> Stuart was a wonderfully good judge of the condition of his horses. When out exploring in splendid grassy country which looked as if water must be near, he without any apparent reason would give orders to return and we found we had just as much as we could do to get back without losing any of our horses or of our men.[48]

Notwithstanding such expertise, on many occasions horses knocked up badly and had to be left behind. Some were later assisted into camp by taking water out to them. Severe dehydration was a common problem, which affected the animals in varying ways. During his third expedition Stuart reported that:

> The little bay mare Polly has become nearly mad, running about among the other horses and kicking them as she passes; even the men do not escape from her heels.[49]

John Forrest's horses suffered badly towards the end of his 1874 expedition. On one occasion, as they were struggling towards a known water supply, thc mob gradually split into three groups. Windich was out in front on the only horse strong enough to ride, looking for the water in the creek lines descending from a rocky range, while Forrest and Kennedy drove the main group along on foot. The leader reported that '... if we halted a minute, many of the horses lay down and we had great difficulty in getting them up again.'[50] Alexander Forrest and two others brought up the rear, quietly pushing along a group which was in even worse condition.

On Giles' second expedition, when east of the Gibson Desert, his horses

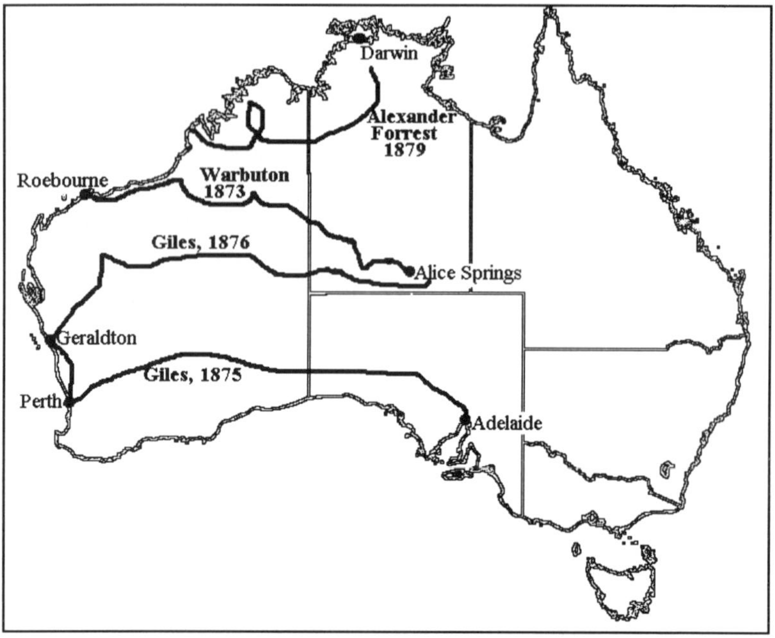

The desert explorers.

were in an appalling state. On one occasion they had not drunk for four days and, as Giles and his men did not reach their camp until late at night, they could do nothing for the horses. At dawn he and Tietkens:

> ... took the shovel and walked to where we heard the horse-bells. Twelve of the poor animals were lying in the bed of the creek, with limbs stretched out as if dead, but we were truly glad to find they were still alive, though some of them could not get up. Some that were standing up were working away with their hobbled feet the best way they could, stamping out the sand trying to dig out little tanks and one old stager had actually reached the water in his tank, so we drove him away and dug out a proper place.[51]

To their credit, Giles, Forrest and Stuart had such an affinity for their horses that they often went to considerable lengths in order to save them.

During this period it was found that experience increased a horse's ability to undergo severe water-stress. On several occasions Stuart noted that his older horses, which had suffered from deprivation on previous expeditions, coped much better than the less experienced animals.[52] Thus, although he felt sorry for his horses when they were suffering badly from thirst early on the second expedition, he saw value in the experience, noting '... I expect they will endure it better next time; they now know what it is to be without.'[53]

Often, when water was finally found, the horses had to be held back and watered carefully and frequently, being allowed only small amounts at a time. Should they be given unlimited access whilst still severely dehydrated they were likely to suffer badly from colic, which Stuart, Giles and Tietkens discovered through experience. With large groups of badly dehydrated horses and small numbers of men, however, keeping them under control at a watering point was not always possible, as Stuart, Kekwick and Head found during the third expedition.

> We had great difficulty in keeping the horses out while we cleared (the soak) ... One of us is required to be constantly with them to keep them back and that he can hardly do; some of them will get away from him do all he can ... [54]

Poisonous plants do not appear to have been such a problem during the 1860s and 1870s, perhaps because most of the plants which deleteriously affected horses were known.[55] This was not the case with camels, which were eating plants that in many instances horses had not previously touched.

The only instance of a new form of poisoning occurred on Alexander Forrest's exploration of the Kimberleys. This event produced the first recorded case of Kimberley Walkabout disease, which was to lead to the deaths of many thousands of horses in that region. On 20 June 1879, Forrest reported:

> One of the horses last night showed symptoms of madness and wandered away ... He was tracked, but was presumed to have stumbled in a creek and been drowned.[56]

This problem stems from the ingestion of the legumes *Crotalaria retusa* and *Crotalaria crispata*, which cause liver failure, the build-up of ammonia in the bloodstream and the consequent intoxication of the central nervous system.[57] As a result, horses become disoriented and walk compulsively until their eventual death from debilitation, or from starvation resulting from the associated loss of vision.

Finally, the quality of horses and horsemanship appears to have improved greatly during this period. Stuart and his associates made several references to the hardiness and reliability of the horses from his sponsor Mr Chambers' property. A number of these horses were taken on several expeditions by

Stuart and their tolerance of heat, water-stress and poor feed was remarkable. According to the explorer, the horses to show out best under the worst conditions were those with some 'blood', an imprecise but tacitly understood notion concerning an infusion of thoroughbred breeding. Such horses were more finely built than other heavier, more coarsely bred types. On physical appearances the coarser, stronger looking types would have been expected to cope better with severe stress, yet such was not Stuart's experience.

> I have had horses that have suffered three times as much privation and yet have held out. The light ones are alright; it is the heavy ones, of the cart horse breed, that feel it most.[58]

That the explorers' horsemanship improved markedly during this period appears indisputable, for one of the most striking features of their journals is the distances covered day after day. Although spare horses were usually taken so that the riding horses could often be given rest days, such was not always the case. The Forrest brothers, for example, were not well provided with horses and their mounts were often ridden for many days in succession. The journals of Giles, the Forrests and Stuart repeatedly mention covering fifty-five to sixty-five kilometres per day, with seventy- and eighty-kilometre days not being at all uncommon. Such an achievement is not readily explainable, for the improvement in horse quality must have been offset by the increasingly difficult country being traversed. On the other hand, the riders appear to have been well aware of the necessity of husbanding their stock's strength. Stuart, for one, had placed in his written instructions that the horses were not to be ridden faster than a walking pace.

Despite such developments, explorers eventually came to realise that horses had reached their limits in the western deserts. On so many occasions, when only 150 to 250 kilometres separated the explorers from their goals, they were unable to continue. Stuart tried desperately in 1860 and 1861, from both Attack Creek and Newcastle Waters, to cover the 220 kilometres which separated him from Gregory's farthest point on Sturt Creek to the west, but was driven back again and again. In 1862, on his final expedition, he abandoned the idea after nine further attempts over six weeks and reached the coast by initally travelling to the north and north-east. John Forrest came to a standstill in October 1874, only about 160 kilometres from W C Gosse's most westerly point, at longitude 126°59'E and to the south of Barrow Range. Although he eventually broke through and found water at the point indicated by Gosse, his horses suffered badly in the process.[59] Giles vividly describes the condition of his surviving horses at the time of his turning back from the fringe of the Gibson desert in 1873.

> The pack-horses now presented a demoralised and disorganised rout, travelling in a long single file, for it was quite impossible to keep the tail (of the mob) up with the leaders ... The real leader was an old black mare, blear-eyed from fly-wounds, forever dropping tears of salt rheum, fat, large, strong, having carried her 180lbs at starting and now desperately thirsty and determined, knowing to an inch where the water was; on she went ... the next was Giant Despair, a perfect marvel. He was a chestnut, old, large-framed, gaunt and bony, ... Life for him seemed but one unceasing round of toil ...[60]

Indeed, because their horses could travel for no more than three to four days without water and could carry only limited quantities with them, which meant their effective reconnoitring radius was 120 kilometres at the absolute maximum, Stuart, Forrest and Giles were forced to admit the limitations placed on them. Frequently deviations had to be made to secure water supplies, even when the goal was within sight. Consequently, on several occasions, all three wished for camels, noting how much easier their tasks would be if they had the extra range that camels would provide. Giles was provided with the clearest possible example of the differing capabilities of both animals on his third expedition, when his horses all died an agonising death from thirst.

> The country we had traversed was the most frightful desert, yet day after day our noble camels kept moving slowly but surely on, with undiminished powers, having carried water for their unfortunate companions the horses and seeing them drop one by one exhausted and dying of thirst; still they marched contentedly on, carrying us by turns and all the remaining gear of the dead horses and finally brought us to water at last.[61]

Just as the usage of bullocks for exploration purposes reached its practical limits in the late 1830s and early 1840s due to the increasingly difficult nature of the terrain being encountered, so too did pack and riding horses prove inappropriate for the arid environment traversed in the 1870s.

In 1874, when John Forrest, after setting out from Geraldton, finally reached Kooringa in South Australia he, his men and their horses were taken by train for a ceremonial march through Adelaide, where they were met by fellow explorers Giles, Warburton and Gosse. Forrest insisted that his horses take part in the parade, noting:

> Eleven of these were the survivors of the expedition and we were desirous that our faithful and hard-worked four-footed

companions should have their share of the attention of our South Australian friends.[62]

Forrest's animals were accompanied by one of the horses from the Burke and Wills expedition and Frank Thring rode a horse which had crossed the continent with Stuart. Thus, in the streets of Adelaide, an appropriate and symbolic farewell was made to horses in Australian exploration. For the remaining few major explorations undertaken by Warburton and Giles, camels were essential.

Charles Eden, Warburton's relative who wrote the foreword to his Journal, notes that in 1846 a man named Horrocks appears to have been the first in Australia to use a camel for exploration purposes. Burke and Wills later took twenty-five camels with them on their ill-fated expedition, but these animals were poorly managed. Realistically, they were not even required in such country, as Howitt, Landsborough, Walker and McKinley demonstrated on their various relief forays. It was not until 1866, when Sir Thomas Elder had 121 camels landed in South Australia, that exploration of the western deserts became feasible. These animals, which were of both baggage and riding breeds,[63] were imported for exploration and cartage purposes and were found to thrive in inland Australia.

Camels were found to be superior to horses in many ways, but especially in their ability to go for long periods without water. Giles' 1875 experience is a good example of this quality. Ten days after setting off from Ouldabinna in South Australia at the start of his successful crossing to Perth, the explorer found his first fair supply of water at Boundary Dam on the Western Australian border. His camels then covered 517 kilometres in seventeen days, with only one small drink from their own supplies along the way, until they found the Queen Victoria Springs, 210 kilometres due east of the future mining town of Broad Arrow, where a plentiful supply of water was encountered.[64] The difference between this exploit and Giles' earlier limited, hesitant and extremely dangerous forays on horseback, is striking. Nevertheless, although camels have a far greater capacity than horses to tolerate waterless conditions, Giles commented that they, like horses, also have to learn to cope with dry periods.

The experience gained from such explorations stood the leaders of the scientific expeditions of the 1890s in good stead. David Lindsay, the leader of the Elder Scientific Expedition, noted that, through fortuitous cool weather and the availability of succulent bushes for grazing, he was able to nurse his camels for thirty-five days over 858 kilometres. During this period the animals had fourteen litres on the second day, eleven litres on the eighth day and eleven on the twenty-fifth day, or only thirty-six litres altogether. This astounding feat of bushmanship owed much to the developmental work of the first users of camels in Australia.[65]

In addition to coping with poorly watered country, camels were found to be superior to horses in that they could survive and even thrive in areas were horses would die of starvation. Being ruminants, they could convert food of a quality insufficient to sustain horses. Furthermore, they were prepared to eat certain Acacia shrubs which horses would not attempt. Finally, their longer necks and greater height meant they had a greater grazing and foraging potential than horses.

The camels, with their immensely superior weight-carrying capacity, could also transport large quantities of water. Loads of 180 kilograms were common. Indeed Giles' camels were laden with an average of 250 kilograms each when they set out from South Australia in 1875. An unexpected advantage of this load size was that Giles' leading camels, with large water containers strapped on each side, smashed a clear path through the mallee scrub, making it easy for the remainder of the team to follow them.

Finally, whereas horses had, on occasion, to be driven up with stock whips before they would enter the spinifex in the mornings, camels were apparently unconcerned. Giles' explanation of this behaviour is particularly interesting.

> In my former journals I mentioned that the spinifex wounded the horses' feet and disfigured their coronets, it also used to take a good deal of hair off some of the horses' legs; but in the case of the camelsalthough it did not seem to excoriate them, it took every hair off their legs up to three feet from the ground and their limbs turned black and were as bright and shiny as a newly polished boot. The camels' hair was much finer then that of the horses, but their skin was much thicker and while the horses' legs were punctured and suppurating, the camels' were all as hard as steel and bright as bayonets.[66]

Although camels had considerable advantages, some problems were encountered in adapting to them, for there was no previous experience in using them. Howitt, for example, had enormous difficulties in coping with the aggressiveness of his bull camel on the Burke rescue operation. In desperation, he tied the aggressive animal's head down close to his knees and short-hobbled him, but the bull still chased all the other camels from the camp. He surmised that it was unwise to take both male and female camels together, for '... one is never safe for a day from their straying and from continual fights between the male camels for mastery.' Nevertheless, Howitt believed that with all-male or all-female teams there would be no more problems than with horses and stated '... I firmly believe in the suitability of camels for exploring.'[67]

Warburton lost fifteen of his seventeen camels during his 1873 expedition. Besides the one which died from complications following an infected saddle gall, several became paralysed, purportedly through their loins becoming chilled at night by the cold desert air, but possibly through eating poisonous plants. He certainly recorded that his old bull died of poisoning, causing the younger bulls immediately to become obstreperous, attempt to break up the herd and drive the cows away.[68] Indeed, a number of his camels did break free and could not be recaptured.

Giles also had handling problems during his first experience with camels, which was on his third expedition. On that occasion a camel calf made a habit of entangling itself in its mother's nose peg. On several occasions it pulled the peg out, causing the cow considerable pain. Worse, the myriad flies present were immediately attracted by the blood and:

> The agony the poor creature suffered from flies must have been excruciating, as after this accident they entered her nostrils in such numbers that she often hung back and would cough and snort until she had ejected a great quantity of blood and flies from her nose.[69]

Once Giles mastered the different technique for hobbling his camels, he became a firm convert to their use. As he noted, whereas his offsider Nicholls had previously called the camels 'ugly, useless, lazy brutes', once the horses had died and the camels were plodding on with 'undiminished powers', he came to appreciate the camels' virtues. Overall, Giles appears to have had little trouble with his camels, merely pointing out that it was critical to keep their saddlery in good condition and well-fitting and that his 'Afghan', Saleh, 'used to do this admirably'. Once the art of managing them had been learnt, they were 'much easier to work than a mob of pack horses.'[70]

After Giles had gained confidence in his camels he made several innovations which improved the ease of travelling. He devised a technique which made loading more convenient and the loads more stable and less wearying for the animals. As well, he had very large leather saddlebags supplied by Sir Thomas Elder, at the bottoms of which were wooden boxes. This innovation meant that 'all books, papers, instruments, glass and etc. were safe.'[71] The use of leather in the construction of saddlebags was a particularly important improvement, for all preceding explorers had used canvas, which required constant repairs in the field.[72]

Without camels, the crossing of the Australian deserts during the 1870s by Warburton and Giles may not have been possible. Warburton was adamant that he would not otherwise have reached the west coast, for the same country had already repulsed Gregory. As he pointed out, '... any man attempting to cross this country with horses must perish.'[73] Alternatively, it is almost certain that traversing the most difficult sections of inland Australia would have been an incremental process whereby permanent water supplies were painstakingly established, so allowing a slow leapfrogging forward. Even so, the Gibson, Great Victorian and Sandy Deserts were not won lightly. Because of the intense heat during the day, for example, Warburton was eventually forced to travel by night in 1873. As a result, he failed to find any of the wells upon which the Aboriginal people depended and upon which he had previously relied. If he pressed on in the daylight the heat would kill his camels. If he travelled by night not only would he eventually die of thirst, but also his journey would be rendered meaningless in geographical terms. Yet notwithstanding the intense difficulties now faced in the central and particularly the western deserts, in most instances white explorers possessed sufficient expertise to enable them to cope.

With the exception of Warburton and the Forrest brothers, explorers rarely enlisted the help of Aborigines after the 1840s. Windich assisted both John and Alexander Forrest considerably in finding water and procuring game but in most cases was merely following up a general line deduced from the topography by the Forrests. Despite Warburton's undoubted bushmanship, his survival would have been difficult without Charley, who in many cases located waterholes by tracking Aborigines to their camps or by carefully monitoring the movements of specific types of birds. On one occasion, after the Aboriginal youth had led the party to water, Warburton was unstinting in his praise.

> To the energy and courage of this untutored native may, under the guidance of the Almighty, be attributed the salvation of the party. It was by no accident that he encountered the friendly well. For 14 miles he followed up the tracks of some blacks, though fatigued by a day of severe work and, receiving a kindly welcome from the natives, he had hurried back, unmindful of his own exhausted condition, to apprise his companions of the important discovery he had made ... I never could have gone on after that night without more food and water ...[74]

Warburton, like Austin some twenty-five years earlier, occasionally captured Aborigines and forced them to lead the expedition members to water. This approach was of limited value, as his experience with one elderly woman indicated.

> We let the old witch go. She was the most alarming specimen of a woman I ever saw; she had been of no use to us and her sex alone saved her from punishment, for under pretense of leading us to some native wells, she took us backwards and forwards over heavy sand-hills, exhausting the camels as well as my small stock of patience.[75]

Stuart had an Aboriginal guide on his first expedition but the man was unfamiliar with the area and eventually ran away. Henceforth the explorer would rely on his own highly-developed sense of placement, plus his surveying skills.

> My doubt of the black fellow's knowledge of the country is now confirmed; he seems to be quite lost and knows nothing of the country, except what he has heard other blacks relate; he is quite bewildered and points all round when I ask him the direction of Wingillpin.[76]

Giles only used an Aboriginal guide during his third expedition in the difficult South Australian lakes country between Fowlers Bay and Elder's Station, Beltana. Jimmy, who was familiar with the area, was of considerable value to the explorer, who was amazed at his almost infallible intuitive sense of placement.

During this period, although Stuart expressly prohibited his men from leaving the line of march without permission, most explorers were not sufficiently concerned about the threat of Aboriginal attacks to avoid splitting into small groups. Not only had their mobility and general skilfulness increased, but also their firearms were now much more efficient. Earlier, the slow rate of fire and inaccuracy of muskets had caused serious problems which affected the explorers' safety. Caley had stressed to Banks the great virtues of a double-barrelled pistol, which:

> ... is very useful in the woods ... as many of the natives are well aware that a gun will only go off once; nay, many of them do not mind a single gun now ...[77]

Major Lockyer was also critical of the quality and efficacy of early weapons. In 1827 he complained that he was disappointed that some Aborigines had not been shot when fired upon by the foot soldiers, for it would have taught them greater respect.[78] Perhaps the clearest example of the problems which such weapons caused the earlier explorers occurred in 1845, when Leichhardt and his men were attacked shortly after dark, near the Mitchell River on the Cape York Peninsula. In part, this attack occurred because of Leichhardt's belief that watches were unnecessary in areas where the Aborigines had not become guileful through association with white people. Nevertheless, on this occasion no firearms could be fired in response until the weapons had been primed with caps. Once Leichhardt had found the caps and provided them to Charley and Brown, they '... discharged their guns into the crowd of natives, who instantly fled ...'[79] In the meantime, however, Gilbert had been killed and Roper and Calvert had been speared several times and severely beaten with waddies. Although an immediate volley would not have saved Gilbert, Calvert and Roper would almost certainly have been spared considerable injuries. Indeed, the remaining expedition members were fortunate to have survived this particular attack.

Firearms were continuously being improved. Although Mitchell had earlier impressed his native guide by shooting an emu at a considerable distance during the first expedition in 1831, it was not until the development and ready availability of integral cartridges and rotary mechanisms, that the effectiveness of firearms increased markedly. Such weapons allowed considerably longer shots to be made to keep the Aborigines away, or rapid volleys to be fired at close range with devastating effect. As early as their surveys of the Darling River region in 1865, Giles and Tietkens were equipped with Schneider rifles and revolvers. On several occasions they were attacked, but as their rifles fired a .577-inch hollow-nosed cartridge, which '... turns inside out when it hits anything and the wound bleeds freely ...',[80] it is hardly surprising that the Aborigines were unable to compete. Moreover, Tietkens made it clear that Giles took care to be well equipped, having '... purchased quite a formidable arsenal of firearms ...' for the second expedition.[81] Consequently they had no difficulties, as Aboriginal attacks were easily repulsed. Tietkens described such situations laconically, commenting on one occasion that:

> The breech loading rifle and revolver had again sent them off with serious loss ... [although] several spears were thrown in the dark. I rushed at them and fired point blank emptying the six chambers of my pistol. A stampede followed and I returned to reload ... I [later] found a considerable quantity of blood but no blacks.[82]

On one occasion in Central Australia during his final expedition, Stuart had sufficient confidence in the skill and weapons of his marksman Auld to order him to fire his rifle at the rock upon which an Aboriginal leader was standing whilst inciting his men to attack. The flying rock splinters which resulted so terrified this man that the attack was aborted.[83] According to Alexander Forrest, his brother John shot and killed an Aborigine at a range of 200 metres during an attack in 1874.[84]

Stuart's men also had revolvers which they carried on their belts, which Stuart felt was safer than strapping them to the saddles, in case the horses got away. Furthermore, the men carried Enfield rifles, breech loading precursors of the Lee-Enfield rifles of the colonial armies of the Boer War and the First and Second World Wars.[85]

Such devastating firepower gave explorers far more confidence in their capacity to cope with Aboriginal attacks to the extent that, during his first expedition, Giles was prepared to leave just one man and a small barking terrier watchdog to guard the camp near Lake Amadeus in the western region of South Australia while he was away reconnoitring for up to a week.[86] Nevertheless, the Aboriginal threat remained, making Stuart, for one, almost obsessive about watch keeping. As Auld comments:

> I omitted to mention before that, when in camp, night and day Stuart was most strict in having a man on guard every two hours. He threatened that if ever he found any of the party asleep on watch he would shoot him dead.[87]

Stuart also stipulated that no man could leave the camp without carrying arms and ammunition, that the men on watch had to be armed, that he or the officer-in-charge were to be called for any incident, 'however trifling', and that all the men had to sleep with their weapons at their sides.[88]

Despite the effectiveness of their firearms, Giles, the Forrest brothers and Stuart were all attacked by Aborigines at different times, largely because the Aborigines and explorers were inevitably forced to compete for the same waterholes. Whereas thirty years previously Sturt had studiously avoided exhausting or fouling Aboriginal watering points, explorers in the 1860s and 1870s often lacked this option. Also, their markedly increased firepower often made them less anxious to avoid conflict. As Giles pointed out in 1874:

> No doubt these Autochthones were dreadfully annoyed to find their little reservoirs discovered by such water-swallowing wretches as they doubtless thought white men and horses to be; I could only console myself with the reflection, that in such a region as this we must be prepared to lay down our lives at any moment in our attempts to procure water and we must take it when we find it at any price, as life and water are synonymous terms. I dare say they know where to get more, but I don't.[89]

Because water was such a scarce resource in the country they traversed, explorers of this period relied on a variety of techniques to locate it. In the main, ranges of hills were sought and followed. In 1874 Forrest, for example, selected probably the only central route feasible for horses by tracing the Gascoyne upstream to its source. He then gambled on finding intermediate uplands until he reached the Barrow and Musgrave Ranges of South Australia which Gosse had explored and mapped and of which details were in his possession. In most cases Forrest, like his contemporaries, never left a watering point before reconnoitring and proving satisfactory supplies ahead.

Warburton also exemplified this approach when commenting on the country he encountered near the point on Sturt Creek, on the north-eastern flank of the Great Sandy Desert, where Gregory had been driven back.

> This is our last chance; if it fails, we must go over those terrible sand-hills again to our last water! It will ruin the camels and place us in an ugly predicament, but there is no alternative. I dare not work them on a chance. What they can do must be all on a certainty of getting water at the end.[90]

By contrast, Giles was willing to gamble. In 1875, he and his men set out from the last known water in South Australia into completely unknown country. Giles admitted that he was risking all: 'I had set my own and all my companions' lives upon a cast and will stand the hazard of the die ...'[91]

Generally, however, explorers of this period realised that the country was too unforgiving to take risks. Even Giles, when skirting Lake Amadeus in 1872, decided to admit defeat and turn back. When Tietkens, who was equipped with camels, visited the same area in 1889, he reflected on the good fortune of his predecessor in the region.

> It cannot be looked upon as otherwise than providential that Gileswas prevented from reaching the west extremity of this lake; for when we reflect upon the character of the country that awaited him had he done so ... it would (have led) into difficulties that might have ended in disaster, perhaps death.[92]

In the Great Sandy Desert, in the absence of uplands and gnamma holes, Warburton fortuitously discovered the presence of a network of wells which the Aboriginal inhabitants had established over thousands of years. According to Eden, such wells were dug with a slight vertical curve so that the water was shaded, thus reducing evaporation. Their average depth was about five feet and they were usually quite inconspicuous.[93] Although sub-surface water clearly existed in this region, Warburton was unable to ascertain the indicators. Indeed, from fifty attempts his party only twice succeeded in finding water.

Digging for water was now very much a feature of Central Australian exploration. Because Stuart's men frequently had to make extensive excavations of creek beds, learning to find promising moist sites became an important skill. Despite having shovels, the labour involved in such excavations was considerable. On his third expedition, Stuart and his two assistants Kekwick and Head continually exhausted themselves while digging for water, especially after they lost their shovel in crossing the Macdonnell Ranges. Stuart commented:

> There is plenty of water under this sand, but having only a small tin dish, the labour is too great. My men have lost all their former energy and activity and move about as if they were a hundred years old; it is sad to see them ...[94]

In his subsequent expedition the effort involved in watering the horses in this way, with the larger number of animals, became even more significant, inducing Stuart to increase the number of men in his party.

Giles' second expedition to the east of the Gibson Desert was characterised by digging for water in creek beds in the vicinity of ranges. Although a shovel was provided for this purpose, on occasions when Giles was reconnoitring, he frequently forgot to take it with him, thus increasing the labour disproportionably, for tools as crude as saddlebags had to be used. Julius Brockman, on his exploration in the 1880s between Roebourne and Broome, expended much energy digging waterholes. He reported that frequently he and his two assistants dug as deep as eighteen feet, dragging the wet sand up in saddlebags.[95] The labour involved was both intense and extremely dangerous, for such excavations often collapsed. Lawrence Wells, leader of the Calvert Expedition in 1894, had similar experiences when, north of Warburton's track and before reaching the Fitzroy River, a well was found when the expedition was in severe danger of dying of thirst. J G Hill's description of this event highlights both the labour and dangers inherent in watering stock from such a supply:

> We reached this well on the 18th and had to spend thirty-six hours in baling fifty-five buckets of water with a pannikin. It was very dangerous work, on account of the probability of the sand bank falling in. Mr. Wells insisted that either he or I should do the work, as it was too dangerous to send the men down.[96]

All the major explorers attempted to carry water, particularly those who had camels and could take advantage of their superb weight-carrying capacity. On leaving Coopers Creek in December 1860, Burke and Wills' camels and horses carried a total of 475 litres.[97] Although Stuart had special waterbags made up for his fifth expedition in 1862, they were not particularly successful, for the inner lining separated and they leaked badly. As well, because each bag only had a single small filler-hole, filling them took up to half a day.[98]

The quality and quantity of equipment supplied for the explorations during this period ranged from the sub-minimal to the superfluous. Burke and Wills' expedition exemplified the latter, with approximately twenty-one tonnes of equipment being carried. The gross load was so heavy that initially the horses and camels were unable to cope and wagons were hired to take a proportion of the goods. This tremendous burden not only demonstrated Burke's inability to distinguish among the essential, the desirable and the dispensable, but also hindered the expedition severely, for its mobility was greatly curtailed. The superfluous equipment he carried included a stationery cabinet, a Chinese gong, oaken camp stools and an oaken camp table with a cedar top. The only other Australian explorer previously known to have taken tables was Mitchell, who also included lace tablecloths made by his mother-in-law![99]

Burke also took forty-eight spare sets of spur rowels, which is extremely difficult to understand, given that spur rowels almost never wear out and rarely ever break or become lost, and that for much of the way Burke made his expedition members walk and thus they would have not been wearing spurs. In addition, Burke had several complete sets of grooming equipment of sufficient quality to prepare and present his horses and camels for an Agricultural Society show. All he really required were several stiff body-brushes to take out dried sweat and perhaps one or two pairs of clippers. Finally, in what is perhaps the most bizarre example of all, Burke took air pillows to support his camels' heads in case he had to swim them across rivers!

In contrast to Burke and Wills, Stuart, Forrest, Giles and Warburton attempted to reduce the weight and bulk of their equipment to an absolute minimum. They were all experienced bushmen, well aware of the conditions their horses and camels would have to endure.

From Stuart's journal, however, there is evidence that he was over-preoccupied with lightness and mobility. As a consequence, he and his men were for most of the time on short rations and suffered accordingly.[100] Should Stuart have carried an antiscorbutic agent, for instance, rather than relying on finding native plants, he would almost certainly have avoided the scurvy which almost killed him on the fifth expedition. Of their overall food supply, Stuart himself admitted:

> I find the quantity of rations is not enough; five pounds of flour

> per week is too little for many weeks together. It may do very well for a month or so, but when it comes to the length of time we have been out, we all feel it very much; and the dried meat that I brought with me being very young, it has not half the strength in it that old meat has.[101]

A shortage of meat appears to have been a problem with all of the major explorers of this period. Giles overcame it on his second expedition by slaughtering and smoking the meat from those horses which were failing.[102] In order to prepare this smoke-dried meat for consumption, it was boiled, pounded with an axe head or shoeing hammer and then cut into small pieces. The resulting material was then wetted and mixed with dampened flour to form a horsemeat damper, which was cooked on coals. The bones, hoofs, shanks, skull and so on were used to make soup, being boiled up overnight until they:

> ... resolved themselves into a consistent jelly that stank like rotten glue, and at breakfast at least, when this disgusting stuff was in a measure coagulated, we would request one another with the greatest politeness to pass the gluepot.[103]

Warburton was so long in the field that he ran out of flour, tea, sugar and meat. To overcome the meat problem he slaughtered those camels which were failing. As there was no salt, the meat was sun-dried. Warburton commented that they were not in a position to be squeamish and nothing at all was wasted.

> ... every single scrap was greedily devoured ... No shred was passed over; head, feet, hide, tail, all went into the boiling pot, even the very bones were stewed down for soup first and then broken for the sake of the marrow they contained ... The head was steadily attacked and soon reduced to a polished skull, tongue, brains and cheeks all having disappeared; the foot was much esteemed as a delicacy (and the preparation entailed scraping and singeing as much hair off as possible) ... Having done this, stick the end into the glowing coals, burn it for some considerable time and then, withdrawing it, place it on its side on the ground and strike the other side smartly with the back of a tomahawk, when, if charred enough, the sole will come off, [leaving] a large flat slab composed of tough spongy horn ... Having got the sole off, place the foot in a bucket and keep it steadily boiling for thirty-six hours ... then at last you may venture to hope that your teeth — if good — will enable you to masticate your long deferred dinner.[104]

Such experiences reflected the forbidding nature of the tasks the desert explorers set themselves, rather than the quality or adequacy of their equipment. Indeed private sources were now playing a considerable role in providing funding. All of Stuart's expeditions were backed, in whole or in part, by Messrs Chambers and Finke. Forrest's expeditions were supported by a mixture of government funding, private donations and grants from scientific societies. Warburton was financed by Sir Thomas Elder, who also provided the camels for both his and Giles' expeditions. Giles' five expeditions were funded by himself and his brother-in-law, von Mueller, and the South Australian Government. No matter who paid the bill for the equipment, such expeditions lacked nothing which the leaders felt was essential. Giles noted, when setting out on his fourth expedition, that he had nineteen camels, provisions for eight months and 'a perfect equipment for carrying water.'[105] Similarly, once the South Australian Government became involved in Stuart's expeditions, it was determined to 'place Mr Stuart in the position to go out again with such an equipment as would be sufficient ...'[106]

Nevertheless, cost and competence were clearly unrelated. Forrest was able to mount his central Australian expedition with £400 from the Government and approximately £200 of private funding. The anticipated cost of Alexander Forrest's Kimberley expedition was approximately £950. By contrast, the Burke and Wills expedition, together with the subsequent rescue parties and the chartering of vessels, finally cost approximately £35,000.[107]

Despite the unquestionable development of bushmanship to this point, not all explorers were yet confident of their innate sense of placement and direction. When Stuart was in the extremely flat and occasionally thickly timbered country south of Daly Waters, he commented that it would be terrible country in which to be lost, for there were no landmarks and the ground was often too hard or stony to show tracks. Consequently horses which would follow their tracks back to the last camp became greatly valued. One evening, when uncertain of the direction of a camp near Newcastle Waters on Stuart's fifth expedition, Frank Thring tried out several horses until he found one which possessed this ability. Because he had previously only been used as a packhorse, he bucked when Thring first mounted him. Fortunately '... he then settled down to running his tracks back to camp (in the dark), where we wound up about ten o'clock.'[108]

Thring used this horse almost incessantly thereafter and, on one occasion when a member of the party had become lost, volunteered to search for him. When Thring, who had almost given up and was ready to return to camp, fortuitously found the unfortunate man, he:

Alexander Forrest's well-equipped, well-mounted 1978 expedition picks its way through the Leopolds. (From Forrest's North West Exploration)

> ... dropped his horse's reins and put his arms around my neck and sobbed and cried. It was some time before I could pacify him.[109]

Thring later recollected that, because of the nature of the country, he would have been particularly reluctant to '... have volunteered to go back myself if I had not been riding Gloag on this trip.'[110]

Later, on the journey home, when Stuart's health declined so rapidly that Thring had full responsibility for navigating, Gloag proved invaluable. The horse carried out his task by no single skill or sense, but used a combination of sight, smell and a sense of placement and direction. According to Thring:

> ... the horse ran his tracks back from camp to camp. Sometimes

> in going over stony country there were no signs of our tracks, but the horse seemed to be so confident of his movements that I did not interfere with him and the old camping grounds used to turn up all right.[111]

On the same expedition Auld also found cause to value the same uncanny sense in his own mount for, after stopping on one occasion, he found that the main body of the expedition had moved ahead and left no tracks on the hard, rocky ground. Auld later wrote that he lit his pipe, put his hands in his pockets so as not to interfere with the course the pony was picking and said 'now Teaser, my boy, you find the tracks.'[112] The pony put his nose to the ground, made a few diversions, then soon started cantering northwards, bringing him shortly within earshot of the horse-bells of the main team. In appreciation, Auld bought the horse at the dispersal sale in Adelaide after the completion of the expedition and kept him for the remainder of his life.[113]

Like the Gregory brothers who preceded them, the major explorers of this period were intensely professional. During John Forrest's Central Australian Expedition, for example, the reconnoitring and the movement of the main body of the expedition were carried out in complete unison, so much so that Forrest later commended his brother for his unremitting attention to detail.

> To my brother, Mr. Alexander Forrest, I am especially indebted for his assistance and advice on many occasions, also for his indomitable energy and perseverance. Every service entrusted to him was admirably carried out. He never disappointed me. When absent for a week, I knew to a few minutes when we should meet again. Whether horses or loads had to be abandoned, it mattered not to him, he always carried out the service ...[114]

Thus Forrest could keep moving ahead, continually reconnoitring, leaving only notes attached to trees, knowing that his brother would be carrying out his part of the operation as instructed.[115] Having an equally skilled second-in-command, such as Stuart had with Thring, Giles with Tietkens and Warburton with his son Richard, meant that much of the incessant pressure which earlier leaders such as Eyre and Leichhardt had complained of was eliminated.

Stuart, who reconnoitred continuously and comprehensively, intuitively felt his way across much of Central Australia. So attuned was he to soil types, accompanying vegetation and the almost imperceptible lie of the land which would reveal the eventual course of water flow, that he seemed

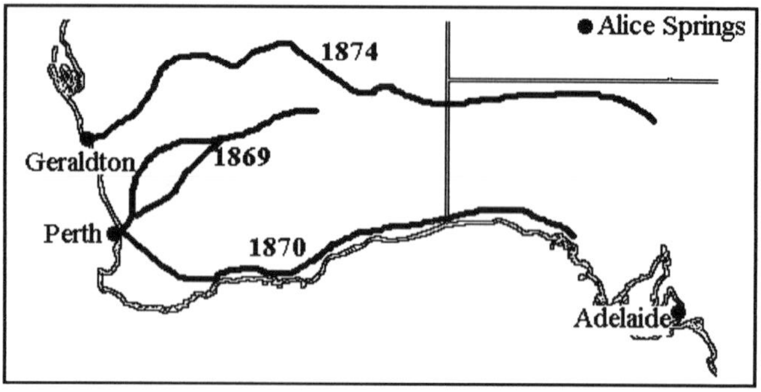

John Forrest's three expeditions.

subconsciously to know the best course to take. This skill, combined with his experience and organisational skills, made his expeditions run like clockwork. His written orders for his men give the clearest indication of his minute attention to detail. He insisted, for example, that nothing was to be removed from a saddlebag without Kekwick's knowledge and furthermore, should any object be taken out it was to be rewrapped and replaced in exactly the same position, in the same bag. As a result, Kekwick always knew precisely where to find articles.

Thring was in charge of the horses on Stuart's final expedition. According to Auld, the animals were divided into groups of eighteen, with specific saddles and numbered saddlebags allotted to each horse. Auld records that within a short time the horses knew their groups and places within each group and, when driven in the mornings, would line up in the correct positions. Stuart's men were thus spared the wearying and temper-fraying ordeal of carrying up to fifty pack-saddles and a hundred saddlebags weighing up to thirty-five kilograms each around a constantly milling mob of horses and re-adjusting the girths, breast-plates and britchings of every saddle each day.

Giles, with his experienced men, his rapidly acquired knowledge of camels, his experimentally devised techniques, his specifically designed saddlebags and his transportable canvas water trough which made watering far easier than with buckets, was able to move with pertinacity across the Great Victorian Desert. In describing his progress the explorer was so moved that his customary wit, but not his command of language, temporarily deserted him.

> But this expedition, as organised, equipped and intended by Sir Thomas Elder, was a thing of such excellence and precision, it

> moved along apparently by mechanical action; and it seemed to me, as we conquered these frightful deserts by its power, like playing upon some fine new instrument ...[116]

By the end of 1870s explorers knew exactly the equipment they required. Water bags and containers had been developed to suit expected conditions. Water-finding skills and equipment and the expertise necessary to husband stock through long waterless stages were now being applied. When it became clear that horses and horsemanship had reached the limits of their usefulness, the skills necessary to use camels were rapidly developed. Firearms and camping equipment were now of superb quality. The sense of direction and placement had been improved to the point where Aboriginal guides were seen as being of little or no value. Techniques for deterring hostile Aborigines were clearly understood. All in all, the explorers, who were pushing always to the limits, had become consummate professionals.

So the initial exploration of Australia and the associated development of bushmanship were complete. Thereafter, field work would be a process of refinement and of painstaking, scientifically oriented research. This landmark change in emphasis was encapsulated by Giles on the last page of his journal, where he wistfully marked the passing of a romantic era.

> The history of Australian exploration, though not yet quite complete, is now so far advanced towards its end, that only minor details now are wanting, to fill the volume up; and though I shall not attempt to rank myself amongst the first or greatest, yet I think I have reason to call myself, the last of the Australian explorers.[117]

8

THE FINAL TASK — THE DESERTS OF WESTERN AUSTRALIA

Exploration in Australia during the 1890s was of a completely different nature from that of the preceding decades. The last unknown areas were now being closed in and the overall approach was changing towards an emphasis upon field research. There were four major expeditions in this decade. In late 1889, Giles' former lieutenant, Tietkens, closely explored the Lake Amadeus, Ayers Rock and Mount Olga regions. The Elder Scientific Exploring Expedition of 1891–2 traversed the eastern portion of the Gibson Desert, moved across to Giles' Queen Victoria Springs, then travelled via Southern Cross to the mouth of the Murchison. There it was prematurely disbanded after covering 4,392 kilometres of previously unexplored country and suffering severely from water shortages and exposure to summer heat. The Calvert Scientific Exploring Expedition set off in 1894 from Mullewa, a hundred kilometres east of Geraldton in Western Australia, and headed north and north-north-east, eventually reaching the Fitzroy River after a desperate struggle.[1] Finally, the 1896 Horn Scientific Exploration made a close examination of the Macdonnell Ranges region, which included the Alice Springs area.

Easily the single most important factor influencing the changes in the nature of field research was a gradual move away from economic motives, although the earlier expeditions of this period were still primarily economically oriented. This shift of emphasis had been foreshadowed in the opening address to the 1887 Congress of the Australian Association for the Advancement of Science, when H C Russell argued:

> ... we must not take the vulgar view, which only sees the necessity for cultivating those branches of science that are direct producers of gold and minerals.[2]

Tietkens' venture was funded by the Central Australian Exploring and

Prospecting Association.[3] Although the expedition was under the control of the South Australian branch of the Royal Geographical Society of Australasia, and it was envisaged, inter alia, that experiments would be made in central Australia with date palm seeds,[4] the emphasis was undeniably economic. Tietkens corroborated this, pointing out on one occasion that:

> As a geographer, I would much like to continue on until the west coast is reached and so decide beyond all doubt and forever, the nature of the country, but my instructions direct me to endeavour to discover minerals and pastoral areas.[5]

Consequently the party often stopped and spent days gathering mineral samples, as Tietkens' diary frequently indicates. His entry for 12 April 1889, for example, reads:

> Tuesday April 9th — all of us out prospecting ... Wednesday April 10th — prospecting all day ... Saturday April 12th — had trial holes put down, intending to pan off the stuff from the bottom ... [6]

The Elder Expedition, although funded and equipped solely by the prominent pastoralist and entrepreneur, was ostensibly the first expedition to be mounted with purely scientific motives. While economic returns possibly influenced Elder's interest, such considerations were not particularly apparent in the official outline, which expressed the supposedly non-economic nature of the project:

> The object of this Expedition is to make an exhaustive Scientific Exploration of these regions and to determine and map with certainty and accuracy the position and nomenclature of all geographical physical features and ascertain the nature of its fauna, flora, geological structure and climatic conditions ... the unexplored and unknown country in South Australia, the Northern Territory and Western Australia, situated near as well as between the routes of previous Explorers Forrest, Giles, Warburton and Gosse ... (comprises) an area of about a million square miles. It is desired that the exploration shall be as complete and exhaustive as possible.[7]

Yet although these instructions were professional and scientific in tenor, the desire for economic return was undeniable, as the instructions to the geologist showed:

> The scientific work which the Geologist will undertake is of primary importance and may result in discoveries of great value

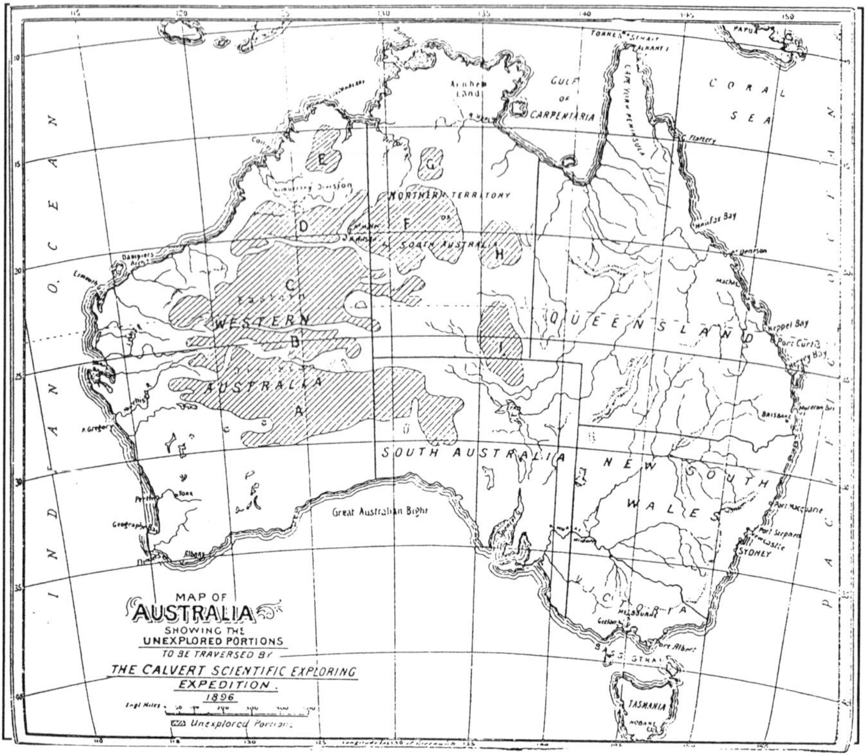

> ... No opportunity should be missed for washing likely drift for gold, tin, or gem stones ...[8]

Following the disbandment of the Elder Expedition, those areas designated on a map prepared for the South Australian branch of the Royal Geographical Society as C, D, E, F, H and I (see above) were still unknown and a close analysis of them was seen as desirable. It was for this purpose that the Calvert Expedition was mounted.

It was not until the Horn Scientific Expedition, which was easily the most rigorously planned, controlled and executed field project to date, that an unarguably scientific and non-commercial major exploration was undertaken. This expedition was formed to investigate the premise that the Macdonnell Ranges had been an island when Australia was earlier submerged and:

> ... that consequently older forms of life might be found in the more inaccessible parts ... I resolved to organise and equip a party, composed of scientific men, to thoroughly explore this

> belt of country ... In order to secure the best men in Australia, I decided to make it a semi-national undertaking and to this end invitations were extended to the Premiers of the Principal Colonies, asking them to nominate scientific representatives.[9]

So different in nature was this expedition, with its tightly delimited area of research, its purely scientific interest and the high quality of its scientific staff that, according to Baldwin Spencer, the public believed it was a search for gold:

> ... they could not understand a body of scientific gentlemen going into a desert country, giving up their time and services and submitting to all the dangers, discomforts and hardships attendant upon the life for any other reason ... The real objects of the Expedition (were) the scientific examination of the country from Oodnadatta to the Macdonnell Ranges; the collection of specimens illustrative of the fauna, flora and geological structure and mineralogical resources of that region and the illustration by photography of the Aborigines in their primitive state, the collection of information as to their manners, customs and languages and the reproduction of their paintings.[10]

A second element underlying the change of emphasis during this decade was the fact that these expeditions were now filling in the final broad geographic details of the continent and, as a consequence, frequently crisscrossing previous explorers' tracks. Because existing information on water supplies was vital, all the leaders of these scientific explorations took pains to be conversant with it. In 1889, when Tietkens was rained out in one camp for some days, he commented '... the only reading I have is Mr Gosse's diary and if it rains much longer I shall know it off by heart'.[11] Exploring parties saw and crossed the tracks of their predecessors and photographed their blazed trees with amazing frequency. Tietkens, for one, was continually identifying features mapped earlier and, at one particular campsite, found trees marked by Giles, Gosse, Carmichael and Chewings.[12] Lawrence Wells, the leader of the Calvert Expedition, remarked that he had crossed the tracks of Forrest, Giles and Warburton as his party headed northwards from Meekatharra.

Because, in most instances, water supplies and the nature of the country to be crossed were known from other explorers, scientific expeditions were able to concentrate on their given tasks. As Spencer of the Horn Expedition commented:

> Though away from beaten tracks we only traversed country

> previously explored and had practically no serious difficulties to contend with. We had, however, more time to devote to an examination of the different features — zoological, botanical, geological and meteorological — of the country than was possible in the case of the original explorers.[13]

The expeditions of the 1890s also benefited from Australia's expanding transport and communications network. Samples could now often be sent much of the way home by train, ship or carriage, thus enabling them to arrive in considerably better condition. Lindsay, for one, sent ten boxes of samples from his depot at Fraser Range, through the port of Esperance on the south coast of Western Australia,[14] so allowing him to 'relieve at least two camels.'[15] Furthermore, on occasions expedition animals and equipment were carried some distance by train to an inland setting-off point. Should Stuart, for example, have enjoyed this benefit, he would have saved considerable time and effort as he retraced his steps northwards on his third, fourth and fifth expeditions in the late 1850s and early 1860s.

A further factor enabling the emphasis of field exploration to change during the 1890s was the quality of the expedition leaders and many of their staff, who were highly experienced men. By 1889 Tietkens had not only accompanied Giles on two major expeditions, gaining considerable experience with camels in the process, but also had a further ten years' field experience in inland Australia. Lawrence Wells, who was second-in-command of the Elder Expedition, also had considerable experience as a surveyor in inland South Australia. A few years later, partly on the strength of David Lindsay's warm recommendation, he was seconded from the South Australian Crown Lands Department and appointed leader of the Calvert Expedition. His cousin, C F Wells, who was also an experienced surveyor in inland South Australia and the Northern Territory, was appointed Second-in-Command. Finally, the Horn Expedition's collector and taxidermist, George Keartland, had had previous field experience on the Calvert Expedition.[16]

Finally, because supply requirements had been steadily established through the preceding hundred years of exploration, their provision was now adequate to say the least. Tietkens' quite small expedition, for example, had two camels out of twelve specifically engaged in carrying water.[17] The Elder Expedition employed fourteen men and forty-four camels, of which ten were for riding and thirty-four for packing purposes. More than 1,800 litres of water were carried in almost forty containers, ranging in capacity from 120-litre kegs to individual waterbags.[18] The quantity of food and water, the numbers of pack animals, the expertise to manage these animals, the cooking and camping equipment — all requirements were understood and calculated with exactitude. The Elder Expedition's rations were sufficiently sophisticated to include dried peas, compressed vegetables, currants, raisins, dried apples and apricots.[19] Furthermore, the explorers soon heeded Tietkens' 1889 comments on the dangers of camel poisoning.

> ... future travellers to these regions should be supplied with some simple remedies for these cases of vegetable poisoning ... Darby [his riding camel] has answered his last call and is now at rest ...[20]

The increasing scientific emphasis of exploration eventually led to a reduction in scope and a changed approach. Whereas the Elder and Calvert Expeditions were planned on an immense scale, the Horn Expedition was designed to examine methodically a specific area of feasible dimensions, given the constraints of time, water supply, academic study leave and scientific rigour. Instead of being preoccupied with maximum mobility over a basically straight-line course, it epitomised the radical notion of thoroughness of examination and sampling. Tietkens and his men often spent full days photographing topographical features and collecting and classifying botanical and geological specimens.[21] The expedition leader even commented that, after visiting Mount Sonder, he was dissatisfied with the thoroughness of his survey and intended to make a closer examination on a future occasion.[22]

This philosophical shift was exemplified in the instructions issued to the staff of the Elder Scientific Exploring Expedition.

> It is desired that the exploration shall be as complete and exhaustive as possible ... it will, therefore, be necessary to depart very largely from the usual manner of determining the route to be traversed when the task of the explorer is to proceed by the most direct practicable route through unknown regions.[23]

The Elder Expedition was the first to increase the thoroughness of analysis by sending small parties off in various directions to answer specific questions and to cover the country more comprehensively.[24] This technique was subsequently employed on both the Calvert and Horn Expeditions where, particularly in the latter case, straight-line mobility was of little importance because of the limited geographic scope of the operation. After establishing a new depot within a designated area of study, the expedition, at times, had up to three separate groups out working simultaneously, so that comprehensive scientific analyses could be achieved.[25] Lindsay's instructions outlined the benefits which were expected to accrue from this approach:

> ... the surrounding country may be elaborately examined by radial traverses, thus making absolutely certain that no important topographical or other physical feature is left undiscovered.[26]

While smaller groups were away working, members of the main body remained at the depot and carried out essential report-writing, analysis and preparation of samples and further collecting in the vicinity of the camp. On several occasions Lindsay commented on the productivity of such activities.

> Mr Streich has had some opportunities today to study the geological features, whilst Mr Helms is kept very busy indeed, as, owing to the rains, both insect and plant life are plentiful ... Mr. Helms has quite an array of stuffed [wallabies'] bodies hanging up.[27]

Camps were also established in areas which were seen as potentially productive and daily stages shortened accordingly. On one occasion, for example:

> [We camped early] ... because there was a large rock face covered with native drawings, which we wished to sketch.[28]

Although this approach slowed the rate of progress, Lindsay was not concerned. Indeed, on one occasion he commented:

> Mr. Helms and I got on capitally, although his searching for plants and etc., often delayed us and made our journeyings short. Still I did not object to that as his work was having good results, as shown by the large parcels of various botanical specimens, besides birds' eggs, reptiles and insects.[29]

By the time of the Horm Expedition this sea change of emphasis was complete, leading Spencer to comment that:

> The actual route was to be determined upon by the four members of the scientific staff and upon Mr Winnecke devolved the responsibility of carrying out the wishes of the scientific staff so far as he judged them to be consistent with the safety of the Expedition.[30]

To take advantage of the improved opportunities for scientific research, the quality of scientific personnel improved rapidly. While the Elder Expedition, whose leader David Lindsay was a Fellow of the Royal Geographical Society, was perhaps marginally inferior in terms of

Sartorial elegance in the outback: members of the Horn Scientific Expedition.

scientific personnel to Augustus Gregory's earlier North Australian Expedition, the Horn Expedition was extremely well staffed. It included Professor Baldwin Spencer of the University of Melbourne, who was responsible for the zoological research and photography; J A Watt of the University of Sydney, who was involved in geological and mineralogical work; Professor R Tate FLS, of Adelaide University, who undertook geological and botanical research; Dr Edward Stirling FRS, of the same institution, who carried out anthropological studies; and C A Winnecke FRGS, a qualified surveyor, who undertook the surveying and meteorological observations and data collection. F W Belt and G A Keartland worked in the field as collectors and taxidermists and two experienced prospectors assisted with the sinking of sample holes and the collecting and preparation of mineral samples.[31]

In order to maximise the scientists' research efforts, expeditions during this decade carried increasing numbers of support staff. A photograph taken on the Horn Expedition, shows the full-time camp cook standing near the fire while the other expedition members are still asleep, the obvious comfort of their mattresses contrasting strongly with the hard ground their predecessors had had to endure. In another photograph, the quite formal attire of the scientists, which contrasts with the standard bush uniform of moleskin trousers, denim shirts and cabbage tree hats, also illustrates the changes which had occurred. The contrast between these situations and the experiences of the scientists on Augustus Gregory's North Australian Expedition and of F G Waterhouse on Stuart's fifth expedition, is remarkable.

Scientific expectations increased as the quality of field work improved. Indeed, the Elder Scientific Exploring Expedition members could justifiably have groaned under their burdens. Von Mueller, South Australian Government Astronomer Charles Todd and J G Tepper of the Adelaide Museum contributed copious instructions on the means and techniques necessary to achieve the standards they expected. Lindsay was expected to keep an elaborate journal, with special emphasis on the mapping and placement of topographical features such as ranges, water courses, drainage channels and water supplies, as well as ethnographic material on the Aboriginal people. His was an integrating task, incorporating the data supplied by the expedition's scientists. To allow this material to be presented in a succinct manner, he was instructed to complete a specific form daily.[32]

Surveyor Lawrence Wells, who afterwards led the Calvert Expedition, was expected to provide complete geographical coordinates, magnetic variations, course bearings, altitudes, distances travelled and natural features, in a detailed field map.[33] F J Elliot, the medical officer, was required to collect ethnographic data, including the numbers of Aborigines, their diseases, physiques and colour shades, plus measurements of a 'considerable number'. Information on tattoo marks, mythology, totems, initiations, customs, natural food, signals, commerce and so forth was also requested. Furthermore, as complete a vocabulary as possible was to be collected.[34] In addition, Elliot was instructed to produce a photographic record of highlights of the journey, including portraits of individuals and illustrations of the geographical and botanical features of the country. The Aborigines photographed had to have a standard measuring stick alongside them and each photograph was to have location details recorded.[35]

Geologist, mineralogist and meteorologist F P V Streich was perhaps the hardest-worked of all. Data recorded had to be sufficiently comprehensive to allow for the compilation of a detailed map showing the site of origin of all the samples. Such samples had to be packed separately and assigned a number, date and locality and at least four complete sets of samples, each of about twenty cubic centimetres, were to be collected. The artesian water potential was also to be given special attention.[36]

Meteorological observations were to be made exactly at 9.00 a.m., 3.00 p.m. and 9.00 p.m. when possible, using the appropriate instruments. Maximum and minimum temperatures, relative humidity, the amount and types of clouds, wind speed and direction and the general state of weather were all to be recorded.

Naturalist and botanical collector R Helms was similarly hard-worked. Von Mueller, who was particularly concerned with the gathering of a comprehensive collection, instructed Helms to collect even fungi. He further directed that specimens of all plants thought to be poisonous were to be collected for later analysis. Sufficient samples of all specimens were to be gathered to allow for the later making up of '... many separate complete collections. Of rare specimens at least ten or twelve should be obtained if possible.'[37] Specimens had to be labelled according to locality, date, colour of flower, scent, colour of fruit, taste, height, appearance of bark and nature of wood.[38] As von Mueller pointed out:

> It is usual for explorers to simply record the names of the various species discovered; this is not an example to be followed as the value of the botanist's journal will be greatly enhanced if it contains a discriminative description of the botanical physical aspect of the country and the conditions which govern the existence of the various species of timber trees and plants.[39]

Von Mueller also gave advice on the drying, preparation and packing of plant specimens. Tepper of the Adelaide Museum provided two and a half pages of advice on the collecting of botanical samples and ten pages of information on preparing zoological specimens, including techniques for skinning, stuffing, drying and packing and for preparing arsenical soap for birds, fishes, reptiles, land shells, fresh water shells and crustacea. He also instructed that specimen labels should include date, locality, sex and the colour of eyes, bills and legs. Information on the nature of the country where each specimen was collected, including vegetation, geology, time of year, altitude, Aboriginal names and so forth, was also required. In the case of insects, a dozen specimens of each should, if possible, be procured.[40]

Yet despite their increasing sophistication, field researchers during the 1890s were still very much at the mercy of the environment and of the limitations of their pack and riding animals. The heat and aridity of inland Western Australia, which forced Lindsay to stay close to the settled regions and caused Sir Thomas Elder to abort his expedition, were the most telling factors. Two years later, the Calvert Expedition was lucky not to perish in such conditions. Due to water shortages, Wells was forced to:

> ... abandon five of ... [the camels] together with all his surplus gear, firearms, ammunition, specimens, photographic cameras and survey plant. These effects included Mr Keartland's collection of about 3,000 specimens ... Owing to the intensity of the heat and the terrible condition of the camels they had to traverse the last 170 miles by night.[41]

Using animals for conveyance also meant that the daily rate of travel was slow, restricting the time available to scientists for research purposes. Spencer commented on this problem, pointing out that, of the 125 days which the Horn Expedition spent in the field, less than twenty were devoted totally to research. During the remainder, only the '... odd hour or two were available for collecting.'[42] In addition, problems such as breakages of scientific instruments, spoilage of samples by buffeting and wetting and the selection of research areas according to the availability of water supplies would not be resolved until reliable motor transport became available.

Notwithstanding such difficulties, some outstanding scientific results were obtained during the 1890s. According to the South Australian Government Geologist H Y L Brown, Tietkens' 100 rock specimens gave '... a good idea of the geology of a part of the interior which hitherto was unknown ...'[43] On the other hand, von Mueller appraised the explorer's collection of 250 plant species as 'somewhat disappointing'.[44] Nevertheless, Tietkens was awarded £250 by the South Australian government and was elected Fellow of the Royal Geographical Society.

During the Elder Expedition, Lindsay and his men explored and mapped 130,000 square kilometres[45] and forwarded ten crates of samples from Esperance. Overall, however, this was a scientifically disappointing expedition for, apart from the extensive field work carried out in the eastern Gibson Desert area, little else was accomplished. Lindsay made a direct line from this region to the Queen Victoria Springs and then, because of water problems, headed straight for Fraser Range Station, north-east of Esperance. The expedition then skirted settled areas until it reached the Murchison, where a valuable six-week reconnaissance was carried out while Lindsay was reporting to Elder in South Australia, prior to the decision to abandon the expedition. Although a huge distance was covered over much previously unexplored country, the scientific results were limited.

The Horn Expedition can be seen as the culmination of over a hundred years of patient and often painful accumulation of the knowledge and skills necessary to mount and sustain such expeditions. After the return of this expedition to Adelaide in 1896, it took two years to analyse and report on the results, which were finally released in four volumes.[46] They were the work of erudite men, who also possessed the necessary measure of practical expertise. The accuracy and sophistication of their results are in total contrast to the vague reports, some eighty years earlier, of George Evans who, it may be remembered, was forced to apologise for his lack of cleverness.[47]

Thanks to a combination of highly developed bushmanship, the virtual completion of geographical exploration and the application of more sophisticated techniques and methodology, field research in Australia had finally come to realise the expectations of the scientific societies.

ENDNOTES

(NB. *The Historical Records of New South Wales* and *The Historical Records of Australia* will hereafter appear as *HRN* and *HRA*, respectively. The Mitchell Library, Sydney, is referred to by the initials ML. The J S Battye Library of West Australian History is referred to by the initials BL. *Exploration Diaries* refers to the six-volume bound typescript held by the Battye Library. Reference is also made to the author's Field Notes Supplement to his doctoral thesis, copies of which are held by the Battye Library and Curtin University library.)

Chapter One

1. Marie Boas Hall, *All Scientists Now: The Royal Society in the Nineteenth Century* (Cambridge University Press, 1984), Andrew Thomas Gage and William Thomas Stearn, *A Bicentenary History of the Linnean Society of London* (London: Academic Press Ltd, 1988), and Neil Campbell and R Martin Smellie, *The Royal Society of Edinburgh (1783–1983): The First Two Hundred Years* (Edinburgh: The Royal Society of Edinburgh, 1983).
2. Hall, p. IX.
3. Hall, p. IX.
4. Hall, p. X.
5. Gwendy Caroe, *The Royal Institution: An Informal History*. (London: John Murray Ltd, 1985) p. 12.
6. Caroe, p. 29.
7. Patrick O'Brian, *Joseph Banks: A Life* (London: Collins Harvill, 1987) pp. 221–2.
8. A B Rendle, 'Banks as Patron of Science' *Proceedings of the Linnean Society of London, 1918*. (Piccadilly: The Linnean Society, 1918) p. 11.
9. O'Brian, p. 227.
10. Rendle, p. 10.
11. E C K Gonner, 'The Settlement of Australia' in *The Founding of Australia: The Argument About Australia's Origins*. (Edited by Ged Martin) (Sydney: Hale and Iremonger, 1978) p. 31. Gonner based this assessment on Banks' testimony as reported in the Commons Journals, Vol XXXVII, p. 314.
12. 23 Aug 1783. *HRN:* V1 P2, pp. 1–6.
13. 23 Aug 1783. *HRN:* V1 P2, p. 3.
14. Sydney to the Lords Commissioners of the Treasury, 18 Aug 1786. *HRN:* V1 P2, p. 17.
15. Sydney to the Lords Commissioners of the Treasury, 18 Aug 1786. *HRN:* V1 P2, p. 19.
16. Ged Martin, 'Economic Motives Behind the Founding of Botany Bay' in Martin, p. 250.
17. Martin, 'Economic Motives', p. 239.
18. G C Bolton, 'The Hollow Conqueror' in Martin, p. 103.
19. Ged Martin, 'The Founding of New South Wales' in *The Origins of Australia's Capital Cities*. (Edited by Pamela Statham) (Sydney: Cambridge University Press, 1989) p. 42.

Chapter Two

1. Phillip to Sydney, 13 Feb 1790. *HRN:* V1 P2, p. 306.
2. Banks to King, 15 May 1798. *HRN:* V3, p. 382.
3. Banks to King, 13 Dec 1798. *HRN:* V3, p. 516.

4. Portland to the Governor of the Settlement of New South Wales (acknowledged by Acting-Governor King), 26 Feb 1800. *HRA:* S1 V2, p. 499.
5. Portland, 26 Feb 1800. *HRA:* S1 V2, p. 500.
6. Hunter to Portland, 10 Jan 1798. *HRN:* V3, p. 347.
7. Hunter to Portland, 10 Jan 1798. *HRA:* S1 V2, p. 118.
8. Portland to Hunter, 21 Dec 1798. *HRA:* S1 V2, p. 241.
9. King to Portland, 21 Aug 1801. *HRA:* S1 V3, p. 169.
10. King to Hobart, 20 Dec 1804. *HRA:* S1 V5, pp. 204–5.
11. King to Hobart, 7 Aug 1803. *HRA:* S1 V4, p. 357.
12. Phillip to Sydney, 15 May 1788. *HRN:* V1 P2, p. 128.
13. Phillip to Sydney, 15 May 1788. *HRN:* V1 P2, pp. 128–135.
14. Captain Watkin Tench, *Sydney's First Four Years: being a reprint of A Narrative of the Expedition to Botany Bay and A Complete Account of the Settlement at Port Jackson.* (Sydney: Library of Australian History, 1979) p. 66.
15. Tench, p. 66.
16. Tench, p. 175.
17. Hill to Wathen, 26 July 1790. *HRN:* V1 P2, p. 371.
18. Tench, pp. 67–8.
19. Captain John Hunter, *An Historical Journal of Events at Sydney and at Sea: 1787–1792.* (FACS ED) (Edited by John Bach) (Sydney: Angus and Robertson, 1968) p. 49.
20. Hunter, p. 48.
21. p. 47.
22. George Caley, *Reflections on the Colony of New South Wales.* (Edited by J E B Currey) (Melbourne: Lansdowne Press Pty. Ltd., 1966) pp. 63–4.
23. Banks to King, 13 Dec 1798. *HRN:* V3, p. 515.
24. Caley to Banks, 12 Mar 1804. Cited in Caley, p. 71.
25. Caley to Banks, 12 Mar 1804. Cited in Caley, p. 71.
26. Appendix A of *HRN:* V5 consists of a seventy-six-page Journal of Ensign Barrallier's attempts to cross the Blue Mountains in Nov and Dec 1802. Opposing pages are in French or English. p. 781.
27. King to Portland, 21 Aug 1801. Enclosure No. 2. *HRA:* S1 V3, pp. 173–4.
28. King to Hobart, 9 May 1803. Enclosure No. 12. *HRA:* S1 V4, p. 107.
29. King to Portland, 10 Mar 1801. Enclosure No. 2. Instructions to Lieutenant Grant by Phillip Gidley King. *HRA:* S1 V3, p. 65.
30. Hobart to King, 24 Feb1803. *HRA:* S1 V4, pp. 36–7.
31. Caley to Banks, 12 Oct 1800. *HRN:* V4, p. 240.
32. Caley to Banks, 7 July 1808. *HRN:* V6, p. 695.
33. Caley to Banks, 25 Aug 1801. Cited in Caley, p. 65.
34. The Admiralty to the Navy Board, 15 Apr 1801. *HRN:* V4, p. 344.
35. Banks to unstated (possibly William Milnes), 20 Jan 1801. *HRN:* V4, p. 291.
36. Banks to unstated (possibly William Milnes), 20 Jan 1801. *HRN:* V4, p. 291.
37. Brown to Banks, 30 May 1802. *HRN:* V4, p. 779.
38. Caley to Banks, 3 June 1799. It should be noted that this letter was written by Caley in regard to one of the several land excursions he made at ports-of-call on his voyage to Australia. The principle was, however, the same during his excursions in New South Wales. *HRN*: V3, p. 677.
39. Flinders to Banks, 24 Jan 1801. That extra space was available was perhaps fortunate for botanical science, for Gage and Stearn note that Brown eventually returned to England in 1805 with nearly 4000 plant specimens. While a number of these would have been collected subsequent to the *Investigator* voyage, Flinders' preparations showed considerable foresight, and an appreciation of what was to become a major problem for inland researchers. *HRN*, V4, p. 291.

40. Brown to Paterson, 4 Mar 1804. *HRA:* S3 V1, p. 490.
41. Brown to Greville, 30 May 1802. *HRN:* V4, p. 775.
42. Brown to Banks, 30 May 1802. *HRN:* V4, p. 777.
43. Macquarie to Bathurst, 28 Apr 1814. Enclosure No. 4. *HRA:* S1 V8, p. 171.
44. Macquarie to Bathurst, 30 June 1815. *HRA:* S1 V8, pp. 610–11.
45. Hill to Wathen, 26 July 1790. *HRN:* V1 P2, p. 368.
46. Appendix C, The Journal of Lieutenant King. Nov 1787 to Mar 1788. *HRN:* V2, p. 530 and p. 544.
47. Paterson to Dundas, 21 Mar 1795, *HRN:* V2, p. 286.
48. Hunter to Portland, 18 Nov 1796. *HRN:* V3, p. 182.
49. Hogan to Portland, 23 Sept 1797. *HRN:* V3, p. 300.
50. The Duke of Northumberland Papers, Aug 1806. The imported 17 h. h. British stallion 'Northumberland' was reported to have thrown stock '... much larger than any that were in the colony before his arrival and (which) will be found of very essential service to the colony'. *HRN:* V6, p. 182.
51. The Duke of Northumberland Papers, Aug 1806. *HRN:* V6, p. 182.
52. King to Hobart, 1 Mar 1804. Statement of Bills drawn up by Commissary Palmer. *HRA:* S1 V4, p. 474.
53. Barrallier's Journal, 6 Nov 1802. *HRN:* V5, p. 751.
54. Phillip to Sydney, 15 May 1788. *HRN:* V1 P2, p. 133.
55. Phillip to Sydney, 15 May 1788. *HRN:* V1 P2, p. 134.
56. Tench, p. 223.
57. Tench, p. 227.
58. Tench, p. 237.
59. Tench, p. 224. This information is given in the form of a footnote.
60. Tench, p. 228. The problem of an inability to gain a view of the country ahead was a feature of much of the exploration of Australia. Hunter first commented on this factor, pointing out that '... in a country like this you may travel many miles through the woods and not get sight of very high land, though it may not be half a mile from you.' (p. 343). Leichhardt commented similarly, over 50 years later, pointing out that although 'the ground is undulating and hilly, ... you very seldom catch sight of, or enjoy a view from, an outstanding eminence.' Marcel Aurousseau (ed), *The Letters of F W Ludwig Leichhardt, in Three Volumes.* (Cambridge University Press, 1968) Vol 2, p. 597.
61. Ludwig Leichhardt, *Journal of an Overland Expedition in Australia, from Moreton Bay to Port Essington, a Distance of Upwards of 3000 Miles, During the Years 1844–1845* (FACS ED) (Sydney: Macarthur Press Pty Ltd, first published in 1847) p. 65.
62. Tench, p. 225.
63. Tench, p. 225.
64. Tench, p. 226. Blaxland in 1812 also found Aboriginal guides to be of little value once beyond their home territory, and commented that in future he intended '... not to take them again on my more distant expedition. Very little information can be obtained from any tribe out of their own district, which is seldom more than about 30 miles square.' Gregory Blaxland, 'A Journal of a Tour of Discovery across the Blue Mountains in New South Wales' in *Blaxland — Lawson — Wentworth, 1813* (Edited by Joanna Armour Richards) (Hobart: Blubber Head Press, 1979) p. 65.
65. Tench, p. 225.
66. Appendix C, Journal of a Second Journey, 14 Mar 1798. *HRN:* V3, p. 824. This appears to be the John Wilson cited on p. 610 of Volume II of the *Australian Dictionary of Biography.* (Edited by Douglas Pike) (Melbourne: Melbourne University Press, 1967). John Wilson was convicted in 1785 and transported to Australia where, soon after his sentence expired, he took to the bush and lived with Aboriginal people for several years. He was later involved in differing excursions and, on this

occasion, apparently saved the lives of his companions through his bushmanship.

67. Appendix C, Journal of a Second Journey, 23 Mar 1798. *HRN:* V3, p. 827. The youth involved also commented that, on an earlier occasion, their food situation was so poor that they had had '... nothing to eat for two days, but one rat about the size of a small kitten ... (and I was) very sick, and wished myself at home ...' (p. 822).

68. Caley to Banks, 1 Nov 1802. *HRN:* V4, p. 881.

69. Footnote to Barrallier's Journal, 10 Dec 1802. *HRN:* V5, p. 815.

70. Caley to Banks, 1 Nov and 8 Nov 1802. *HRN:* V4, pp. 882 and 887.

71. Caley to Banks, 26 May 1802. Cited in Caley, p. 53.

72. Banks to Caley, 25 Aug 1808. Cited in Caley, p. 190.

73. Caley to Banks, 1 Nov 1802. *HRN:* V4, p. 882. It is interesting to contrast this degree of confidence with his earlier lack of knowledge. Prior to leaving for Australia, Caley wrote to Banks stating that he had been told he should purchase a reliable watch as people had been lost in New South Wales for want of one. Although every twentieth-century Boy Scout knows that, by using a watch on the sun, it is possible to establish the cardinal points with considerable accuracy during the daylight hours, there is no evidence that Caley was aware of this technique. Indeed, he and his advisers clearly saw exploration as an event of a single day's duration and that by having a timepiece, explorers would know at what time of the day they should begin to return, for fear of being caught in the bush by unexpected nightfall. Caley to Banks, 9 Feb 1799. *HRN:* V3, p. 535.

74. Caley to Banks, 16 Feb 1809. Cited in Caley, p. 177.

75. King to Banks, 2 Nov 1805. These papers provide a copy of Caley's journal of his excursions to the Carmarthan Mountains area, and King's overview of his achievements. *HRN:* V5, pp. 724–5. The reward promised to the men chosen to accompany Caley was half a pint of spirits per day for the convicts, and various articles for the free settler. King based this decision on his belief that '... these excursions must be rewarded some ... way, as an encouragement to similar efforts'. King to Bligh, 22 Aug 1806. *HRN:* V6, p. 172.

76. Bligh to Castlereagh, 8 July 1809. *HRA:* S1 V7, p. 161.

77. Caley to Banks, 1 Nov and 8 Nov 1802. *HRN:* V4, p. 882 and pp. 887–8.

78. Macquarie to Bathurst, 28 Apr 1814. Enclosure No. 4. *HRA:* S1 V8, pp. 169–70.

79. Lachlan Macquarie, *Journals of His Tours in New South Wales and Van Diemen's Land 1810–1822.* (FACS ED). (Sydney: Library of Australian History, 1979). p. 145.

80. Augustus Charles Gregory and Francis Thomas Gregory, *Journals of Australian Explorations.* (FACS ED). (Victoria Park, Western Australia: Hesperian Press, 1981). pp. 84–5.

81. Alexander Harris, *Settlers and Convicts: or Recollections of Sixteen Years' Labour in the Australian Backwoods.* (FACS ED). (Melbourne University Press, 1964). p. 25.

82. Peter Cunningham, *Two Years in New South Wales: A Series of Letters, Comprising Sketches of the Actual State of Society in that Colony: of its Peculiar Advantages to Emigrants: of its Topography, Natural History, and etc., and etc , in two volumes.* (FACS ED). (Adelaide: Libraries Board of South Australia, 1966). V2, p. 166.

83. Of this incident, Leichhardt commented that '... it was quite a misery to hear its dull jarring sound, instead of the former cheerful tinkling'. *Journal*, p. 382. For details of the location of the campsite see pp. 447–8, V3 of the Field Notes Addendum.

84. Tench, p. 237.

85. A letter from Sydney, British Museum Papers. 24 Mar 1791. *HRN:* V2, p. 776.

86. Phillip to Sydney, 15 May 1788. *HRN:* V1 P2, p. 134.

87. Phillip to Nepean, 9 July 1788. *HRN:* V1 P2, p. 155.
88. Tench, pp. 269–70.
89. Collins to Bligh, 18 Oct 1806. 'It was extremely fortunate for us that the Kangaroo was to be found in such abundance as we experienced, for without such an Aid the majority of the People must have been without Food.' *HRA:* S3 V1, p. 380.
90. Barrallier's Journal, 12 Nov 1802. *HRN:* V5, p. 771.
91. Caley to Banks, 12 Oct 1800. Caley further commented that such muskets were '... very heavy, and swallow too much shot and powder for to load them'. *HRN:* V4, p. 240.
92. A M Low, *Musket to Machine-Gun*. (London: Hutchison and Co. Ltd, 1942) p. 29.
93. Low, p. 22.
94. Macquarie to Bathurst, 28 Apr 1814. Enclosure No. 4. *HRA:* S1 V8, p. 170.
95. Macquarie to Bathurst, 28 Apr 1814. Enclosure No. 4. *HRA:* S1 V8, p. 170.
96. Tench, p. 270.
97. Phillip to Sydney, 15 May 1788. *HRN:* V1 P2, p. 136 and p. 134.
98. Caley to Banks, 1 Nov 1802. *HRN:* V4, p. 881.
99. Macquarie to Bathurst, 28 Apr 1814. Enclosure No. 4. *HRA:* S1 V8, p. 170.
100. Brisbane to Bathurst, 16 June 1825. Enclosure. *HRA:* S1 V11, p. 647.
101. Collins to Sullivan, 24 Dec 1802. This despatch included a two-page list of equipment considered essential for the establishment of a new settlement at Port Phillip. *HRN:* V4, p. 923.
102. Leichhardt, *Journal*, p. XVIII.
103. Tench, pp. 223–4. On one occasion one of Tench's party: '... knocked up, ... and had not a soldier, as strong as a pack-horse, undertaken to carry his knapsack, in addition to his own, we must either have sent him back, or have stopped at a place for the night which did not afford water.'
104. Caley to Banks, 25 Aug 1801. Cited in Caley, p. 48.
105. Hunter, p. 108.
106. Barrallier's Journal, 27 Nov 1802. *HRN:* V5, p. 803.
107. Allan Cunningham, in *Early Explorers in Australia: From the Log-Books and Journals, including the Diary of Allan Cunningham, Botanist, from March 1, 1817, to November 19, 1818.* (Edited by Ida Lee) (London: Methuen and Co Ltd, 1925) p. 226.
108. Caley to Banks, 12 Oct 1800. Fustian is a thick-twilled, short-napped cotton cloth. *HRN:* V4, p. 241.
109. Darling to Hay, 22 Dec 1827. Included an enclosure from Hely to McLeay. *HRA:* S1 V13, pp. 663–4.
110. Of this problem Leichhardt wrote on 17 Sept 1845, that the '... few shirts which we had taken with us became so worn and threadbare, that the slightest tension would tear them. To find materials for mending the body, we had to cut off the sleeves, and, when these were used, pieces were taken from the lower part of the shirt to mend the upper. Our trowsers became equally patched: and the want of soap prevented us from washing them clean. We had, however, saved our shoes so well, by wearing mocassins while travelling along the eastern coast, that every one was well provided, particularly after the death of Mr. Gilbert, whose stock of clothes I divided among my companions.' *Journal*, p. 408.
111. Barrallier's Journal, 9 Nov 1802. *HRN:* V5, p. 759.
112. Barrallier's Journal, 12 Nov 1802. *HRN:* V5, p. 773.
113. The *Glatton* carried 2000 yards of No. 3 Brown stout canvas to New South Wales on or before 21 May 1802. *HRA:* S1 V4, p. 28. Also, according to King, canvas was being manufactured in New South Wales as early as 1804, for in that year he forwarded samples for analysis to Under-Secretary Sullivan. *HRA:* S1 V5, p. 143.
114. Macquarie to Bathurst, 28 Apr 1814. Enclosure No. 4. *HRA:* S1 V8, p. 169.
115. Macquarie to Bathurst, 30 June 1815. Enclosure. *HRA:* S1 V8, p. 617.

116. Barrallier's Journal, 22 Nov 1802. *HRN:* V5, p. 791.
117. Tench, p. 275.
118. Webster noted, for example, that on Stuart's final expedition: 'Most of the group selected by Chambers (one of Stuart's sponsors), presumably with Stuart's approval and assistance, were very young men ... Nearly all were under twenty-one at the time of their engagement. Mona Stuart Webster, *John McDouall Stuart.* (Melbourne University Press, 1958) p. 185.
119. King to Camden, 1 Nov 1805. Enclosure No. 3. *HRA:* S1 V5, p. 586. As well as being tidal inlets, for example, creeks also became 'brooks and small Rills that are deeply seated in the Ground and the Sides or Banks (are) very Steep.'
120. Tench, p. 154.
121. Caley to Banks, 10 Dec 1804. *HRN:* V5, p. 508.
122. Caley to Banks, 22 Dec 1800. Cited in Caley, p. 42.

Chapter Three

1. Jack Morrell and Arnold Thackray, *Gentlemen of Science: Early Years of the British Association for the Advancement of Science.* (Oxford: Clarendon Press, 1981) pp. 5–19.
2. Gage and Stearn, p. 30.
3. Hall, p. 6.
4. Hall, p. 18.
5. Hall, p. 23.
6. Hall, p. 14.
7. Hall, p. 47.
8. Herschel to Young, 30 Aug 1828. Herschel papers 18:345. Cited in Morrell and Thackray, p. 43.
9. Ann Mozley Moyal, *Scientists in Nineteenth Century Australia: A Documentary History.* (Cassell Australia, 1976) p. 107.
10. Darling to Huskisson, 10 Apr 1828. *HRA:* S1 V14, pp. 130–1.
11. Davy to Bathurst, 21 Nov 1823. *HRA:* S1 V11, p. 202.
12. Brisbane to Bathurst, 11 Aug 1826. *HRA:* S1 V12, p. 707.
13. Hay to Darling, 11 Jan 1827. *HRA:* S1 V13, p. 16.
14. Bathurst to Macquarie, 18 Apr1816. Instructions for Exploring Expeditions. *HRA:* S1 V9, p. 115.
15. Bathurst to Macquarie, 18 Apr 1816. Instructions for Exploring Expeditions. *HRA:* S1 V9, p. 116.
16. Darling to Murray, 19 Nov 1828. *HRA:* S1 V14, p. 472.
17. Darling to Murray, 24 Apr 1829. *HRA:* S1 V14, p. 722.
18. Macquarie to Bathurst, 30 Apr 1814. *HRA:* S1 V8, p. 211.
19. Macquarie to Bathurst, 30 Apr 1814. *HRA:* S1 V8, pp. 211–12.
20. Macquarie to Bathurst, 18 May 1818. Enclosure No. 2. Oxley to Bathurst. *HRA:* S1 V9, p. 805. cf Evans to Macquarie, 1 Feb 1815. Enclosure No. 8. *HRA:* S1 V8, pp. 475–6.
21. Bathurst to Brisbane, 21 Aug 1824. The two geodesists nominated by Bathurst were Messrs Finch and Rodd. *HRA*, S1 V11, p. 350–1.
22. Twiss to Darling, 31 May 1829. Enclosure. *HRA*: S1 V14, p. 899.
23. Bathurst to Macquarie, 4 Dec 1815. *HRA*: S1 V8, p. 639.
24. The Commentary on Despatches elaborates on this point in note 132, which relates to pages 556 and 619. *HRA:* S1 V13, p. 871.
25. In the Commentary on Despatches, a brief outline is provided in note 141 of the background to the notions of an inland sea, or a great river. *HRA:* S1 V8, pp. 682–3. As early as 1819 the idea of an inland sea was being challenged. William Wentworth argued that the extremely hot and dry north-westerly winds during summer could only occur by gathering heat 'from the immense tract of country which they traverse'. William Charles Wentworth, *Statistical, Historical and Political Description of the Colony of New South Wales and its Dependent Settlements in Van Diemen's Land: with a Particular Enumeration of the Advantages which these Colonies Offer for Emigration, and their Superiority in Many Respects Over*

those Possessed by the United States of America. (FACS ED) (Adelaide: Griffin Press Ltd, 1978) p. 37.

26. Bathurst to Macquarie, 18 Apr 1816. *HRA:* S1 V9, p. 114.
27. Bathurst to Macquarie, 18 Apr 1816. *HRA:* S1 V9, pp. 114–15.
28. These maps were later redrawn by Arrow-smith, the British Government Cartographer, and are works of art. It is interesting to study these early maps, for they could only indicate known features, beyond which were large though diminishing blank areas.
29. J R Whitehead, *An Investigation of John Oxley's Journey in the Coonabarabran District 1818.* (Coonabarabran: Warrumbungle Historical Society, 1970) pp. 11–12.
30. A Cunningham, in Lee, p. 174. W G McMinn, *Allan Cunningham: Botanist and Explorer* (Melbourne University Press, 1970) covers Allan Cunningham's experiences in Brazil on pp. 8–10.
31. Macquarie to Bathurst, 15 Dec 1817. *HRA:* S1 V9, p. 729.
32. John Oxley, *Journals of Two Expeditions into the Interior of New South Wales: Undertaken by Order of the British Government in the Years 1817–18.* (Australiana Facsimile Editions No. 6). (Adelaide: Libraries Board of South Australia, 1964) p. 314.
33. Charles Sturt, *Two Expeditions into the Interior of Southern Australia During the Years 1828, 1829, 1830, and 1831: With Observations on the Soil, Climate, and General Resources of the Colony of New South Wales, in two volumes.* (Australiana Facsimile Editions No. 4). (Adelaide: Public Library of South Australia, 1963). Vol I, p. 63. That this was Charles Fraser appears unlikely for, in a memorial to the Colonial Secretary in 1829, he listed the nine expeditions he had been involved with up until 1828 and Sturt's was not among them. Darling to Murray, 9 Oct 1829. Enclosure No. 1. *HRA:* S1 V15, p. 200.
34. J H L Cumpston, *Charles Sturt: His Life and Journeys of Exploration.* (Melbourne: Georgian House, 1951) p. 14.
35. Sturt, *Two Expeditions*, Appendix No. 1, Letter of Instructions. Vol I, p. 184.
36. Sturt, *Two Expeditions*, Vol I, p. 63.
37. Oxley, p. 31.
38. That spare parts for some scientific and surveying equipment were readily available can be seen in the 1831 equipment manifest for the Western Australian Department of Lands and Surveys. For example, spare glasses for circumferentors, theodolite level-ling screws, ivory plotting scales, barometers, thermometers and quicksilver (mercury) were all kept in store, to cater for the demands of the field staff. MS BL Archive note, AN3 Registry. 330/284.
39. Oxley, p. 255.
40. Brisbane to Bathurst, 16 June 1825. Enclosure — the Memorial of George William Evans, Surveyor-General of Van Diemen's Land. *HRA:* S1 V11, p. 647.
41. Darling to Murray, 19 Nov 1828. *HRA:* S1 V14, p. 472.
42. Sturt, *Two Expeditions*, Vol I, p. 22.
43. Sturt, *Two Expeditions*, Vol I, p. 42.
44. Appendix 1, Macquarie's Instructions to Oxley, Oxley, p. 356.
45. Leichhardt commented on this problem in a letter to the Reverend J D Lang of Sydney, on 9 Apr 1846, pointing out that 'When I was in Moreton Bay, I witnessed several cases of ague, ... (and) the rheumatic complaints were frequent. The fact is that everybody is so careless, so spoilt by the fine climate, that he thinks it is almost impossible his body could suffer by any exposure, particularly at the commencement of the rainy season. The master as well as the servant, think it not worth while to change their clothes, when they are drenched with rain, or to have a cloak or a poncho to prevent it. The consequence is, that they are punished by rheumatism, or occasionally

by an attack of ague ...' Aurousseau, Vol 3, pp. 850–1.

46. Lachlan Macquarie, MS List of Provisions and Equipment for John Oxley's 1817 Expedition. Archives Office, Lands Department NSW: 24 Mar 1817.

47. During the underlying fieldwork carried out in Queensland in 1992, I spoke with several stockmen of the Taroom area, and was advised of the above policy. Mr Mark Groves pointed out that the desirability of this approach had been brought home to him when, on one occasion, a tin of golden syrup had leaked, covering the inside of his saddle-bag and its contents with a sticky mixture. Worse still, the residue of this concoction of syrup, flour and so forth had later attracted flies and ants.

48. Sturt's memorandum on the equipment for his first expedition lists the cooking utensils taken, which included three iron boilers, two long-handled frying pans and an iron kettle. Cited in Cumpston, *Charles Sturt*, Appendix B, pp. 170–174. A list of equipment sent to the colony in 1803 is similar in content, viz '200 iron Pots, 200 do. Kettles, 2, 3 and 4 Gallons'. Hobart to Collins, 7 Feb 1803. Enclosure No. 6. *HRA:* S3 V1, p. 8.

49. Sturt, *Two Expeditions*, Appendix No. 1, Letter of Instructions. Vol I, p. 187.

50. Cook to Stephens, 12 July 1771. Containing an enclosure from Perry to Cook. *HRN:* V1 P1, p. 339. Inspissated juices are condensed or thickened versions of the original, while saloup is a hot drink made from an infusion of powdered salep, which is nutritive meal, starch or jelly made from the dried tubers of various orchidaceous plants.

51. Smyth to Darling, 30 Oct 1827. *HRA:* S3 V5, p. 817.

52. Information gathered while carrying out related field research in 1992.

53. Peter Cunningham's and Wentworth's comments on the prices of horses by the late 1820s are of considerable relevance to the mobility of exploration parties. Wentworth is adamant that by 1819 good riding horses were available for £20 to £30 and, because of the very rapid increase in horse numbers by 1819 they could often be bought for one-half to one-third of the quoted sale price. (p. 101) Cunningham disagrees, noting that in 1827 '... no good saddle, gig, or cart horse can be had for less that £40 ...' (Vol 1, p. 297). The latter figure appears more accurate, given Governor Darling's 1827 figure of £55 for horses for the mounted police. Nevertheless, as noted in the earlier outline of horse numbers and costs, by the mid 1820s horses were relatively cheaper and there were considerably more available for exploration purposes.

54. Sturt, *Two Expeditions*, Vol I, p. 13.

55. Similarly on the second expedition, where Oxley notes that there were sixteen men, and food supplies for twenty-four weeks. Working on the earlier noted ration of one kilogram per man per day of flour and salted pork, an approximate figure of seven kilograms is realised per man per week. Sixteen men by seven kilograms per week by twenty-four weeks equals 2688 kilograms of food. In allowing seventy kilograms per pack-horse (see Endnote No. 57), Oxley would, therefore, have required 41 packhorses, and this number does not include the additional animals necessary to carry the cooking equipment, clothing, bedding, ammunition, tents and scientific equipment. He had nineteen. Worse, he had sent three back from the depot, deeming them the weaker of the collection, despite being able to calculate his requirements.

56. A Cunningham, in Lee, p. 214.

57. As early as the late 1850s the Gregory brothers had established the load which packhorses could be expected to carry for a sustained period. On the 1858 expedition in search of Leichhardt, Augustus Gregory pointed out that: '... the total weight of the equipment was about 4,600 lbs, exclusive of the saddles and harness, which gave an average load

of 150 lbs as the net load carried by each pack-horse.' (Gregory, *Journals*, p. 201)

Similarly with the Jardine brothers who, on their gruelling cattle drive across the Cape York Peninsula during a severe wet season in 1864, adjusted their loads so that the 18 sets of saddlebags weighed 'at the start about 150 lbs each'. The Messrs Jardine, *Narrative of the Overland Expedition of the Messrs Jardine, from Rockhampton to Cape York, Northern Queensland.* (Edited by Frederick J. Byerley) (Brisbane: J W Buxton, 1867) p. 7.

Finally, during his second expedition, when attempting to break through from South Australia to Perth, Giles noted that: 'Our horses' loads were very heavy at starting, the greater number of the horses carrying 200 lbs.' Ernest Giles, *Australia Twice Traversed: The Romance of Exploration, being a Narrative Compiled from the Journals of Five Exploring Expeditions into and through Central South Australia, and Western Australia, from 1872–1876, in two volumes.* (Australiana Facsimile Editions No. 13). (Adelaide: Libraries Board of South Australia, 1964.) Vol 1, p. 139.

58. Oxley, p. 39.
59. Research into salt pork containers, as freighted on the ship *Ruby* in 1812, indicates that pork was then carried in barrels with a net weight of 318–320 pounds — Invoice of Provisions. *HRA* S3 V1, p. 514. A further entry for beef barrels, from the ship *Diana* in 1800, shows each cask weighed 200 pounds, so it is possible that the pork casks weighed only 200 pounds. King to Portland, 10 Mar 1801. Enclosure No. 3. *HRA:* S1 V3, p. 72.
60. Oxley had the pork repacked in smaller casks, before leaving the depot at Mount Harris, presumably so that one cask could be strapped on either side of a horse. Oxley, p. 242.
61. Oxley, p. 247.
62. Oxley, p. 249.
63. Oxley, p. 256.
64. Oxley, p. 269 and p. 307.
65. Oxley, p. 310.
66. Oxley, p. 54.
67. Sturt, *Two Expeditions*, Vol I, p. 99.
68. Normally, stockmen periodically listen for their horses' bells during the night, in order to determine the direction in which the animals are grazing. In the morning, should the horses not be visible nor their bells audible, the stockmen are aware of the general direction in which to commence searching. By following this line the horses can usually be located, once the stockmen are within hearing range of their bells.
69. Simpson and Weiner, Vol xvi, p. 102.
70. A Cunningham, in Lee, p. 216.
71. A Cunningham, in Lee, p. 219.
72. The name 'Peel's Range' is not in modern Gazetteers of Australia. It was described in 1848 as 'a range of mountains situated in the district of Lachlan, New South Wales'. William Henry Wells, *A Geographical Dictionary and Gazetteer of the Australian Colonies, 1848.* (FACS ED) (Sydney: Council of the Library of New South Wales, 1970) p. 335. Possibly the name refers to the Warrumba Range, West of Cowra, which is not mentioned in Wells' dictionary.
73. Oxley, pp. 155–6.
74. A Cunningham, in Lee, p. 228.
75. A Cunningham, in Lee, p230.
76. Leichhardt determined on this course of action on 10 Jan 1845, about 100 days after setting off. As he pointed out: 'To prevent unnecessary loss of time by my reconnoitring excursions, and to render them less fatiguing to myself, I arranged that both the blacks should go with me: in order that I might send one back from the first favourable camping place, to bring the party on, whilst I continued to explore with the other.' Leichhardt, *Journal*, p. 103.
77. Oxley, p. 256.
78. Sturt, *Two Expeditions*, Vol I, p. 45.
79. Sturt, *Two Expeditions*, Vol I, p. 79.
80. Sturt, *Two Expeditions*, Vol I, p. 73.

81. Sturt, *Two Expeditions*, Appendix No. 2., List of Stores Supplied for the Expedition. Vol I, p. 190.
82. Sturt, *Two Expeditions*, Vol I, p. 95.
83. A Cunningham, in Lee, p. 248.
84. Oxley, p. 350.
85. Sturt, *Two Expeditions*, Vol II, p. 204.
86. Sturt, *Two Expeditions*, Vol II, p. 194.
87. Sturt, *Two Expeditions*, Vol II, p. 194.
88. Sturt, cited in Cumpston, *Charles Sturt*, p. 25.
89. Oxley, pp. 45 and 71.
90. A Cunningham, in Lee, p. 273.
91. A Cunningham, in Lee, p. 299.
92. Oxley, p. 74.
93. Oxley, p. 261.
94. Oxley, p. 264.
95. Sturt, *Two Expeditions*, Vol I, p. 15.
96. Sturt, *Two Expeditions*, Vol I, p. 145.
97. Sturt, *Two Expeditions*, Vol I, p. LXVIII.
98. Sturt, *Two Expeditions*, Vol I, p. 108.
99. Sturt, *Two Expeditions*, Vol I, pp. LVII, LVIII.
100. Lockyer to Macleay, 2 Apr 1827. *HRA:* S3 V6, p. 480.
101. Major Edmund Lockyer, 'Journal of Major Lockyer: Commandant of the Expedition Sent from Sydney in 1826 to Found a Settlement at King George's Sound, West Australia'. *Exploration Diaries*: Vol 1, p. 20.
102. Captain James Stirling, 'State of the Colony of Swan River 1st Jan 1830: Read at the Geographical Society of London, and Accompanied by a Chart'. *Exploration Diaries*: Vol 1, p. 141.
103. Dr T B Wilson, 'Exploration to the North West and West of King George's Sound by Dr. T. B. Wilson, Dec 1829'. *Exploration Diaries*: Vol 1, p. 117.
104. Macleay to Lockyer, 4 Nov 1826. *HRA:* S3 V6, p. 455.
105. Sleeman to Macleay, 25 Mar 1829. *HRA:* S3 V6, p. 525.
106. Captain James Stirling, 'Captain James Stirling: Narrative of Operations, 1827.' *Exploration Diaries*: Vol 1, p. 34.
107. Robert Brown, 'General View of the Botany in the vicinity of Swan River', Addendum to Captain Stirling's 'State of the Colony.' *Exploration Diaries*: Vol 1, p. 155.
108. Stirling, 'Captain James Stirling'. *Exploration Diaries*: Vol 1, p. 35.
109. Jane Eliza Currie, 'Relevant Extracts from the Diary of Jane Eliza Currie, Wife of Captain Mark Currie W. A. Archives'. *Exploration Diaries*: Vol 1, p. 67.
110. Dr T B Wilson. 'Journal of Dr. T. B. Wilson of an Excursion up the Canning River Oct 1829'. *Exploration Diaries*: Vol 1, p. 81.
111. Captain Thomas Bannister, 'Extracts from a Journal Kept by Thomas Bannister in Charge of a Party from Swan River to King Georges Sound'. *Exploration Diaries*: Vol 1, p. 225.
112. Field research related to the assessment of Leichhardt's mapping accuracy, carried out in Queensland in 1992, was often hampered by dense understorey thickets, despite Leichhardt noting in his *Journal* that such areas had been park-like when he passed through in 1844–45. Mitchell also observed this phenomenon and commented on it as early as the mid-1840s: 'The ommission of the annual periodical burning by natives, of the grass and young saplings, has already produced in the open forest lands nearest to Sydney, thick forests of young trees, where, formerly, a man might gallop without impediment, and see whole miles before him. Kangaroos are no longer to be seen there: the grass is choked by underwood: neither are there natives to burn the grass, nor is fire longer desirable there amongst the fences of the settler. The occupation of the territory by the white race seems thus to involve ... an inevitable result ...' Major Thomas Livingstone Mitchell, *Journal of an Expedition into the Interior of Tropical Australia in Search of a Route from Sydney to the Gulf of Carpentaria.* (London: Longman, Brown, Green and Longman, 1848). p. 413.
113. Dr T B Wilson, 'Journal of Dr. T. B. Wilson of an Excursion up the Swan

River Oct 1829'. *Exploration Diaries*: Vol 1, p. 78.

114. Stirling, 'State of the Colony'. *Exploration Diaries*: Vol 1, pp. 142–3.

115. Wilson, 'Journal of Dr. T. B. Wilson of an Excursion up the Canning River Oct 1829'. *Exploration Diaries*: Vol 1, p. 88.

116. Wilson, 'Exploration to the North West'. *Exploration Diaries*: Vol 1, p. 109.

117. Wilson, 'Exploration to the North West'. *Exploration Diaries*: Vol 1, p. 108.

118. Wilson, 'Exploration to the North West'. *Exploration Diaries*: Vol 1, p. 114.

119. Wilson, 'Exploration to the North West'. *Exploration Diaries*: Vol 1, p. 114.

120. Wilson, 'Exploration to the North West'. *Exploration Diaries*: Vol 1, p. 125.

121. Dr T B Wilson, 'Extract of a Letter Received from Dr. T. B. Wilson, R. N. Dated King George's Sound, 15th Dec 1829'. *Exploration Diaries*: Vol 1, p. 140.

122. Bannister, 'Extracts'. *Exploration Diaries*: Vol 1, p. 231.

123. Ensign Robert Dale, 'Mr. Dale's Journal of an Expedition whilst Exploring the Country Eastward of the Darling Range, 1830'. *Exploration Diaries*: Vol 1, p. 187.

124. *Perth Gazette*, 23 Mar 1833. p. 6.

125. Wilson, 'Journal of Dr. T. B. Wilson of an Excursion up the Canning River'. *Exploration Diaries*: Vol 1, p. 87.

126. John Septimus Roe, 'Government Notice Issued Mar 22nd, 1830'. *Exploration Diaries*: Vol 1, p. 170.

127. Wilson, 'Journal of Dr. T. B. Wilson of an Excursion up the Canning River'. *Exploration Diaries*: Vol 1, p. 84.

128. John Wall Hardey, 'Journal of an Expedition over General Darling's Range, 100 miles east from Swan River. Oct 1830 — John Wall Hardey'. *Exploration Diaries*: Vol 1, p. 206.

129. Hardey, *Exploration Diaries*: p. 206. The necessity for tents appears soon to have passed in Western Australia though, for George Fletcher Moore — ever in the vanguard of the innovative early Western Australian explorers — commented in his exploration north of Perth in 1835 that the Aborigines he was travelling with had shown him how to make a hut thatched with grass-tree leaves. According to Moore, such a hut was water- and wind-proof, was readily made and, with dry foliage for bedding, protected one from rheumatism caused by cold, wind, rain or dew. '[With such] a hut over the head, and fire at your feet, there is little to be apprehended from exposure in the bush.'Excursion to the Northward. From the Journal of George Fletcher Moore Esq. 14th Apr 1835'. *Exploration Diaries*: Vol 2, p. 319.

130. Hardey, *Exploration Diaries*: Vol 1, p. 217.

131. Dale, 'Mr. Dale's Journal'. *Exploration Diaries*: Vol 1, p. 186.

132. Hardey, *Exploration Diaries*: Vol 1, p. 216.

133. John Septimus Roe, 'Government Notice'. *Exploration Diaries*: Vol 1, p. 175.

134. Darling to Bathurst, 5 May 1827. *HRA:* S1 V13, p. 275.

135. A small example of an ailment which, under suburban conditions would be tolerable, yet becomes insufferable under constant riding, is that of haemorrhoids. Leichhardt suffered from this problem on his second expedition and, combined with '... mosquitoes, sandflies and hornets (they) ... contributed to make myself extremely miserable.' Cited in Colin Roderick, *Leichhardt the Dauntless Explorer* (North Ryde, NSW: Angus and Robertson, 1988) p. 411. Similar problems occurred during the field research underlying the Field Notes, in Queensland in 1992. At one stage I was suffering from haemorrhoids, an abscessed tooth, heartburn arising from gastric reflux, and back problems. Individually, or in suburbia, these ailments would have been of little consequence. Collectively, and in the

bush where treatment was not readily available, as well as being continually worsened by constant riding, they became a problem.

136. P Cunningham, Vol II, p. 158.

137. P Cunningham, Vol I, p. 316.

138. Anglophiles of the day apparently strove to deny the influence of the better environment in Australia, by denigrating the quality of the usually taller Colonial offspring of British parent-stock. It was claimed that the Australian-bred product grew precociously, but had less substance and was weaker, thus the term 'corn-stalk' for Colonial youths. Sollicker, the stolid British-born boundary rider in *Such is Life*, claimed similarly, pointing out in heavy dialect that the climate 'plays ole Goozeb'ry wi heverythink hout 'ere', and that Colonial products, including his horses and even his son, possessed no more chest than a greyhound. Tom Collins, *Such is Life: Being Certain Extracts from the Diary of Tom Collins* (Sydney: Angus and Robertson, 1975) p. 179.

139. Harris, p. 25.

140. Horton to Darling, 20 Oct 1827. Enclosure No. 2. *HRA:* S1 V13, pp. 556 and 558.

141. P Cunningham, Vol II, p. 165.

142. Darling to Murray, 24 Apr 1829. Sub-enclosure No. 1 — The Memorial of William Hilton Hovell, Free Settler. *HRA:* S1 V14, p. 726.

143. Hay to Darling, 22 Oct1826. Enclosure — *HRA:* S1 V12, p. 656.

Chapter Four

1. Edward John Eyre, *Autobiographical Narrative of Residence and Exploration in Australia 1832–1839, by Edward John Eyre.* (Edited by Jill Waterhouse). (London: Caliban Books, 1984) p. 194.

2. Morrell and Thackray, p. 9.

3. See footnote 136, cited in Morrell and Thackray, p. 64.

4. 1833 BAAS Report, p. 471; 1834 Report, p. XX; 1837 Report, p. XXVIII. Cited in Morrell and Thackray, p. 329.

5. Herschel to Whewell, 7 Feb 1835. Whewell papers a 207. Cited in Morrell and Thackray, p. 424.

6. BAAS address by Whewell, 1836. Cited in Morrell and Thackray, p. 273.

7. Hall, pp. 80–82.

8. Major Thomas Livingstone Mitchell, *Three Expeditions into the Interior of Eastern Australia: with Descriptions of the Recently Explored Region of Australia Felix, and of the Present Colony of New South Wales, in two volumes.* (FACS ED.) (Adelaide: The Public Library of South Australia, original copy printed in 1839.) Vol 1, p. 149.

9. Mitchell, *Three Expeditions*, Vol 2, p. 2.

10. Captain George Grey, *Journals of Two Expeditions of Discovery in North-West and Western Australia, During the Years 1837, 38, and 39, Under the Authority of Her Majesty's Government: Describing Many Newly Discovered, Important, and Fertile Districts, with Observations on the Moral and Physical Condition of the Aboriginal Inhabitants, and etc, and etc, in two volumes.* (FACS. ED.) (Western Australia: Hesperian Press, 1983.) Vol 1, p. 5.

11. Mitchell, *Three Expeditions*, Vol 2, p. 42.

12. The Scientific footnotes, appendices and cataloguing were provided by Dr. Lindley (botany), Professor Owen (palaeontology), and Mr. Ogilby (zoology). *Three Expeditions*, Vol 1. p. iv.

13. Grey, Vol 1, p. 50.

14. See particularly Chapter 13: 'Financial Embarrassment', Rica Erickson, pp. 95–102.

15. Grey, Vol 1, p. 1.

16. Grey, Vol 1, pp. 274–6.

17. Mitchell, Three Expeditions, Vol 1, p. 3.

18. Gipps to Russell, 28 Sept 1840. *HRA:* S1 V20, p. 844.

19. Gipps to Russell, 28 Sept 1840. *HRA:* S1 V20, p. 844.

20. Gipps to Russell, 28 Sept 1840. *HRA:* S1 V20, p. 844.
21. Sir James Stirling, 'Notes by His Excellency Sir James Stirling of an Expedition to King George's Sound, undertaken in Oct 1835.' *Exploration Diaries*: Vol 2, p. 373.
22. Mitchell, *Three Expeditions*, Vol 1, p. p2–3.
23. Mitchell, *Three Expeditions*, Vol 1, p. 107.
24. See note 141 in the Commentary on the text. *HRA:* S1 V8, pp. 682–3.
25. Macquarie to Bathurst, 15 May 1818. Enclosure No. 2. *HRA:* S1 V9, pp. 780–1.
26. Darling to Bathurst, 22 May 1826. enclosure Report on The Church and School Establishments by Archdeacon Scott, 1 May 1826. *HRA:* S1 V12, p. 314.
27. Darling to Bathurst, 22 May 1826. Enclosure — *HRA:* S1 V12, p. 312.
28. Darling to Bathurst, 3 Feb 1827. Sub-enclosure No. 3. *HRA:* S1 V13, p. 70.
29. Goderich to Darling, 12 Jan 1831. *HRA:* S1 V16, pp. 22–4.
30. Goderich to Darling, 12 Jan 1831. The details of this proposal were provided to Darling in Enclosure No. 1. 'Outline of a prospectus of an Academical Institution which it is proposed to establish in Sydney, N. S. Wales.' *HRA:* S1 V16, p. 24.
31. Glenelg to Bourke, 17 Apr 1836. *HRA:* S1 V18, p. 406.
32. Bourke to Goderich, 24 Dec 1832. Enclosure No. 2. *HRA:* S1 V16, p. 828.
33. Bourke to Stanley, 24 Oct 1833. *HRA:* S1 V17, p. 248.
34. Mitchell, *Three Expeditions*, Vol 1, p. 18.
35. Mitchell, *Three Expeditions*, Vol 1, p. 77.
36. Mitchell, *Three Expeditions*, Vol 2, pp. 210–11.
37. Mitchell, *Three Expeditions*, Vol 2, p. 204.
38. Mitchell, *Three Expeditions*, Vol 2, p. 208.
39. Eyre, *Autobiographical Narrative*, p. 135.
40. Mitchell, *Three Expeditions*, Vol 1, p. 301.
41. Mitchell, *Three Expeditions*, Vol 2, p. 13.
42. Mitchell, *Three Expeditions*, Vol 2, p. 246.
43. Mitchell, *Three Expeditions*, Vol 1, p. 297.
44. John Septimus Roe, 'Journal of an Expedition from King Georges Sound, overland to Swan River, via York, by J. S. Roe, Surveyor General.' *Exploration Diaries*: Vol 2, p. 570.
45. George Fletcher Moore, 'Excursion to a River to the Northward. From the Journal of George Fletcher Moore Esq.' *Exploration Diaries*: Vol 2, p. 404.
46. Refer to data indicated on Figure 3.
47. Mitchell, *Three Expeditions*, Vol 2, p. 1.
48. John Septimus Roe, 'Journal of an Expedition from Swan River overland to King Georges Sound, by J S Roe Esquire, Surveyor General, 1835.' *Exploration Diaries*: Vol 2, p. 438.
49. Mitchell, *Three Expeditions*, Vol 1, p. 166.
50. Mitchell, *Three Expeditions*, Vol 2, p. 4.
51. Mitchell, *Three Expeditions*, Vol 1, p. 332.
52. Grey, Vol 1, pp. 127 and 131.
53. Charles Sturt, *Journal of the Central Australian Expedition 1844–1845 and An Account of the Sea Coast and Interior of South Australia.* (FACS ED. of Charles Sturt's Narrative of an Expedition into Central Australia: Volume Two, 1849.) pp. 145–286 (Edited by Jill Waterhouse.) (London: Caliban Books, 1984.) p. 44.
54. Mitchell, *Journal of an Expedition.* pp. 7 and 23.
55. Mitchell, *Three Expeditions*, Vol 2, p. 2.
56. Mitchell, *Three Expeditions*, Vol 2, p. 2.
57. Mitchell, *Three Expeditions*, Vol 1, p. 58.
58. Mitchell, *Three Expeditions*, Vol 1, p. 216.

59. Mitchell, *Three Expeditions*, Vol 1, pp. 338–9.
60. Mitchell, *Three Expeditions*, Vol 1, p. 337.
61. Roe, 'Journal of an Expedition from Swan River'. *Exploration Diaries*: Vol 2, pp. 439–40.
62. Alfred Hillman, 'Journal of an Expedition to Nornalup Undertaken by Mr. Alfred Hillman 3rd July 1833, from the Settlement at Albany — K. G. Sound.' *Exploration Diaries*: Vol 2, p. 277.
63. Alfred Hillman, 'Mr. Hillman's Journal of an Expedition to explore the country intervening between Kelmscott and the Williams and thence to the Avon River in Oct 1835.' *Exploration Diaries*: Vol 2, pp. 342–3.
64. Mitchell, *Three Expeditions*, Vol 1, p. 17.
65. Mitchell, *Three Expeditions*, Vol 1, p. 28.
66. Mitchell, *Three Expeditions*, Vol 1, p. 201. An example of the desirability of this practice occurred when one of Mitchell's men went forward on his own and inadvertently severely offended the Aborigines camping around a waterhole, by failing to warn them of his approach. Even worse, he erroneously partook of their food as a sign of friendship. The man was fortunate to escape uninjured and Mitchell commented that Hawking's '... debut [was] outrageously opposed to their ideas of etiquette, which imperatively required that loud 'cooys' should have announced his approach, before he came within a mile of their fires.' *Three Expeditions*. Vol 1, p. 87.
67. Mitchell, *Three Expeditions*, Vol 2, p. 135.
68. Mitchell, *Three Expeditions*, Vol 1, pp. 273–4.
69. Mitchell, *Three Expeditions*, Vol 2, p. 103.
70. Mitchell, *Three Expeditions*, Vol 1, p. 111.
71. Mitchell, *Three Expeditions*, Vol 1, p. 96.
72. Pike (Editor), Volume 2, p. 240.
73. Mitchell, *Three Expeditions*, Vol 1, p. 274.
74. Mitchell, *Three Expeditions*, Vol 2, p. 304.
75. Mitchell, *Three Expeditions*, Vol 2, p. 114.
76. Mitchell, *Three Expeditions*, Vol 2, p. 290.
77. Mitchell, *Three Expeditions*, Vol 2, p. 290.
78. Grey, Vol 1, p. 67.
79. Grey, Vol 1, p. 68.
80. Grey, Vol 1, pp. 68–9.
81. Grey, Vol 1, p. 70.
82. Grey, Vol 1, p. 86.
83. Grey, Vol 1, p. 76.
84. Grey, Vol 1, p. 121.
85. Grey, Vol 1, p. 121.
86. Grey, Vol 1, p. 35.
87. Grey, Vol 1, p. 83.
88. Grey, Vol 1, p. 212.
89. Grey, Vol 1, p. 147.
90. Grey, Vol 1, p. 150.
91. Grey, Vol 1, p. 124.
92. Grey, Vol 1, p. 236.
93. Grey, Vol 1, pp. 236 and 207.
94. In fact, when Roe finally reached the survivors whom Grey had left behind while he pushed on to Perth, the men were standing on the beach. Because of malnutrition and debilitation they were incapable of surmounting the rocky headland which they had reached and were more or less awaiting their fate.
95. Mitchell, *Three Expeditions*, Vol 1, p. 168.
96. Grey, Vol 1, p. 123. Knee haltering appears to be tying the ponies' heads down from their halters to their knees to prevent them moving quickly, yet still allowing them to graze. Something similar has been done in stock camps for over 100 years, when fresh packhorses are tied down to a hobble strap on one leg in order to prevent them bolting with valuable pack-saddles and loads.
97. Roe, 'Journal of an Expedition from Swan River'. *Exploration Diaries*: Vol 2, p. 472.
98. Grey, Vol 1, p. 131.
99. Grey, Vol 1, p. 160.

100. Personal communication, Dr Kimberley Rose, BSc, BVMS, Ascot, Western Australia.
101. Grey, Vol 1, p. 180.
102. Gregory, *Journals*, p. 72.
103. Gregory, *Journals*, p. 71.
104. Gregory, *Journals*, p. 75.
105. Mitchell, *Three Expeditions*, Vol 2, p. 27.
106. Mitchell, *Three Expeditions*, Vol 1, p. 129.
107. Grey, Vol 1, p. 228.
108. Grey, Vol 1, p. 153.
109. J G Bussell, 'Mr. Bussell's Journal of an Expedition to the River Vasse, from the Blackwood. *Exploration Diaries*: Vol 1, p. 317.
110. Grey, Vol 1, p. 224.
111. Roe, 'Journal of an Expedition from King Georges Sound.' *Exploration Diaries*, Vol 2, p. 548.
112. Mitchell, *Three Expeditions*, Vol 1, p. 293.
113. Bussell, *Exploration Diaries*: Vol 1, p. 307.
114. Sir James Stirling, *Journals of Several Expeditions Made in Western Australia During the Years 1829, 1830, 1831, and 1832: Containing the Latest Authentic Information Relative to that Country, Accompanied by a Map.* (FACS ED.) (Perth: University of Western Australia Press, 1980.) p. 227.
115. Stirling to Murray, 30 Jan 1830. *HRA:* S3 V6, p. 619.
116. Mitchell, *Three Expeditions*, Vol 1, pp. 98–9.
117. Percussion caps were sealed capsules con-taining highly explosive potassium chloride, which were ignited when struck by a spring-loaded firing pin or hammer, thus setting off the powder charge in the barrel, and expelling the ball or shot. Although their use marked a considerable advance on the flintlock tech-nique, where misfires were frequent, even the sealed caps were deleteriously affected by the constantly high humidity. Not until the general introduction of integral cartridges in the 1860s and 1870s would this problem be completely overcome.
118. In Volume 2, Chapter 14, of Grey's *Journal* is the first detailed exposition of exactly how specific foods were gathered by Aborigines, which was the most extensive treatment of the subject to that point. He found that, although seasonal excesses of one food not uncommonly led to a monotonous diet, overall the Aborigines were not 'greatly pressed for want of food.' (p. 259) See also Vol 2, p. 263, for a list of the foods available in southern Western Australia.
119. This description referred to central New South Wales, where Mitchell observed an Aborigine catch a bee, attach a light feather with some gum resin and follow the now highly visible insect back to its hive. This technique was in contrast to the incompetence of Mitchell and his men who were 'inexpert clowns', and to whom the bees were 'inaccessable, and indeed invisible'. Mitchell, *Three Expeditions*, Vol 1, p. 173.
120. Roe, 'Journal of an Expedition from King Georges Sound.' *Exploration Diaries*, Vol 2, pp. 558–9.
121. Grey, Vol 2, pp. 13–14.
122. Grey, Vol 2, p. 262.
123. Grey, Vol 2, p. 261.
124. On numerous occasions Mitchell's expeditions were caught short of water by nightfall, which meant he had the option of continuing to travel by night, a choice the explorer was loath to exercise given his men's lack of bush skills. In fact he often had no choice, for the bullocks were frequently exhausted and unable to continue. Mitchell, *Three Expeditions*, Vol 1, p. 68.
125. Mitchell, *Three Expeditions*, Vol 1, p. 70.
126. Mitchell, *Three Expeditions*, Vol 1, p. 69. Leichhardt also commented on this phenomenon, examples of which were also noticed during the related field work carried out in Central Queensland in 1992.
127. Mitchell, *Three Expeditions*, Vol 2, p. 28.

128. George Fletcher Moore, 'Excursion to the Northward'. *Exploration Diaries*, Vol 2, p. 329.
129. Moore, 'Excursion to the Northward'. *Exploration Diaries*, Vol 2, p. 330.
130. Moore, 'Excursion to a River'. *Exploration Diaries*, Vol 2, p. 394.
131. Moore, 'Excursion to a River'. *Exploration Diaries*, Vol 2, p. 401.
132. Stirling, 'Notes by His Excellency'. *Exploration Diaries*, Vol 2, p. 370.
133. Roe, 'Journal of an Expedition from Swan River'. *Exploration Diaries*, Vol 2, p. 477.
134. Moore, 'Excursion to the Northward'. *Exploration Diaries*, Vol 2, p. 319.
135. Mitchell, *Three Expeditions*, Vol 1, p. 31.
136. Eyre, *Autobiographical Narrative*, p. 75.
137. Eyre, *Autobiographical Narrative*, pp. 75–6.
138. Eyre, *Autobiographical Narrative*, p. 85.
139. Eyre, *Autobiographical Narrative*, p. 85.
140. Eyre, *Autobiographical Narrative*, p. 151.
141. Eyre, *Autobiographical Narrative*, p. 159.
142. Eyre, *Autobiographical Narrative*, p. 190. Eyre's development of bushmanship during the 1830s was not unique for, by the end of the decade, overlanding of stock was an established practice and large numbers were being moved. Grey, (Vol 2, p. 189) points out that in fifteen months from 1839 to 1840 overlanders shifted 11,200 cattle, 230 horses, and 60,000 sheep from New South Wales to South Australia. Grey, perhaps romatically, described the overlanders as resolute, undaunted, self-confident in difficulties and dangers, and 'a fund of accurate information'. Vol 2, p. 184. These men had to learn to cope with very large outfits of stock, while ideally keeping them fit, sound and thriving. An indication of the size of these outfits can be gained from one overlander's team of sixty-two horses alone. Grey, Vol 2, p. 189.
143. Gipps to Glenelg, 6 Apr 1839. *HRA*: S1 V20, p. 91. In this light Gipps later reported to Russell in 1839 that dispersion was a fact of life, with an area 900 miles long by 300 miles deep being occupied. *HRA:* S1 V20, p. 839.
144. Gipps to Russell, 28 Sept 1840. Gipps noted ironically that these numbers were almost certainly an understatement. *HRA:* S1 V20, p. 839.

Chapter Five

1. Edward John Eyre, *Journals of Expeditions of Discovery into Central Australia, and Overland from Adelaide to King George's Sound, in the Years 1840–1: Sent by the Colonists of South Australia, with the Sanction and Support of the Government: Including an Account of the Manners and Customs of the Aborigines and the State of Their Relations with Europeans, in two volumes* (London: T and W Boone, 1845). Vol 1, pp. 126–7.
2. Eyre, *Journals*. Vol 2, pp. 131–2.
3. Of Eyre's decision to press ahead, Favenc commented that '... he could not bear the thought of returning to Adelaide a beaten man. Whilst one can give a meed of admiration to the obstinate courage that characterised this resolution, we are also astonished at his persistence in a course that, whilst inevitably entailing the greatest possible suffering on men and horses, could lead to no good nor useful result. With his small party and equipment it would at best be only a struggle for life around the coast, giving no more information than had been acquired by the Marine Surveys. Even the wild attempts of Grey look comparatively reasonable beside this march of Eyre's ... as it was, his trip was bound to be profitless and resultless.' Ernest Favenc, *The History of Australian Exploration from 1788 to 1888: Compiled from State Documents, Private Papers and the Most Authentic Sources of Information.* (FACS ED).

(Holland: Meridian Publishing Co, 1967) p. 132.
4. Eyre, *Journals*. Vol 1, pp. 178–9.
5. Sturt, *Journal*. p. 87.
6. Sturt, *Journal*. p. 47.
7. Sturt, *Journal*. pp. 73–4
8. Leichhardt, *Journal*, pp. 475–6. While water was not a great problem, on occasions they suffered thirst through poor mobility. The convict Phillips noted that in August 1845 they were forced back to the Nicholson River near Burketown, and that by the time they reached water his tongue had turned black and swollen so badly that it was protruding from his mouth. William Phillips, 'The Journal of One of the Party who Accompanied Dr. Leichhardt on his First (Successful) Expedition to Port Essington.' (MS. ML Accession Number, C165) p. 83.
9. Gregory, *Journals*. pp. 204–5.
10. Robert Austin, 'Report from Mr. Austin's Expedition to Shark's Bay'. *Exploration Diaries*, Vol 4, pp. 349–50. The emphasis is Austin's.
11. Ian Cameron, *To the Farthest Ends of the Earth: The History of the Royal Geographical Society 1930–1980.* (London: McDonald and Janes, 1980) p. 275: and Gregory, *Journals*, p. 52.
12. Hall, p. 187.
13. Cameron, pp. 262–3.
14. Caroe, pp. 71 and 97.
15. *The Illustrated Australian Encyclopaedia*. (Sydney: Angus and Robertson, 1925–6) p. 398.
16. Introduction *HRA:* S1 V23, p. xiii–xiv.
17. Moyal, p. 221.
18. Moyal, p. 110, p. 172 and pp. 108–9, respectively.
19. Moyal, p. 109.
20. Moyal, pp. 120 and 122.
21. Moyal, p. 109.
22. Alexander Sutherland, *Victoria and its Metropolis: Past and Present, Volume I — Early History and Culture*. (FACS. ED.) (Melbourne: Today's Heritage, first published in 1888.) pp. 532–3. See also Pike, Vol 5, pp. 306–8: and D H Borchardt and Victor Crittenden, *Australians: A Guide to Sources*, Volume 9. (Edited by D H Borchardt and Victor Crittenden) (NSW: Fairfax, Syme and Weldon Associates, 1987) p. 95.

In regard to the increased awareness of the necessity for qualified staff it is useful to look at the Museum of Economic Geology Entry Book of Correspondence (MS. ML Accession Number M1186) where entries can be found for 1846, acknowledging the discovery of gold in the Adelaide hills, and for 1849, that specimens of lead ore had been found in the Murchison district of Western Australia, as well as a request for texts on mining and metallurgy. (GSM1/2 pp. 156–7, p. 368, and pp. 175–6). A further entry for Mar 1849 notes the discovery of copper, lead, iron and gold in New South Wales, and that geologists were required to carry out surveys. (GSM1/5, pp. 181–4) Later entries indicate the appoint-ment of a Government Surveyor and a Government Geologist for South Australia (GSM1/6, pp. 98–103), and also include a letter from Sir Roderick Murchison, President of the Royal Society, recommending that all Colonial Governments employ geologists (GSM1/7, pp. 266–8).
23. Borchardt and Crittenden, pp. 89–90.
24. Gipps to Stanley, 9 Mar 1846. Enclosure No. 1. *HRA:* S1 V24, p. 810.
25. Gipps to Stanley, 7 Dec 1843. *HRA:* S1 V23, p. 246.
26. Eyre, *Journals*, Vol 1, p. ix.
27. Gregory, *Journals*, p. 53.
28. For details on Elsey, see Pike, Vol 4, p. 139.
29. Given that Bentham had access to all the 8125 Australian specimens which had been collected and forwarded over the years, he was perhaps not an unreasonable choice. Moyal, pp. 172–5.
30. Eyre, *Journals*, Vol 2, pp. 137–8.
31. Eyre, *Journals*, Vol 2, p. 134.
32. Eyre, *Journals*, Vol 2, pp. 134–5.
33. Leichhardt, *Journal*, p. 220.
34. Sturt, *Journal*, p. 225.

35. Gregory, *Journals*, p. 101. Moyal (p140) notes that geology was seen in the earlier years as being almost exclusively of commercial interest and that professionals appointed from Britain chafed under their narrow and restricted role.
36. Augustus Gregory was advised, in the 'Official Instructions to the North Australian Expedition', that to find additional grazing lands would be of 'incalculable advantage' to the colonies of South and Western Australia. *North Australian Exploring Expedition: Copy of Correspondence*. (Melbourne: John Ferres, Government Printer, 1855) pp. 11–12.
37. Gregory, *Journals*, p. 14.
38. Gregory, *Journals*, p. 52.
39. Eyre, *Journals*, Vol 1, p. ix.
40. Eyre, *Journals*, Vol 2, pp. 113–4. Leichhardt, similarly poorly equipped and staffed, also suffered from this problem and, in the Taroom area of Southern Queensland, commented in 1844 that: 'I could not decide, to my entire satisfaction, whether my views were right: for the country was difficult for reconnoitring: and I was necessarily compelled to move quickly on, to accomplish the object of my expedition: but it is a very interesting point for geographical research, and I hope, if I am not anticipated by other explorers, to ascertain, at some future period, the course of these creeks and rivers.' *Journal*, p. 43.
41. Gregory's Instructions requested that he provide '... general Superintendence to the Scientific branch of the Service as will Stimulate those under your command to use their utmost endeavours ... ' Gregory, *North Australian*. p13. In this light, Gregory provided von Mueller with the quietest riding horses, for he was not a competent rider, and attempted to care for the packaged samples, but this was not always possible.
42. Gregory, *North Australian*. p. 11.
43. Elsey to his sisters, 12 Aug – 4 Sept 1855. MS ANL, Cited in Wendy Birman, p. 104. See also Elsey to Tom, 19 May 1856. MS ANL. Cited in Wendy Birman, *Gregory of Rainworth: A Man in His Time*. (Perth: University of Western Australia Press, 1979) p. 142.
44. Bennett to Owen, 4 Feb 1833. Cited in Moyal, p. 76.
45. Gilbert to Gould, Port Essington, 19 Sept 1840. Cited in Moyal, p. 66.
46. Leichhardt, *Journal*, p. 445.
47. Gregory, *North Australian*, p. 9.
48. Gregory, *North Australian*, p. 9.
49. Leichhardt, *Journal*, p. 469. Of this incident Leichhardt wrote on 24 Oct 1847, that the bullock carrying his botanical specimens was swimming for a quarter of an hour. (Aurousseau, V3, p. 969) Aurousseau notes in Vol 3, Item 188D that J Decaisne, whom Durando had appointed to prepare and catalogue the remnants of the collection, wrote on 5 Feb 1850, that the specimens were consequently too badly damaged for exact study.
50. See Elsey and Mueller's comments on the problem of conveying scientific samples by packhorse, in Birman, p. 155.
51. Eyre, *Journals*, Vol 1, p. 85.
52. Gregory, *Journals*, p. 160.
53. Eyre, *Journals*, Vol 1, p. vii. Perhaps more importantly, on this expedition Eyre took John Baxter, who had worked for him for several years on his grazing and overlanding exploits and was perhaps as experienced as Eyre. Edward Scott, who had '... travelled with me overland from King George's Sound to Swan River' (Vol 1, p. 11) was appointed as a 'companion'. Corporal Coles, who was seconded from Captain Frome, had accompanied Grey on all his Western Australian explorations. He was also a wheelwright by trade which was a particularly important skill given that drays were being taken (Vol 1, p. 13). In addition, one of the dray drivers had also worked on Eyre's sheep stations. Finally, the two Aboriginal men taken along had been with Eyre for

several years on his overlanding expeditions, and working on his stations.

54. Sturt, *Journal*. p. 118.

55. Sturt, *Journal*. pp. 107–8. Consequently Sturt's Central Australian Expedition included John McDouall Stuart, Louis Piesse and James Pool, who had all previously been employed by Sturt on inland survey work. John Browne, appointed as medical officer, botanist and naturalist, had had previous exploration experience. Robert Flood, who '... had a good reputation for handling horses had (also) been head stockman of Sturt's overlanding party in 1838.' Finally, David Morgan had accompanied Sturt on his expedition along the Murray River. Sturt, *Journal*, p. 103.

56. Roe to Gregory, 16 Dec 1854. WA. SDF v49/428 No. 386 BL. Cited in Birman, p. 74. Of further interest in the sense of a Roe legacy, is that the Gregory brothers once surveyed on William Forrest's property at Picton, near the port of Bunbury. Forrest's sons John and Alexander, who were enthralled by these men, later followed in their footsteps, first as surveyors, then as explorers. Thus a clear line of development can be seen from Roe's earliest, tentative explorations of the immediate surrounds of Perth, to the explorations of the barren, waterless expanses of Cooper Creek and the Great Sandy Desert region of north-western Australia.

57. Wilson had also had some years' field experience in the Californian goldfields. Wilson to Shaw 23 Nov 1854. LBR MSS NAE. 1/7 RGS. Cited in Birman, p. 82.

58. Eyre, *Journals*, Vol 1, p. 73.

59. Eyre, *Journals*, Vol 1, p. 104.

60. Charles Sturt, MS. ML Accession number FM4/1541, p8.

61. Sturt, *Journal*. p. 97.

62. Augustus Gregory, MS. ML Accession number Q437, Item 7, p. 14.

63. Mitchell, *Journal*, p. 5.

64. Mitchell, *Journal*, p. 86.

65. Mitchell, *Journal*, p. 63.

66. Mitchell, *Journal*, p. 88.

67. Leichhardt had originally intended to use packhorses, for he had had eighteen months' field experience in New South Wales prior to setting off, and appreciated that drays would be impracticable in the bush. That he changed to pack bullocks appears to have arisen from incorrect advice that their carrying capacity was approximately 110 kilograms: forty-five kilograms greater than that of horses. As Leichhardt was particularly short of funds, bullocks would therefore have seemed an attractive alternative, for he could have carried the same load with fewer animals. Leichhardt unfortunately found that the bullocks' carrying capacity over an extended period proved no greater than that of horses. *Journal*, p. xix.

68. John Septimus Roe, 'J. S. Roe Esq, Surveyor General, from Perth to Cape Riche.' *Exploration Diaries*, Vol 4, p. 92.

69. Roe, 'J. S. Roe Esq ...', *Exploration Diaries*, Vol 4, p. 92.

70. John Septimus Roe, 'Report by J. S. Roe, Esq, Surveyor General, of his Expedition to Explore the Interior country South Eastward from York, between Sept 1848 and Feb 1849.' *Exploration Diaries*, Vol 4, p. 136. Eyre had been placed in a similar position on his crossing of the Bight, when his horses were critically knocked up by three long waterless stages. He abandoned almost everything that was not edible and, when the southern winter began to encroach, he and Wiley suffered severely. Leichhardt was similarly placed on his first expedition, due to an increasingly critical shortage of pack animals, and on several occasions revised his loads. At the Staaten River (approximately one kilometre from the present homestead) he abandoned his spare horse shoes and two gun barrels in a freshwater billabong. (*Journal*, p. 320) He left Gilbert's rock collection at the Limmen Bight River and, after the disastrous loss

of four horses in two days on the Roper River, burnt the majority of his and Gilbert's plant collections.

71. Gregory, *Journals*, p. 151.

72. Gregory, *Journals*, p. 119.

73. Augustus Gregory, MS. ML Accession number Q437, Item 7, p. 14.

74. Leichhardt, *Journal*, p. 31. Heat exhaustion also affected Mitchell's bullock drivers, particularly when caught without water on his first and second expeditions. On 13 April, during the fourth expedition, Mitchell established yet another depot and again split his expedition, then set out on horseback while his men were walking in 105°F heat. *Journal*, p. 125. It may well have been that, because Mitchell always rode, he took many years to come to appreciate the necessity of having all his men adequately mounted.

75. Leichhardt, *Journal*, p. 159.

76. Augustus Gregory, MS. ML Accession number Q437, Item 7, p. 13.

77. Augustus Gregory, MS. ML Accession number Q437, Item 7, p. 12.

78. This advantage is shown by the fact that Stuart, the Gregory's, Giles and other explorers of the 1860s and 1870s rarely had difficulties with Aborigines attacking repeatedly, as occurred with the Jardines, whose rate of travel was determined by the pace of the cattle they were droving.

79. Mitchell, 'Major Mitchell's Expedition into the Interior of Australia', *The Journal of the Royal Geographical Society of London*, Vol 7, 1837. (London: John Murray, 1837) p. 284. Mitchell's preoccupation with measurement at the expense of mobility can be seen in the advice he gave to Kennedy, when sending him back to trace the course of the 'Victoria River' (ie. the Barcoo), on how to calculate his distances: 'If you count the strokes of either of your horse's fore feet, either walking or trotting, you will find them to be upon an average, about 950 to a mile. In a fieldbook, as you note each change of bearing, you have only to note down also the number of paces (which soon becomes a habit): and to keep count of these, it is only necessary to carry about thirty-five or forty small pieces of wood, like dice (beans or peas would do), in one waistcoat pocket, and, at the end of every 100 paces, remove one to the empty pocket on the opposite side. At each change of bearing, you count these, adding the odd numbers to the number of hundreds, ascertained by the dice, to be counted and returned at each change of bearing to the other pocket. You should have a higher pocket for your watch, and keep the two lower waistcoat pockets for this important purpose.' (Mitchell, *Journal*, pp. 409–10) The difficulties associated with negotiating rough country and ascertaining and keeping a course whilst simultaneously juggling beans or peas from pocket to pocket warrant no further comment.

80. Captain Frome, 'Capt. C. E. Frome's Report on the Country Eastward of Flinder's Range', *The Journal of the Royal Geographical Society of London*, Vol 14, 1844. (London: John Murray, 1844) p. 285.

81. J L Cumpston, *Sir Thomas Mitchell*, p. 150. Cited in Birman, p. 88.

82. Roe, 'Report by J. S. Roe, Esq ...'. *Exploration Diaries*, Vol 4, p. 157.

83. Gregory, *Journals*, p. 82.

84. Gregory, *Journals*, p. 163.

85. Roe, 'Report by J. S. Roe, Esq ...'. *Exploration Diaries*, Vol 4, p. 137.

86. As Leichhardt noted: 'The death of our spare horses did not allow us any more to relieve the others by alternate rests, and we became soon aware of their increasing weakness. This was considerably aggravated by the necessity under which we were of keeping two horses tethered near the camp.' (*Journal*, p. 455.) However, not all green feed was beneficial, particularly when stock were unaccustomed to it. One of Leichhardt's bullocks, for example, was badly affected on one occasion: '... the poor beast was scarcely able to crawl before us. His weakness had been occasioned by a diarrhoea brought on by the green feed

and the brackish water at Seven Emu River: and I congratulated myself on not having remained there longer, as probably all my bullocks would have been equally affected. (*Journal*, p. 404)

87. Gregory, *Journals*, p. 105.
88. Eyre, *Journals*, Vol 1, p. 113.
89. Of Eyre's claims, Giles later wrote: 'This journey of Eyre's was very remarkable in more ways than one: its most extraordinary incident being the statement that his horses travelled for seven days and nights without water. I have travelled with horses in almost every part of Australia, but I know that after three days and three nights without water horses would certainly knock up, die, or become utterly useless, and it would be impossible to make them continue travelling.' (Vol 1, p. xxviii) Perhaps more tellingly, on John Forrest's retracing of Eyre's route in 1870, he found that after only four days without water in exactly the same country, his horses were in a critical state: 'I have never seen horses in such a state before, and hope never to do so again. The horses, which four days ago were strong and in good condition, now appeared only skeletons, eyes sunk, nostrils dilated, and thoroughly exhausted. Since leaving Eucla to getting water at this spot, a period of nearly ninety hours, they had only been allowed one gallon of water each, which was given them from our water drums. It is wonderful how well they performed this journey: had they not started in good condition, they never could have done it.' John Forrest, *Explorations in Australia: [1] Exploration in Search of Dr. Leichhardt and Party. [2] From Perth to Adelaide, Around the Great Australian Bight. [3] From Champion Bay Accross the Desert to the Telegraph and to Adelaide.* (FACS ED) (Adelaide: Libraries Board of South Australia, First Published in 1875) p. 122.
90. Eyre, *Journals*, Vol 1, pp. 100–101.
91. Sturt, *Journal*, pp. 99–100.
92. Gregory, *Journals*, p. 91.
93. Sturt, *Journal*, p. 95.
94. Gregory, *Journals*, p. 82.
95. Eyre, *Journals*. Vol I, p. 37.
96. Edward M Curr, *Pure Saddle Horses, and How to Breed Them in Australia: Together with a Consideration of the History and Merits of the English, Arab, Andalusian, and Australian Breeds of Horses.* (Melbourne: Wilson and Mackinnon, 1863.) p. 292. The emphasis is Curr's.
97. Eyre, *Journals*, Vol 1, p. 32.
98. Augustus Gregory, MS. ML Accession number Q437, Item 1.
99. Gregory, *Journals*, p. 205.
100. Gregory, *Journals*, p. 177.
101. Hillman, 'Mr Hillman's Journal'. *Exploration Diaries*, Vol 2, p. 350.
102. Roe, 'Report by J. S. Roe, Esq ...' *Exploration Diaries*, Vol 4, pp. 213–4.
103. Austin, *Exploration Diaries*, Vol 4, p. 348.
104. Gregory, *Journals*, p. 11 and p. 51.
105. Gregory, *Journals*, p. 161.
106. That expedition member Murphy's pony almost certainly died from poisoning can be found from the Journal of the Jardine brothers' expedition in the Lynd-Mitchell Rivers area twenty years later. On this occasion, they eventually lost over ten of their best horses, and described the effects of the poison as it ran its course on their stock. (P. 46). More importantly, they noted that: 'Leichhardt mentions (p. 293) the loss of Murphy's pony on the Lynd, which was found on the sands, "with its body blown up and bleeding at the nostrils". Similar symptoms showed themselves in the case of the horses of this expedition, proving pretty clearly that the deaths were caused by some noxious plant.' (Messrs Jardine, p. 20).
107. Leichhardt, *Journal*, p. 319.
108. Leichhardt, *Journal*, pp. 248 and 278. Leichhardt's lack of horsemanship was manifested when, of this problem, he later commented: '[The horses were] shod at our leaving the Downs, but they soon lost their shoes: and, as our stages were short, and the ground soft, I did not think it necessary to shoe them again. In travelling along the Burdekin, however,

and the upper Lynd, they became very footsore: but still there was a sufficient change of good country to allow them to recover ... ' (*Journal*, p. 319.)

109. Phillips, p. 49.

110. Sturt, *Journal*, p. 86.

111. Sturt, *Journal*, p. 90.

112. Eyre, *Journals*, Vol 1, p. 93.

113. Eyre, *Journals*, Vol 1, p. 180.

114. Roe, 'Report by J. S. Roe, Esq'. *Exploration Diaries*, Vol 4, p. 184.

115. Gregory, *Journals*, p. 68.

116. Gregory, *Journals*, p. 162. One of the few occasions that Gregory's horses were unshod occurred on the Leichhardt expedition, when their shoes had been removed '... to enable them to traverse the mud plains.' Gregory, *Journals*, p. 206. This is a not uncommon problem in Queensland, particularly in black-soil country, where an accumulation of clay builds up inside the horseshoe until it protrudes an inch or so beyond them, and the animal is walking on an unstable convex surface. Unfortunately, shortly after the clay area had been passed, Gregory's horses struck rocky ground and their '... hoofs were soon worn to the quick', so necessitating re-shoeing. Gregory, *Journals*, p. 206.

117. Augustus Gregory, MS. ML Accession number Q437, Item 1.

118. Edward M Curr, *Recollections of Squatting in Victoria: Then Called the Port Phillip District (from 1841 to 1851)*. (Melbourne, Sydney, and Adelaide: George Robertson, 1883) p. 117.

119. Rev Henry William Haygarth MA, *Recollections of Bush Life in Australia: During a Residence of Eight Years in the Interior*. (London: John Murray, 1864) p. 78.

120. Curr, *Pure Saddle Horses*, p. 178.

121. W H L Ranken, *The Dominion of Australia: An Account of its Foundations*. (Piccadilly: Chapman and Hall, 1874) p. 124. The actual construction of such saddles was never a problem, for Wentworth noted as early as 1819 that saddlers and harness-makers were working in the colony. (p. 111)

122. W H Tietkens, MS. ML Accession number 1352–2, p. 115.

123. Macquarie, Archives Office, Lands Department files, 24 Mar 1817. Bannister's comment on his 1830 expedition from Perth to Albany, of '... the necessity of having some description of pack-saddle for such expeditions ...' in order to prevent poorly fastened loads moving the saddles and causing severe galling, is strong evidence that British military pack-saddles were probably not used in the exploration of Australia. Bannister, 'Extracts', *Exploration Diaries*, Vol 1, p. 231.

124. William Landsborough, *Journal of Landsborough's Expedition from Carpentaria, in Search of Burke and Wills: With a Map Showing his Route.* (FACS ED) (Adelaide: State Libraries Board of South Australia, 1971) p. 23.

125. Leichhardt, *Journal*, pp. xix, 5 and 8.

126. Roe, 'Report by J. S. Roe Esq.' *Exploration Diaries*, Vol 4, p. 151.

127. Gregory, *Journals*, p. 19.

128. W B Lord and T Baines, *Shifts and Expedients*. pp. 30–1. Cited in Birman, pp. 119–20.

129. Gregory, *Journals*. p. 120.

130. Gregory, *Journals*. p. 198.

131. Augustus Gregory, MS. ML Accession number Q437, Item I.

132. Gregory, *Journals*. p. 198. The condamine bell had a leather strap inserted in its mouth to immobilise the clapper during the day, for the bells are left around the horses' necks as they travel and, without this strap, stockmen would be annoyed by the incessant clanging, particularly where several horses are belled. Plate 19B shows two bay horses with bells, with the strap in position. Once a camp has been established and the horses hobbled for the night, the leather muffling strap is removed, so allowing the clapper full movement and thus the bell to work unimpeded. The strap is replaced the next morning when the horses have been brought in for re-saddling.

133. Augustus Gregory, MS. ML Accession number Q437, Item I.
134. Leichhardt, *Journal*, p. 26.
135. *Royal Geographical Society Journal* (London) V18, p. 117. Cited in Birman, p. 154. Nevertheless, Gregory and his men made considerable use of the wildfowl they shot, and also used Portulaca as a vegetable. Gregory later commented that this plant was found over the whole of Northern Australia and it proved 'a very valuable article of food.' *Journals*, p. 116.
136. Leichhardt, *Journal*, p. xviii.
137. Leichhardt, *Journal*, p. 400.
138. Leichhardt, *Journal*, pp. 401 and 407.
139. Leichhardt, *Journal*, p. 407.
140. Leichhardt, *Journal*, pp. 120, 247, 284–5, 298 and 411.
141. Leichhardt, *Journal*, pp. 108 and 120.
142. Leichhardt, *Journal*, p. 148.
143. The tops of corypha palms were also baked in hot coals and eaten as a vegetable. *Journal*, pp. 40–41.
144. Leichhardt, *Journal*, p. 77.
145. Sturt's men affected with this disease suffered appallingly. Poole, for example, '... lost the use of his lower extremities, the skin of his legs turned black, large pieces of flesh hung down from the roof of his mouth and he was at once reduced to perfect helplessness.' Sturt, *Journal*, p. 52. The list of native foodstuffs consumed on the 1844–5 expedition, which Leichhardt prepared upon his return in 1846, included: 'The bean of the McKenzie; Sterculia seeds, Convolvulus root, the lower part of the Typha Nymphaea seeds, stems and tubes Fruit of Correya arborea, Eugenia scarlat, rose large to small Nacuna (the vine bean of the roper), Little gooseberry tree, The gum of Acacia of Expedition Range — it's seeds vomitis, Salicornia shoots, Capparis, Jibong, Exocarpus latifolia, Yellow fig, Hairy fig, Clustered fig, Nelumbium stalks and seeds, Allamur, Imbebus and Cabbage palms.' (Leichhardt, MS. ML Accession number C154, p. 5)
146. Leichhardt was well aware of the necessity of caring for his dog, but lacked the means to carry water during the daily stages, for he had not taken sufficient containers with him. *Journal*, p. 393.
147. Gregory, *Journals*, p. 109.
148. Mitchell, *Journal*, p. 125.
149. Leichhardt, *Journal*, pp. 27 and 275.
150. Leichhardt refers to this technique on p. 79 of his *Journal*, pointing out that they dried the meat like 'the charqui of the South Americans', and Aurousseau notes that he may have gathered the idea from employees of the Australian Agricultural Company, for he passed through the Company's property in May 1844. At this time the Company had imported mules and horses from Chile. Aurousseau, Endnote 118A, Vol 3, p. 1040.
151. Leichhardt, *Journal*, p. 37.
152. Leichhardt, *Journal*, p. 247.
153. Phillips, p. 48.
154. Leichhardt, *Journal*, p. 527.
155. For an amusing description of the usually unsanitary techniques of salting and smoking, it is useful to consult Tom Cole, *Hell West and Crooked* (Sydney: Collins Publishers Australia, 1988) pp. 30–1.
156. Leichhardt, *Journal*, pp. 168–9.
157. Leichhardt, *Journal*, pp. 416–7.
158. Leichhardt, *Journal*, p. 84.
159. Gregory, *Journals*, p. 91.
160. Leichhardt, *Journal*, p. 117.
161. Leichhardt, *Journal*, p. 343.
162. Leichhardt, *Journal*, p. 46.
163. Augustus Gregory, MS. ML Accession number Q437, Item I.
164. Mitchell, *Journal*, p. 148.
165. Mitchell, *Journal*, p. 29.
166. Leichhardt, *Journal*, p. 128.
167. Eyre, *Journals*, Vol 1, p. 183.
168. Mitchell, 'Major Mitchell's Expedition', Vol 7, 1837, p. 283.
169. Gregory, *Journals*, p. 97.
170. John Septimus Roe, 'Report on Champion Bay and its Vicinity. By J. S. Roe Esq. Surveyor General.' *Exploration Diaries*, Vol 4, p. 31.

171. Roe, 'Report by J. S. Roe, Esq'. *Exploration Diaries*, Vol 4, pp. 166, 152 and 146, respectively.
172. Roe, 'Report by J. S. Roe, Esq'. *Exploration Diaries*, Vol 4, pp. 146 and 152.
173. Roe, 'Report by J. S. Roe, Esq'. *Exploration Diaries*, Vol 4, p. 152.
174. Gregory, *Journals*, pp. 4 and 7. Trap is a dark-coloured eruptive rock of columnar structure, and thus Gregory's comment that its fissures negated any chance of water storage is understandable.
175. Leichhardt, *Journal*, pp. 182–3.
176. Sturt, *Journal*, p. 44.
177. Sturt, *Journal*, p. 63.
178. Frome, Vol 14, 1844, p. 283.
179. Sturt, *Journal*, p. 98.
180. Leichhardt, *Journal*, p. 159.
181. Leichhardt, *Journal*, p. 162.
182. Leichhardt, *Journal*, pp. 375 and 379.
183. Gregory, *Journals*, p. 198.
184. Mitchell, *Journal*, p. 336.
185. Leichhardt, *Journal*, pp. 18 and 65.
186. Mitchell, *Journal*, p. 280.
187. Leichhardt, *Journal*, p. 75.
188. Leichhardt, *Journal*, p. 371.
189. Leichhardt, *Journal*, p. 118.
190. Eyre, *Journals*, Vol 2, p. 217.
191. Mitchell, *Journal*, pp. 252–3. It should be noted that this quotation is selectively abbreviated, and that Mitchell expressed mitigating factors.
192. Gregory, *Journals*, p. 14.
193. Leichhardt, *Journal*, p. 340.
194. Gregory, *Journals*, p. 25.
195. Gregory, *Journals*, p. 28.
196. Gregory, *Journals*, p. 31.
197. Gregory, *Journals*, p. 57.
198. Gregory, *Journals*, p. 44.
199. Gregory, *Journals*, pp. 58 and 85.
200. Gregory, *Journals*, pp. 42 and 91.
201. Edward John Eyre, MS. ML Accession number 1235, p. 1012.
202. Macquarie, Archives Office, Lands Department files, 24 Mar 1817: and Augustus Gregory, MS. ML Accession number Q437, Item I.
203. Augustus Gregory, MS. ML Accession number Q437, Items 1 and 5.
204. Augustus Gregory, MS. ML Accession number Q437, Items 1 and 5.
205. Augustus Gregory, MS. ML Accession number Q437, Item 1.
206. Augustus Gregory, MS. ML Accession number Q437, Item 3.
207. Eyre, *Journals*, Vol 1, p. 4.
208. Gipps to Stanley, 7 Dec 1843. *HRA:* S1 V23, p. 246.
209. Gregory, *Journals*, pp. 74 and 154. See also Birman pp. 89–90 where, in a letter written to his brother Francis in 1855, Augustus Gregory pointed out the danger of being left isolated on the North Australian Expedition.
210. Gregory, *Journals*, p. 197.
211. In preparing to leave the Victoria River, to set off eastward on the second section of his North Australian Expedition, Gregory outlined to a nicety how the horses available could carry five months' provisions for nine men and thus the 'party proceeding to the interior must not exceed nine in number'. Gregory, *Journals*, p. 119.
212. Augustus Gregory, MS. ML Accession number Q437, Item 7, p. 13.
213. Gregory, *Journals*, p. 121.
214. Gregory, *Journals*, p. 59.
215. Gregory, *Journals*, p. 59.
216. Gregory, *Journals*, p. 89.
217. Leichhardt, *Journal*, p. 299.
218. Leichhardt, *Journal*, p. 130.

Chapter Six

1. Roderick, p. 7.
2. Giles, Vol 1, p. xxx.
3. Giles, Vol 1, pp. xxx–xxxi.
4. A H Chisholm, *Strange New World: The Adventures of John Gilbert and Ludwig Leichhardt* (Sydney: Angus and Robertson, 1941) p. x.
5. Chisholm, p. xi.
6. Chisholm, p. 316.
7. Chisholm, pp. 338–40.
8. Favenc, p. 155.
9. Favenc, pp. 166–7.
10. Henry Stuart Russell, *The Genesis of Queensland: An Account of the First Exploring Journeys to and Over the Darling Downs; The Earliest Days of Their Occupation; Social Life; Station*

Seeking; The Course of Discovery, Northward and Westward; and a Resume of the Causes which led to Separation from New South Wales with Portraits and Facsimiles of Maps, Log, and etc, and etc. (FACS ED) (Toowoomba: Vintage Books, 1989) p. 359.
11. Russell, p. 371.
12. Russell, p. 376.
13. Robert Logan Jack, *Northmost Australia, Volume One* (Melbourne: George Robertson, 1922) pp. 200–201.
14. Chisholm, p. 279.
15. Leichhardt, *Journal*, p. 450.
16. Roderick, p. 274.
17. Roderick, pp. 271–2.
18. Roderick, p. 271.
19. Chisholm, p. 237. Refer also to pp. 294–300 of Vol 2 of the Field Notes Addendum.
20. Leichhardt, *Journal*, pp. 249 and 252.
21. Roderick, p. 244.
22. Refer to the Data Summary Sheets at the front of Volumes 1–3 of the Field Notes.
23. Gilbert, cited in Chisholm, p. 248. See also p. 234.
24. Roderick, pp. 379–80.
25. Kathleen Fitzpatrick, *Walkabout*, October, 1963. (Melbourne: Australian National Travel Association) p. 14.
26. Roderick, p. 8.
27. Jack, p. 201.
28. E H Carr, *What is History?* (England; Penguin, 1987) p. 12. See Chapter I, pp. 7–30 for a broader exposition of this problem.
29. Roderick, pp. 49, 54, 59, 62 and 79.
30. Roderick, p. 77.
31. Roderick, p. 77.
32. Roderick, p. 79.
33. Roderick, p. 79.
34. Roderick, pp. 79–80.
35. Roderick, p. 82.
36. Henry Turnbull, cited in Roderick, p. 234.
37. Aurousseau, Vol 3, p. 845. Leichhardt notes that his entire expedition cost him 'hardly 900 rix dollars'. He later provided the necessary conversion rate, pointing out, for example, that £600 equalled 4200 rix dollars. (V3, p. 929). As this is a ratio of 7:1, his expediture of 900 rix dollars on the Port Essington expedition would have been approximately equal to £130.
38. Eyre, MS. ML Accession No. 1235, pp. 1009–1011.
39. Leichhardt, *Journal*, p. xiv.
40. Aurousseau, Vol 3, p. 969.
41. Leichhardt MS, ML Accession No. A2541, p. 54.
42. Aurousseau, Vol 3, p. 969.
43. Aurousseau, Vol 3, p. 869.
44. Aurousseau, Vol 3, p. 982.
45. Aurousseau, Vol 3, p. 986.
46. Aurousseau, Vol 3, p. 870.
47. Aurousseau, Vol 3, p. 969.
48. Aurousseau, Vol 3, p. 892.
49. Chisholm, p. 340.
50. Chisholm, p. 211. While Chisholm is correct in asserting that the Burdekin was first discovered by the Aboriginal assistant Charley on 1 April (John Gilbert, MS. ML Accession No. A2587), Leichhardt does not specifically state in his Journal that the Burdekin was first seen on 28 March. Although the observation is recorded on the entry for March 28, it is quite clear that Leichhardt was encompassing the findings of several days under this one date. For a more detailed analysis of Chisholm's criticism of this aspect of Leichhardt's writings see the paragraph immediately following Endnote 40 in the text.
51. Chisholm, p. 340.
52. Aurousseau, Vol 2, p. 521.
53. Aurousseau, Vol 2, p. 456.
54. Aurousseau, Vol 2, p. 697.
55. Aurousseau, Vol 2, p. 481.
56. Aurousseau, Vol 2, pp. 479 and 481.
57. Aurousseau, Endnote No. 54, Vol 2, p. 801.
58. Aurousseau, Vol 2, p. 546.
59. Aurousseau, Endnote No. 107, Vol 2, p. 818.
60. Aurousseau, Endnote No. 91, Vol 2, p. 814.
61. Aurousseau, Endnote No. 109A, Vol 2, pp. 818–19.

62. Aurousseau, Endnote No. 109A, Vol 2, p. 819.
63. Aurousseau, Endnote No. 109A, Vol 2, p. 819.
64. Mitchell, cited in Roderick, p. 452.
65. Aurousseau, Vol 3, p. 994.
66. Paul Carter, *The Road to Botany Bay*. (New York: Alfred A Knopf, 1988), pp. 119–122.
67. Aurousseau, Vol 3, p. 873.
68. Aurousseau, Vol 3, p. 969.
69. Chisholm, p. 253.
70. Aurousseau, Endnote No. 177b, Vol 3, p. 1062.
71. Aurousseau, Endnote No. 186b, Vol 3, p. 1064.
72. Jack, p. 196.
73. Chisholm, p. 173.
74. Chisholm, p. 241.
75. Roderick, p. 314.
76. Whitehead, p. 9.
77. John Lort Stokes, *Discoveries in Australia; with an Account of the Coasts and Rivers Explored and Surveyed During the Voyage of HMS* Beagle *in the Years 1837–38–39–40–41–42–43. By Command of the Lords Commissioners of the Admiralty. Also a Narrative of Captain Owen Stanley's visits to the Islands of the Arafura Sea, in two volumes.* (London: T and W Boone, 1846) Vol 1, p. 397.
78. Whitehead, p. 10.
79. J L Cumpston. *Sir Thomas Mitchell* cited in Birman, p. 88. See also Birman p. 187 for details of how Gregory found Mitchell's placement of the junction of the Alice and Barcoo Rivers to be in excess of five miles north of its true position.
80. Whitehead, p. 10.
81. Whitehead, p. 10.
82. Stokes, Vol 1, p. vi.
83. For further details on this question refer to J E D Williams, *From Sails to Satellites* (Oxford University Press, 1992) pp. 95–6 and especially p. 100.
84. Whitehead, p. 12.
85. Mitchell, MS. ML Accession No. A2166, p. 275.
86. Allan Cunningham, MS. ML Accession No. FM4 A3802, p. 9.
87. Stokes, Vol 1, p. 377. See also Vol 2, pp. 121 and 224.
88. Favenc, p. 154.
89. Favenc, p. 140.
90. Webster, p. 91.
91. Webster, p. 227.
92. Hill, p. 18.
93. Aurousseau, Vol 3, p. 942.
94. See the Introduction to the Field Notes Addendum for an explanation of the problems underlying longitude determination of Leichhardt's campsites in the Gulf region.
95. Given the previously outlined problems inherent in establishing longitude by celestial observation in the nineteenth century, these were satisfactory results, especially given the paucity of Leichhardt's equipment.
96. Refer to the Data Summary Sheets at the front of volumes 1 to 3 of the Field Notes Addendum.
97. Roderick, Footnote, p. 320.
98. Jack, Footnote, p. 192.
99. Aurousseau, Vol 3, p. 853.
100. Chisholm, p. 277.
101. Roderick, p. 351.
102. Sheet 73, pp. 428–435, Vol 3 of the Field Notes Addendum provides a detailed exposition of this question. (See also Enclosure 2, following p. 435)
103. Chisholm, pp. 241–2.
104. Roderick, p. 306.
105. Gilbert, cited in Roderick, pp. 309–310.
106. W B Clarke, *The Spectator*, 1846, p. 284. MS. ML Accession No. MDQ 079/119.
107. Leichhardt, *Journal*, p. 303.
108. p. xii.
109. p. 86.
110. Russell, p. 361.
111. pp. 364–5.
112. Favenc, p. 165.
113. Chisholm, p. 93.
114. p. 306.
115. Favenc, p. 121.
116. Aurousseau, V2, p. 634.
117. Aurousseau, V2, p. 662.
118. Aurousseau, V2, p. 748. See also V2, pp. 746–7.
119. Chisholm, p. 92.

120. Aurousseau, V2, pp. 672–3. See also Endnote No. 87b, V2, p. 813.
121. Darling to Twiss, Enclosure No. 1. 12 February 1830. *HRA*: S1 V15, p. 374.
122. Eyre, *Journals*, V1, p. 106.
123. Mitchell, *Journal*, p. 42.
124. Mitchell, *Journal*, p. 116.
125. Russell, p. 362.
126. Aurousseau, V3, p. 922.
127. Aurousseau, V2, p. 746.
128. Aurousseau, V2, p. 781.
129. Aurousseau, V2, p. 781. Furthermore, Leichhardt earlier stated that he intended taking six pack mules and twelve riding horses, 'for every person'. Vol 2, p. 770. Presumably, economics dictated his final choice but Chisholm's claim does not withstand scrutiny.
130. Aurousseau, Endnote 114A, V3, pp. 1036–7.
131. Leichhardt, *Journal*, p. xvii.
132. Aurousseau, V3, p. 918.
133. Aurousseau, V3, p. 918.
134. Leichhardt MS. ML Accession No. AL 69–1, p. 5.
135. Aurousseau, V3, p. 891.
136. Aurousseau, V3, p. 936.
137. Chisholm, p. 214.
138. Aurousseau, V3, p. 998.
139. Leichhardt, Journal, p. 373. This feat says perhaps as much, or more, for Leichhardt's horse.
140. Richard and Helen Walker, *Curtin's Cowboys; Australia's Secret Bush Commandos*. (North Sydney: Allen and Unwin Pty Ltd, 1986) pp. 52–54.
141. Aurousseau, V3, p. 982.
142. Aurousseau, V3, p. 877.
143. Aurousseau, V3, p. 885.
144. Aurousseau, V3, p. 938.
145. Aurousseau, V3, p. 1004.
146. Aurousseau, V3, p. 1004.
147. Aurousseau, V3, p. 918.
148. Aurousseau, V3, p. 1002.
149. Gilbert, cited in Chisholm, p. 141.
150. Leichhardt, *Journal*, p. 393.
151. Favenc, pp. 165–6.
152. Roderick, pp. 220–22. See also Aurousseau, V2, pp. 591 and 721, and V3, p. 826.
153. Aurousseau, V1, p. 391.
154. See Aurousseau, V3, p. 845 for details of the cost, and V3, p. 929 for the conversion rate.
155. Aurousseau, V3, p. 845.
156. Aurousseau, V3, p. 913.
157. Aurousseau, V3, p. 964.
158. Aurousseau, V2, p. 780.
159. Aurousseau, V3, p. Pp. 891–2. See also V3, p. 907 regarding the 1000 pounds of flour provided for the eight men for two years, on the third expedition, at an effective rate of 1.3 pounds per day.
160. See Aurousseau, V3, pp. 839–40 for details of the drying process, and Endnote 118a, V3, p. 1040 on the possible origins of Leichhardt's knowledge of this technique.
161. Aurousseau, V3, p. 892.
162. Aurousseau, V3, p. 929.
163. Aurousseau, Endnote 87b, V2, p. 813.
164. Aurousseau, V2, p. 600.
165. Stuart, p. 353.
166. Aurousseau, Endnote No. 90b, V2, p. 814.
167. Chisholm, p. 129.
168. Aurousseau, V3, p. 880.
169. Aurousseau, V2, p. 512.
170. Chisholm, p. 94.
171. Jack, pp. 200–201.
172. Aurousseau, Endnote 118h, V3, p. 1042.
173. Chisholm, p. 188.
174. Chisholm, p. 297.
175. Chisholm, p. xv.
176. Gilbert, cited in Chisholm, p. 259.
177. Aurousseau, V2, p. 660.
178. Aurousseau, V3, p. 1005.
179. Aurousseau, V3, p. 931.
180. Aurousseau, V3, p. 931.

Chapter Seven:

1. Moyal, p. 175.
2. Tim Bonyhady, *Burke and Wills: From Melbourne to Myth* (Sydney: David Ell Press Pty Ltd, 1991) p. 68.
3. Bonyhady, pp. 51–2.
4. William John Wills, *A Successful Exploration Through the Interior of Australia, from Melbourne to the Gulf*

of Carpentaria. (London: Richard Bentley, 1863) p. 69.
5. Burke to Standish, 4 Oct 1860, cited in Bonyhady, p. 98.
6. The Royal Commission Report, cited in Wills, p. 215, noted that '... it does not appear that Mr. Burke kept any regular journal, or that he gave written instructions to his officers.'
7. Wills, p. 240.
8. Moyal, p. 55.
9. Alexander Forrest, 13 Oct 1879, MS. BL Accession number AR 519.
10. John Forrest, pp. 70–1.
11. Giles, Vol 2, p. 203.
12. W P Auld, *Recollections of McDouall Stuart.* (Adelaide, 1984) p. 54.
13. Auld, p. 54. Furthermore, the old bugbear of equipment breakages still occurred during this period, although explorers had had eighty to ninety years to improve their equipment, horsemanship and saddlery. On one occasion Stuart's equipment was damaged because the backgirth on his packhorse slipped backwards into the horse's flanks, so effectively acting as a flank rope and causing the horse to bolt. Some refinements had been made, however. This particular horse, for example, was led thus overcoming, in considerable part, the problems encountered by earlier explorers such as Oxley, who had left loose the horses carrying important equipment. Nevertheless, '... the instruments were very much injured, in fact very nearly ruined.' John McDouall Stuart, *Explorations in Australia: The Journals of John McDouall Stuart during the Years 1858, 1859, 1860, 1861, and 1862, When he Fixed the Centre of the Continent and Successfully Crossed it From Sea to Sea — Second Edition.* (London: Saunders, Otley, and Co, 1865) p. 134.
14. John Forrest, p. 156.
15. John Forrest, p. 21.
16. Alexander Forrest, MS. BL Accession number AR 519, p. 3.
17. Wilkie, Mueller and Macadam, *Progress Reports (1–6) and Final Report of the Exploration Committee of the Royal Society of Victoria.* (Melbourne: Royal Society, 1863) First Report, p. 2.
18. Wilkie, Mueller and Macadam, Sixth Report, p. 3.
19. Wilkie, Mueller and Macadam, Fourth Report, p. 3.
20. Wilkie, Mueller and Macadam, Sixth Report, p. 3.
21. Charles Eden, 'Introduction', in Colonel Peter Egerton-Warburton, *Journey Across the Western Interior of Australia.* (FACS ED) (Edited by H W Bates) (Perth: Hesperian Press, 1981) pp. 7–8.
22. Eden, in Warburton, p. 128.
23. Eden, in Warburton, pp. 131–2.
24. Giles, Vol 2, p. 341.
25. Cameron, pp. 264–5.
26. John Forrest, p. 22.
27. Giles, Vol 1, p. xxiv and p. xxv.
28. Giles, p. xxvi. See also Curr, *Recollections of Squatting in Victoria,* pp. 181–3 for his description of the country traversed by Sturt and his thoughts on why Sturt found the region so oppressively hostile.
29. Auld, p. 15 and p. 62.
30. Bates, in Warburton, p. 240.
31. Giles, Vol 1, p. 98.
32. W H Tietkens, MS. ML Accession number 1352–2, p. 133.
33. W H Tietkens, MS. ML Accession number 1352–2, p. 133.
34. Giles, Vol 2, p. 115. Several other examples can be found in the major explorers' journals of horses burning their lips as, in desperation, they attempted to lift boiling pannikins off the fire. See Howitt, 'Howitt's Journal', in Robert O'Hara Burke and William John Wills, *The Burke and Wills Exploring Expedition: An Account of the Crossing the Continent of Australia, from Cooper's Creek to Carpentaria, with Biographical Sketches of Robert O'Hara Burke and William John Wills* (Melbourne: Wilson and Mackinnon, 1861) p. 7. See also Auld, p. 74.
35. Giles, Vol 1, pp. 290–1.
36. Giles, Vol 1, p. 291.

37. Giles, Vol 1, p. 56.
38. Giles, Vol 1, pp. 56–7.
39. Ranken, p. 8.
40. Webster, p. 127.
41. Eden, in Warburton, pp. 133–4.
42. Stuart, p. 190.
43. Auld, p. 39.
44. Auld, p. 40.
45. Stuart, pp. 251–2.
46. Stuart, p. 33. See also Giles, Vol 1, pp. 46–48.
47. CL and IO 662/1863. Cited in Webster, p. 248.
48. Auld, p. 43. Compounding the horses' weakness brought on by dehydration was the fact that feed was a problem, particularly after Stuart's time, when the western deserts were being attempted. For much of the Forrest brothers' route through central Western Australia they saw almost only spinifex. Maintaining their horses was, therefore, a difficult task. Many of the horses which died did so principally as a result of malnutrition and debilitation. Indeed, Alexander Forrest later pointed out that he walked over 1600 of the 2900 kilometres covered, '... owing to our horses not being able to carry us'. Alexander Forrest, *Diary of Alexander Forrest 1874*. (Perth: Battye Library, 1975) p. 27.
49. Stuart, p. 201.
50. John Forrest, p. 247.
51. Giles, Vol 1, p. 231.
52. Stuart, p. 425.
53. Stuart, p. 47. Even these experienced horses had, however, definite limits and on the final expedition, when Stuart was desperately seeking a way beyond Newcastle Waters, he drove his horses terribly hard. At this time he was forced to comment that: 'Even my old horses that are inured to hardship are unable to be longer than three days without water, owing to the heat of the sun, the dryness of the feed, and the softness of the country.' (p. 309)
54. Stuart, p. 175. See also Tietkens, MS. ML Accession number 1352–2, p. 125, and Howitt, 'Howitt's Journal', in Burke and Wills, p. 8.
55. More so in temperate southern Australia. In the north of Western Australia, the Northern Territory and northern Queensland, which were often quite different botanically from the southern regions, explorers were coming up against unknown species. One of the few instances of exploration animals being affected by poison during the 1860s and 1870s was that of the horse Barratt, on Stuart's Central Australian Expedition. Stuart later surmised that many of his horses had eaten some injurious plant at the Roper River on the return journey during the fifth expedition, for many of them fell away badly and could neither carry weight, nor cope with sustained journeyings. Whatever the truth of the matter, no plant was isolated. Stuart, p. 425.
56. Alexander Forrest, *North West Exploration: Journal of an Expedition from DeGrey to Port Darwin.* (Perth: Richard Pether, Government Printer, 1880) p. 21.
57. Milton Moore (ed), *Australian Grasslands.* (Canberra: Australian National University Press, 1972) p. 389.
58. Stuart, pp. 177–8.
59. John Forrest, pp. 243–246.
60. Giles, Vol 1, pp. 288–9.
61. Giles, Vol 2, p. 122. For similar comments on the limitations of horses in the Western Deserts see John Forrest, pp. 161 and 265, and Alexander Forrest, *North West Exploration*, p. 9.
62. John Forrest, p. 269.
63. Eden, in Warburton, p. 121.
64. Giles, Vol 2, p. 197.
65. David Lindsay, 'Final Report', *Journal of the Elder Scientific Exploring Expedition, 1892: Equipped Soley at the Cost of Sir Thomas Elder GCMG for the Purpose of Completing the Exploration of Australia, and Placed Under the Control of the Royal Geographical Society of Australasia, South Australian Branch* (Adelaide: C E Bristow, Government Printer, 1893) pp. 108–117.
66. Giles, Vol 2, p. 181.

67. Howitt, 'Howitt's Journal', in Burke and Wills, p. 12.

68. Warburton, pp. 213–4. Bates, in Warburton, notes in a footnote how there is normally a dominant bull camel who keeps the other males under control. Once subordinate males realise that the dominant male is ailing for some reason, the established hierarchy disintegrates almost immediately, and fighting for females commences.

69. Giles, Vol 2, pp. 95–6.

70. Giles, Vol 2, p. 283.

71. Giles, Vol 2, p. 136.

72. As Giles noted on his second expedition, just to the east of the Gibson Desert: 'We always have a great deal of sewing and repairing of the canvas pack-bags to do, and a day of rest usually means a good day's work.' (Giles, Vol 1, p. 204.) Stuart, on his fourth expedition, after attempting to force a passage through hundreds of miles of scrub country, also suffered from this problem, pointing out that: 'The two tarpaulins that I brought from Mr Chamber's station for mending the bags, are all used up some time ago, and nearly all the spare bags: the sewing twine has been used long since, and we are obliged to make some from old bags.' (p. 321.)

73. Warburton, p. 194.

74. Warburton, pp. 250–1.

75. Warburton, p. 208.

76. Stuart, pp. 10–11.

77. Caley to Banks, 12 Oct 1800. *HRN:* V4, p. 240.

78. Lockyer, *Exploration Diaries*, Vol 1, p. 16.

79. Leichhardt, *Journal*, p. 309.

80. Attributed to James Twigg of Western Australia, in 1891. Cited in Patrick O'Farrell, *Letters From Irish–Australia 1825–1929.* (Edited by B Trainor) (Sydney: New South Wales University Press, 1984) pp. 86–7.

81. W H Tietkens, MS. ML Accession number 1352–2, p. 113.

82. W H Tietkens, MS. ML Accession number 1352–2, pp. 97 and 107.

83. Auld, pp. 37–8.

84. Alexander Forrest, *Diary of Alexander Forrest 1874.* p11.

85. In a section entitled 'Stuart's Rifles', Webster notes that one of them was an Enfield Carbine. p. 292.

86. Giles, Vol 1, p. 92.

87. Auld, p. 40.

88. Auld, pp. 31–2.

89. Giles, Vol 1, pp. 212–3.

90. Warburton, p. 195. See also Sturt's recon-noitring between 6 May and 10 July when he made eleven attempts to break through to the north and north-west, towards the country Gregory had earlier explored along the Victoria River.

91. Giles, Vol 2, p. 188.

92. W H Tietkens, *Central Australia Exploring Expedition, 1889, Under Command of W. H. Tietkens.* (Adelaide: C E Bristow, Government Printer, 1891) p. 50.

93. Bates, in Warburton, p. 179.

94. Stuart, p. 234.

95. Julius Brockman, *He Rode Alone: Being the Adventures of Pioneer Julius Brockman from His Diaries.* (Edited by Joan Brockman) (Perth: Artlook Books, 1987) p. 80.

96. J G Hill, *The Calvert Scientific Exploring Expedition (Australia, 1896).* (London: George Philip and Son, Ltd, 1905) pp. 16–17.

97. Burke and Wills, p. 32.

98. Auld, p. 43.

99. Major Thomas Livingstone Mitchell, MS. ML Accession number CYA 295–2, p. 85.

100. Auld, p. 34.

101. Stuart, p. 213.

102. For details on the smoking, which was a quite sophisticated process, given that Giles had minimal equipment and was completely isolated, see Giles, Vol 2, p. 64.

103. Giles, Vol 2, pp. 64–5.

104. Bates, in Warburton, pp. 217–8.

105. Giles, Vol 2, p. 160.

106. *South Australian Parliamentary. Debates*, 9 Oct 1860. Cited in Webster, p. 159.

107. Wilkie, Mueller and Macadam, Final Report, p. 3.
108. Auld, p. 68.
109. Auld, p. 70.
110. Auld, p. 70.
111. Auld, p. 69. A similar experience occurred in 1991 whilst carrying out field research on Leichhardt's route through Expedition Range in Southern Queensland. On this occasion one of the riding horses retraced its steps almost precisely, by employing both sight of the tracks, and scent when the tracks were lost on rocky ground.
112. Auld, p. 200.
113. Auld, p. 200.
114. John Forrest, p. 266.
115. Alexander Forrest, *Diary of Alexander Forrest 1874*, p. 13.
116. Giles, Vol 2, p. 247.
117. Giles, Vol 2, p. 342.

Chapter Eight:

1. At this point it was gradually realised that two members of the expedition, who had set off earlier on a tangential exploration, were overdue. After several months of very considerable, arduous and particularly dangerous searching by a variety of private and governmental groups, their remains were found and eventually taken back to Adelaide for burial.
2. AAAS Report, 1887, Vol 1, pp. 8–14. Cited in Moyal, p. 119.
3. Tietkens, *Central Australian Exploring Expedition*. p. 1.
4. Tietkens, *Central Australian Exploring Expedition*, p. 2. Unfortunately the date palm seeds did not arrive before the expedition set off.
5. Tietkens, *Central Australian Exploring Expedition*, p. 35.
6. Tietkens, *Central Australian Exploring Expedition*, pp. 10–11.
7. Lindsay, 'Instructions'. pp. 3–5.
8. Lindsay, 'Instructions'. pp. 12–13.
9. Baldwin Spencer (ed), *Report on the Work of the Horn Scientific Expedition to Central Australia — In Four Volumes*. (Melbourne: Melville, Mullen and Slade, 1896) Vol 1, p. v.
10. Spencer, Vol 1, pp. v and vi.
11. Tietkens, *Central Australian Exploring Expedition*, p. 20.
12. Tietkens, *Central Australian Exploring Expedition*, p. 17.
13. Spencer, Vol 1, p. 2.
14. Lindsay, *Journal*, p. 127.
15. Lindsay, *Journal*, p. 93.
16. Hill, pp. 7–8.
17. Tietkens, *Central Australian Exploring Expedition*, p. 2.
18. Lindsay, *Journal*, p. 15.
19. Lindsay, *Journal*, p. 126.
20. Tietkens, *Central Australian Exploring Expedition*, p. 54. Two years later the Elder Expedition carried considerable quantities of Epsom salts and castor oil, and routinely drenched poisoned camels in order to purge them. (Lindsay, p. 56.)
21. Tietkens, *Central Australian Exploring Expedition*, pp. 6–10.
22. Tietkens, *Central Australian Exploring Expedition*, p. 10.
23. Spencer, Vol 1, p. 48.
24. Lindsay, 'Final Report', p. 6.
25. Spencer, Vol 1, p. 112.
26. Lindsay, 'Instructions', p. 5.
27. Lindsay, *Journal*, p. 19 and p. 82.
28. Lindsay, *Journal*, p. 33.
29. Lindsay, *Journal*, p. 35.
30. Lindsay, 'Instructions', p. 5.
31. Spencer, Vol 1, pp. v and vi, and p. 2.
32. Lindsay, 'Instructions', p. 7.
33. Lindsay, 'Instructions', p. 10.
34. Lindsay, 'Instructions', pp. 11–12.
35. Lindsay, 'Instructions', p. 12.
36. Lindsay, 'Instructions', p. 13.
37. Lindsay, 'Instructions', p. 18.
38. Lindsay, 'Instructions', pp. 17–19.
39. Lindsay, 'Instructions', p. 17.
40. Lindsay, pp. 21–34. Tepper also provided two pages of information on the preparation of entomological specimens. These notes specified that small specimens were to be packed in sawdust while larger ones were first to be rolled in paper, with the limbs straightened, and the specimen to be then dried by fire or sun. The ends of the rolls then had to be squeezed, and the rolls packed in tins so they could not

shake or be broken by pressure. Naphthalene or camphor was to be applied to keep insects away. These tins were then to be firmly sealed in brown paper, which had been found to keep insects out while allowing moisture to escape. Small moths were to be pinned in cork-lined boxes, '... as they otherwise get so injured by transport as to make them almost useless'. The sawdust or bran used for packing was to be heated and stirred before use, to kill all insects. (Lindsay, pp. 33–34.)

41. Hill, p. 11.

42. Spencer, Vol 1, p. 3.

43. Tietkens, *Central Australian Exploring Expedition*. p. 68.

44. Von Mueller based this assessment on the belief that Tietkens had gathered many of the specimens 'without due discrimination as to flower and fruit'. Tietkens, *Central Australian Exploring Expedition*. pp. 69–70.

45. During this period they also covered 4409 kilometres of previously unexplored country, and 6889 kilometres altogether. (Lindsay, Final Report, p. 12.)

46. Volume One contained a 136-page outline and comment by Baldwin Spencer on procedures, persons involved, problems and highlights. It was informative and readable, for Spencer appreciated the problems which predecessors such as Stuart had had to overcome in writing of often repetitive events and almost unvarying country. Skilfully intermingled were detailed general notes on many of the specimens encountered. Presumably Spencer was able to encompass this range of material as deftly as he did through discussions with the differing scientists of the background and implications of their findings, during nightly talks around the campfires. Such was his literary sophistication that he encompassed science, humdrum daily travel and humorous descriptions of their opinions of the camels with equal facility.

Spencer then went on to provide summaries of the zoological, botanical, geological and palaeontological data, and a twenty-eight-page conclusion.

Volume Two, being 420 pages of the zoological findings and analyses, encompassed mammalia, aves, reptilia, amphibia, pisces, molluscia, crustacea, lepidoptera, coleoptera, orthoptera, and so on. Geography and geology were dealt with in Volume Three, and embraced physical geography in twenty-five pages, general geology in forty-nine pages, economic geology in six pages, petrology in fifteen pages, palaeontology in seventy-three pages and botany in twenty-four pages. Finally, in Volume Four, 196 pages were devoted to the anthropological findings. (Spencer, Vols 1–4)

47. Macquarie to Bathurst, 28 Apr 1814. Enclosure number 4 — Assistant-Surveyor Evans' *Journal*, 1813–1814. *HRA*: S1 V8, p. 171.

INDEX

Aboriginal peoples: and deserts, 247; and explorers, 33, 39, 47, 73, 74, 112, 248, 249, 250, 259; Barrallier, 45, 49, 172; deteriorating relationships with, 174; early descriptions by, 22, 24; Eyre, 127; Forrest (J), 249, 250; Gilbert, 173; Giles, 159, 250; Gregory (A C), 173; Gregory brothers, 173, 174; Grey, 93, 114, 115, 116, 120; guides, 34, 36, 37, 123, 124, 148, 171, 210, 247, 248, 259; Kennedy, 133, 173; Leichhardt, 173, 183, 184, 248; Mitchell, 92, 110, 111, 112; Stuart, 248, 250; Sturt, 74, 75; trust, 172; Warburton, 247; and firearms, 249; and food-gathering, 44, 45, 86, 122, 123; and Governor Phillip, 21; and horses, 42; and inland sea, 138; and poisonous plants, 164; and Royal College of Physicians, 58; and water supplies, 72, 124, 125; indications of, 72, 124; wells, 251; bush skills, 50, 172, 248; deaths, 111; driven from hunting grounds, 81; friendship, 78, 81; in Western Australia, 78, 85; perceived lifespan, 51; research, 268; sense of orientation, 171

acacia beans, 213

Acacia pendula (myall scrub), 71, 124

Adelaide Museum, 268, 269

Adelaide Philosophical Society, 136

apples, native, 164

Astronomical Society, 53

atriplex (fat-hen), 164

Audouin, Jean Victor, 187

Auld, W P, 228, 232, 238, 239, 249, 250, 257, 258

Aurousseau, Marcel, 185, 191, 192, 217, 219, 220

Austin, Robert, 134, 143, 155, 247

Australian Agricultural Company, 210

Australian Association for the Advancement of Science, 260

Australian Library, 101

Babbage, of Stuart's party, 198, 237

Babbich, Charles, 54

Baines, Thomas, 144, 175

bandicoot as food, 89

Banks, Joseph (Sir), 23; and Cook, 14; and *Investigator*, 26, 27; and Matra, 15; and NSW colony, 15, 16, 19; and research, 13, 14, 20; and Royal Society, 11, 53, 54; at Botany Bay, 14; collections, 13, 23; decline, 53; early career, 13; position, 14; recipient of botanical specimens, 22; reports from Caley, 38, 39, 45, 48

Bannister, Thomas, 81, 83, 84; and horses, 84

Barker, Collet (Captain), 80, 86

Barney, of Mitchell's party, 124

Barrallier, Francis (Lieutenant), 48; and Aboriginal peoples, 37, 39, 49, 172, 173; expeditions, 25, 40, 44; Blue Mountains, 18, 37, 50; equipment, 49; methods, 32, 38; reports, 29; supplies, 86; journals, 24

Bass, George, 18

Bathurst, Earl of, 51, 56, 58, 59, 90; and Evans, 59, 60, 62; and Macquarie, 68; and research, 58, 59, 60; and schools, 100

Baxter, John, 79, 173

Becker, of Burke and Wills' party, 61, 226, 227

Beckler, of Burke and Wills' party, 226, 227
Becquerel, Antoine Cesar, 187
Bedart, commentator on Gregory (A C), 173
bells on stock, 43, 162
Belt, F W, 267
Bennett, George, 140, 220
Bentham, George, 137
Billiatt, of Stuart's party, 232
billy cans, 65
Blaxland, Gregory, 35, 40; and Blue Mountains, 18; and dogs, 46
Blue Mountains, 29, 32, 149; and Barrallier, 24, 25, 32, 37, 50; and Dawes, 18; and Evans, 29, 47; and Phillip, 18; as barrier, 35; crossing, 32, 51, 62
Board of National Education, 135
Board of Science, 135
Boecking, Henry, 210
Bolton, G C, 16
boots, 49
Bourke, Richard (Governor Sir), 101
Bowman, of Gregory (A C)'s party, 144
Brisbane Museum, 136
Brisbane, Thomas (Governor Sir), 55, 56, 136
British Association for the Advancement of Science, 94
British Museum, 54, 95
Brock, D, 189
Brockman, Julius, 252
Brongniart, Adolphe, 187
Brongniart, Alexandre, 187
Brown, Charley's companion, 148, 170, 172, 249
Brown, H Y L, 270
Brown, Harry, 210, 218
Brown, of Gregory (F T)'s party, 153
Brown, Robert, 27, 28, 79, 98, 193; reports, 29; scientific shortcomings, 28, 29; specimen preserving techniques, 28
Browne, John, 78
Browne, Sturt's assistant, 132, 152
Bryan, W H (Professor), 192
bullocks, 42, 104, 141, 154; and bushmanship, 63; and explorers, 43; Barrallier, 32; expeditions, 102, 103, 104, 105, 109, 126; Leichhardt, 132, 160, 210; and poisonous plants, 155; as food, 165; as haulers; best when warm, 153; as pack carriers, 67; fettering, 42; galling of, 154; hobbling, 70; importation of, 30; limits of, 243; pack, 67, 105; preserving, 164; shortage of, 29
Bunce, Daniel, 210, 217
Burke and Wills. *See* Burke; Robert O'Hara; Wills, William John
Burke, Robert O'Hara, 43, 61, 160, 198, 224, 227, 244; aims and plans, 225; expedition, 227; camels, 244; cost of, 255; equipment, 253; goal, 229; water, 252; qualifications, 226
Burton, David, 23
bush food. See food
bush skills. *See* bushmanship
bushcraft. *See* bushmanship
bushmanship, 70, 89, 225; and Aboriginal peoples, 36, 86, 110, 172; lessons from, 50; and explorers, 44; Caley, 38; camels, 245; Eyre, 93; Giles, 238; Gregory brothers, 134; in early expeditions, 33; lack of, 33, 51, 77, 109, 110, 112, 122; Leichhardt, 205, 206, 207, 208, 218, 219; bullocks, 63; defined, 33; development of, 18, 33, 36, 39, 40, 62, 63, 70, 79, 81, 82, 85, 86, 87, 88, 91, 92, 128, 130, 142, 144, 232, 255, 259, 271; dissemination, 77; dogs, 73; finding water, 72; food-gathering, 73, 122; importance, 110; water-finding, 72
bushrangers, 40, 88
Bussell, John, 120, 121

calabashes, 164, 170

Caley, George: and Aboriginal peoples, 39, 248; and bushmanship, 38, 39; and directional skills, 39; and horsemanship, 38; and weapons, 45; evaluation of work, 26; expeditions, 25, 29, 32; Blue Mountains, 18; equipment, 25, 32; methods, 38, 40; reports to Banks, 38, 39, 45, 48; specimens, 32; supplies, 86; hardships, 47, 50, 52; scientific shortcomings, 23, 26; sense of alienation, 178
Calvert Scientific Exploring Expedition, 198, 252, 260, 262, 263, 264, 265, 268, 270
Calvert, James, 148, 249
camels, 227, 237, 244, 264; and deserts, 246; and Elder, 230, 244, 255; and explorers, 89, 107; Burke and Wills, 244; Giles, 243, 246, 258; and galling, 233; and horses, 238, 244, 245; and poisonous plants, 241; and spinifex, 245; and water, 252; as food, 254; hobbling, 246; loads, 245; problems of, 245, 246; range of, 243; rate of progress, 244; saddles, 246
Campbell, John, 210
Carmichael, desert explorer, 263
Carr, E H, 186
Carter, Paul, 193
Central Australian Exploring and Prospecting Association, 261
Chambers, Stuart's backer, 229, 241, 255
Charley, Leichhardt's Aboriginal assistant, 35, 148, 170, 171, 172, 218, 221, 249
Charley, Warburton's Aboriginal assistant, 247
Chewings, desert explorer, 263
Chisholm, Alec, 179, 180, 181, 183, 184, 185, 186, 190, 191, 194, 195, 199, 201, 202, 205, 206, 207, 209, 210, 212, 214, 215, 217, 218, 219, 220, 221, 222
Clark, Manning, 42
Clarke, W B (Reverend), 136, 203
clothing. *See* supplies
cockatoos: and water, 124; as food, 86, 122, 166
Collins, David (Lieutenant-Governor), 44
Cook, James (Captain), 14, 15; and vitamin C, 66
crocodiles, 114, 156, 164
Crotalaria crispata, 241
Crotalaria retusa, 241
crows: as food, 166
crupper, 84, 159, 161
Cunningham, Allan, 49, 188, 189, 197; and inland sea, 59; and Oxley, 48, 60; and scurvy, 73; expeditions, 98; equipment, 189; food-gathering, 75; horses, 68; research, 60, 61, 98; water supplies, 71, 72
Cunningham, Peter, 89, 90; and tethering of stock, 42
Cunningham, Richard, 95, 173; death, 110
Curr, Edward, 80, 153, 158, 159
Currie, Jane, 80
cycad, 164

Dale (Ensign), 85, 87
Darling, Ralph (Governor Sir), 56; and expeditions, 61, 63, 67; and schools, 99; and Sturt, 57, 65; reports, 49; research, 58
Davy, Humphrey, 13
Dawes, Lieutenant, 18, 22
de la Beche, Henry (Sir), 137
Denison, Governor, 226
direction of travel, 121
dogs, 47; and Aboriginal peoples, 47; and explorers, 164; food-gathering, 73; hunting, 46; kangaroos, 46; Leichhardt, 214; care of, 164
Drummond, James, 81, 96
Durando, Gaetano, 193

Eden, Charles, 181, 230, 231, 244, 251
Egerton-Warburton. *See* Warburton

Elder Scientific Exploring Expedition, 260, 261, 262, 264, 265, 266, 268, 270
Elder, Sir Thomas, 231, 258, 261, 269, 270; and camels, 244; and expeditions, 230, 244; and Giles, 231, 246; and Warburton, 231, 255; background, 230
Elliot, F J, 268
Elsey, Joseph, 137, 140, 142, 175
emus: and dogs, 73; as food; fried, 165; roasting for fat, 166
Endeavour, 14, 15, 66
equipment, stores and supplies, 55, 56; and Aboriginal peoples, 34; Bannister, 84; bushmanship, 33; Caley expeditions, 32; cost of, 90; developments of, 174; explorers, 43; Burke and Wills, 227, 253; cost of, 90, 106, 175; Dale, 85; Eyre, 126, 128, 188, 176; Forrest (J), 253; Giles, 253, 255; Gregory (A C), 154, 175, 176; Gregory (F T), 176; Grey, 93, 115; Leichhardt, 188, 206, 215, 216; mobility, 66; Oxley, 58, 60, 64, 67, 70, 160; Stuart, 238, 253; Sturt, 61, 64, 73, 163, 238; Warburton, 253; firearms, 64; for horses, 31; for research, 26, 27, 38, 57, 59, 61, 62, 137, 142, 175; loading, 62; poor quality, 47; quality of, 174; shortages, 25, 26, 51; stores; clothing; and Leichhardt, 217; tents; in hot weather, 90; tents and flies, 49, 87; Evans, 49
Evans, George, 271; and bushmanship, 62; and Earl of Bathurst, 60; and Oxley, 48, 58, 66, 76; and packhorses, 68; and tents, 64; background, 95; clothing, 64; expeditions, 29, 47, 49; Blue Mountains, 149; food, 46; Lachlan River, 18; Macquarie River, 18, 59; methods, 101; reports, 29; hardships, 47, 48; horsemanship, 40, 41; journals, 59; saddles, 160
Eyre, Edward John: achievements, 220; and Aboriginal peoples, 127, 173; and Gipps, 137; and ophthalmia, 208; and Sturt, 138; awards, 135; background, 93, 125; bush skills, 125, 128, 142; directional skills, 119, 198; droving, 103, 127; expeditions, 92, 130; and Aboriginal peoples, 172; and inland sea, 138; cost of, 188; difficulties, 231; distances covered, 144; equipment, 142, 174, 188; horses, 126, 127, 128, 144, 150, 151, 152, 153, 154, 157; in the Centre, 130; livestock, 106, 107, 126, 127, 214; methods, 149, 257; saddles, 160; stores, 176; supplies, 145; water supplies, 128, 167, 168, 170; pressures on, 139

Favenc, Ernest, 181, 198, 206, 207, 215, 217, 232
figs, native, 164
Finke, Stuart's backer, 229, 255
firearms, 250; and explorers, 47; early, 45; improvements in, 249
Fitzpatrick, Kathleen, 185
flies, 86, 115, 232, 233, 246; and horses, 154; and ophthalmia, 208
Flinders, Captain Matthew, 27, 28, 59, 201
flying fox: as food, 166
food, 126, 163, 194; and dogs, 82; and explorers; Barrallier, 45; Leichhardt, 73, 163, 164, 166, 219; Mitchell, 164; Oxley, 66, 73; preservation, 46; problems, 50; Sturt, 65, 70, 73; bandicoot, 89; birds, 166; bush, 219; emus, 46, 165, 166; flying foxes, 166; game, 36, 38, 44, 47; and explorers, 44, 46; Evans, 46; and firearms, 45; and Phillip, 44; in W A, 83, 86; preserving, 165; gathering, 73, 89, 122; Aboriginal peoples, 86; by explorers, 163; horses, 165; preserving, 165; hunting, 44; kangaroos, 44, 46, 47, 165; problems shooting, 46; of Aboriginal peoples, 44; possums, 89; preserving, 164, 165; fats, 166; shortages, 76, 78

Forrest brothers see also Forrest, Alexander and Forrest, Sir John: achievements, 220
Forrest, Alexander, 228, 250; achievements, 220, 224; and Forrest (J), 257; and Roe, 93, 143; background, 237; expeditions, 161, 236, 239; and Aboriginal peoples, 247; difficulties, 234; funding, 255; goals, 229; horses, 241; poisonous plants, 241; rate of progress, 242; research, 227
Forrest, Sir John (first Baron Forrest of Bunbury), 52, 91, 255, 261, 263; achievements, 220, 224; and Aboriginal peoples, 250; and Forrest (A), 257; and Roe, 93, 143; awards, 231; background, 237; expeditions, 236; and Aboriginal peoples, 247, 250; equipment, 253; funding, 255; goals, 229, 231; horses, 70, 239, 240, 242, 243, 244; methods, 257; rate of progress, 242; research, 227, 228; water, 251; search for Leichhardt, 231
Fraser, Charles, 60, 61, 77, 79, 80, 95, 189
Frome, Captain, 149, 170, 198

galling of horses, 41, 68, 102, 150, 153, 154, 158, 160, 161, 177, 213
game. *See* food
Gay-Lussac, Joseph Louis, 187
Geographical Society. *See* Royal Geographical Society
Gibson, Alfred, 233
Gilbert, John, 185; and Gould, 141; and Leichhardt, 49, 143, 184, 194, 200, 202, 203, 214, 217, 220, 222; collections, 140; death, 173, 202, 249; equipment, 188; expeditions; food-gathering, 164; hardships, 50; journal, 184; research, 137, 189; views on, 183
Giles, Ernest, 52, 91, 243, 251, 261, 263, 264; achievements, 220, 224; and Aboriginal peoples, 248, 250; and Elder, 230; and Eyre, 151; and Gibson, 233; and Leichhardt, 179, 180; and Sturt, 232; awards, 231; background, 238; bushmanship, 238; expeditions, 236, 259; attacked by Aboriginal peoples, 159; camels, 244, 245, 246, 258; difficulties, 232, 235; equipment, 253; firearms, 249; funding, 255; horse and camel teams, 107; horses, 233, 234, 235, 239, 240, 241, 242; horses as food, 254; methods, 257; rate of progress, 242; research, 227, 228; spinifex, 245; water, 251, 252
Gipps, George (Governor Sir): and Eyre, 137; and inland settlement, 128; and Leichhardt, 215; and Mitchell, 97, 215; research, 98
Glenelg, Lord, 101
Glynn, Peter, 190
Gosse, William Christie, 242, 243, 251, 261, 263
Gould, John, 136; and Gilbert, 141, 220
Goyder, George Woodroofe, 198
Grant, Lieutenant, 24, 25
grasses, native: loss of, 81
Gregory brothers see also Gregory, Augustus Charles and Gregory, Francis Thomas: achievements, 220; and Aboriginal peoples, 173, 174; and poisonous plants, 156; and Roe, 143; as bushmen, 178; expeditions, 144; horses, 157, 177; packhorses, 148; sense of orientation, 171; stores, 176; water supplies, 169
Gregory brothers see also Gregory, Augustus Charles and Gregory, Francis Thomas see also Gregory, Augustus Charles and Gregory, Francis Thomas, 257
Gregory, Augustus Charles: achievements, 220; and Aboriginal peoples, 33, 112, 173; and Geographical Society, 135, 137; and Kennedy, 149; and Mitchell, 149; and Mueller, 136; and Roe, 93, 143; and Sturt, 145; and water supplies, 133;

awards, 135; expeditions, 88, 133, 247; bells on stock, 163; biscuits, 147; cost of, 90, 175; difficulties, 231; dogs, 164; equipment, 142, 174, 175; food, 167; preserving, 165; supplies, 148; game, 163; horses, 67, 68, 150, 151, 154, 157, 165, 176, 177; livestock, 211; methods, 134, 149; packhorses, 149; pack-saddles, 162; rate of progress, 212; research, 137, 139, 140, 144, 267, 268; saddles, 160; search for Leichhardt, 144, 154, 162, 176; search for pastures, 139; sense of orientation, 171; stores, 176; supplies, 163, 175, 189, 216; water, 251; supplies, 170; horsesmanship, 151
Gregory, C F, 173
Gregory, Francis Thomas, 133; achievements, 220; and Aboriginal peoples, 33, 112, 174; and Geographical Society, 135; and Roe, 93, 143, 147; awards, 231; expeditions; achievement, 177; cost of, 175; equipment, 176; flying foxes, 166; horses, 42, 118, 150, 152, 153, 157, 177; methods, 134; rate of progress, 105; research, 137; search for arable land, 139; sense of orientation, 171; Shark Bay, 144; water supplies, 167, 168, 177
Gregory, Henry, 133, 143
Grey, George (Sir): and Aboriginal peoples, 75, 93, 115, 120, 173; and Geographical Society, 96, 98, 134; and Roe, 93; background, 92, 95; expeditions; attacked by Aboriginal peoples, 93, 115, 120; calculating distances, 120; direction of travel, 121; food-gathering, 122, 123; horses, 114, 117, 118; lack of bush skills, 122; livestock, 116, 117, 119; methods, 101, 106, 112, 113, 114, 116, 119, 121; research, 95, 96; goals, 99; hardships, 113, 114, 115, 116; journals, 96; wounded, 116
Halloran, Lawrence, 100
Hardey, John Wall, 86, 87
Harris, Alexander, 42, 89
Haygarth, William (Reverend), 158
Head, Benjamin, 237, 241, 252
Healy, Hovendon, 210
Helms, R, 266, 269
Hentig, Arthur, 210
Herschel, 55, 94
Hill, Captain, 29
Hill, J G, 252
Hill, of Forrest (A)'s party, 227, 228
Hillman, Surveyor, 109, 155
Hobart, Lord, 24
hobbles, 42, 70, 117; for camels, 246
Hooker, William (Sir), 137, 220
Horn Scientific Expedition, 194, 260, 262, 263, 264, 265, 267, 270
Horrocks, user of camels, 244
horsemanship, 150, 153; and bells, 162; and mobility, 157; and plants, 154; and saddles, 159; explorers; Gregory (A C), 151; lack of, 112; Leichhardt, 213; Oxley, 67, 69; quality of, 241, 242; tethering, 42
horses, 238, 241, 243, 244, 257, 258; and bells, 43; and camels, 238, 244, 245, 247; and directional skills, 255, 256, 257; and explorers, 43; Bannister, 84; Forrest (J), 239; Giles, 234, 235, 239; bogged, 233; Gregory (A C), 140, 176; Gregory (F T), 152, 153; Gregory brothers, 177; Grey, 117, 118; Leichhardt, 132, 210; loads, 177; Oxley, 69, 177; Stuart, 238, 239; Sturt, 70; and poisonous plants, 155, 156, 241; and saddles, 158, 159; and sanding, 118; and spinifex, 235, 245; and water supplies, 131, 134; and water-stress, 240, 241; as food, 165, 254; best when warm, 153; care of, 153, 154, 177; dehydration, 239; flies, 154; galling, 41, 68, 102, 150, 153, 154, 158, 160, 161, 177, 213; shoeing, 156, 157; cost of, 31, 67, 89, 106; cruppers, 159;

equipment, 160; footsore, 118; from Timor, 114; importation of, 31; in Western Australia, 85; Kimberley Walkabout disease, 241; limits of, 242, 243, 259; loading, 154; mobility, 67; original stock, 31; packhorses; and expeditions, 31; and explorers; Gregory (A C), 68; Leichhardt, 67; Oxley, 67, 68, 69; Sturt, 67; Blue Mountains, 32; Darling, 67; in W A, 86; loading, 65; loads, 68; mobility, 67; packsaddles, 159; picquetting, 85; population of, 30, 31, 105, 129; quality of, 241; released in Kimberleys, 116; saddlebags, 90; saddles, 159; sense of orientation, 171; shoes, 64, 65; shortage of, 29, 30, 32, 33; skins as footwear, 48; specilling, 71; tethering, 41, 42, 43, 85, 117; tracking of, 42, 43; treatment, 70

Hovell, William Hilton: and Hume, 90

Howitt, seeker for Burke and Wills, 244, 245

Hume, Hamilton: and busk skills, 109; and Earl of Bathurst, 90; and Hovell, 90; and Sturt, 63, 70, 90; and water supplies, 73; bushmanship, 63, 70

Humphrey, William H, 25

Hunter, John (Governor), 18, 20, 30, 231; and expeditions, 22, 36; hardships, 48, 50; reports, 23

hunting, 46; and dogs, 46; by Aboriginal peoples, 44; early efforts, 45; skills, 47

inland sea, 59, 137; and Gregory (A C), 133; and Grey, 97; and Leichhardt, 191; and Mitchell, 97

Investigator, 26, 27, 28, 29, 98

Isaac, F N, 199

Jack, Robert Logan, 182, 184, 185, 195, 200, 220, 221

Jimbour, 132, 163

Jimmy, of Giles' party, 248

Johnston, James Wingate (Surgeon), 121

Kaiber, 123

Kakadu National Park, 132

kangaroo dogs, 47

kangaroos, 22; and dogs, 46; dried, 165; skins for footwear, 48

Keartland, George, 264, 267, 270

Kekwick, of Stuart's party, 237, 241, 252, 258

Kennedy, Edmund, 133, 146, 149, 173, 208, 239

Kew Botanical Gardens, 13, 14, 23, 137

Kimberley Walkabout disease, 241

King, Governor: and expeditions, 39

King, P P, 192, 201, 213

King, Philip Gidley (Governor), 19, 20; and botanical collecting, 23; and expeditions, 24, 32, 37; and George Caley, 38; sense of alienation, 51

King, Stephen, 237

kurrajong, 164

Landsborough, William, 160, 244

Lawson, William, 35, 40; and Blue Mountains, 18

Leichhardt, Ludwig: achievements, 220, 223; and Aboriginal peoples, 173, 248; and bushmanship, 208; and Charley, 221; and Gilbert, 49, 143, 220; and Giles, 180; and mules, 213; and native grasses, 81; and ophthalmia, 208, 209; appreciation of country, 178; assessments, 222; at Jimbour, 132; awards, 135; background, 191; bush food, 219; bushmanship, 217, 218; collections; loss of, 32; death, 192; directional skills, 35, 119, 197–205, 217, 218; equipment; clothing, 48; expeditions, 31, 133, 187; bullocks, 210, 216; calculating distances, 120; calculations, 183; clothing, 217; cost of, 209, 216; determining longitude, 197; dogs, 164, 214, 215; equipment, 146, 147, 162, 188, 189; experience, 207, 213; food preserving, 164, 165, 166; food-gathering, 73, 163, 164, 166;

funding, 188, 190, 216; horses, 151, 154, 156, 210; bells, 43; inland sea, 191; journal, 184; livestock, 106, 211, 214; members, 190, 194, 209, 217; men lost, 171; methods, 111, 212, 257; mobility, 148, 210; mules, 147, 211, 214; names, 184, 194, 201; obstacles, 108; pack animals, 190; packhorses, 67; pack-saddles, 160; rate of progress, 212; reports, 193; research, 137, 138, 179, 189, 193, 194, 197; scurvy, 66, 73; sense of orientation, 171; specimens, 32; stock, 211; supplies, 203, 215, 216, 217; water supplies, 72, 167, 168, 170; water-finding skills, 169; fate, 180; game, 45; goal, 222; horsemanship, 41, 213; journal, 192, 194; loss of collections, 141; pressures on, 139; qualifications, 186, 187, 188, 191, 192, 207, 219, 222; search for, 144, 149, 154, 162, 176, 225, 229, 231; specimen-preserving techniques, 28; view of life, 222; views on, 179, 180, 181, 182, 183, 184, 185, 186, 187, 190, 192, 195, 205, 206, 207, 219, 220, 221; weapons, 45

limes, native, 66, 164

Lindsay, David, 198, 244, 264, 265, 266, 268, 269, 270

Linnean Society, 12, 13, 14, 53, 54, 136

Lockyer, Edmund (Major), 77, 78, 79, 248

Logan-Jack, Robert. *See* Jack, Robert Logan

McCoy, Frederick, 136

McCoy, William, 136

McKinley, John, 244

Macquarie, Lachlan (Governor): and botanic samples, 60; and Earl of Bathurst, 68; and Evans, 149; and expeditions, 29, 64; and exploration, 29; and Macquarie River, 59; and Oxley, 160; and schools, 99; research, 57; tours, 41

Mann, John, 42, 56, 210

marjoram, wild, 164

Marsden, Samuel, 99

Martin, Ged, 16

Matra, James Maria, 15

Mitchell, Thomas (Major Sir): and Aboriginal peoples, 33, 75, 111, 172, 173; and firearms, 249; and Gipps, 97, 215; and Gregory (A C), 150; and Kennedy, 133; and Leichhardt, 179, 192, 193; and Oxley, 92; and Richard Cunningham, 110; and scientific staff, 95; background, 92, 95; evaluation, 92; expeditions, 31, 92, 101; and Aboriginal peoples, 110, 111, 112; and Fort Bourke, 108; and livestock, 106; boats, 104, 105; bullocks, 145, 153; cost of, 90, 97, 106, 175, 216; determining longitude, 196; direction of travel, 121; directional skills, 197, 199; distances travelled, 149; dogs, 164; equipment, 106, 253; experience, 207; finding water, 123; food preserving, 164; food-gathering, 122; horses, 146; inexperience, 102; lack of bush skills, 109, 122; livestock, 107, 117, 119, 126, 214; members, 209; men lost, 171; methods, 101, 103, 105, 106, 107, 108, 109, 111, 112, 117, 119, 120, 121, 149; ophthalmia, 208; rate of progress, 105, 212; research, 96, 137, 189; sense of orientation, 170; supplies, 145; to Port Essington, 133; water supplies, 123, 124, 125, 167, 168; first trigonometrical survey of NSW, 58; goals, 97, 98, 108; journal, 95, 106; qualifications, 188; sense of alienation, 178; views of, 221

Mokare, 78, 82

Moore, George Fletcher, 105, 125; and water supplies, 124; expeditions; horses, 117; indications of water, 124; water supplies, 125

Moyal, Ann Mozely, 56, 136, 224, 227

Mueller, Ferdinand, 136, 137, 142, 144, 188, 231, 255, 268, 269, 270; and Gregory (A C), 136; and horses, 150; and poisonous plants, 156; appointment, 136
mules, 90, 156, 211, 212, 214; and galling, 213; and Leichhardt, 147, 190, 210; equipment, 214
Murchison, Roderick (Sir), 137
Murphy, of Leichhardt's party, 184, 185, 200
Museum of Natural History, 58
muskets. *See* firearms

National Museum of Victoria, 136
Nicholls, Giles, 246

ophthalmia, 208
orientation, sense of, 170, 171
Orton, William, 205
Overland Telegraph Line, 225, 234, 237
Owen, Professor, 96, 136
Owen, Richard, 140
horses, 66
Oxley, John: and Aboriginal peoples, 74; and bush skills, 109; and Evans, 76; and Fraser, 79; and hobbles, 70; and Mitchell, 92; and scurvy, 73; background, 58; death, 92; equipment, 62, 64; expeditions, 48, 56, 59, 60, 61, 62, 72; directional skills, 197; distances covered, 75; distances travelled, 149; equipment, 160, 174; food-gathering, 73, 75; horses, 62, 66, 67, 69, 70, 71, 162, 177; methods, 101; packhorses, 68; readings, 196; research, 96; supplies, 175; water supplies, 71, 72, 124; qualifications, 188; sense of alienation, 76, 178

packhorses. *See* horses
pack-saddles, 159, 160, 161, 162
Palmer, Commissary, 31
pandanus, 164
Parr, William, 60
Paterson, Colonel, 40
Perry, James, 66, 210
Phibbs, of Gregory (A C)'s party, 144
Phillip, Arthur (Governor): and Aboriginal peoples, 44; and equipment, 47, 49; and expeditions, 33, 43; expeditions, 18, 22, 33, 34, 44; hardships, 50; reports, 21, 23; research, 87
Phillips, of Leichhardt's party, 185, 200
Philosophical Society of Australasia, 55
Philosophical Society of New South Wales, 135
picquetting horses, 85
Pierre, Tommy, 234, 237
plants, poisonous, 154; and Aboriginal peoples, 164; and camels, 241, 246; and horses, 156, 241; and Leichhardt, 164; *Crotalaria crispata*, 241; *Crotalaria retusa*, 241; gastrolobium spp, 156
poisonous plants. *See* plants, poisonous
Poole, Sturt's assistant, 164
Portland, Duke of, 19, 20, 30
portulaca, 164, 232
Preston, Lieutenant, 81

Rhagodia dilatata, 75
Richardson, John, 95
Roach, John, 95
Roderick, Colin, 137, 179, 181, 183, 184, 185, 186, 187, 191, 192, 195, 199, 200, 202, 207, 221, 222
Roe, James, 144
Roe, John Septimus: and Aboriginal peoples, 112; and bush skills, 125; and Gregory (A C), 144; and Gregory brothers, 133; and pupils, 143; background, 95; expeditions, 93; direction of travel, 121; equipment, 106, 109, 147; experience, 207; food-gathering, 122; horses, 117, 147, 150, 151, 154, 155, 157, 160; indications of water, 124; methods, 121, 143, 149; poisonous plants, 155; rate of progress,

105, 212; water supplies, 125, 168, 169; goals, 98; Swan River, 80
Roper, of Leichhardt's party, 35, 132, 185, 249
Royal College of Physicians, 58, 208
Royal Geographical Society, 78, 81, 88, 137, 195, 231, 266, 270; and Gregory (A C), 134, 137; and Gregory (F T), 135, 168; and Grey, 96, 98, 134; establishment, 94
Royal Geographical Society of Australasia, 261, 262
Royal Institution, 13, 14
Royal Society, 11, 13, 14, 53, 54, 55, 56, 94, 95, 135, 136; achievements, 12; and Banks, 11, 13; and *Endeavour*, 14; beginnings, 11
Royal Society of Edinburgh, 12
Russell, H C, 260
Russell, H W, 205, 207, 209
Russell, Henry, 182, 209
Russell, Lord, 98

saddles and saddlebags see also pack-saddles, 157, 159, 160; for camels, 246, 258; for mules, 213; pack; lining of, 41
Saleh, Giles' saddler, 246
sanding in horses, 118
schools, 99
Scott, A W, 205, 207
Scott, Helenus, 207
Scott, Walker, 207
scurvy, 66, 73, 164, 219, 232; and Stuart, 253
Selby, of Gregory (A C)'s party, 144
Sleeman, Lieutenant, 79
Smythe, H W H, 84
Society for Promoting Natural History, 12
sonchus (sowthistle), 164
specimen-preserving techniques, 28
Spencer, Baldwin (Professor), 29, 194, 263, 267, 270
spencilling, 71
spinifex, 245
Stanley, Captain, 196
Stanley, Lord, 143
Stephenson, William, 137
Stirling, Edward (Dr), 267
Stirling, James (Governor Sir), 61, 79, 80; and Aboriginal peoples, 78; and food-gathering, 86; and game, 80; booklet, 121; expeditions; equipment, 109; water supplies, 125; goals, 98; report to Geographical Society, 81, 88
Stokes, John Lort, 141, 196, 197, 201
Streich, F P V, 266, 268
Strzelecki, Count, 135, 136
Stuart, John McDouall, 52, 213, 244, 250; achievements, 220, 224; and Aboriginal peoples, 112, 248, 250; and scurvy, 253; and Sturt, 237; awards, 231; collapse of health, 232, 237; expeditions; and Aboriginal peoples, 249; and directional skills, 255; directional skills, 198, 218; equipment, 253; firearms, 250; food, 238; funding, 255; goals, 229; horse and camel teams, 107; horses, 70, 238, 239, 240, 241, 242, 258; members, 252; methods, 257; rate of progress, 242; research, 189, 227, 228, 268; scurvy, 164, 232; watches, 250; water, 252; waterbags, 252
Sturt, Charles, 90, 213, 232; and Aboriginal peoples, 33, 74, 75, 111, 127, 250; and bush skills, 109; and Eyre, 138; and Giles, 232; and Governor Darling, 57; and Gregory (A C), 145; and Hume, 63, 70, 90; and Leichhardt, 179; and Stanley, 143; and Stuart, 237; awards, 135; bush skills, 142; bushmanship, 77; equipment, 64, 65; expeditions, 31, 57, 61, 63, 66, 77, 98, 132; clothing, 87; cost of, 90, 106; difficulties, 231; equipment, 61, 174; experience, 207; firearms, 65; food-gathering, 73; game, 65; hobbling, 70; horses, 67, 70, 145, 150, 151, 152, 156; in the Centre, 130, 131; inland sea, 138; livestock, 106, 107; methods, 111;

ophthalmia, 208; packhorses, 67; rate of progress, 212; research, 137, 188, 189; scurvy, 164; stores, 153; supplies, 145, 163, 175, 216; vitamin C, 65; water supplies, 72, 73, 123, 132, 134, 170; water-finding skills, 170; firearms, 64; hardships, 131; qualifications, 143; sense of alienation, 77; lessens, 76, 77; views of, 221
supplies. *See* equipment
Swan River Colony/Settlement, 50, 61, 77, 79, 80, 93, 116, 222
Sydney Mechanics Institute, 101
Sydney, Lord, 15

Tasmanian Society of Natural History, 55
Tate, R (Professor), 204, 267
temperatures, 177, 239; cold, 34; high, 50, 76, 113, 116, 167, 170; recording, 24
Tench, Watkin (Captain): and Aboriginal peoples, 51; and water supplies, 43; equipment, 48; expeditions, 18, 33, 34, 35, 36; game, 46; hardships, 51; lack of bush skills, 44; reports, 21, 22, 23, 34
Tepper, J G, 268, 269
Thring, Frank W, 237, 244, 255, 256, 257, 258
Tietkens, W H, 159, 233, 234, 238, 240, 241, 249, 251, 257, 260, 261, 264, 265, 270
Todd, Charles, 268
Turnbull, Henry, 210

University of Adelaide, 267
University of Melbourne, 135, 136, 267
University of Sydney, 135, 267

Victorian Institute for the Advancement of Science, 136
Victorian Philosophical Society, 136
vitamin C, 65, 164
von Mueller, Ferdinand. *See* Mueller, Ferdinand

Walcott, P, 137
Walker, Frederick, 95, 207, 244
wando, 124
Warburton, Peter Egerton, 91, 198, 224, 227, 233, 243, 244, 246, 247, 252, 261, 263; achievements, 224; and Aboriginal peoples, 247; and Elder, 231; awards, 231; background, 237; expeditions, 233, 236; and Aboriginal peoples, 247; camels, 244, 246; as food, 254; difficulties, 232; equipment, 253; funding, 255; horse and camel teams, 107; method, 257; night travel, 247; research, 227, 228; water, 251; journal, 230, 231
Warburton, Richard, 257
watches, 83, 140, 173, 177, 249, 250
water, 243; and camels, 252; and explorers; Cunningham (A), 71; Eyre, 127, 128, 170; Giles, 243; Gregory (A C), 133, 169; Gregory (F T), 168; Gregory brothers, 169; Leichhardt, 72, 119, 167, 168, 170; Mitchell, 105, 123, 124, 125, 167; Moore, 124; Oxley, 66, 71, 72; Roe, 124, 168, 169; Stuart, 237, 250; Sturt, 70, 72, 132, 170; Tench, 43; Wilson, 83; and horses, 131, 134; and livestock, 107; and Phillip, 33, 43; avoiding, 72; cartage, 72, 170; digging for, 252; finding, 72, 169, 170, 250, 259; indications of, 72, 73, 124, 169; Aboriginal axe-marks, 72; Acacia pendula (myall scrub), 71, 124; wando, 124; purifying, 125; shortages, 260; causes, 43; wells, 251, 252
waterbags, 170, 253, 259
Waterhouse, F G, 189, 227, 228, 268
Watt, J A, 267
weapons. *See* firearms
Webster, Mona Stuart, 198
Wells, C F, 264
Wells, Lawrence, 198, 252, 263, 264, 268, 270
Wentworth, William Charles, 35, 40; and Blue Mountains, 18; hardships, 51

Whewell, William, 94
Whitehead, John, 60, 196, 197
Whitehouse, F W (Dr), 192
Wills, William John, 61, 160, 198, 244; aims and plans, 225; expedition, 227; camels, 244; cost of, 255; equipment, 253; goal, 229; water, 252; qualifications, 226; research, 226
Wilson, James, 137, 139, 144, 175
Wilson, T B (Dr), 78, 80, 81, 82, 83, 86; and Aboriginal peoples, 86; and clothing, 87
Windich, of Forrest (J)'s party, 237, 239, 247
Winnecke, C A, 266, 267
Wommai, of Leichhardt's party, 210